CONTEMPORARY COMPOSITION

Contemporary Composition

FOURTH EDITION

Maxine Hairston

UNIVERSITY OF TEXAS AT AUSTIN

HOUGHTON MIFFLIN COMPANY • BOSTON

DALLAS • GENEVA, ILL. • LAWRENCEVILLE, N.J. • PALO ALTO

Printed in the U.S.A.
Library of Congress Catalog Card Number: 85-80769
ISBN: 0-395-35729-2

ABCDEFGHIJ-H-89876

Text Credits

We are grateful to the following authors and publishers for permission to quote from their works:

American Heritage Dictionary. Definitions from *The American Heritage Dictionary*, Third Edition, reprinted by permission of Houghton Mifflin Company.   Aristotle. Lane Cooper, *The Rhetoric of Aristotle*, © 1932, renewed 1960, pp. 132–133, 134–135. Adapted by permission of Prentice-Hall, Inc., Englewood Cliffs, N.J.   General Libraries. Materials prepared by librarians in the undergraduate library reprinted by permission of General Libraries, University of Texas at Austin.   Garrett Hardin. "Lifeboat Ethics: The Case Against Helping the Poor," reprinted with permission from Psychology Today Magazine. Copyright © 1974. (APA)   Excerpts from pages 79, 80, 84–85 "Letter from Birmingham Jail, April 16, 1963" from *Why We Can't Wait* by Martin Luther King, Jr. Copyright © 1963 by Martin Luther King, Jr. Reprinted by permission of Harper & Row, Publishers, Inc., and Joan Daves.   Alfred McClung Lee and Elizabeth Briant Lee, *The Fine Art of Propaganda* (New York: Harcourt, Brace and Institute for Propaganda Analysis, 1939, and Octagon Books, 1972; San Francisco: Institute for General Semantics, 1979), pp. 23–24, by permission of the authors who are the copyright owners. Copyright renewed 1967.   Joe McGinness, Extracts from *The Selling of the President 1968* copyright © 1969 by Joemac, Inc. Reprinted by permission of Simon & Schuster, Inc., and Sterling Lord Literary Agency.   William Raspberry. From the *Austin American-Statesman*, © 1984 Washington Post Writers Group, reprinted with permission.   Carl Rogers. Selections from *On Becoming A Person*, copyright 1961, reprinted by permission of Houghton Mifflin Company.   Gary Saretsky & James Mecklenburger. "See You in Court" © 1972 Saturday Review magazine. Reprinted by permission.   Tom Tiede. "Does the Devil Make Us Do It?" reprinted by permission of Newspaper Enterprise Association, Inc.   From *I Can Sell You Anything*, by Carl P. Wrighter. Copyright © 1972 by Ballantine Books, a Division of Random House, Inc. Reprinted by permission of the publisher.   Brian Vachon "Hey, What Did You Learn in Reform School?" © 1972 Saturday Review magazine. Reprinted by permission.   Philip Wylie. "Science Has Spoiled My Supper," copyright © 1954 by The Atlantic Monthly Company, Boston, Massachusetts. Reprinted by permission of Harold Ober Associates.   "Failing in Fitness" from *Newsweek*, April 1, 1985, copyright 1985 by Newsweek, Inc. All rights reserved. Reprinted by permission.

Illustrations

We are grateful to the following individuals for permission to reproduce their photographs in this text:

Cover photo: "Constellation IV" © Alan Magee 1983. Watercolor, 40 by 60 inches.

Chapter openers:

Chapter 1: Peter Menzel/Stock, Boston   Chapter 2: Bruce Davidson/Magnum   Chapter 3: Clemens Kalischer   Chapter 4: Stanley Rowin/The Picture Cube   Chapter 5: Werner H. Müller/Peter Arnold   Chapter 6: Mark Antman/The Image Works   Chapter 7: Franklin Wing/Stock, Boston   Chapter 8: Hena Hammid/Photo Researchers   Chapter 9: George Holton/Photo Researchers   Chapter 10: Ulrike Welsch   Chapter 11: Peter Mauss/Esto Photographs   Chapter 12: Jonathan A. Meyers

CONTENTS

The fourth edition of this book has a new name, *Contemporary Composition,* one chosen to reflect the text's increased emphasis on all the elements of the composing process. My purpose in showing the range of options open to writers when they face different kinds of writing tasks is to bolster students' confidence and demonstrate to them that the ability to write is not a mysterious power or a magical gift granted only to a few. Ordinary people who are willing to invest energy and time and to engage in disciplined practice can learn to write clearly and effectively. This text provides practical strategies and realistic writing assignments that will help them achieve that goal.

The text is still rhetorically based; that is, it sets each writing task in a context that requires students to think about why they are writing and to pay attention to their readers' needs and expectations. It also continues to stress that students need to become critical readers and analytical thinkers as well as competent writers, and it retains the argumentative edge that it has featured through the first three editions. In fact, the argumentative portion of the book has been updated and made more accessible to students by dropping the rather traditional section on deductive logic and substituting an illustrated section on informal logic or Toulmin argument, the approach to argument now featured in most texts on argumentation. The section on fallacies and propaganda has been retained.

The fourth edition features several other major changes and additions.

• It is now available in two formats: a hardcover edition, which includes a greatly expanded and clairfied handbook, and a softcover edition, which omits the handbook.

• It begins with an explanation of the ways in which writing serves as a major mode of learning in all college courses.

• It introduces a fresh conceptual approach about different kinds of writing and the processes by which they are done.

• It combines two chapters on rhetorical theory into a single chapter titled "The Elements of Rhetoric."

• It features a completely new chapter on revision that explains revising as part of the composing process, sets priorities for revising, and demonstrates the revision process by including drafts and the final versions of two student papers.

• It introduces students to the concept of peer groups and gives guidelines to help them work together.

• It includes a new section on sexist language, discussing its implications and suggesting ways of avoiding it.

• It concludes with a completely rewritten, expanded, and updated chapter on the research paper that treats research as an ongoing learning activity pertinent to everyone's life. The section on documentation explains and illustrates new MLA style and APA style.

• Writing assignments throughout the book have been revised and updated to include the components of audience and purpose for each one.

I believe the changes in the fourth edition reflect changes and improvements in my own teaching of writing in the past four years and also reflect new knowledge and significant advances in the profession. I believe strongly that the two professional organizations that have done the most to bring about those changes and improvements are the National Council of Teachers of English and its subsidiary organization, the Conference on College Composition and Communication. I offer my thanks and appreciation to my colleagues in those organizations who have invested so much energy, talent, and commitment in the teaching of writing to all students.

I would also like to thank the following individuals for thoughtful suggestions for and reviews of this edition: Dorothy Bankston, Louisiana State University; Mark Bracher, Kent State University; Thomas J. Campbell, Pacific Lutheran University; Richard A. Cox, Abilene Christian University, TX; Ann Dobyns, Ohio State University; Kathleen E. Dubs, University of San Francisco; William D. Dyer, Mankato State University, MN: Arra M. Garab, Northern Illinois University; Penny L. Hirsch, Northwestern University, IL; Ralph R. Joly, Asbury College, KY; Carl D. Malmgren, University of New Orleans; Judith A. May, Edison Community College, FL; Twila Yates Papay, Hofstra University, NY; Barbara Stout, Montgomery College, MD; and Darlene Harbour Unrue, University of Nevada, Las Vegas.

Maxine Hairston

CONTEMPORARY COMPOSITION

1 · Writing: An Overview, Part 1

CHAPTER

Why Write in College?

As a college student, you are almost certainly going to have to write many papers during your years in school, and when you enter a profession after graduation, you will probably have to continue to write. A major purpose of this book is to help you to become an effective writer who can write clear, well-organized papers for your courses and then carry that skill over into your professional life.

Writing in college has another significant function, however: it is a major tool for learning. When you write, you do so to practice expressing ideas and to demonstrate to your instructors that you have mastered the material in their courses. But there are additional reasons for writing that may be even more important:

1. Writing is a tool for discovery. We stimulate our thought processes by the act of writing and tap into information and images we have in our unconscious minds. Writing helps us to "harvest" what we know.
2. Writing generates new ideas by helping us to make connections and see relationships.
3. Writing helps us to organize our ideas and clarify concepts. By writing down ideas we can arrange them in coherent form.
4. Writing down our ideas allows us to distance ourselves from them and evaluate them.
5. Writing helps us to absorb and process information; when we write about a topic, we learn it better.
6. Writing enables us to solve problems; by putting the elements of the problem into written form, we can examine and manipulate them.

7. Writing on a subject makes us active learners rather than passive receivers of information.[1]

So as you become a more confident and facile writer, you will reap benefits that you may not have anticipated and find that writing can be a rich and productive experience.

Purposes of the Writing Course

People who are starting to write need to know a number of things all at once, because even relatively simple writing tasks require the mastery of several skills. But no one can master all these skills at once, so we have to set priorities and focus first on those that seem to be the most important for the novice writer. In my judgment they are as follows:

Priorities for novice writers

1. Recognizing and appreciating good writing.
2. Understanding the writing process.
3. Learning how to get started writing.
4. Learning how to organize writing.
5. Learning how to unify writing.

The first two chapters of this book will give you guidelines for developing these basic abilities, and once you grasp the main principles, you should be able to approach writing your first papers with some confidence. At least you will understand what you are supposed to be doing even if you do it rather awkwardly and slowly the first few times. Gradually, as you master these skills and begin to supplement the early lessons with more complex ones, you will begin to write easily without always consciously thinking about what you are doing. But studied practice has to come first.

You already have good communication skills

In fact, you are probably already fairly well prepared to write that first paper even if you have not done much writing in high school, because all writing starts with the mind and the emotions, not with a pencil or typewriter or word processor. For a long time you have been using your interpersonal skills to communicate with people in conversations or letters. You have ideas or opinions, and you tell

[1] List adapted from an article by Maxine Hairston, "Speculations About Writing Programs in the Eighties," *Association of Departments of English Bulletin* 67 (Spring 1981): 12.

people about them by using language that comes naturally to you. You state your position on issues and support it by drawing on your experience or on another natural skill, the ability to reason.

This strong desire that all of us have to make others understand us should serve you well as you write. Now you just need to organize your ideas more carefully and to think deliberately about how you can use the right words and the right examples to make your points. The process is necessarily slower and more painstaking than talking, and no one claims that if you can talk well you can also automatically write well. But the two processes are closely connected, and you can use those already well-developed communication skills when you start to write. And remember that even beginning writers do many more things right than they do wrong.

What Is Good Writing?

All expository writing has an audience and a purpose

The purpose of this section is to give you a working definition of good writing that will help you to set standards by which you can judge your writing and to understand some important goals of a college writing course. The definition is limited in that it refers only to *expository writing* — that is, nonfiction writing that presents and explains ideas. Expository writing always takes place in a specific situation: someone writes it for a specific audience and for a specific purpose. Thus, we have to make our first judgments about any piece of expository writing by asking this question: does it achieve its purpose for its intended audience? If it does, it is effective writing; if it does not, it is ineffective, no matter how attractive it may seem when considered out of context. So when we judge a piece of writing we must first try to decide if it accomplishes what the author intended. After we decide that question, we can look for other features that affect its general quality.

Characteristics of Good Writing

Fortunately, it is not difficult to identify characteristics that are common to good expository writing and to pinpoint the features that most readers want to find.

First, they want writing to be *significant*. It should tell them something they want or need to know.

Second, they want writing to be *clear.* They don't want to have to reread it several times to find out what it means.

Third, they want writing to be *unified* and *well organized*. They don't want the author to lead them off in several directions so that they get no sense of an underlying plan.

Fourth, they want writing to be *economical*. They don't want to feel that the writer is being unnecessarily long-winded and wasting their time.

Fifth, they want writing to be *adequately developed.* They want the author to support key points and keep any promises he or she makes.

Sixth, they want writing to be *grammatically acceptable.* They don't want to find distracting mistakes in usage or mechanics.

These characteristics are basic to any kind of effective nonfiction writing. But for nonfiction writing to be not only satisfactory and efficient but also a pleasure to read, it should have at least one more quality: vigor. That term is easier to illustrate than to define, but in general one can say that vigorous writing makes the reader sense the writer's presence. Often it has a visual quality and a definite rhythm, and it reflects the writer's energy and his or her interest in the topic.

Writing is significant when the reader enjoys it, learns something from it, or fills some need by reading it. When writing serves any of those purposes, it is worth doing, even if it is not profound or original. As a student writer, you shouldn't underestimate your own resources for making your writing significant. You have had experiences that other people would enjoy hearing about, and almost certainly you have valuable information about some activity or interest that someone would like to read about. You also hear the news, read the papers, and react to events and issues. You can incorporate all of this material into your writing to make it interesting and significant to your readers.

What most readers are apt to consider insignificant and trivial, a waste of their time, is "canned writing," writing that states the obvious or only repeats conventional ideas or sentiments that are already so familiar to the reader that they make no impression. Such writing is pointless. The student who produces it usually has no real interest in the topic and is just going through motions in order to meet a requirement. The instructor who reads it does so for the same reason: to meet a requirement. Papers written under these conditions are really "teacher papers." Full of generalities and clichés, they bore both the people who write them and the people who read them. Here is a rather typical opening paragraph from a "teacher paper":

> A person's basic morals are formed during childhood. Almost from the time you are born you are told what is right and what is wrong. The family is the most dominant force in the shaping of a child's morals. Parents try to guide their children according to their own morals. Society is another strong force in shaping morals, and people tend to have those values which society had while they were growing up. Today the media also have a strong influence on morals.

Although the writing is clear and correct, the content is so hackneyed that no reader would voluntarily continue past the first two sentences. And students shouldn't expect their writing instructors or their fellow students to read such papers either — they're not worth anyone's time.

In contrast, here is an opening paragraph on a comparably broad topic, but it engages the reader's interest and promises to say something worth reading:

> The demonstrations and riots of the 1960s dramatically brought civil rights issues home to Americans. Fifteen years ago it was not uncommon to hear of a man who had lost his life because he believed that black Americans should have the same rights as white Americans. Today the battlefields are quiet, and to a casual observer, it might appear that the civil rights movement has obtained its objectives. How accurate would such a statement be? To put it another way, is America now totally "color blind"?

Probably the best way to make your writing worth reading is to choose a topic that interests you, one that hasn't been written about so often that there's nothing new to say about it. If you can't do that, at least try to find something personal and specific to say about the assigned topic.

Qualities of clear writing

Clarity   When people complain about bad writing, they frequently single out lack of clarity as the fault that annoys them most. When writing is vague and obscure, it taxes their patience and wastes their time, and if they have no strong incentive for trying to figure out

---

what the writer is saying, they'll quickly stop reading. Clarity is relative, of course; informed and skilled readers with large vocabularies often have no trouble reading material that many other readers would find confusing. But even very skilled readers value clarity; they don't want their reading to be any harder to understand than it must be, given the subject matter.

Most writers would tell you that nothing is more important than writing clearly, and nothing is more difficult. To write clearly you have to pay attention to everything: audience, sentence structure, diction, organization, transitions, choice of examples, and half a dozen other considerations. So much is involved that most of the writing advice in this book is really advice on how to write clearly. Learning to do so may be a long process, but it is not a mysterious one. With persistence, most writers can master it.

Unity and Organization   When you go to hear someone give a talk and leave thinking, "That speaker really got to the point. She was easy to follow and didn't waste anyone's time," you have heard a unified speech. When you read a piece of writing that stays directly on the topic and moves purposefully from one point to the other without jolts, interruptions, or digressions, you get the same impressions. That kind of writing is satisfying to read and usually easy to understand.

Qualities of unified writing

In tightly unified writing, each sentence in a paragraph develops or supports the main idea of the paragraph and connects in some way with any sentences that come before and after it. All the sentences seem to fit with each other in a logical sequence. In poorly unified writing, however, the sentences often seem to be jumbled; they could be moved around and rearranged without its making much difference. The paragraphs in tightly unified writing also fit with each other logically. Just as no irrelevant sentences go off at a tangent in a good paragraph, no disconnected paragraphs pop up unexpectedly in a good essay.

We call this quality in writing *coherence*, a word that comes from the verb *cohere*, which literally means "to stick together." Writers create coherence in their writing in four principal ways, ways that will be explained in the next chapter.

Economy   Many student writers find it difficult to believe that they should write economically because they so often have been asked to write papers of a specified length — 1,000 words, 2,500 words, 10 pages, and so on — and have worried about finding enough to say to produce the required number of words. Consequently, they have acquired the habit of thinking that they should write as much as they can, and they may find it hard to realize that their wordiness is more likely to annoy readers than to impress them. But it's true. To busy people — and that includes your writing instructor — time is their most valuable commodity, and they resent having to wade through puffed-up writing that takes twice as long as it needs to make a point. Thus it pays for student writers to learn to think in terms of maximum, not minimum, numbers of words and to cultivate the writing and rewriting habits that will help them to overcome wordiness. Later chapters will suggest specific ways to do this.

Adequate Development   Early in any piece of writing, the writer establishes a contract with the reader. That contract can take various forms: a title that predicts, an opening question that must be answered, a thesis statement to be developed, or an anecdote or reference to be explained. The contract becomes the writer's *commitment,* an obligation to the reader. Good writers meet that obligation by answering the questions they have raised and by explaining and developing the assertions they have made.

  In other chapters of this book, you will find an expanded discussion of this important component of any writing task and suggestions about how to set up your writing commitments and how to meet them. For this introductory discussion it is enough to say that good writers don't make extravagant commitments that they can't meet in the space they have to work in, and they follow through on any commitments they do make. They achieve these goals by keeping two cautions in mind. First, they choose limited topics, and second, they make limited commitments. And in both instances they develop their main ideas with reports, anecdotes, evidence, and specific details that help their readers to visualize the problem and grasp the issues. Other sections of this text will explain and demonstrate how one goes about this kind of development.

Acceptable Usage   I recently did a survey of professional people like bankers, lawyers, business executives, judges, and administrators to find out how they reacted to grammatical mistakes in the writing that they had to read in the course of their work. Although

---

most of them indicated that the quality they valued most in writing is clarity, all agreed that they also expect writers to know and observe the rules of good English usage and that they get upset when they don't. A survey made at the University of Texas a few years ago showed that professors in every discipline felt the same way.

The responses of these people don't mean that they expect the grammar and mechanics to be perfect in every report or paper; in fact, they probably aren't sure what "perfect" grammar is. They do, however, expect writers to have as good a command of the conventions of English usage and punctuation as the average educated public speaker or writer has. They want writing to meet the standards that they — and you — learned as high school and college students.

Mechanics

Students who make major errors in writing often do it not from ignorance but from indifference, carelessness, or forgetfulness. They are simply not convinced that writing correctly is important enough to justify the amounts of time and effort it requires. It would be reassuring to agree with those who say that mechanics are really not important, that what you write and how you put your words together matter far more than such details as a comma fault, an occasional sentence fragment, or a misplaced modifier. Such an assertion is partially justified. Focusing your attention on saying something worthwhile and saying it forcefully and clearly *are* much more important than devoting most of your energies to turning out an absolutely "correct" composition. A paper can be totally trivial even though the spelling, handwriting, and grammar are flawless. But it is poor logic to say that because content is more important than mechanics, then mechanics do not matter. They do, and for several reasons.

First, poor grammar and punctuation in a paper draw a disproportionate amount of attention to themselves. In some ways the situation is analogous to that of running a household: more than one person has complained that the most frustrating thing about housekeeping is that much of the time you are doing invisible work. No one notices it unless it is *not* done.

When reading your papers, college teachers seldom think, "What nice punctuation!" or "This student certainly spells well." They take those skills for granted and concentrate their attention on other elements of your writing: clarity, coherence, and sound thinking. If, however, you have neglected the niceties of grammar and spelling, the errors will divert their attention from what you are doing right to what you are doing wrong — and that is certainly not where you want it. Both you and the housekeeper have a better chance of getting credit for the important things you do if you take care of the relatively unimportant ones as a matter of course.

The toleration level of teachers varies. Some are fairly permissive about the more common lapses in grammar; some are very strict. Most college teachers, however, have reasonable standards. They no longer worry about all the fine points of usage. Nevertheless, they still frown on comma splices and sentence fragments, insist that you differentiate between adverbial and adjectival forms, and want subjects and verbs to agree and modifying phrases to come in the right place. And they care about spelling, not because they equate intelligence with good spelling, but because they know other people do.

Form good habits now

The second reason you should be concerned about writing correctly is that you need to form good habits now when the penalties for writing incorrectly are not so severe as they will be later. In a composition course, you will be writing several papers; if you have problems, you have a chance to solve them as you go along and gradually bring your work up to the level of standard English. In upper-division courses, however, your grade may depend on the one or two papers you turn in. Under those circumstances, a poorly written paper can cost you dearly.

The crucial test comes when you begin to write the letters and applications that could affect your future. At that point careless grammar and misspelling may cause your prospective employer or the admissions officer to think, "Here is a sloppy and irresponsible person who is totally indifferent to the impression made on me." Harsh and unreasonable as such a judgment may seem, it is a predictable one. People in authority do judge you by your writing.

Poor mechanics interfere with communication

The final hazard of faulty mechanics is that they can interfere with communication. The failure to put commas in the proper places can completely alter the sense of a statement. Misplaced modifiers can make sentences comically ambiguous. Run-on sentences or the failure to insert quotation marks where they are needed can confuse your readers. Thus, faulty mechanics not only distract and annoy your readers, they can also deceive them.

Spelling   Pay attention to your spelling. After eight or ten years of studying spelling, you should know whether you are a reasonably competent speller. If you are not, don't just shrug off your deficiencies by saying, "Well, I never could spell." If you had mastered all the skills required to drive a car except that of backing it, you wouldn't say, "Oh, I'll just settle for this. Backing up is too hard." You would practice backing up until you mastered it because you would be handicapped in your driving if you did not. You will be equally handicapped in your writing if you refuse to do whatever is necessary to correct your spelling.

There are several steps you can take to improve your spelling. First, invest in one of the standard dictionaries and keep it on your desk or work table. Get in the habit of looking up any word about which you have the slightest doubt. If you are not sure whether there are two *r*'s in *embarrass,* look it up; if you are confused about whether *pursue* is spelled with a *u* or *e,* check it. Words with unaccented vowel syllables, such as "sep-*a*-rate," "com-*pro*-mise," "mil-*i*-tant," and "ul-*ti*-mate," are frequent troublemakers because there is no way to be sure which vowel to use without checking. Most word endings with an *ize* sound are spelled *ise,* but *emphasize* is not, so you may have to check on those too. All this is a nuisance, of course, but absolutely necessary if you are serious about improving your spelling.

Keep a list of words you misspell

You should also form the habit of keeping a list of the correctly spelled versions of words you have missed on papers. The flash card system is handy since it allows you to consult them in alphabetical order, or you may put the list in the back of your English notebook. In addition, make it a practice to pay particular attention to the spelling of key words in an assignment. Teachers have little patience with the student who is so careless as to consistently spell Hemingway with two *m*'s, to write a paper on John Stuart Mill and use the spelling "Mills" throughout, or to forget to put in the second *l* every time *syllogism* is used.

Find a study skills program

There may be some spelling aids available on campus. Ask your teacher if your college offers a study skills program that includes instruction in spelling, if there is an English laboratory set up to help you, and if the bookstores carry inexpensive, programmed workbooks for improving your spelling. As a last resort, you can always find one of those fortunate souls who are naturally good spellers and ask for help. And if you write on a computer, you can use its spelling checker, although they have serious limitations (see p. 135).

Finally, if you consistently have difficulty with punctuation or spelling don't worry about mechanics while you are writing your first draft. Once you get started writing, if the ideas are coming quickly and you're forming your sentences rather easily, stopping to fret about whether everything is correct may make you lose the creative energy you've worked up. You will do better to keep going until you have finished the first draft and to put off editing for mistakes until the final stages of the writing process.

The Problem of Models for Student Writing

Most people would agree in principle with these standards for good writing — after all, when they *read* they want the material to be significant, clear, unified, economical, and adequately developed, and they expect correct usage and spelling. Many college students, however, don't seem to believe that their instructors really want them to write clearly and economically and to say something honest and direct. Instead, they think college professors expect them to produce polished writing on scholarly topics and major issues, using an abstract and high-level vocabulary and a complex and elegant style. No wonder students are afraid to write! Very few people, including their professors, are qualified to do what students frequently expect of themselves, and yet students often assume that they are the only ones who can't live up to these high expectations.

Misconceptions about models for writing

Such misconceptions about "college-level writing" come from a number of sources. First, many students have read little contemporary nonfiction except for their high school textbooks, so they have no models of effective persuasive or explanatory expository writing by which to judge their own efforts. Even if they do read clear and interesting articles in magazines like *Esquire, Ebony, Newsweek,* or *Sports Illustrated,* they do not think of them as good models to imitate because they are popular, not scholarly. In fact, however, such articles often make excellent models for college writers because their authors have mastered the art of writing readable prose.

A second reason that students have trouble identifying models for their own writing is that they sometimes encounter wordy and ponderous writing in their textbooks or academic journals and assume that the style is typical of academic prose. Moreover, often it is just the article that students find the hardest to read that impresses them most. And because they are inexperienced readers, they seldom say to themselves, "I am having a hard time reading this book or article because it is badly written." Rather they say, "I must be stupid because I am having such a hard time reading this article. What's more, this must be important stuff because the author uses so many big words and long sentences."

Although an essay or book may be important and worth reading *even though* it is hard to understand, no one should be impressed by a piece of writing *because* it is hard to understand. Readers who allow themselves to be dazzled and intimidated by overblown and confusing writing are like the people in the Hans Christian Andersen fairy tale who were afraid to say that the emperor, who was supposed to be wearing a robe of beautiful cloth, actually was naked. Because these spectators had been told that the robe was made of a wonderful fabric that was invisible to those who were stupid or not fit to hold office, they did not have the nerve to say they couldn't see the fabulous robe. In the same way, timid readers are sometimes afraid to say, "I don't understand what that means" for fear they will be thought stupid or unfit to be around educated people. So by their silence they help to encourage unclear writing — worse, they sometimes try to imitate it to impress people.

As a student, you will almost inevitably have to read much writing that is dense and difficult to understand — for example, works by Marx, Dewey, Kant, Hegel, and others. Although there is little use in complaining — after all we can't go back and ask those thinkers to write more clearly — you certainly shouldn't think that such cumbersome prose is a good model. Above all, don't try to imitate it.

Use clear writing as a model

What you should use for models are those serious books and articles that you can read and understand with comparatively little trouble, and there are certainly many of those. Historians like Bruce Catton and Arthur Schlesinger, philosophers like Bertrand Russell, economists like John Kenneth Galbraith, and literary critics like Wayne Booth and Cleanth Brooks demonstrate that you don't have to write badly to say something important.

You can also learn something about clear writing from the simple language of magazine articles written for people who have similar interests but who come from a wide variety of educational backgrounds. For instance, here are two examples from vastly different magazines:

> Everyone who has ever taken up a fishing pole or a hunting piece has known hunters and fishing types who are invariably

lucky when the rest of us are coming home empty-handed. A little investigation would show, I'm convinced, that almost all of that habitual "luck" is an ancient mixture of toil and guile. To be sure, the most innocent tenderfoot townie alive can bag a ten-point buck once in a while without actually having the remotest notion of what he's doing. But the man who brings his deer or turkey home every season when most of his buddies are sitting around a stove somewhere cracking their knuckles and bemoaning the lack of game does not depend on luck. Fishing and hunting reward the chap who knows where to be, at what hour, and what to do after he gets to that place to be.[2]

The man who began the King Ranch and one of America's most durable families had no family ties himself. In 1833, at the age of nine, he was apprenticed to a jeweler in New York City. He never saw his family again and never divulged anything about them except that they were Irish. The young boy could not abide the close, tedious work of the jeweler's shop or the rigid medieval bonds of apprenticeship. Even at that age he was drawn toward open spaces. At eleven he stowed away on a sailing ship bound for Mobile and for the next ten years he worked on steamboats in the rivers and coastal waters of the eastern Gulf of Mexico. The steamboaters were his parents and the frontier was his schoolroom. The boy learned its tough and demanding lessons well, and he grew into a young man with a quick mind and quicker fists.[3]

The language in both examples is clear, simple though not elementary, and seems to flow as naturally as everyday speech. In most cases, that is the kind of language you should use when you write. Don't switch over to a complicated, stilted style and use words you're really not familiar with just because you are putting those words on paper.

In fact, one way to test the readability of your prose is to read a sentence out loud after you've written it and ask yourself, "Does that sound like me? Would I talk like that, even in serious conversation?" If the answer is no, you should revise and simplify the sentence.

As you take more college courses, you will be reading more and

[2]Richard Starnes, "Dry Run," *Field and Stream* July 1976: 10.
[3]William Broyles, Jr., "The Last Empire," *Texas Monthly* Oct. 1980: 158.

more nonfiction of all kinds, and if you read critically you will learn to distinguish good writing from poor writing. You know now what to look for. In informative or persuasive prose, those features of good writing combine to produce one quality: *readability*. If you put your best efforts into reading a piece of writing — and that is an important "if" — and if the subject is not so complicated or specialized that it is over your head, you have a right to expect that you will be able to understand what the writer is saying. So trust your instincts about good writing and also your taste. If you like what you're reading, it is probably well written.

What Happens When People Write

People who are taking writing courses in the 1980s are lucky because they are nearly the first generation of students who have the chance to benefit from the research and investigation into the writing process that has been done in the past ten years. That research, which is continuing, has helped us to understand at least partially how writers work and what happens during the writing process. We are also beginning to identify some of the significant differences between the writing behaviors of skilled and unskilled writers and to draw some conclusions that can help apprentice writers work more effectively. And as we find out more about how writers work, we also find out more about how they don't work. As a result, we can

now dispel some of the popular myths that seem to surround the act of writing for many people.

Dispelling Some Myths

The Myth About Inspiration   Many nonwriters believe that "real" writers are gifted people who write in a frenzy of inspiration. They are so talented that they do not have to spend much time or effort on their writing. Instead, they wait around until they are in the mood to write and then when an idea strikes them, they pour the words out onto the paper in a spurt of creativity. The myth also holds

that because such people are geniuses, their inspired writing is always good. They don't have to revise their work or write anything more than once; they get it right the first time. And the more inspired they are, the better their writing is.

We might call this view of the writing process the Magic Touch Theory. Even in the past, practicing writers would have told you that this is a fairy tale, and now research confirms what they knew from experience. But some people like to believe the fairy tale because it gives them a good excuse for not working at their writing. Since they're not geniuses and never have any inspirations, they reason, no one should expect much of them. But the myth of the Magic Touch is almost pure fantasy. Those of us who write and teach writing know that very ordinary people can and do become good writers.

The Myth About Rules   At the other extreme are people who believe that they would be good writers if they just knew enough rules. They think that writing is a rule-governed activity and that if they could learn all the rules that professional writers know they would not have any more problems with their writing. These people frequently excuse their poor writing by saying that they are still working at learning the rules; they assume that once they master them, they will become good writers.

Writing is not a rule-governed activity

Practicing writers can also demolish this myth. No writer ever produced good work because he or she worked hard at memorizing rules or formulas. Although it's certainly true that effective writers must be able to spell, punctuate, and construct correct sentences, most writers don't think about rules as they write. They may think about them as they *rewrite,* but rules have no power to help writers generate ideas or organize them into readable form.

The Habits of Writers

Most good writers are not geniuses who write in bursts of inspiration, nor are they human computers who produce discourse according to a set of rules. Rather, the average productive writer is a steady worker who acts pretty much as other people do when they have a job to do. And though different individuals have different ways of approaching writing tasks, my research has convinced me that we can draw these generalizations about how effective writers behave:

How good writers work

1. Effective writers don't count on inspiration; they write whether they feel like it or not. They write regularly, and usually they write according to a schedule.

2. Effective writers usually write in a specific place, and they like to use the same tools each time — word processor, typewriter, or pencil. The details of writing are important to them — the kind of paper, the location of their desk, the clothes they wear, the atmosphere of the room — so they try to create a favorable environment for their work.

3. Effective writers depend on deadlines to keep them working; they make commitments that will force them to write and to get their work in by a certain date.

4. Effective writers often procrastinate about writing and feel guilty about doing so.

5. Effective writers usually work slowly. Many of them consider 1,500 words (five double-spaced, typed pages) a good day's work.

6. Effective writers usually make some kind of plan before they start to write, but they keep their plan flexible and replan as they work.

7. Effective writers often have trouble starting to write, but many of them have developed strategies for overcoming this problem.

8. Effective writers expect to get new insights as they work; they know that writing is an act of discovery, and they develop their ideas by writing.

9. Effective writers stop frequently to reread and reflect on what they have already written; they know that such rereading stimulates them to continue writing.

10. Effective writers revise their work *as* they write, and they expect to do two or more drafts of their writing.

11. Effective writers are careful observers, and they have a system for collecting ideas or material that may be useful to them.

12. Effective writers do not always enjoy writing — usually they can find something else they would rather be doing — but they get satisfaction from *having written*.[4]

All these data suggest that when people write they engage in a process that is inexact, messy, sometimes unpredictable, often astonishing, and frequently tedious. By its nature, it defies precise analysis; nevertheless we can find certain patterns in the writing process, patterns that seem to correspond to those common to other creative

[4]The bibliography of works from which these conclusions were drawn is on pp. 37–39.

endeavors in fields such as art, music, architecture, or scientific discovery.

The Stages of the Writing Process

Researchers and theorists who study and speculate about the creative process believe that it occurs in four stages: preparation, incubation, illumination and execution, and verification. For writers, those stages seem to have the following characteristics:

Preparation   Preparation to write can be thought of in two steps. The first step is *long-range* preparation. It includes every experience or relationship a person has had before starting to work on a writing assignment — reading, work, sports, travel, friendships, illness, school, marriage. Everything that has gone on in a person's life becomes potential material that can be drawn on, and the more alert and thoughtful a person is about experiences in his or her life, the better prepared that person is to write.

Preparation is both long-range and immediate

The second step is *immediate* preparation, which takes place after the writer identifies and commits to the writing task at hand. This step may include choosing and narrowing a topic or clarifying an assignment made by someone else. It also includes identifying the audience and purpose: *who* is the paper for and *what* is it for? When the writer has answered that question, he or she can begin to employ various strategies for generating material, strategies that will be explained at length in Chapter 2. The writer may also begin to think about ways to organize and develop his or her material; Chapter 2 focuses on those concerns. The activity at this stage of the process may be compared to feeding information into a computer that one will later use to write a program or solve a problem.

Incubation   After spending as much time as they need — or can afford — in the preparation stage, many writers try to stop working or thinking directly about their material and just let it *incubate* or "cook" in their subconscious mind. They turn their attention to something else, but beneath the level of consciousness the subconscious faculties are busy processing, evaluating, sorting, and combining the information, impressions, and memories the writer has stored. This stage resembles "sleeping on a problem."

Your material may need to "cook"

Illumination and Execution   After preparation and incubation, a writer can usually return to the job of writing with a sense of *illumination*. That is, he or she has what seems to be a workable idea or a valid thesis and also has some plan about how to put it into writing. The writer begins to *execute* that plan, and at the end of this stage the writer has a draft. The execution stage of the creative process is probably the hardest to analyze and describe because it varies so widely, not only from writer to writer but from writing task to writing task for the same writer. This stage of the process can be painfully slow, or it may move along briskly. Writers may do extensive revising at this stage, having additional flashes of illumination as they work, or they may write quickly, making few changes. They may write six drafts, or they may write only one.

Writers execute their plans in various ways

Verification   Finally, like a scientist checking the results of an experiment or an architect inspecting his or her final drawing, the writer has to *edit* what has been written — check that there are no inconsistencies or failures to follow through on commitments, that sources are cited accurately, that proper grammar has been used, and that names are spelled correctly. A final proofreading comes here as well — the writer checks for misspellings and usage and punctuation mistakes. Notice that proofreading is the *last* thing to do. Writers shouldn't allow themselves to be distracted by worrying about these details at the execution stage.

Making the final check

The Flexible Nature of the Writing Process

Different Kinds of Writers

This overview of the writing process is very generalized. In actuality, the stages can be highly flexible and their characteristics vary greatly depending on the temperament or experience and ability of individual writers. Some writers like to invest a lot of time in the preparation stage, reading, taking notes or making outlines, rehearsing different approaches in their mind, and mulling over what they are going to do. When they get to the execution stage, they can turn out a first draft quickly and efficiently. I know one writer who thinks about an article for a month or more but does little actual writing during that time. When he does start to write, however, he can turn out an acceptable draft in two or three writing sessions. Other writers prefer not to spend a lot of time on preparation at first, because they know from experience that they work better by jotting down some rough notes to capture their main ideas and getting to the actual writing fairly quickly. They do, however, move back to the preparation stage from time to time by stopping to plan and make additional notes.

Writers also differ in how much incubation time they like to allow. Some, particularly experienced writers like journalists, don't require large chunks of time for incubation but seem to be able to move directly from planning to execution, especially when they have to meet a tight deadline. Other writers need idle time to allow their ideas to generate and just can't force the process. Writers even vary in the amount of time they need for verification. Those who are able to suspend completely the internal monitor for spelling and punctuation as they write need to allow substantial time for the cleanup phase; others, who are either naturally good spellers and punctuate instinctively or who cannot resist fixing the little things as they go, can often get by with a quick proofreading at the end.

Find your working method

So all writers have their individual methods of working, and you should learn yours. You will enjoy writing more if you stick to the method that suits you best, at least for your first draft. But even if you like to put considerable time and effort into your first draft, I would caution that you not invest so much in it that you will be reluctant to make changes. You *may* be satisfied with your first attempt, but the chances are good that you won't be, and you shouldn't close out your options too soon. Through revision you may be able to develop your paper into one far more interesting than you could have anticipated when you began. And through revision you may also find that you can't write the paper you planned to write, and you will have to change your topic or your approach.

Different Kinds of Writing

I think individual writers also use different writing processes according to the kinds of writing they are doing — that is, no writer does all of his or her writing in the same way or at the same speed. Rather, all of us vary our methods to fit the particular kind of writing task we are doing and the circumstances under which we are writing. I classify the kinds of writing tasks into three broad categories.

Message Writing   First, we do *message* writing — the kind of writing all of us must do for routine, everyday writing tasks such as brief memos at the office or casual notes at home. Ordinarily we don't have to spend much time on this kind of writing because we know what we are going to say, and we write as quickly and straightforwardly as possible. To be sure, a writer must occasionally take special pains with a message to be sure that it is accurate and to get the tone right, but most of the time a literate person has no trouble with this kind of writing. Messages constitute an important kind of writing, particularly in business and the professions, but they seldom require much preparation or incubation time from writers.

Self-Contained Writing   Second, we do *limited* or *self-contained* writing. This category is quite broad, containing many different kinds of writing, including case studies, technical reports, most essay exams, writing samples on competency exams, and papers or articles that summarize and present information. The identifying feature of limited or self-contained writing is that the person writing it already knows most of what he or she is going to write or at least knows where to find it. The writer's main task is not to discover what he or she wants to say, generating most of the content during the writing process, but to organize already-known content and present it in a clear and effective style.

A typical example of self-contained writing is the kind of article that professional writers write for general audiences: for instance, an article in *Newsweek* about the apparent link between diet and cancer or an article in an airline magazine on walking trips through Scotland. To write such articles, writers do not have to discover their content; it already exists in research findings or travel books. The challenge they face is to select and organize the specific material they want to use and to present it clearly and in a way that will hold their audience's attention. Most of the writing that people do in business and industry is self-contained writing. It is not necessarily easy to do, and, because it is often important writing, doing it well can require considerable time and thought.

Another typical example of self-contained writing is a writing sample in a placement exam or the writing students do on essay exams. In situations like these, writers have to draw on what they already know or can remember; they have little time to probe their experiences, reflect on them, and come up with fresh ideas. They cannot write discovery drafts, set them aside to "cook," and then rethink what they want to say. Under circumstances like these, the competent writer jots down notes as a memory aid, quickly decides on a format, and writes as clearly as he or she can, doing comparatively little revising. These are the times when a reliable formula can be valuable: state your thesis, give and develop your supporting points, and summarize in a conclusion.

Self-contained writing is not necessarily formulaic

But self-contained writing is by no means always formulaic. When writers work on term papers, case studies, reports, or papers that present the results of an investigation, they must consider how to select their material and how best to present it. Sometimes they get fresh insights while they are working. The process can certainly be creative. Nevertheless, writers who are doing self-contained writing often can't allow much time for incubation — particularly in business — and usually have to move ahead with their work once they have settled on content. They may do considerable revising if they have time, but when they do they focus on rearranging or cutting or on trying to get the tone right.

Reflective Writing   We also do a third kind of writing that I call *reflective* or *emergent* writing. This is also a broad category that includes several kinds of writing: personal experience papers in which writers recall events in their lives and reflect about their meaning, exploratory or speculative articles in which writers give data or information and theorize about implications or consequences, articles in which writers theorize about the future, or original, thoughtful papers of almost any kind. Of course there are innumerable examples of reflective writing; among those you may encounter are Alice Walker's "In Search of Our Mothers' Gardens," an essay in which she recalls the gardens her mother used to make and reflects on their meaning, and George Orwell's "Marrakech," an essay in which he describes the poor people of that city and theorizes about what their situation says about the culture in which they live. A further example is an editorial in which a writer speculates about how women's new career aspirations have affected the teaching profession.

Often when students write papers in which they discuss the effect of an experience or recall an important event in their lives, they are doing reflective writing. Writing an original comment on a book or essay or theorizing about the long-range impact of a new technology also may be reflective writing. And student writers do reflective writing when they collect information, synthesize it, and draw conclusions from it. Both papers at the end of Chapter 4 on revision represent this kind of writing. In business, the people who write prospectuses and research proposals are usually doing reflective, emergent writing, and judges who write judicial opinions also do reflective writing.

Content emerges during reflective writing

The identifying characteristic of reflective writing is that the writer begins with little more than an idea or a strong "felt sense" of what he or she wants to say and only a general idea of the content or how that content will be organized. The writers count on most of their content emerging as they write and stimulate their thought processes, and they expect their writing to take form as they work.

When writers do reflective writing, the amount of time they spend on preparation varies considerably according to their work habits. Some spend almost no time on direct preparation; rather, they spend a lot of time thinking about their project, letting their impressions germinate. Finally they begin to write, expecting to formulate their ideas during the execution stage. Others may do extensive reading and note taking, brainstorm to help themselves get started, allow considerable incubation time, and, as they write, move back and forth between planning and execution. In either case, the illumination and execution stage usually takes much longer for reflective writing than it does for self-contained writing because writers have to harvest and pay attention to the information they coax from their subconscious. Usually, they also have to write several drafts to settle finally on their purpose and shape their thesis.

Cautions

This system of classifying different kinds of writing and writing processes must inevitably oversimplify a highly complex process and create pigeonholes that are too neat and limited. The analysis also suggests that readers can examine a finished written product and infer the processes a writer used to create that product. That's a risky assumption. A report that seems straightforward and factual might, in fact, have required considerable original thought and reflection; a seemingly reflective essay about a personal experience might have been turned out quickly from ideas the writer had already articulated to him or herself. Nevertheless, it can be useful to think about writing in these classifications and realize that writers frequently have to adjust their writing processes according to the tasks they are doing.

There is a parallel to these classifications in at least one other creative field. An architect friend tells me that sometimes, when a client wants him to design a building, the elements of the problem are straightforward and predictable and he can create a good design quickly, particularly if he has done other buildings of the same kind. He doesn't have to discover a fresh approach and try out several designs in order to find out what he wants to do. He has reliable strategies he can draw on to do a perfectly satisfactory job. At other times, however, the client may bring him a problem that requires him to reflect and experiment extensively in order to come up with a good design. He has to discover what he wants to do as he works. People working on problems in other areas such as science or engineering or medicine make the same observation: some problems are more difficult to solve than others and take more time and reflection.

Using the Different Kinds of Writing

Most writers need to do all three kinds of writing in their personal, professional, and academic lives. They have to know how to write clear, succinct messages in order to communicate primary information to others. They have to know how to take information they have, evaluate and organize it, and present it to their readers efficiently and effectively. Being able to do this kind of self-contained writing and do it well is an important part of a writer's craft. And they also need to know how to develop a piece of thoughtful, reflective writing in which they discover new ideas and insights and articulate them for others.

All three kinds are necessary

So all three kinds of writing are useful and necessary, and one is not more important than another. Probably most writers do more message writing and self-contained writing than reflective writing because there is simply more of it to be done. And it's a good thing that usually it doesn't take as much time or energy as reflective writing. Most of us could not afford the processes of reflective writing for every writing task, just as my architect friend couldn't afford to come up with an original idea and several exploratory designs for every building for which he accepted a commission.

Most people who write frequently agree that reflective writing is the most difficult to do but also the most rewarding; it causes the most anguish but also brings the most satisfaction. Certainly it carries the highest risk. But that's part of the reason that it is the most fun.

The Generative Power of the Process

This sketchy overview of the stages of the writing process may make the act of writing seem more straightforward than it really is most of the time. In reality, it's often messy and frequently unpredictable, particularly when one is working on a complex, open-ended project. Then the stages often mingle, overlap, or alternate, and a great deal of revision goes on as a writer works.

Probably most writers begin with some kind of plan, making preliminary outlines or sketching their general ideas. Many, however, do not plan their projects completely ahead of time because they do not want to close out new ideas that may come to them. Also, they know from experience that a clearer vision of their goal will come to them as they write; thus, they plan, write, stop and replan, and then write again. If they get stuck, they may pause for short periods of incubation, leaving their desks for a few minutes and hoping for a flash of insight that will get them moving again. So the stages of the writing process are not linear; that is, very few writers start at stage 1 and move in a straight line through stage 4, even if they are doing strictly self-contained writing for which they have a fixed plan. The evolution of any creative work — a building, a musical composition, a painting, or an essay — is often like this, a slow, uneven process with frequent detours and backtracking.

For instance, if we look at the working sketches for the painting *Hotel Lobby* by Edward Hopper, we can infer a good deal about the process by which the painting developed. In Figure 1 we see a rough sketch, comparable to an early draft of a piece of writing. Clearly, at this stage Hopper has in mind the main features and overall design of his painting; he has a felt sense of what he wants to do but evidently has not yet decided on the mood of the picture or what the relationship of the figures in the picture will be. At this stage, the figure sitting alone at the right of the picture seems to be a man, but we can tell little about him or about the man and woman at the left of the picture except they seem to be talking to each other.

Writing is not a linear process

Analogy between writing and painting

Figure 1

Figure 2

Figure 5 *Hotel Lobby*

In Figure 2 Hopper has started to reshape or *revise* his painting. Now the figures become clearer and the relationship among them begins to emerge. We sense an air of intimacy between the man and the woman on the left as the man puts his arm on the woman's chair and leans toward her. This intimacy emphasizes the isolation of the other two figures in the painting; the man at the right looks particularly despondent. Hopper also gives more attention to the background and composition of the picture, adding strong vertical lines and dark shadings.

Figures 3 and 4 show Hopper's practice sketches for individual details in the picture. One might compare these to individual passages that a writer might give special attention to — for example, an anecdote used to illustrate a point or a character sketch of a key figure in an article. They represent a kind of *spot* revision. These sketches also show another of Hopper's changes; they replace the man of Figure 2 with a young woman and suggest that Hopper is going to contrast the isolated pose of the older woman with the assured pose of the younger one.

Figure 5 shows the final version of the painting, substantially different from the earlier ones. Now the man stands upright, paying no attention to the older woman, apparently his wife. The woman reading in the chair ignores the couple, and the second woman on the left has disappeared. As one critic put it, "In the evolution from drawing to final painting, Hopper apparently tried to accentuate the sense of non-communication, to reveal a poignant lack of emotional interaction."[6] Like a writer, Hopper began with an idea and worked it out through drafts, finding his focus as he worked. With each succeeding draft — and there may have been more than are shown here — the work of art developed, culminating in the final, rich version.

In the same way, the writer who wants to create a thoughtful and original piece of writing usually begins with only a rough plan for the final product and discovers his or her focus by working through several drafts, letting the paper emerge through revision. Of course, no one who writes frequently has time to do several drafts of every piece of writing, and, as we have seen, not every writing task warrants that kind of investment. But when a writer is committed to doing a first-rate job on a piece of work, he or she is most apt to succeed by following this general creative process.

[6]Gail Levin, *Edward Hopper: The Art and the Artist* (New York: Norton, published in association with the Whitney Museum of American Art, 1980): 49.

Think of Yourself as a Writer

As you write your papers, try to get in the habit of thinking of yourself as a creative person, a working writer. Experiment to find out what kind of tools suit you best and where and when you work best. Establish a routine for writing and condition yourself to think of writing a paper as a process by which you write and revise. Most professionals — lawyers, engineers, business executives, accountants, professors — spend a high percentage of their time writing, and if you can start now to develop the attitudes and habits of a good writer, you will be ahead when you have to start writing as a professional.

Exercises

1. *What is good writing?* Here are several paragraphs taken from both professional and student writing. Which paragraphs are good, and why? What are the features that detract from the paragraphs you do not like?

   a. A revolution is under way. Most Americans are already well aware of the gee-whiz gadgetry that is emerging, in rapidly accelerating bursts, from the world's high-technology laboratories. But most of us perceive only dimly how pervasive and profound the changes of the next twenty years will be. We are at the dawn of the era of the smart machine — an "information age" that will change forever the way an entire nation works, plays, travels, and even thinks. Just as the industrial revolution dramatically expanded the strength of man's muscles and the reach of his hand, so the smart-machine revolution will magnify the power of his brain. But unlike the industrial revolution, which depended on finite resources such as iron and oil, the new information age will be fired by a seemingly limitless resource — the inexhaustible supply of knowledge itself. Even computer scientists, who best understand the galloping technology and its potential, are wonderstruck by its implications.[7]

   b. Almost every city today has a number of western stores. These stores sell nothing but western clothes, and you can find a large

[7]"And Man Created the Chip," *Newsweek* 30 June 1980: 50.

selection of cowboy boots there. Prices range from about one hundred dollars to five or six hundred dollars a pair. For a good pair of bull or cowhide boots, you should plan to spend $125–$150. If you wait for a good sale, you can get these same boots for $90–$100. In addition, some individuals will hand-make your boots. These are considerably more expensive, usually $200–$225 minimum but if you have the money they are well worth the price. A good bootmaker will have you come in before he even starts on the boot. He will measure your foot in every direction and then custom fit the boot to your foot. A custom made boot will last a lot longer than a machine made boot. [*student paragraph*]

c. Scholarships provide a chance for underprivileged and independent students to go to college. Furthermore they seek out people of intelligent potential who wouldn't have thought of going to college. Many people because of their past environment and background don't consider going to college until scholarship agencies contact them through schools, advertisements, and other various means. This includes the basic function of scholarships which is to allow people to go to college that can't afford it. Also young people who wish to make it on their own find it possible through scholarships. All of these various opportunities that all types of scholarships offer emphasizes the importance of personal achievements and therefore promotes it. [*student paragraph*]

d. If a culture is restricted from keeping pace with society, the individuals of that society lose their definition and sense of purpose. They have no choice except to search for meaning in an outmoded cultural reference that does not account for any new symbols and ideas a society conceives and adopts over time. The society becomes confused and stumbles awkwardly, out of step with reality. . . . Any fiber that clashes with the status quo is discarded in deference to strands that complement the reactionary web that is suffocating the life out of our democracy.[8]

e. You've seen them along the highway. Those cars and trucks parked sporadically along the major thoroughfares of the state and overflowing with anything and everything under the sun.

---

[8]Mark McKinnon, "Slouching Toward Camelot," *The Daily Texan* 16 Oct. 1980: 2.

Home-painted signs saying "FRESH FRUIT — GREAT BUYS" or "FRESH SEAFOOD — FROM $1.99 A POUND" entice weary travelers to stop and shop for a bargain. Other merchants don't need signs to point to their wares — you can spot their purple and red polka-dotted bean-bag chairs or their ten foot stuffed Pink Panther dolls from a mile away. [*student paragraph*]

2. *Models*

a. Find a paragraph that seems to you to be particularly well written. Clip it out and tape it to a sheet of paper, or copy it onto a sheet, being sure in either case to give the source. Beneath it write a short paragraph explaining why you think the paragraph is a good one.

b. From a book or magazine select a paragraph that you find difficult to understand and try to analyze why you are having trouble with it. Does the problem seem to be with you because you do not have adequate background or reading skills, or with the author because she or he does not write well? Can you think of a way in which the author could have made the paragraph easier to understand?

3. Rewrite these sentences to make them clearer and more vigorous:

a. The size of the growth rate will depend on consumers' perception of the quality of the available product as well as on the effectiveness of marketing strategies.

b. I cannot account for the accuracy of the depiction of such emotions.

c. Students would be cognizant of the fact that they had command of the technique.

d. The rules may not be enforced unless and until there is a finding of public health necessity.

e. Raising the interest rate is required in order to assure the continued viability of the credit union movement and to assure the availability of consumer loans.

4. In a sentence or two write out an example that you could use to support each of these abstract statements:

a. Addiction to television strikes all age groups.

b. Prosperity is a relative term.

c. Owning a foreign car can be a real headache.

d. Social competition starts very early.

e. The word *busing* has taken on new meaning in the last few years.

5. Comment on the quality and the readability of the following two student papers. Do they meet the criteria set up for good writing (pp. 5–16), and are they comparatively easy to read? Give reasons for your answers.

Paper A was written for an audience of ten- to twelve-year-old children to explain what computer programmers can do. Paper B was written for a general audience, such as readers of an airline magazine.

A. Computer Programming: May the Force Be With You

Imagine yourself the pilot of a two-billion dollar rocket ship, with R2D2 and C3PO at your side. All around you flies the mysterious black beauty of space. Your mission: travel to Einsteina, a newly discovered planet in the Andromeda galaxy. You will record information about the planet's geology, biology and chemistry. On your trip back to the earth, you will use the ship computer to determine if Einsteina would support a colony of scientists. Your skill as a computer programmer will determine the success of the mission.

In today's world and in the future, women and men who program computers are important to almost all areas of life. Here is a list of just a few things you can do as a computer programmer:

- Create special effects for movies like *Star Wars*
- Help design cities of the future
- Keep library or business records
- Create computer-designed art
- Help design a submarine
- Develop new methods of teaching

As you can see, programmers are involved in solving problems in most areas of life. Since good problem solvers are needed everywhere, programmers can work for almost any type of business, government or educational institution. Whether you want to live in Hawaii, France, Egypt, or in the U.S.A., your skills as a programmer will find you a job.

By now you may have decided that you might enjoy being a computer programmer. So let's talk about what a programmer actually does at work.

Computer programmers solve problems. Then they teach the computer to solve the same kind of problem. You see, computers can only do what they are told to do — sort of like a dumb robot. But they think much faster than people do. And once you tell a computer how to do something, it will remember it until it is told to forget it.

So there are four basic steps to programming:

1. Solve the problem
2. Write the steps to the solution
3. Write the steps in computer language
4. Teach the steps to the computer

Computers don't read English or Spanish. Computers read a special language. Actually there are many computer languages. Cobol is a computer language used to solve business problems. Scientists use a computer language called Fortran. These languages are like English, but shorter. They are also like math.

Let's look at a simple computer program.

Program Addition (This program adds numbers.)

A = 5;
B = 10;
C = 16;
D = A + B + C
Print D

Now this program is typed to the computer on a keyboard that looks like a typewriter keyboard. The computer will read the program and remember the value of each letter. When it sees the word "print", the computer will type out the number 31 on the screen. This program is one that you could do without a computer, but as the problems become more difficult, you can see the value of using a computer. You could ask the computer to add one thousand numbers, and it would print the answer faster than you can turn on a light switch.

Solving more difficult problems requires more time and thought on the programmer's part. But once the program is "fed" into the computer, the computer will print the answer in a very short time. And the next time you want to solve the same problem, you don't have to start at the beginning. Just ask the computer. It will still have the answer stored in its memory.

You can see that computers save people time and energy. So you can understand that people who program computers are important to many different parts of life. The next time you turn on the television, or ride in the car, or talk on the phone, remember: a computer programmer was one of the people who made it possible.

Mike Williams

B. The Wild West Hero: America's Oldest Cover Up

You are watching a western on TV when an uneasy feeling creeps down your spine as two gunslingers approach each other on a deserted, dusty street. A haunting silence falls over the town as horrified townspeople watch quietly from their hiding places. The wind kicks up and time stands still as you are shown the icy-cold eyes of the gunfighters staring through one another. You sit up in your chair as you peer at the faces of two hard men; two poker-faced men who are putting each other through a bittersweet hell. The picture shifts to two hands nervously hovering above their guns, when all at once they both draw. Gunshots are heard, smoke is seen and you watch as an angry, unbelieving man with gritted teeth falls in slow motion with hand over heart. A cloud of dust arises upon impact with the ground and as the dust slowly filters back to the ground, our villain dies. A feeling of relief gradually replaces your uneasiness and you smile because your hero, Quick Carl, is still alive.

Somehow, the preceding gunfight seems terribly beautiful when seen on television, but unfortunately gunfights probably very seldom happened that way. In fact, most modern beliefs about western legend and heroes are not quite true, even though we might wish them to be so. Legend builds many champions of the west up to be brave, rugged and always ready for a challenge. In reality, many western heroes appear to be quite pathetic when you contrast what they were supposed to be with what they really were.

For example, let's take the case of Calamity Jane, best remembered out of Hollywood in the figure of Jean Arthur. According to a Robert Sherrill book, *The Saturday Night Special,* legend portrays Jane as being a crack shot, a scout for the Army, a pony express rider and also being very beautiful. Unfortunately, Sherrill says, accurate history tells another story: her real name was Martha Jane Canary; her mother, Charlotte Canary, ran a brothel called "The Bird Cage," in which Calamity Jane apprenticed. Jane was not the gun-toting beauty she is now made out to be. Sherrill tells us that historian Bruce Nelson who specializes in studying her adventures cites that "her services to the Army were in a quite different capacity from that mentioned" in her autobiography. "Citizens of Deadwood who knew Jane well described her as a common harlot — and one of such coarse and forbidding appearance as to frighten away all save the tipsiest miner."

"Coarse and forbidding" are two adjectives historians might have also used in describing Belle Starr, yet another heroine of wild west fame. The legendary Belle Starr (Myra Bill Shirley) epitomized the frontier woman, gracious but with a will of iron, and always loyal to her man. According to legend, Belle was quite handy with a six-gun and rifle; however, the manner of her death seems to question that. She was shot down from behind by her son who used a charge of buckshot to knock her off her horse and a charge of turkeyshot to finish her off. Sherrill's *Saturday Night Special* also tells us that the real Belle Starr was a known whore and an ugly one at that. She had two illegitimate children — a boy who grew up to be her incestuous lover and murderer, and a girl who followed in mother's prostitute footsteps.

Belle Starr's son was not the only backshooter in the west. A young man named Billy the Kid, about whom Hollywood has made no fewer than twenty-one movies, was also a come-from-behind artist. In each of Hollywood's movies about him, the hero is represented by tall, handsome actors such as Paul Newman, who was the last person to portray Billy the Kid. A more accurate description of Billy, according to Peter Lyon in

The Wild, Wild West, would be a "slight, short, buck-toothed, narrow-shouldered youth whose slouch added to his unwholesome appearance." As mentioned earlier, Billy usually killed from ambush; his only recorded face-to-face gun murder was of an unarmed man.

The Wild Bill Hickok legend began at Rock Creek, Nebraska, where Bill had supposedly wiped out singlehandedly the "McCanles Gang" of nine "desperadoes, horse-thieves, murderers, and cutthroats," according to Harper's Monthly. Using six-gun, rifle, and Bowie knife, Hickok supposedly took on the gang and received eleven bullets in his body.

However, once again Sherrill's *Saturday Night Special* gives a more correct version of the story; it seems that Hickok was hiding behind a calico curtain in a trading post when he gunned down Dave McCanles. The other members of the "gang" consisted of McCanles' twelve-year old son, a young cousin, and a young employee who blundered into the fight. The son did nothing more than run to his dying father while the other two were wounded in the gunplay and attempted to run away. The latter two were not successful as some of Hickok's friends murdered one boy with a hoe and the other with a shotgun blast. Ironically, Hickok's triumph over the "McCanles Gang" has been referred to sometimes as being "the greatest one man gunfight in history." In later years, Sherrill finds Wild Bill in Abilene Kansas in 1871 where he had been hired to enforce the law. Some say he spent most of his nights sleeping with the whores in the section of Abilene called "Devil's Half Acre," while others complained that he spent the rest of his time protecting "professional gamblers, madams, and saloonkeepers from irate and dissatisfied customers who thought they had been cheated — as indeed they probably had."

If after reading this you feel like you've been cheated by Hollywood and possibly previous history courses, you're probably right. However, don't feel bad; Hollywood has taken practically everyone for a ride, and the problem of legend being passed off as fact is still with us today. Our present society has the tendency to dramatize personalities and happenings in movies and on television. Who will be the heroes of tomorrow? Possibly the "Godfathers" and hoodlums of today, but it is really hard to say. It isn't hard to guess that whoever they are, they will be given more credit than they deserve.

Reggie Rice

Writing Assignments

Paper 1

One of the major reasons we write is to enrich our associations with other people by sharing our impressions, our experiences, and our knowledge with them. This writing assignment gives you a chance to tell other people about a sport or activity you enjoy, an interesting or unusual experience you have had, or some information that might be useful to them. The challenge of the assignment is to write an account that your readers will find interesting and informative, perhaps even useful in their own lives.

Before you start the main part of your paper, write down the specific person or group interested in reading it and give their reasons for being interested. Then write a one-sentence statement of your purpose for writing to them; that is, state what you hope to accomplish with your readers. Perhaps you just want them to understand why you enjoy a particular activity, or perhaps you want to convince them to try a sport or consider taking a job. You may want to give them enough information on some product to help them make a decision.

The paper doesn't have to be long, perhaps between 300 and 400 words, brief enough to be part of a letter or to serve as a short talk in a speech class.

Possible Topics

1. Juggling child care and class schedules.
2. The fun of wind surfing.
3. Coping with the university student aid office.
4. Trying out for the band or the baseball team.
5. Carrying out groceries at the supermarket.
6. The pros and cons of regulation black bicycling pants.
7. Working as a cat- and dog-sitter.

Your particular interests and experience will probably suggest other possible topics that would work well for such a short piece. Try to use specific personal and visual details that will hold your readers' attention.

Paper 2

This writing assignment gives you an opportunity to express an idea or an opinion that you think is worth discussing with someone else. It doesn't call for you to construct an extended and careful argument or use data to support your points; think of it as something you might write for an informal orientation program or a short talk.

Before you start to write the paper, write down your audience for the paper and the reasons they have for reading or listening to what you write. Also state your purpose in writing. What do you want to accomplish by giving your explanation or opinion for these readers?

Possible Topics

1. Most college students spend more than they need to on clothes.
2. Being an older college student has certain advantages.
3. The university should pay more attention to its commuter students.
4. The college book store should get its act together.
5. You're better off to bring a bike to school than to bring a car.
6. What life in the fast-food lane will do to you.
7. Finding a place to study on campus is becoming a major problem.

You can probably think of similar topics out of your own experience and concerns. Whatever topic you choose, develop it with specific and personal touches that will make it come alive for your readers.

Bibliographical Sources for Pages 17–18 (The Habits of Writers)

Barzun, Jacques. "A Writer's Discipline." *Writing, Editing, and Publishing*. Chicago: U of Chicago P, 1971. 5–17.

Britton, James. "The Composing Processes and the Functions of Writing." *Research in Composing.* Ed. Charles Cooper and Lee Odell. Urbana: NCTE, 1978. 13–28.

Cowley, Malcolm, ed. *Writers at Work: The Paris Review Interviews,* 1st ser. New York: Viking, 1958.

Didion, Joan. "On Keeping a Notebook." *Slouching Towards Bethlehem.* New York: Delta, 1968. 131–40.

———. "Why I Write." *New York Times Book Review* 5 Dec. 1976: 2, 98–99.

Emig, Janet. "A Review of the Literature." *The Composing Processes of Twelfth Graders.* Urbana: NCTE, 1971. 7–27.

Galbraith, John Kenneth. "Writing, Typing, and Economics." *Atlantic Monthly,* March 1978: 102–105.

Kazin, Alfred. "An Interview with Alfred Kazin." *Composition and Teaching.* San Jose, Ca.: San Jose State University, 1978. 2–29.

McPhee, John. Introduction. *The John McPhee Reader.* New York: Vintage, 1977. xiv–xxvii.

Murray, Donald. *A Writer Teaches Writing.* Boston: Houghton, 1968. 2nd ed. 1985.

Pianko, Sharon. "Reflection: A Critical Component of the Composing Process." *College Composition and Communication,* Oct. 1979: 275–78.

Plimpton, George, ed. *Writers at Work: The Paris Review Interviews,* 2nd ser. New York: Viking, 1963.

———, ed. *Writers at Work: The Paris Review Interivews,* 3rd ser. New York: Viking, 1967.

———, ed. *Writers at Work: The Paris Review Interviews,* 4th ser. New York: Viking, 1976.

Publishers Weekly staff, eds. *The Author Speaks.* New York and London: Bowker, 1977.

Robertson, Nan. "Barbara Tuchman: A Loner at the Top of Her Field." *The New York Times* 27 Feb. 1979: C10.

Sommers, Nancy. "Revision Strategies of Student Writers and Experienced Adult Writers." *College Composition and Communication,* Dec. 1980: 378–88.

Stallard, Charles. "An Analysis of the Writing Behaviors of Good Student Writers." *Research in the Teaching of English* (Summer 1974): 206–18.

Steinbeck, John. *Journal of a Novel.* London: Pan, 1970.

2 · Writing: An Overview, Part 2

Preparing to Write

The advantage of an early start

Probably the best break you can give yourself when you need to write a paper is to start early enough so that you can allow ample time for preparation. Professional writers have recognized this for years, and consequently many of them spend more time preparing to write than they do actually writing. They know that brainstorming their topic, sketching out a plan, or making preliminary notes helps them generate ideas and discover insights they didn't know they had. Amateur writers, in contrast, often wait until the last minute before they start writing and thus do not give themselves time to tap their creative powers and to let their ideas develop. They don't realize what rich resources they have within themselves, nor do they know how to get to these resources. But there are strategies both for developing those resources and for tapping them. This chapter will explain what they are.

Preparation: Stage One

Strategies for finding material

People who must write a lot have developed special strategies for adding to their reserves of material and keeping themselves well prepared for whatever writing tasks they may need to do. For example, many writers keep a file of clippings they have built up by regularly scanning newspapers and magazines for items of special interest. Most of them also have some system for taking notes and are never without pen or pencil and something to write on, usually a small notebook. Many working writers also make special efforts to break out of their regular routines occasionally so that they can observe and talk to people whose jobs and style of living are very different

from theirs. They seek experience and try to develop a kind of personal radar system that picks up signals from everything that is going on around them.

As an apprentice writer, you can enrich your own stock of working material by cultivating the same kinds of habits. Moreover, doing so doesn't necessarily require that you travel widely or spend a great deal of money. Rather, you need to learn to mine your environment for everything it has to offer. Talk to the person who fixes your dishwasher or refrigerator; listen to the conversation going on next to you in the airport; pick up a foreign language magazine on the newsstand or in the library and see how its ads and illustrations differ from ours; check your campus newspaper to see what unusual outings the recreational sports department is offering; go to a meeting of the Sierra Club or the Prelaw Association and find out what they talk about; pay special attention to the signs you see on campus or in public buildings. In other words, put your intellectual antennae out to discover what is going on around you — you'll be surprised at how much activity you find, and how many anecdotes, narratives, and examples you can draw from it later on.

Preparation: Stage Two

So your general preparation to write goes on all the time, and the more involved you are with the world around you, the better prepared you will be to write. Specific preparation to write starts when you choose or are given a definite writing task. At that point you need to do three things.

Define the task

First, *define your writing task as precisely as possible.* If the assignment gives you several options, choose the one you find most interesting or the one that gives you a chance to write about something you know. Then think about how you can limit the topic until it is narrow enough to treat adequately in the number of pages allotted for the paper — that will probably be narrower than you think at first. For some good ways of narrowing your topic, see the discussions of treeing (pp. 46–48) focusing (pp. 119–121).

Define your audience

Second, *define your audience.* Two of the most important questions that working writers ask themselves are "Who is my audience for this piece?" and "Why are they going to read it?" No writer can really make intelligent decisions about his or her writing without knowing the answers to those questions; yet inexperienced writers often start a paper without giving a thought to who, other than their composition instructor, would be reading it. They "blue-sky" it, throwing their words to some vague and general reader who puts no demands or limitations on them, and the result bores everyone, including themselves.

The problem of audience is so important that it will be a major concern in Chapter 3. For now, just keep in mind that identifying your audience specifically is an essential part of getting ready to write.

Define your purpose
Third, *define your purpose*. Ask yourself, "Where am I going with this paper? What do I hope to accomplish?" If the assignment is one that calls for straightforward exposition on a topic about which you already have most of your information or know where to find it, you probably have a strong sense of what you need to do.

Suppose, for example, that you have one hour in which to write a short essay for a placement exam into second-semester English. The assignment asks you to write an editorial for the college newspaper in which you argue for or against a current proposal to raise the student activity fee next year in order to build a new outdoor swimming pool. You know that your real purpose in the essay is to demonstrate that you can organize and develop a short piece of writing in acceptable English. To do that you need only to take a definite position, call on knowledge you already have to find logical reasons for your stand, and develop those reasons with some kind of evidence. You don't have to ponder your purpose.

On the other hand, if you are writing a less clear-cut kind of paper, perhaps one in which you are trying to convince your parents that you want to transfer from the college of engineering to the college of architecture, your broad purpose is obvious, but you might feel less certain about how you can specifically accomplish it on paper. Should you try to convince them that you are unhappy? Is that a good enough reason for changing? Or should you try to persuade them that you don't have the aptitude to be an engineer, or that architecture offers more creative options than engineering? You will have to explore as you write, and from that exploration the specific purpose for your paper will emerge.

If, however, you start out with no sense of what you want to accomplish in your paper, you're likely to waste time on writing without any direction. Chapter 3 says much more about purpose: how you find it, how you sharpen it, and how you use it as a guideline when you are revising.

Strategies for Discovery

Stocking your brain with a wide variety of experiences and information takes time, but it's a satisfying process, particularly if you're a naturally curious person and like to talk to people and to read. But one does not accumulate a stock of resources for writing in an orderly fashion, and consequently the data that you may want to draw on for a specific writing task often cannot be called up on command. They may lie hidden in dark corners, maybe close to the bottom of your mind, or may have gotten wedged in with other information you don't want. The problem is how to get to them and bring them to the surface of your mind, where you can examine them and see if you want to use them.

The problem is an important one, especially for inexperienced writers who must work on a schedule that doesn't allow them time to consider a topic at their leisure and wait to see what may develop from it. They need exploratory strategies that will help them probe into their memories and information banks and stir up some intellectual action that will generate ideas for their writing. Those strategies should be comparatively simple so that they can be put to use immediately, and they should yield results quickly. The strategies described here meet both these requirements.

Strategy 1: Writing   As every practicing writer knows, writing itself is the best device anyone has for generating and discovering ideas. The very act of writing, of seeing words on paper, seems to help stimulate the brain and help writers make connections that they had not seen before. If there is any magic about writing, this is the moment at which it seems to be working. For this reason, sometimes the best tactic for getting started is just to start writing and see what develops. Even if your first efforts don't lead anywhere, almost certainly they will help you break the inertia barrier. And once you realize what a powerful generative device writing can be, you will expect to get new insights and inspirations as you work.

The magic of writing

But the magic of this kind of writing is unreliable, and writers who wait until they start writing to think about what they want to say often find that inspiration fizzles out before they can complete their work. For that reason, it's a good idea to try several other kinds of probes and have a stock of strategies at your disposal when you start to write.

Learning to brainstorm

Strategy 2: Brainstorming Brainstorming is a free-association technique for stirring up intellectual energy. Writers can engage in it singly or in groups, but either way the method is essentially the same. You begin with a word or an idea and start writing down everything and anything that it brings to mind. You continue free associating at an intense pace for a predetermined period of time — usually fifteen to twenty minutes — recording your thoughts as you go.

In group brainstorming, one person acts as recorder and writes down everyone's ideas. No one worries about correct grammar or spelling or about explaining or justifying anything that is said. The important thing is to get down a lot of ideas as quickly as they can surface. Individuals who brainstorm by themselves go about it the same way, writing down their ideas as fast as they come.

Two principles govern brainstorming:

First, everything that comes out in a brainstorming session is a right answer. You should not dismiss any suggestion as trivial, irrelevant, impractical, or inappropriate. At this point in the discovery process, writers haven't yet discovered what they want to say or exactly what they want to do, so how can any suggestions be "wrong"?

Second, ideas piggyback on each other. When those who are doing the brainstorming come up with an idea, they are not necessarily responding to the original stimulus; rather, they may be taking off from a second, third, or fourth level of association that may seem remote from the original. One of the benefits of brainstorming is that it starts chains of thought, and sometimes those chains lead to places that are more interesting than the original starting point.

Strategy 3: Focused Freewriting You probably know from experience that sometimes original ideas and insights seem to pop into your head when you are engaged in casual conversation with someone. Such revelations can really be astonishing; you find that you didn't know what you were thinking until the words came out of your mouth. Apparently the very act of putting words together stirs up your subconscious mind and brings to the surface useful bits of information that fit with the topic you're discussing. That's one principle underlying brainstorming.

Casual, unstructured writing, or freewriting, can produce the same results. When you freewrite, you sit down at the typewriter with a supply of cheap paper or at a desk with a reliable pen and lined paper or a notebook. Then you just start writing whatever comes into your head and keep going for at least ten minutes. If you stall and can't think of something to say, just write "I'm stalled, I'm stalled — can't think of anything" until something comes into your head. Usually that won't take long.

Sometimes writers will write about just anything that comes into their head when they are using freewriting as a strategy for breaking through a temporary writing block. But when you are using it to generate material on a particular topic, you need to do *focused* freewriting. At the top of your paper write down your topic, even though it's a broad one, and take off from there.

In freewriting it's important to keep moving and keep skimming off the ideas that come into your head. Don't stop to edit or correct your writing or to pause and reflect on what you have written. If you stop to think about what you're writing and cross out something or decide to change a word or a phrase, you might censor out some thought that could start a productive chain of ideas. At this point you don't want to make any decisions about what's right or wrong, useful or not useful. You just want to generate material.

Peter Elbow, the teacher who introduced the idea of freewriting in a book called *Writing Without Teachers,* suggests that after a session of freewriting you stop to sum up the main point of what you have written in just one sentence; he calls that summary the "center of gravity" in the piece. Then after resting, start freewriting again, using that "center of gravity" as the take-off point for the next ten- to fifteen-minute freewriting session. You can continue this for three or four sessions until you have discovered some points you want to make in your writing and worked up momentum to get started.

Strategy 4: Treeing   Treeing is a "top-down" way of dividing and subdividing a broad topic in order to narrow it and find out what possibilities it offers that might be worth developing. It is also a good

way to generate material on any of those subtopics. For example, if you know a good deal about photography and would like to write a paper about it, you can start out by treeing the topic into subtopics: commercial photography and amateur photography. Each of these

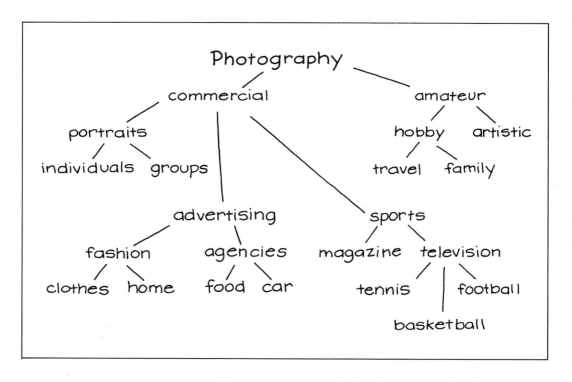

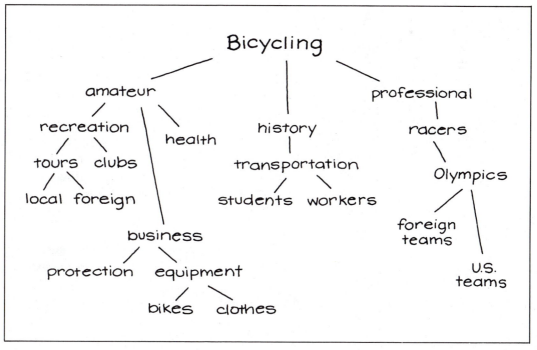

in turn can be subdivided into additional topics: you can divide commercial photography into sports photography, portrait photography, and advertising photography, as well as several other subtopics. Amateur photography can be divided into subtopics such as hobby and artistic. All of these subtopics can also be subdivided, as the diagram on the preceding page shows.

As you subdivide, you will probably create a division of your topic that offers possibilities to do something interesting in an area you already know something about. For example, if you are interested in tennis as well as photography, you could join those interests and write about tennis photography. Now you have narrowed your topic enough so that you can write a specific and concrete paper from which both you and your reader will learn.

The second diagram illustrates how to use the strategy of treeing on another topic.

Strategy 5: Journalists' Questions   Reporters or Journalism students who are learning to write for newspapers are often given this list of key questions to use as a guideline for getting the information *Asking key questions*   they need for their news stories.

1. Who is involved?
2. What happened?
3. Where did it happen? (Or where is it happening?)
4. When did it happen? (Or when will it happen?)
5. Why did it happen?
6. How did it (or does it) affect people?

Other writers can also use these questions to generate material from which to start working. For example, if a writer has chosen to write about the problem of illiteracy in America, starting off with these questions would yield the following information:

1. Who is involved? Thirty million Americans.
2. What happened? These people are functionally illiterate — that is, they do not read well enough to participate in mainstream society.
3. Where is it happening? All over the US, but especially in the South.

4. When did it happen? Right now, at a time when we claim to be educating everyone.
5. Why did it happen? We have given literacy low priority; there is poor support for public schools; teachers may not be using the right techniques.
6. How does it affect those involved? Illiterates are economically handicapped and virtually excluded from modern society.

With this start, a writer can focus on some aspect of the topic — for instance, describing a local program to teach illiterates or attacking a government proposal to cut funds for adult education — and begin to plan his or her paper.

Using a narrative to get started

Strategy 6: Anecdotes or Narratives   Sometimes it is possible to get started writing on a subject by focusing on a person or event connected with it and creating an anecdote or narrative that will suggest a line of thought that you want to pursue. People who write novels sometimes work this way. For instance, Joan Didion describes one such incident in her writing career:

> This second picture [that suggested a situation] was of something actually witnessed. A young woman with long hair and a short white dress walks through the casino at the Riviera in Las Vegas at one in the morning. She crosses the casino alone and picks up a house telephone. I watch her because I have heard her paged and recognize her name: she is a minor actress I see around Los Angeles from time to time, in places like Jax and once in the gynecologist's office in the Beverly Hills Clinic, but have never met. I know nothing about her. Who is paging her? Why is she here to be paged? How exactly did she come to this? It was precisely this moment in Las Vegas that made *Play It As It Lays* begin to tell itself to me.[1]

The way in which Didion noticed this scene and responded to it illustrates that kind of personal radar mentioned at the beginning of this chapter. Didion makes the process sound rather mysterious, but actually the strategy can work just as well for a person writing non-fiction. Primarily it requires that you train yourself to be alert to what

[1]Joan Didion, "Why I Write," *New York Times Book Review* 10 Dec. 1975: 3.

is going on around you and that you think of everything as potential material for your writing.

Strategy 7: Prism Thinking   At some time you may have seen a movie or read a book in which several narrators relate the same event, each recounting it from his or her point of view. Lawrence Durrell's set of novels *The Alexandria Quartet* is a famous example. Such works dramatize the fact that people's accounts or interpretations of an event vary tremendously according to their own set of perceptions and their degree of involvement in the event. When we are in an action or situation, we view it as a *participant*; if we are watching someone else who is involved, we view it as a *spectator*; if we are distanced from the event and are only recording what happens, we view it as a *reporter.*

Looking at a topic from three angles

I call this strategy of viewing an event or topic from three different perspectives *prism thinking.* It works well as a device for generating an angle from which to start writing. For example, someone who wanted to write about the illiteracy problem outlined in Strategy 5 might do an effective paper if she were able to talk to two or three people who can't read and write about what it is like to be an illiterate in our society. Or she could take the spectator view of the problem by interviewing volunteers who teach in a local program and getting their perceptions of what needs to be done. As you can see, she could not adopt the view of a participant; it is not always possible to approach a topic from all three perspectives of the prism.

Strategy 8: Research and Serendipity   Sometimes the best way to start preparing to write a paper is to do the obvious: go to the library and start researching your topic to get some idea of its possibilities. In Chapter 12, on the research paper, you will find a detailed explanation of how to get started on your research, as well as guidelines to the resources available to you in most libraries.

Finding ideas by happy accidents

But your most valuable asset for research is one not found in any library or stored in any computer. It is *serendipity,* the ability to find good things, apparently by accident. This ability goes beyond being lucky; it is a cultivated talent for being in the right place at the right time and discovering something that — although you didn't know it was there — you aren't exactly surprised to find. The person who has happy accidents is the one who scans the environment, listening and talking to people and picking up signals about what may be useful.

To cultivate serendipity you need to practice being curious. Browse in the library or bookstore; talk to people you meet waiting at airports or standing in line at the post office. Stay alert, watching what goes on at the periphery of your world, and be open to stimuli coming from unexpected directions. Developing your talent for serendipity is like developing a talent for soccer or kayaking; the more you practice, the luckier you get. The more curious you are and the more information you accumulate in any area, the more likely you are to make happy discoveries in that area.

Organizing Your Writing

Why you should plan ahead

As you have been generating ideas for writing and gathering material to support those ideas, you may also have been considering how you could organize your thoughts into an effective paper. Like any other complex activity that involves coordinating several parts or steps into a unified whole — for example, building a boat, planning a trip, or creating a fine meal — writing a paper requires that you make some kind of plan. Only geniuses in any field should try to "wing it," that is, count on inspiration and sheer luck to guide them as they improvise step by step. The rest of us are likely to wind up in disaster if we don't plan ahead.

Five Planning Strategies

Giving a pattern to your writing

But insisting that you need a plan does not mean that you must use only the traditional organizing devices, the sentence outline and the thesis sentence. Rather, it means that you need to work out some method for giving a *pattern* to your writing, for imposing order on it so that your reader can follow your ideas without getting lost. Professional writers have several strategies for developing a plan, but the ones they rely on most often are the outline, the thesis sentence, the preliminary abstract, the section-by-section summary, and the working list. Let's take a look at how each of these works and what their advantages are.

The Outline   Only a few professional writers use outlines, but those who do swear by them. The eminent psychologist B. F. Skinner, for instance, says that he makes an outline that winds up being so detailed that it is almost like the finished prose. The *New Yorker* reporter and essayist John McPhee uses an elaborate system of taking notes on index cards, then arranging the cards into the parts of what he calls a "logical" outline that controls the structure of his essay.

For the person who enjoys making an outline, it is probably the ideal organizational tool. Outlines force you to think through your whole paper before you start and to decide whether you have enough supporting material, which points you want to use, and how you are going to arrange them. Also, if you make a careful and detailed outline, you will probably save yourself substantial writing time because you will have to do less revising. A formal sentence outline for a paper about college women might look like this:

Writing a formal outline

Changing Trends Among College Women

I.   In the past fifteen years, the number of women going to college has steadily increased.
   A.   Now, for the first time, more than half of all college students are women.
   B.   The greatest percentage increase has been among women from 25 to 34.
   C.   The number of women getting preprofessional and graduate degrees has doubled in ten years.
      1.   Women's applications to law and medical schools are up dramatically.
      2.   Women now enroll in traditionally all-male institutions like the Harvard Business School and the Wharton School of Finance.
II.   This change in patterns has come about for several reasons.
   A.   The women's movement of the 1970s encouraged women to seek economic independence.
      1.   More and more women have realized that marriage does not guarantee security.
      2.   Women have begun to realize that without an education they can get only low-status, low-paying jobs.
   B.   Also as a result of the women's movement, more women plan careers as part of their long-term life plans.

   C. The rising divorce rate has caused many women to go back to school to seek new interests and improve their job credentials.

   D. Our society is now putting more stress on education for everybody.

  III. This change in patterns is affecting colleges and universities in several ways.

   A. Schools are under pressure to change their curricula to provide more courses on topics of interest to women.

   B. Schools are under pressure to provide more flexible course scheduling to accommodate women students who cannot live on campus.

   C. Schools are going to have to provide some kind of subsidized child-care facilities for student parents or they will lose enrollment.

For long, complex writing tasks, this kind of outline works particularly well because it gives you a feeling of having your subject under control before you start, and you shouldn't have much trouble starting to write after you have put this much time into thinking out your organization. You have also generated good material.

  Formal sentence outlines have their drawbacks, however. Many of us can't seem to sustain the drive to follow one through all the way to the end of a project, and we feel constrained by the requirements to have all the bits of our composition fit into symmetrical patterns — the requirement that you can't have an "A" without a "B" seems particularly irksome. And we feel that outlines constrain our thinking, too — they are like blueprints that don't allow room for change or innovation as a piece of writing progresses. For that reason a less formal and more adaptable kind of outline seems to work best for many people. For instance, a writer might find it more practical to plan the paper just outlined with this kind of informal outline:

Making an informal outline

Changing Trends Among College Women

More women than ever going to college:
 Biggest increase among 25 to 34
 More women in law school and med school — more in graduate school

Places that used to be all-male now enroll women (give examples)

Reasons for increase in women in college:
Women's movement — economic independence, sense of own identity
Finding out marriage no guarantee — average woman works 25 years out of her life
See other women stuck in low-paying jobs like clerks and typists
Degrees women got 10 or 20 years ago are outdated
Increased divorce rate making women go back to college — previously many were discouraged from going by husbands and families. Now it's necessary.

What it will do to the colleges:
Administrators will have to pay more attention to women students and be more flexible about some of the rules
Women are going to want day-care centers on campus

This kind of loose structure will still give you a good organizational plan, but it's much easier to construct because you don't have to make everything fit into slots. And because you don't have so much time and energy invested in it, you will probably be more willing to make changes in it as new ideas occur to you.

Thesis Sentences   Another kind of organizing tool that can be extremely useful is the thesis sentence. It should be a tight, though not necessarily brief, statement that summarizes the main points you are going to make in your paper. You do not have to begin your paper with it, or even use it in your writing, but it does provide a working guideline that can keep you on the track. For example, a thesis sentence for a paper on better safety at city swimming pools could read:

Constructing thesis sentences

> In order to improve safety and prevent drownings at our city pools, the city should hire only guards who are certified through the Red Cross Water Safety Instruction Course and who are mature enough to get respect and obedience from swimmers; we should also hire enough guards to cover every area of the pools at all times and require that they stay on their guard stations while they are on duty.

If you followed this thesis through and expanded each section with supporting details and illustrations, you should be able to turn out a tight and logically developed paper.

Here are some other good thesis sentences taken from student papers:

> Although the government should not ban the advertising of alcoholic beverages on television, the TV industry and the Federal Trade Commission should work together to put some controls on such advertising because alcohol has almost no nutritional value and can damage people's health.

> Local police should stop arresting people for "victimless crimes," such as prostitution, nude dancing, using drugs, and gambling because such acts cause no damage to other people or property, they persist regardless of penalties, and making them crimes encourages more serious crimes, such as blackmail and bribery.

> Students starting college should realize the importance of academic achievement, of not carrying more courses than they can handle well, of attending class regularly, and of pacing their studying.

If you write such a thesis sentence *ahead of time,* you should have little trouble turning out a well-organized paper.

A poor thesis sentence, however, is little help to the writer, regardless of when it is written. For example, the following thesis sentences show that their authors have very little idea of how they are going to organize their papers.

> The Open Records Law of 1974 has caused many problems.

> I am going to describe some of the ways women are oppressed.

> The United States should not withdraw from the United Nations.

Sentences like these give a writer no guidance for organization since they are really no more than undeveloped statements of opinion.

Preliminary Abstracts   A tight, one-paragraph preliminary abstract of your paper can, *if written ahead of time,* serve the same organizing function as a thesis sentence. It may even work better because you have room to include more details. Moreover, writing this kind of summary paragraph can be useful in another way; when you learn to write concise abstracts of your work, you are getting practice for writing the kind of abstract or précis that you need to prepare when you are writing technical reports, proposals, or articles to submit for publication or to a meeting. And although a good abstract is difficult to write because it usually requires that you condense all your main points into about one hundred words, you have developed a valuable skill once you have mastered this art of condensation. The ability to condense material into capsule form is also a real asset for newspaper, radio, and television reporters.

Writing an abstract

A person roughing out a summary paragraph for the paper on better safety at the city swimming pools might produce one like this:

> The best way to improve safety and prevent drownings at our city pools is to hire more lifeguards and to be sure all guards are well trained, mature, and responsible. In the past, several people have drowned because there were not enough guards at crowded pools. Also, in the past many guards had no training in water safety procedures, and they were not mature enough to maintain the discipline that one must have for a safe pool. More mature guards would also be more likely to stay at their stations and not mix with the swimmers. Such a hiring program would be more expensive, but it would save lives.

Section-By-Section Summary   This device works especially well for longer papers that you want to block out but are really not ready to outline in detail. Suppose, for example, that you were going to write a paper on the local real estate market for your economics class. You choose as your audience the employees of a national company that is moving its plant to your city; your purpose is to give them complete and accurate information about what to expect if they plan to buy houses. Your summary would look something like this:

Summarizing by sections

1. The price of houses in the area is at about the national average. Prices are not yet as inflated as they are in California or some parts of Texas, but they have been increasing at a rate of about 12 per cent a year.
2. Fairly difficult to finance a house unless purchaser can make a down payment of about 20 per cent to 25 per cent. If you can

afford a large down payment, some property on which mortgages can be assumed at a lower than the going interest rate exists. Current interest rate running about four points below the prime rate.

3. Not easy to find good rental houses in the city; apartments also scarce because of large student population. Anyone planning to rent should start looking early and sign a lease as soon as possible. Give approximate rents.

4. Good buys in houses available if you are willing to live in south or east part of town, the less fashionable areas. Also some large, four-bedroom, three-bath houses available at reasonable prices if you are willing to live about 15 miles out of town and commute. Give typical prices. Warn that public transportation in the area is poor — not really practical to plan to ride the bus.

5. Suggest that someone in family come to the city several months ahead of time to negotiate for a house or apartment.

This kind of plan gets down your main points on paper, where you can study them and think about how you want to add to or modify them. After you write them out, you may also decide to rearrange them. For instance, in this summary, the fourth section might work better as the second section. Also, the very act of writing out a summary will help you generate ideas for developing your paper.

Preparing a working list

A Working List   A final method of organization is to make a list of the points you want to cover, grouped or subdivided in some way. This method is perhaps the most open-ended and flexible because you can add to various parts of the list as you work or rearrange and regroup items if you find an unexpected pattern developing. It's rather like making an elaborate packing list when you are moving or going on a trip. You write down your categories, leaving plenty of space under each one. Then as you prepare to write, you jot items down under the proper heading. Sometimes you get them down in the order you want to use them, but sometimes you have to shift them. And even after you begin to write, it's a good idea to keep the list close at hand and add new points to it when you think of them.

For me, this system seems to work best for almost any kind of writing. Combined with freewriting and brainstorming, it helps me to generate a body of material and get it into usable form more quickly than any other method I've tried. I am not an outliner, and

I used to feel guilty because I wasn't. Now, however, I've discovered that I am a much more efficient writer when I make lists than I am when I outline, and I realize that individual writers have to choose the methods that best suit their temperament.

For example, here is the working list I used to organize this section of Chapter 2:

Need for planning

Need a pattern to let your reader know what to expect

Complex activities require a plan or they bog down

Need to be flexible — not a blueprint

Different kinds of plans work for different people — don't always have to outline

Other helps to organization

Need a title to condition reader's expectations

Have a pattern — classification, comparison/contrast, etc.

Plans shouldn't get too elaborate or you get attached to them

Lead-in to next section on cohesion

Ways to organize

Outlines — formal, informal, sometimes cause problems

Thesis sentences

Preliminary abstracts

Section-by-section summary

Open-ended lists

If you were to check the text of this section against this list you would find it does not correspond exactly, but it comes very close. Since I was writing the list only for myself, I didn't worry about parallel structure or complete sentences. I just put down ideas as they came to me, but I made the wording complete enough so that I wouldn't forget the point I wanted to make. In the actual writing, I changed the order of points a little and added some other points that I didn't think of until I began to write; however, the essentials of the section are on the list.

Other Aids to Organization

Titles   When you give your paper a title that accurately reflects its content, you increase your chances of writing a well-organized paper. A title, after all, is a promise to the reader, and if you make that promise before you begin to write, you are more likely to stick to the point. At this preliminary stage, your title will be a tentative one, a working guide that may have to be rewritten later, but it will help you to anchor your paper.

Controlling Patterns   Writers and teachers sometimes talk about *structure* in an essay, a term that describes the way a piece of writing is put together or its underlying pattern or design. Writers plan their writing in order to give it this structure, which acts as a controlling pattern that holds it together. If, as a writer, you can decide ahead of time what kind of controlling pattern you want to use, you will find that you have a powerful organizational device that will almost take over and plan your paper for you.

Chapters 9 and 10 talk about the patterns of exposition you can use to develop assertions and arguments: *definition, cause and effect, classification, comparison, induction,* and *claims.* These patterns, and others — for instance, *question and answer* or *problem and solution* — parallel our natural thought processes. We are familiar with them, and our minds move easily along the tracks that they lay down. We sense an underlying design, a path that leads us along to a destination. And if you establish any of these patterns in your writing and hold to it (or them) as you work, your writing is not likely to get out of control. So when you are planning your paper, think about these natural patterns. Would any of them work well with your topic? If so, you are already ahead on your organizing tasks.

A Caution About Planning

But now that I have made the case for planning as an important part of most writing tasks, I want to add a caution: don't invest so much time and energy in your plans that you are unwilling to discard them if you don't like the way they are working out or if a better one

occurs to you. A plan shouldn't be like an elaborate blueprint that commits you to executing it to the last detail. If you labor over a plan too long and include an excessive number of details, you may get attached to it and not be able to see its shortcomings when you actually put it into operation. Also you are less likely to have your personal radar extended to catch any unexpected creative "blips" that might come your way or to be ready for serendipity to lead you in a new direction. If you were planning a trip, you would probably be cautious enough not to put down such a big deposit that you couldn't afford to cancel if you changed your mind; think of your writing plans in the same way.

When you start planning, also keep in mind what kind of writing you are doing. Is your writing task essentially self-contained? For example, your history professor may have asked you to locate and compare two contradictory historical accounts of Custer's battle at Little Big Horn, and then decide which is truer to the facts of the situation as they are now known. You are being asked only to locate accounts that already exist, note their contents, and compare them to a modern interpretation of the evidence (if your professor has not given you that interpretation, you will of course have to find it also). The assignment does not ask you to speculate about why the accounts differ. So the assignment is self-contained and instructive, and you are not writing for discovery. In such cases, making a careful plan as to how you want to organize your material is a good idea, because once you find your data and decide how to present it, you should be able to write the paper without too much trouble.

If, however, for a political science course you want to write a paper in which you explore reasons why our political system seems to discourage highly qualified people from running for office, you may not want to do detailed advance planning. You might start brainstorming by asking yourself why Americans have elected an ex-actor as president and a former basketball star as senator? Why aren't obviously bright and talented business leaders ever mentioned as presidential or congressional possibilities? When you start the paper, you honestly don't know the answers to such questions, and in that case it would be a mistake for you to try to make a detailed outline ahead of time. Elaborate planning would only cut off discovery.

Finally, the conflict between careful planning and a creatively flexible approach to writing that doesn't close out options comes down to the traditional tension between freedom and discipline, or

The "loose/tight" approach to planning

what a best-selling book on business management, *In Search of Excellence,* calls simultaneous "loose/tight" management structure. Before starting on any substantial writing project you need to make plans that will help you to focus on what you want to do and suggest strategies for doing it. You need to take those plans seriously and consult them as you work to help keep you on track. But you also need to be flexible and remain open to new ideas and insights, ready to adjust your plans when a better idea emerges. And you need to recognize those times when a strong plan is likely to be useful and productive and those when it might actually keep you from doing a good job.

Unifying Your Writing

Four Unifying Strategies

Readers are perverse creatures who, if given the slightest opportunity, will manage to get lost when they are reading. If they encounter a gap between one point and the next, they lose track of the narrative or argument. If they don't get clear directional signals to guide them between sentences and between paragraphs, they will head off in the wrong direction. If the author does not put in the right word to show the relationship between ideas, they will put in the wrong one. And if they cannot sense an underlying pattern in a piece of writing, they are likely to get confused and quit reading.

Remember that your reader can easily get lost

The truth is that most readers are lazy, and they won't work at trying to follow what they read. And because they won't, as a writer you have to take the responsibility for making your writing so well unified, so coherent, that a reader will move through it without losing his or her way. You can use a variety of strategies to give your writing that kind of unity.

Structural Design   The best unifying devices for any writing are the natural thought patterns mentioned in the previous section. A paper built around a cause-and-effect pattern or an assertion-and-support pattern, for example, will often hold together with little or no transitional "glue," just as a carefully constructed rock fence holds together because the pieces of rock fit, not because of the mortar that has been applied from the outside.

Designs help to control writing

In addition to using what seem like natural designs, you can also use stylistic patterns such as *parallel structure*. Notice that the first paragraph in this section uses this device, starting several consecutive sentences with "If they . . . ."

Downshifting (pages 204–206) and *commitment and response* (pages 221–223) are also two structural designs that act as powerful unifiers; more on them in the chapter on paragraphs.

Predictions Another way to tie the parts of your paper together is to make a series of predictions to your reader and then carefully follow through on them. For example, James Austin, who writes about chance and creativity, begins a key paragraph: "We can readily distinguish four varieties of chance. . . ." He then goes on to talk about Chance I, Chance II, Chance III, and Chance IV. As long as he follows through on his prediction, he will probably not lose his reader. A writer can get the same effect with ordinal numbers — *first, second, third,* and so on — or with sequence words: *next, subsequently, finally,* and so on.

Repetition Most of us consciously try to avoid repeating the same word or phrase in several consecutive sentences and dig into our memories to come up with substitutes because we don't want our writing to sound monotonous. But repetition can serve as an effective linking device if we use it deliberately with an eye to creating a pattern. See the previous example of parallelism, for instance. A writer can also consciously repeat a key word in order to furnish readers a series of cues or signals that will keep them moving in the right direction, as in this example (italics added):

> *Nowhere* will you see more people standing in queues and doing so more uncomplainingly, than in England. *Nowhere* will you find taxi drivers and salespeople more polite or customers more willing to smile through difficulties and delays. *Nowhere* will you meet better-behaved children or sense a greater reverence for public ceremony. *Nowhere,* in short, will you find a place in which the notions of self-control, responsibility, and restraint have been more faultlessly woven into the social fabric. And *nowhere,* it follows, will you find a greater zest for the berserk, combustive humor that blows that fabric all to hell, for the comedy of explosive release. *England, for all her* dignity, is convulsed by buttock jokes and bowel noises. *England, for all her* polished manners, adores the spectacle of overtried patience crossing the line into desperate, sanguinary rage.[2]

A writer can also use a repeated pronoun to create a pattern and

[2]Lawrence Shames, "God Save John Cleese," *Esquire* April 1984: 60.

a continuity that will hold writing together, as in this paragraph (italics added):

> *She* has daydreams of a privileged life. . . . *She* is rather glad to imagine herself without a job. *She* would get up at seven-thirty, not five-thirty. *She* would see her husband off, her children off, maybe drive the latter to school herself, then have a quiet breakfast. *She* would delight in her aloneness — no one on either side of her, working the assembly line. *She* would watch television, meet a friend at a shopping mall, have lunch with her, come home and do some planting or weeding or "fixing" food or "just plain relaxing." That last option is the one *she* favors most when *she* evokes her daytime dreams while standing and inspecting an endless stream of towels.[3]

Unify with a metaphor

A third effective way to use repetition as a unifying device is to build a passage around a central image or metaphor. Notice, for example, Martin Luther King's skillful use of financial imagery in this passage from his "I Have a Dream" speech (italics added):

> In a sense we have come to our nation's Capitol to *cash a check.* When the architects of our republic wrote the magnificent words of the Constitution and Declaration of Independence, they were signing a *promissory note* to which every American was to fall heir. This note was a promise that all men, yes, black men as well as white men, would be guaranteed the inalienable rights of life, liberty, and the pursuit of happiness.
>
> It is obvious today that America has *defaulted* on this *promissory note* insofar as her citizens of color are concerned. Instead of honoring this sacred obligation, America has given the Negro people a *bad check*; a *check* which has come back marked "*insufficient funds.*" But we refuse to believe that the *bank of justice* is *bankrupt.* We refuse to believe that there are *insufficient funds* in the great *vaults* of opportunity of this nation. And so we've come *to cash this check* — a *check* that will give us upon demand the *riches* of freedom and the security of justice.[4]

[3]Robert Coles and Jane Hallowell Coles, *Women of Crisis* (New York: Dell, 1978): 234–35.
[4]Martin Luther King, Jr., "I Have a Dream," copyright 1963 by Martin Luther King, Jr.

We can classify the three unifying strategies just discussed as *indirect* strategies, for they grow out of the style and structure of the passages themselves rather than from deliberate attempts to join the parts of writing. Most of the time you should rely on these indirect strategies as much as you can because writing seems smoother and tighter when its unity comes from the underlying structure rather than from the more obvious external devices that we call transitions. But such external devices are also necessary and fill important functions for all writers.

Choosing the right transition words

Hooks, Links, and Directional Signals   All writers rely on transitional, or linking, words and phrases to show relationships between sentences and paragraphs and to give clues that point readers in the right direction. It's important to remember, however, that different transitional terms send different signals to readers, and writers have to be careful to choose the correct ones. When you need a linking word, you cannot, figuratively speaking, just reach into a sack of assorted transition words and use the first one that comes to hand. Transition words notify readers to expect certain points to follow. If these points don't follow, you will frustrate your readers.

So simply knowing a general list of transition terms is not enough. You have to think about what you are saying — whether, for example, you are pointing out a contrast or a similarity or demonstrating a cause-and-effect sequence. Some of the most common transitional words and phrases are:

Words that show *consequence:*
   therefore, consequently, thus, as a result
Words that show *contrast:*
   but, however, on the other hand, nevertheless, yet, although
Words that show *similarity:*
   likewise, in the same way, similarly
Words that show *causation:*
   since, because, for,
Words that show *sequence:*
   next, finally, first, in conclusion

When you pick the right transition words, you move your readers along from one idea to the other, giving good directional signals and gently nudging them in the direction you want them to go. Here are two student paragraphs that show how it's done. Transitional and repetitive words and phrases are italicized.

The attitudes I take toward Frisbee are dual. *First,* I consider each flight as an individual act, unrelated to how badly or well I threw the disc last time. *Second,* I try to achieve a balance between concentrating too much and not concentrating enough. *If* I lack the first attitude, I feel a little ashamed when the Frisbee fails to reach its intended target; *this feeling* can make me throw even worse the next time, specifically *because* of my fear that *that* will happen, *and so on* in a vicious circle. *On the other hand, if* I congratulate myself too much on a good throw, I'm inclined to demand the *same* performance from myself each time. *This* is *also* self-defeating. *Therefore,* I try to isolate each flight as something to be experienced anew.

Other dangers are not as immediately recognizable *although these* are hazards you face every time you dive. Yet *these* dangers — *such as* nitrogen narcosis, the bends, and air embolism — are easily avoided by a diver who has successfully completed a diver training certification course. *This training* is available from many places, *some* of which are local dive shops, *some* university courses, and *some* YMCA's. Without *this certification* you cannot rent equipment or have scuba tanks filled.

Here is a choppy student paragraph in which the writer fails to keep the reader moving along smoothly by putting in good links and directional signals.

Practically anybody can get diabetes. Diabetes overlooks sex, race, creed, and color. Diabetes does seem to have a special preference for women over 30. One of the most unusual aspects of the disease is the apparent link to marriage and motherhood. The highest number of deaths from diabetes is among married women. The more children a woman has the more susceptible she is to diabetes.

The writer also has problems with wordiness and order, and the poor transitions magnify them.

Tying It All Together

Even very experienced writers seldom completely master all the diverse strategies for shaping writing into the smooth, easy-flowing, and apparently effortless prose that is the mark of a skillful writer. Most of us admit that we have to revise and tinker with sentences and paragraphs for a long time, patching here and joining there in order to get them to hang together reasonably well. It's never easy. But if you can keep two principles in mind, they may help.

Two guiding principles for unifying your writing

1. Each sentence or paragraph that you write should leave a little residue, a little trace, out of which the next sentence or paragraph develops. It can be an expectation, a hint, a repeated word, or a pattern, but there should be something. Sentences and paragraphs in a piece of discourse should not be truly separate units that don't relate to each other.
2. Between all the units you construct, you should have some kind of hook, real or implied. It can be repetition, parallelism, sequence, or pattern, or it can be a signal word — *therefore, nevertheless, also,* or one from some other group. Whatever you use, the reader should be able to feel the connection. You should try never to have two units so isolated that if one of them came at the bottom of a page and the next one came at the top of the next page, the reader would do a double take and say, "Is there something missing?"

You can sense both these principles at work in the following passage, in which the writer, Larry McMurtry, has used so many hooking and linking strategies that a diagram of them would look like the wiring in the back of a television set. Yet he has done it so skillfully that the reader moves along, quite unconscious of the signals and hooks.

> People who think cowboys are realists generally think so because the cowboy's speech is salty and apparently straight-forward, replete with the wisdom of natural men. What that generally means is that cowboy talk sounds shrewd and perceptive, and so it does. In fact, however, both the effect and the intention of much cowboy talk is literary: cowboys are aphorists. Whenever possible, they turn their observations into aphorisms. Some are brilliant

aphorists, scarcely inferior to Wilde or La Rochefoucauld; one is proud to steal from them. I plucked a nice one several years ago, to wit: "A woman's love is like the morning dew: it's just as apt to fall on a horseturd as it is on a rose." In such a remark the phrasing is worth more than the perception, and I think the same might be said for the realism of most cowboys. It is a realism in tone only: its insights are either wildly romantic, mock-cynical, or solemnly sentimental. The average cowboy is an excellent judge of horseflesh, only a fair judge of men, and a terrible judge of women, particularly "good women."[5]

Probably McMurtry himself wasn't wholly conscious of putting in ties and links as he wrote. Rather, he made the basic unity of the piece come out of the logical structure and out of the natural development of his topic. At least that's the way it seems. And that's the effect that everyone who is trying to be a good writer should strive for.

Exercises

1. *Gathering information*

   a. Take a small notebook or 3" × 5" cards with you and set out to overhear deliberately some interesting conversations. Some likely listening places are the lounge in the student union, the waiting area at an airport or bus station, the local pizza and beer parlor, the laundromat, or the check-out line at the grocery store.

   b. Interview someone whose job provides opportunities to meet many different kinds of people — for example, a cab driver, an admissions officer at your school, a nurse who works in the emergency room at the hospital, or a bartender in a local bar. Talk with that person about his or her job and find out what kinds of experiences make it interesting. Take notes that would help you to write a descriptive anecdote about working at such a job.

[5]Larry McMurtry, *In a Narrow Grave* (New York: Simon, 1968): 148–49.

2. *Preparing to write*

a. Identify the probable audience for each of these written documents and state that audience's reason for reading the document.

- an application for a scholarship
- a brochure on how to establish credit
- an article on women alcoholics

b. Identify the purpose a writer might have in writing the following essays. Compare your answers with those of two other people in your class.

- an article on home computers
- an article on pregnancy among teen-agers
- an article on job opportunities for engineers

3. *Generating ideas*

Here are three topics that could yield some interesting material for a paper:

- buying or building a home in the 1980s
- career goals for women in the 1980s
- dressing for success

Choose the one that you find most interesting and see how much material you can generate by using the following strategies for discovering what you know:

a. *Brainstorming.* For fifteen minutes write down every idea that comes to you about your topic. Remember that in brainstorming no idea is wrong or irrelevant.

b. *Focused freewriting.* Formulate a statement about your chosen topic — for example, "Trends in home buying are going to change in the 1980s" — and then start writing about that statement. Write for ten minutes without taking your pen from the paper or stopping to reflect on what you are writing.

c. *Treeing.* Draw a tree diagram for your topic, dividing it into subtopics and subtopics within subtopics.

d. *Journalists' questions.* Write down brief answers to these questions about your topic: who, what, where, when, why, how?

e. *Anecdotes.* Write down a personal anecdote or narrative of either your own or someone else's experience that you could use to illustrate some point about your topic.

f. *Prism thinking.* Write three sentences about the topic that reflect these three differing viewpoints: that of a participant, that of a spectator, and that of a reporter.

4. *Organizing your ideas*

Write a formal or informal outline, a controlling thesis sentence, a one-paragraph abstract or summary, or a subdivided list that would help you to organize one of these writing tasks:

a. a brochure on nutrition for low-income families

b. a letter to a judge appealing a suspension of your driver's license for receiving four speeding tickets in one year

c. a proposal for expanding and reorganizing student parking facilities on your campus

5. Analyze the controlling patterns of the following student paragraphs. If necessary, review page 59 to refresh your memory about organizational patterns.

a. From small towns to big cities across the United States there is an increasing need for a federally funded day care program to look after the children of the multitude of mothers who work outside the home. According to recent estimates, five out of six million preschool children of working mothers in the U.S. do not have adequate day care facilities. Some children are taken to unlicensed facilities providing substandard care, while others are left at home to provide for themselves. The following statistics dramatize the problem.

• The number of married women with preschool-age children who hold jobs has doubled since 1960.
• Among women who are widowed, divorced, or separated from their husbands, slightly more than half with preschool children are in the labor force.
• In total, about six million preschool children have working mothers, and almost 27 million children under 18 have mothers employed outside the home.

b. If you have ever watched the lid on a saucepan full of boiling water cooking the vegetables for dinner, you may have noticed that the lid moves up and down. This is not magic; it is steam pressure. Imagine kernels in a popcorn popper. When heated, the kernels pop and expand, taking up far more room than before. Water behaves like this when heated also, because steam is just water that takes up more room, expanding and building up pressure unless it can escape. The whistle on a kettle works from built-up steam pressure, which must escape through the spout. The steam engine is like a huge kettle, but the pressure is used to push pistons and turn wheels instead of just blowing a whistle.

c. Have you ever wondered what it would be like to meet San Francisco Forty-Niner Joe Montana? To actually sit down and talk with him for a few minutes? Many people only dream of such an opportunity, but talking to Joe Montana, Martina Navratilova, or Reggie Jackson is just an everyday happening for a sportswriter.

6. Analyze the unifying devices, both direct and indirect, in this complete short essay written to accompany a two-page layout of photographs of oil field workers.

Working the Rigs

   No one really likes the work. No one really likes getting out in the Texas sun and skinning his knuckles on heavy sections of steel pipe or wrestling with a spinning chain or climbing to the top of a rig where a single slip can lead to a ninety-foot fall or mixing drilling mud that gets in work clothes and combines with the grease, sweat, and oil to make a smell that no amount of washing can remove. No one likes to put up a rig in one isolated spot then take it down later only to put it up again in another isolated spot miles away. And no one likes the long hours and graveyard shifts and the endless driving back and forth to the job and coming home, as one roughneck put it, to "warmed over coffee and an asleep old lady."
   Then why do people do it? They may like the money: when there's plenty of work, as there is today, roughnecks can make $15,000 to $25,000 in a year. They may like the people they work with. They may take pride in their toughness and satisfaction from knowing they can do a particular dirty and dangerous job better than the next man. And they may like the life

that surrounds the oil rigs — the high school football games, the fishing trips in a pickup with a camper on the back, the beers on Saturday night, the long Sunday dinners after a morning in the Baptist church. But no one really likes the work.[6]

7. Rewrite these student paragraphs to make them more unified:

a. If you were to change television channels again, you might find a rather innocent type of cartoon such as Walt Disney's Mickey Mouse or Donald Duck. You probably remember watching these when you were a child. This type of cartoon usually contains little or no violence. Often it subtly teaches children a moral. Some of these cartoons may contain a little violence, but it is presented in the form of slapstick comedy. Mickey Mouse and Donald Duck were popular in the '50s and are still popular today.

b. We have found that Braille, the traditional method of teaching the blind to read, is becoming outdated. Learning and using it is a slow procedure. The cost of paper is soaring and once symbols have been punched the paper is not reusable. This causes a large waste of costly material. Books typed in Braille are unusually bulky and hard to handle.

8. Analyze the controlling pattern and the unifying devices in this student paper. Does the paper seem to be well organized and developed? Give reasons for your answer.

Urban Boot Buyers' Relief

"What do I look for when buying a pair of cowboy boots?" Since the onset of the "Urban Cowboy" craze, this is a question many people are asking themselves. The boot industry has flourished in the past two years with record sales all over America. With boots in demand, in order to produce more boots, manufacturers have concentrated on quantity rather than quality. The more time taken in making a pair of boots, the better the quality will be. Some people buy boots for durability and dependability, others for attractiveness only. Regardless of the purpose for buying the boots, someone buying boots for the first time should know how to distinguish a good pair from a bad pair.

[6]*Texas Monthly* Oct. 1978: 124.

First, in order to know the style, one must know what use he or she will have for the boots. If they are to be used for ranch or farm work, the quality need not be as good. A strong, durable cowhide leather will be sufficient. The boot tops should be tall if the boots are to be used while working in areas where snakes are numerous. Tall boot tops also protect the legs from underbrush while on horseback. Most boots come in twelve-, fourteen- and sixteen-inch heights, the sixteen-inch top providing the most protection.

When considering use, the heel is another factor. There are two types of boot heels: the riding heel and the walking heel. The riding heel usually accompanies the sixteen-inch top. The riding heel is a smaller heel and is not sufficient for walking great distances. This heel has a sharper angle on the back, which leaves less heel on the ground. The walking heel, the more standard of the two, is a larger heel and the angle on the back of the boot is not as great, providing better footing. The walking heel is for the person who wears boots for walking and not riding. With riding heels, a person who walks very much may find that these heels will hurt his feet. For the dancing cowboy, the walking heel is best. It gives better footing while dancing, due to the bigger heel.

The boot toe offers yet another style. Toes come in three styles: pointed, semi-round, and round. These features serve no special purpose, but they do affect the outward appearance of the boot. The only advice here is if someone has very wide feet, he or she may want to choose the round or semi-round style because the pointed style will be uncomfortable, and will hurt their feet. Choosing one of these styles depends upon the individual's personal taste more than anything else.

The second consideration is the quality. This is the most misleading factor to the new boot buyer. With the great number of imitation leathers on the market today, genuine leathers have become hard to identify. The boots will have a tag sewn inside to indicate if the leather is genuine or imitation. Imitation leathers look nice while new, but after wear, the color comes off and the boots have a plastic look. Genuine leathers retain their new appearance (if properly cared for) and they are less susceptible to cracking and wrinkling.

Imitation leather boots most always will have a rubber sole.

These do not last long and are rough, which is not good for dancing. The genuine leather boots have a leather sole. This sole lasts twice as long as the rubber sole and is good for sliding the feet while dancing.

The stitching on boots is a very good indicator of quality. The more lines of stitches that are used in designs on the boot top, the better the quality. Stitches are very small and are sewn in lines winding and curving to make designs. Some boots have only one line winding around forming a design, while others have more. The best quality boots will have eight to ten stitches sewn side-by-side in the same pattern to form a design.

The price of boots is another consideration. The brand name is usually a big factor in price. Tony Lama, Larry Mahan, Justin, and Nocona manufacture the best quality boots, and these brands usually cost more. Cowtown, Texas, Acme, Dan Post, and Hondo are lower-quality boots and cost less.

The material used to make boots indicates price also. Dyed leather boots of good quality will cost seventy-five to one hundred dollars. Others may only cost fifty to sixty-five dollars, depending on the brand name. Exotic materials like eel, lizard, shark, snake, calf and others will cost two hundred fifty to three hundred dollars. For the very meticulous person, custom hand-made boots are available for four to five hundred dollars. These are the best boots, but often people do not think a pair of boots made of anything would be worth five hundred dollars.

The last factor to consider is the one people think of the least, but actually is very important. The time a person plans to spend caring for the boots must be considered. Basic dyed leather colors of black, brown, tan, orange and others simply require polish and shine once every week or two. The polish and shine wax come in these colors, so mixing is not necessary. The more exotic materials require care after every use. These boots require special oils and soaps such as mink oil, saddle soap, cavalier lotion, and others. Without proper care an expensive pair of boots can be ruined in less than a month.

These are all factors that should be considered while shopping for boots. The type of boots a person wears are too often used as a social symbol. People believe the more expensive the boots, the better the cowboy. Most often "urban cowboys" will sport the most expensive styles of boots. They wear these to social events, on dates, and to dances, never setting foot on the ranch or farm. The true cowboy can be seen in the old dirty or muddy, worn-out boots most all of the time. The true cowboy buys boots for durability. So, depending on the intentions, the choice is left entirely up to the individual.

Once you have purchased your first pair of boots you will truly love them. Take care of them and you are sure to have something to be proud of the rest of your days on the trail or in the dancehall.

Doni Riddle

Writing Assignments

Paper 1

People often depend on reading what someone has written to get information to help them make decisions, and frequently they find that their best sources are accounts that other people give about their experiences. This assignment asks that you tell your readers about a job you have had and give them enough concrete information to allow them to decide if they would want to apply for that job.

Before starting the main part of your paper, write down who your audience is, what kind of people they are, and what they want to know from reading your account. Also write down your purpose: what do you want to accomplish with this paper? Be more specific than simply saying that you want to tell them about a job you've had: you want to tell them *what* about it?

Possible Jobs to Write About

1. Working in an ice cream store or a doughnut shop.
2. Delivering furniture for a furniture rental firm.
3. Cooking in a fast-food restaurant; for example, McDonald's or Jack-in-the-Box.
4. Shucking oysters in an oyster bar.
5. Being a bell-hop in a hotel.
6. Modeling.

7. Working as a hospital orderly.
8. Running waterfront activities at a summer camp.

Of course, you may choose any other job you know a lot about. Remember to include enough details to give your reader a good sense of the work.

Paper 2

One of the ways in which we learn to handle new situations or decide whether we would like to try a new activity is to read about someone else's experiences. This assignment asks you to write about an experience you have had that someone else could learn from. For example, by writing a vivid and interesting narrative about an experience you had when camping or canoeing, you can point out the dangers of going into a natural setting unprepared for the unexpected.

Before you begin the main part of your paper, write a statement identifying your readers — age, sex, interests, etc. — and listing some of questions they want answered. Also write out your purpose; what do you want to achieve for your readers by writing this account?

Possible Topics

1. Working in a factory or cannery.
2. Traveling in a foreign country.
3. Being in a flood or tornado.
4. Taking children to an amusement park.
5. Buying a used car.
6. Working on an offshore oil rig.
7. Riding a bicycle cross country.

3 · The Elements of Rhetoric

CHAPTER

The art of rhetoric is the art of using language to persuade, to convince, to enlighten, and to discover knowledge. People began to study it seriously about 2500 years ago in ancient Greece when the rise of democracy made it necessary for every citizen to be able to plead his own cause in the public forum. The man — and only men were citizens in those days — who could not argue or discuss ideas effectively was not only at a serious legal disadvantage but could also be sure that he would have little influence in his community.

Why people need to study rhetoric

In some ways the situation of citizens today is not too much different. People still need to be able to express their ideas effectively if they want to communicate them to others, and they still need to know how to construct a persuasive argument if they want to influence their community. And there is more to argument than passionately stating your beliefs and trying to shout down your opposition. The person who argues well is the person who understands the elements of rhetoric and knows how to use them.

What is a Rhetorical Situation?

Whenever you write in order to communicate something to other people, you are involved in a *rhetorical situation*. That is, you are writing in a complex situation that has several elements in it, elements that you need to think about as you write if you want your writing to succeed with your readers. The purpose of this chapter is to show you how to analyze different rhetorical situations, both your own and those of other writers, and to explain how the elements in

these situations function. The elements of any rhetorical situation are these:

1. The purpose or occasion for writing.
2. The audience for whom the writing is done.
3. The persona or assumed role of the writer.
4. The message or content of the writing.

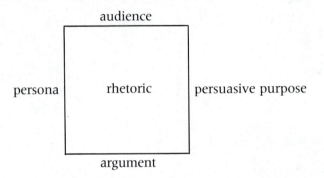

Together these four elements make up the *rhetorical square,* and each of them is necessary to the whole. They are inextricably linked — you don't have an argument unless you have a purpose for arguing, an audience to argue to, and a role that you are playing in making that argument. Moreover, each element affects every other element, and in the last analysis you cannot handle them separately.

All four elements are inextricably linked

The Four Questions

At first, however, when you begin any writing task you should find it helpful to separate these elements and ask yourself these four questions:

Questions to ask yourself when writing

1. What is my *purpose* in writing? What need or occasion is causing me to write?
2. Who is my *audience*? Why are they reading and what important characteristics do they have that I need to keep in mind?
3. What is my *persona* or *voice* in this paper? How do I want to come across to my readers?
4. What is my *argument* or *message*?

Roughing out preliminary answers to these questions will show you what your rhetorical situation is and help you get started on your writing.

When you are reading someone else's writing and need to understand that writer's rhetorical situation, you should turn the questions around and phrase them like this:

Questions to ask about other writers

1. What is the writer's *purpose*? What need or occasion is causing him or her to write?
2. What *audience* does the writer envision? What assumptions does he or she make about that audience?
3. What *persona* is the writer assuming? Does her or she project an authentic voice? (see pp. 92–93)
4. What is the writer's *argument* or *message*?

When you analyze an article or any specific piece of writing by asking these four questions about it, you put it in its rhetorical context and can evaluate how well it succeeds. A smoothly written and witty article might not work at all if it is addressed to readers who are not interested in the topic or if it makes readers angry. Therefore, only when you look at all the elements in a rhetorical situation can you decide if a piece of writing works *in that situation*. It is not really possible to make an intelligent judgment about writing if you don't know its rhetorical content.

Purpose

A writer always needs to begin by asking, "Why am I writing this? What is the need for it and what do I hope to accomplish?" He or she should have a fairly clear idea of goals for the paper, just as a person beginning a trip needs to have some idea of destination — otherwise there is not much point in starting out on either enterprise. Although it is true that in either writing or traveling one can narrow and adapt goals as a situation develops, it is essential to start off with some sense of purpose and direction — otherwise too much effort is wasted.

For students who are writing an assigned paper in college, their first purpose is to fill a requirement — that's the broad goal. Within that, however, they need a more specific goal tied to the content of the specific paper, a goal which, when stated, will help them chart their writing and stay on course. Without such a direct statement to serve as a reminder, writers can easily wander into vagueness.

For example, here is a preliminary statement of purpose that helped a student decide what she wanted to accomplish in her paper.

> To inform young people from ten to thirteen years old of the effects of alcohol on their body and to try to persuade them not to start drinking.

The author, who is the mother of young children herself, started by analyzing what she wanted to accomplish with her young readers. She decided she wanted to educate them so that they could make their own judgments about whether they should drink; to support the educational purpose of the paper, she drew diagrams of the internal organs and showed how alcohol affected them.

With another purpose the writer might have proceeded differently and chosen a different audience. For instance, had she wanted to address the problem of teenage drinking and driving, she would have written for readers over sixteen who are licensed to drive. Then her purpose would have been to make her readers aware of the number of fatal accidents caused by drunk teenage drivers and to persuade them to establish a code for policing their own driving.

Here are other good statements of purpose from student papers; each helped the author to focus his or her writing:

> To help sexually abused teenage girls to realize that they are not to blame for the abuse and to encourage them to seek help.

> To show prospective high school football players and their parents some of the hazards of high school ball and to warn them about exploitative coaches and alumni.

> To inform adolescent girls about the modeling profession. To tell them what training is required, what it is like to model, and how much modeling pays.

On the other hand, here are some ineffective statements of purpose that are too broad and vague to help writers focus their papers:

To open my readers' minds to the advantages of a liberal education. [*The statement is so broad that it almost guarantees a superficial paper. The writer needs to indicate what advantages and for whom.*]

To explain the popularity of running in America. [*Again, the topic is too broad. The writer needs to specify what kind of running and to indicate some of the reasons he will give.*]

Advantages of Identifying Your Purpose

Although deciding what you want to do and spelling it out before you begin to write may seem like an extra nuisance that simply takes up time before you can actually start writing, it can help you in several important ways.

First, it can help you focus your writing. For example, if you are an enthusiastic runner and want to write about the joys and benefits of running, you might start with only a general idea of what you are going to say. In the process of exploring your topic with diagrams or by some preliminary freewriting, you are apt to go off in many directions — there really is a lot to say. That's fine as long as you are only "noodling" your topic, but you need to start narrowing early and decide what you want to do. You can't tell everything you know, so you need to find a specific purpose and try not to digress. As you write, you will probably continue to sharpen and refine that purpose, but it is still important to begin your writing with a definite sense of what you want to accomplish. For example, you can write about how to avoid injuries when you run or about how to train for a marathon, or you can try to explain the phenomenon called "runner's high." Writing out your purpose ahead of time will remind you to stay with your specific topic.

Second, writing out your purpose helps you to see your writing in the context of the rhetorical situation in which you are working and keeps you from writing a "blue sky" or "addressed to occupant" paper, that is, a voiceless paper written only to fill a requirement. When you think about purpose, you have to think about your audience and what you want to accomplish with those readers. Once you start to work in this kind of case-study situation, you'll find writing more interesting. For example, if your purpose is to explain warm-up and stretching exercises to a new runner so that she won't injure herself, you can visualize a specific person for whom you are

Knowing your purpose helps focus your writing

Knowing your purpose puts your writing in context

writing and think about what you want to accomplish for her. That helps make your writing more immediate and interesting than it would be if it were just a set of anonymous instructions.

Knowing your purpose helps you generate material

Third, writing out a statement of purpose can be an excellent generative device that helps you discover some of the points you want to make in your paper. If you invest some time in working out your purpose statement instead of just starting to write, you will probably come up with some ideas you hadn't thought of before. If you were writing a paper for experienced runners about how to train for a marathon, for example, your original purpose might have been to explain how many months one should allow for training and how to plan runs of various lengths. The process of writing out that purpose might trigger additional ideas about avoiding burnout from peaking too early and about ways for runners to pace themselves when they switch from their usual ten- to twelve-mile runs to the twenty-six-mile marathon. If you think of those additional purposes before you start to write, you will be able to organize your paper more efficiently.

In some writing situations — for example when you are writing an assignment that is self-contained (see page 22) or an essay exam — you may have to make a quick, almost automatic decision about purpose and might think you don't have time to write it out. You will find, however, that the few minutes it takes you to write out a statement of purpose is time well spent because it can help you stay on track. Too often students spend the first half of a fifty-minute exam writing *around* the question before they begin to focus on the issue. If instead they spent just a few minutes thinking about their purpose before they started and jotting it down on the back of the exam sheet, they should be able to come to the point more quickly and write a better exam.

Audience

Why Understanding Your Audience Is Important

If you are going to be successful as a writer, you have to cultivate a sure sense of audience — few concerns are as important. Writers must know, as far as possible, who their readers are and what assumptions they can make about them, and they need to keep their readers in mind as they write if they expect their writing to achieve its intended effect. Yet many student writers have never invested any time in identifying and analyzing the audience for whom they are writing. Students often feel that their immediate and only important audience for college papers is their instructor. In one sense they are right. The instructor grades their papers and therefore is the person they must please. But most writing instructors want their students to move beyond this narrow view and get in the habit of writing for a variety of other audiences, real or imagined, so that they can learn the rhetorical skills they need for writing in the many different kinds of writing situations they will encounter outside of college. They want them to work in case-study situations similar to those used in courses in nursing or social work or in law school, addressing a specified audience for a specified purpose. In writing assignments like these, students' grades can depend heavily on how well they adjust their writing to their specified audience.

Learn to write for diverse audiences

Students sometimes find it hard to adapt to this kind of writing assignment. They have never written for any audience but the teacher, and they resist adding this new dimension to their planning. It seems like just another complication, and they would rather write papers that put no special constraints about audience on them. But learning to think about their readers and what those readers want from a piece of writing is as important for writers as learning to anticipate the reactions of judges and juries is for law students or learning to anticipate how patients will respond to treatment is for medical students. Law and medical students learn the skills they will need by practicing in simulated situations; writers need to go through the same kinds of exercises to learn to identify and adapt to their audiences.

Writers also need to keep in mind that often they may have more than one audience for a single paper or document, and they must think about how they are going to satisfy the needs of both groups of readers. For instance, the writer who wrote the paper on cowboy boots on page 71 chose the readers of an airline magazine as his hypothetical audience. He had to think about how much they knew about boots and how much they wanted to know. But he also had to think about the editor of the airline magazine because she is the one who reads the article first and decides whether the magazine's readers would be interested.

Often people who write on the job also have two audiences. An engineer's environmental impact statement about the effects of building a dam might go first to the state bureau of water reclamation but also be used by conservationist groups in a campaign opposing the dam. A doctor's report on an unusual case of mononucleosis might go first into the patient's record but also become part of an article in a medical journal.

Identifying Your Readers and Analyzing Their Needs

All of us adapt our speech or writing almost automatically when we know our audience well and the issue at hand is important to us. For instance, if you want to borrow money from the credit union to finance your car, you're not going to be antagonistic or secretive when you talk to the loan officer, nor are you going to be flippant when you fill out the loan papers. Instead, you anticipate what the officer wants and give it to her. Similarly, if you are trying to persuade your spouse that you should both go skiing over the Christmas holidays, you almost instinctively know what kinds of arguments are likely to persuade him or her. By drawing on your experience with your spouse and the information you have about him or her, you can analyze the rhetorical situation quickly and respond to it most effectively.

Create your audience

When writers write for readers who are less familiar to them, they adopt the same kinds of strategies, but they have to use more thought and imagination to analyze their audience. What they do — and what we all do to some extent when we write for people we don't know well — is to *create* their readers — that is, they make up a composite picture of them and attribute certain characteristics to them just as a novelist creates characters and gives them personalities. First, however, writers get as much information about their audience as they can to help them decide the best approach to take — sometimes, in fact, they have to do substantial research about their readers before they can start writing. It's really the same method an astute job seeker should use before going for an interview — find out as much about the prospective employer as possible before actually facing him or her.

The kinds of information you need about your readers you can get by asking these three questions:

Key questions about your audience

1. Who are they?
2. What knowledge of the topic or attitudes about it do they bring with them to their reading?
3. Why are they reading? What do they need or expect to get from reading what you write?

Who Are Your Readers?   Your first task is to identify specifically and describe your readers. For example:

Describing your readers

> *Audience:* Readers of an airline magazine, mostly male business travelers. The editor of the magazine is also an important audience; he or she wants short, informational pieces on noncontroversial topics.

> *Audience:* Schoolchildren between 10 and 13 who are in science classes and receive a weekly bulletin about new developments in science. They are competent readers.

This kind of description will help you to focus on a particular group of readers and keep them in mind. Remember, however, that *describing* your readers is not the same as *analyzing* them. You need much more information to complete your composite picture.

What Knowledge and Attitudes Do Your Readers Have?   You have to use what your readers know, think, and feel in order to reach them. You can't communicate with people unless you and they have some common background, some common knowledge, and share some beliefs and attitudes. The good rhetorician works at finding out what that common ground is and uses it.

Analyzing your readers

One of your earliest questions about audience should be "What do my readers already know about this topic?" It's often a difficult question, but you have to answer it as best you can to find a starting point for your writing. For example, if you decide you want to explain the binary number system by which computers operate, you have to know whom you are writing for and how much they know. Some readers know so little that you must start from scratch and draw diagrams. With others who have studied symbolic logic you can start at a much higher level. For still other readers, such as computer programmers, you should realize, upon reflection, that they already know what you have to say — you don't have a paper.

So you must find some way to estimate how much your readers know. You need it as a base to build from because you have to use the known to explain the unknown. For instance, in the paper on how to buy cowboy boots on page 71, the writer assumes that the readers know that cowboy boots are popular, have seen such boots, and know a buyer can choose from a bewildering variety of styles and prices. He assumes that his readers do not have more specialized information about cowboy boots: the different styles of heels and toes available, the varieties of decorative stitching, and the various qualities and prices one can choose from. He sets out to give them that kind of information in the paper.

You know from your own experience that readers quickly get bored when a writer tells them something they already know or tells them far more than they want to know or can understand. How does a writer avoid that pitfall? It's not easy. About the only practical way is to think seriously about your projected readers and, using what knowledge and experience you have, try to create an image of them and decide what they would be like. When I am writing textbooks, for example, I think about the many, many student writers I have taught and try to remember what they already knew when they came into my class and what they most needed to learn while they were in it. I have to generalize, of course, because many individual students wouldn't fit the image I create, but I do create a useful picture of the student I want to write to.

The attitudes — that is, beliefs, prejudices, and convictions — that readers bring with them are also crucially important for a writer to keep in mind, particularly when presenting arguments. But knowing something about how your readers *feel* on certain issues is important even when you are writing to inform or entertain. Think about what is important to them, what they are interested in, and what good or bad experiences they have had that might affect the way they respond to your writing.

For example, if you were writing to apply for a scholarship given by a foundation created by an alumnus of your college, you ought to be able to figure out how the people who run the foundation feel about the value of an education and what kind of qualities they look for in scholarship students. If you're writing to the company that manufactured your car to complain about the dealer from whom you bought it, you need to keep in mind how that company feels about its reputation and what it expects from its dealers.

Why is Your Audience Reading and What do They Want to Know?

Why are your readers reading?

All writers should learn to distance themselves from their writing enough to look at it from their readers' point of view. Why are they reading? Why *should* they read? It's not ever a good idea to assume that you have a captive audience, readers who must read a paper whether they like it or not. When someone has to read what you have written, they may stay with it *physically* and trudge through to the end, but they won't stay with it *psychologically* or *intellectually* if you are giving no thought to their needs. So try to cultivate the habit of thinking from your readers' point of view and asking "What is it they want from reading this? How can I meet their needs?"

Often the answer will be that they want to learn something — there is no more powerful motivation for reading. They may also want to be entertained, encouraged, diverted — they may have several reasons for reading. For example, a reader who picks up a copy of *Esquire* and reads an article on clothing styles for young men is reading mainly for information; he wants to know what young men are wearing, what colors and combinations are popular, and which designers are doing the most interesting clothes. But he also wants an article that is pleasant to read and illustrated with good photos.

What questions will your readers have?

It can also be extremely useful to ask yourself "What questions will readers have when they start to read my paper?" After all, readers don't just pluck something to read from out of a vacuum. They form expectations from the context in which they are reading and from the title of the piece. Your history professor, for example, expects certain things from a term paper she has assigned; a company executive expects certain things from a report he has asked for. The professor and the executive have specific questions in mind that the paper is expected to answer; if they are not answered, the readers are going to be dissatisfied. Therefore, you as a writer need to anticipate such questions and be sure that you answer them in your paper. For the paper on cowboy boots, for example, a reader would probably have at least these questions when he or she started reading:

What special qualities do cowboy boots have that make them popular?

What different kinds of boots are there?

What options can one get when buying boots?

What should one look for when buying boots?

How much do they cost?

Where can you buy them?

I have found that listing probable reader questions when I start a writing project helps me greatly. The questions help me generate ideas, and they serve as a kind of tentative outline to follow, one that I find more congenial than a formal outline.

Questions to Ask About Your Audience

Who are my readers?

What is their educational level?

What is their economic level?

Are they men or women? Both?

How old are they?

What is important to my readers?

What values do they have on this issue?

Are they busy? Will they be impatient?

What do my readers already know about this topic?

How much background knowledge can I assume?

How much do I have to explain?

Can I use specialized terminology?

What can I tell them that will interest or inform them?

What attitudes will my readers have on this topic?

How do they feel about this issue?

Are they willing to learn or be persuaded?

Why are they reading?

What do they expect to get?

What questions will my readers want answered?

Keeping Your Audience in Mind

Probably the most common breakdown between you and your audience comes from neglecting to identify it before you start to write or from just forgetting to keep it in mind once you have begun. If you are going to argue that women should no longer settle for the secondary roles in the professions — nurse instead of doctor, bookkeeper instead of investment counselor, secretary instead of executive — you are not likely to make an effective argument unless you decide ahead of time whom you are going to address: women themselves, leaders in the professions, or the faculties of professional schools. Say you determine that your audience is predominantly conservative and practical; if you then allow yourself to go off into an idealistic and emotional argument — and this frequently happens with issues on which people have strong feelings — you are defeating your own rhetorical purpose.

There is, of course, a need for rhetoric that attacks, accuses, and agitates for change. You cannot and should not always try to be pleasant. But the best time to be militant and hostile in your speech or writing is when your real audience is not another person or group that you hope to persuade, but a third audience that you are trying to influence to be for you and against your opponent. For instance, suppose you were participating in a television debate about gun control laws; you are against them, your opponent is for them. Your real audience is the television audience, not the person who favors gun control laws. Under these circumstances you can attack gun control laws as an infringement on constitutional rights and interference with free enterprise. You are certainly not going to convince your opponent by such arguments, but you might influence many people in the viewing audience. So when you begin to compose an angry attack on some person or issue, stop to think who your real audience is. If, for instance, it is a legislator or administrator whom you really hope to influence, don't attack, reason. You simply do not convince people by antagonizing them.

You do not convince an audience by making it angry

Audiences for Student Writing

Students may go about finding their audiences in several ways. Often they may have no problem because the audience is explicitly or implicitly designated in the assignment. You may be asked to prepare for a class a particular report, or to submit to a committee a statement of your reasons for wanting to participate in an honors seminar in history. If you are writing an essay exam, obviously the audience is your professor or the grader; if possible, it may be a good idea to find out which. If, however, your only instructions are to write a paper about your views on credit cards or an argument for or against abolishing the English requirement in your college, you need to find your audience before you begin. One question you might ask yourself is "Who would be interested in this topic?" That will give you a starting place. From there, you can narrow your audience further by concentrating on a group of people about the same age or of a certain educational level. In most cases, it is probably easier and more natural for you to write to other young people.

Identifying your audience for student papers

Reconciling Adaptation to Audience and Authentic Voice

Inevitably when rhetoricians suggest that in order for writers to be effective they must learn to adapt to different audiences, someone cries "Foul" and accuses them of sacrificing integrity for popular appeal. It's an old charge that goes back to ancient Greece, when philosophers accused the rhetoricians known as Sophists of teaching their students how to twist language for their own ends, and it has persisted through the centuries. But those who make such an accusation are being simplistic and misleading. Writers don't have to choose between their integrity and popular appeal. If they are skillful and determined, they can write honestly and still appeal to their readers. They can maintain the authentic voice that is so crucial to good rhetoric (see the next section on persona) and also use effective strategies to get their ideas across. Later chapters in this book focus on ways to do both.

To be sure, writers who try both to be honest and to appeal to their readers have to invest much more time and thought in their work than do writers who take a "no compromise, the readers be damned" attitude and write whatever they like. The "no compromise" stance is the easy way that requires nothing of a writer except that he or she spill out opinions and feelings. Such writers are really writing for themselves — perhaps they just want to blow off steam or write on a favorite topic for the fun of it. But if they want someone else to read and react to what they have written — and they almost always do — they should realize that just because they want to write about an issue doesn't necessarily mean that someone else wants to read about it. Audiences have to be enticed, and writers who work at getting them to read don't have to sell out or compromise principles to succeed. They can use practical strategies and assume a variety of roles, all of which are honest and authentic.

Persona

Once you have defined your audience, your next task is to decide the role that you, as rhetorician, are going to play for your audience. The term *persona* best describes that role because it is a comparatively neutral term. *Persona* derives from the Latin word for the masks worn by the actors in ancient classical drama, masks that immediately classified their roles for the audience: a smiling mask for a comic character, a sorrowful one for a tragic character. Thus, *persona* is an apt word to describe the identity assumed by a writer or speaker.

Role playing is natural

Psychologists have long known that the normal person plays many roles. As a person who lives in a complex and sophisticated culture, you find yourself in a variety of different situations during the course of a day, and you adjust your behavior accordingly. You wear no mask when you are grousing at the alarm clock in the privacy of your room, but you assume one when you get to the breakfast table and want to be at least civil to your companions. In class you assume the role of student; you pay attention, take notes, ask questions. Your instructor is playing the role of teacher, acting quite differently in the classroom than in an office talking to a colleague ten minutes before. Late in the afternoon you may shift to the role of son or daughter when you are talking over the phone with your parents and that evening show another facet of your personality when you are drinking beer with your friends. All this behavior is unaffected and sincere; you are being yourself, but in a flexible way that allows you to choose responses appropriate to your situation and your audience.

How to Decide on Your Persona

Such flexibility is precisely what is involved in establishing your persona in a rhetorical situation. The only difference is that when you

---

are not familiar with your audience, you need to think ahead about your purpose, the make-up of your audience, and the image of yourself that you want to project. In face-to-face situations, you can still rely largely on instinct; common sense tells you that it is all right to act casually at a meeting of student advisers but foolish to do so at a hearing before the dean of students. When you are writing, however, you have fewer clues to guide you; therefore, it is a good idea to think about your persona before you frame an appeal on an important issue.

Why authentic voice is important

The Authentic Voice   A critical ingredient of any successful writer's persona is *authentic voice,* that quality in a piece of writing that makes readers feel there is a real person doing the writing, someone who cares about what he or she is saying and genuinely wants to communicate with readers. An authentic voice individualizes a piece of writing, whether it is a book or a student paper; it is what you *don't* get in those mass-produced, computerized letters that have your name in all the appropriate places but no more uniqueness than a McDonald's hamburger.

In order to project an authentic voice, you have to write honestly and sound genuine in whatever role or persona you adopt. You have to invest something in your writing, care about your topic, and not give the impression that you are hiding behind a mask. The reader wants to be able to *hear* you behind that page of print, to know that there is a real person there. Of course your voice can and does change from one paper to another. At times you can be an ardent spokesman for a project you're involved in, at other times an amused observer of your professor or your employer. In either case, your reader should be able to sense your special voice behind the writing.

Here are two examples that project authentic voice, the first from a professional writer writing about writing, the second from a student writing about animal myths for an audience of young readers.

> The longer I work at the craft of writing, the more I realize that there's nothing more interesting than the truth. What people do — and what people say — continues to take me by surprise with its wonderfulness, or its quirkiness, or its drama, or its humor, or its pain. Who could invent all of the astonishing things that really happen? Therefore I increasingly find myself saying to writers and students: "Trust your material." (William Zinsser, *On Writing Well*)

Ever been stung by a dragonfly? Or held a slimy snake in the palm of your hand? Ever gotten a wart from a toad? If you said "Yes," you're one of the many people who believe in animal myths.

Animal myths are stories men create to explain the qualities of an animal that puzzles them. Myths are fiction, like fairy tales, and are intended to explain certain things in nature which men don't understand. Passed from generation to generation, myths become tradition, believed even after they are proven false. (Steve Bennett)

Notice how clearly the writer's voice comes through in each passage. From reading each, you get a sense of what kind of person the writer is. You should have the same response to the full-length student papers in the following chapters. Each of them has, among other good features, a strong authentic voice.

Ethical Appeal Closely related to authentic voice but subtly different, *ethical appeal* is based on the character, reputation, and expertise of the writer or speaker. As Aristotle pointed out over two thousand years ago in his *Rhetoric,* there is no stronger appeal. If a writer or speaker wins an audience's trust, they instinctively believe him or her and respond favorably. But there is no more fragile appeal, either — if writers or speakers lie to their audience or don't live up to the expectations they raise, ethical appeal can quickly evaporate.

Why ethical appeal is important

In the long run, writers — and everyone else — establish strong ethical appeal only by appearing confident and rational and by consistently behaving in ways that make people trust them. Television anchorperson Peter Jennings and writers Eudora Welty and Lewis Thomas provide good examples of such behavior. But in the short run, even beginning writers can do certain things to convince their readers that they are intelligent, capable, and trustworthy. Some of the ways in which one does this are:

Ways to create ethical appeal

Avoid extreme "always" or "never" statements.

Write clearly so your readers can understand you.

Add the "weight of facts" to your writing by using examples.

Don't overstate your case or claim too much.

Show you have done your homework and know what you are talking about.

The Damaging Effects of Carelessness

Avoid making a bad impression

Writers who have obviously neglected to do sufficient homework before starting to write demonstrate one kind of carelessness, and a serious kind. Readers will turn them off with a contemptuous, "They just don't know what they're talking about." But there are also other kinds of carelessness that can seriously damage the image you want to present to your audience.

Suppose, for instance, that you are applying for a scholarship. You can demonstrate your financial need, show that you are both bright and ambitious, and produce excellent letters of recommendation. You put a lot of thought into the letter of application, but you do not take the time to check the spelling of Optimist Club, so you address the letter to the president of the Jonesville Optomist Club. You will make a bad impression even before the envelope is opened. In the body of the letter, you use *except* when you mean *accept*; you speak of your ambition to be a veterinarian, but spell it as most people pronounce it, *vetinarian*; when you mention a college's fine reputation, you write *it's* instead of *its*; you conclude the letter by saying, "I appreciate your consideration irregardless of your decision."

This letter may well ruin your chance of getting a scholarship because, without your being aware of it, you have established a persona quite different from the one you intended. By careless spelling and grammar you have created the image of someone who is too lazy to look up words and too sloppy to check a letter for errors. You have characterized yourself just as surely as you would by appearing for a formal interview with mud on your shoes, a button off your shirt, and grease stains on your coat. You may be an admirable person in spite of your dirty clothes and a promising student in spite of your bad spelling and faulty diction; but if you start off by establishing an image that annoys people, you will probably never have the chance to demonstrate your real abilities.

You may protest that people who make judgments on the basis of spelling, punctuation, and writing style are being shortsighted and unfair. You have a point. An inability to spell is scarcely an indication of bad character, and a fondness for clichés may not mean that a person is stupid. Nevertheless, the people who decide who will be accepted for law school or the foreign service, who will get scholarships or grants, and who will be chosen for an in-service training program or the position of district supervisor do judge people partially on the basis of their writing. The piece of paper with your words on it and your name at the bottom represents *you*. You cannot change that. And when an administrator or firm receives a flood of applications from well-qualified people, those who have written poor letters will not survive the first screening.

The Content of Argument

The three elements of a rhetorical situation just discussed — purpose, audience, and persona — are essential parts of the rhetorical square because they provide the *context* in which an argument exists. Without them, a written argument is no more than a piece of paper with some marks on it. But the argument is the basis for their existence, too — unless there is content to be argued, a rhetorical situation cannot exist.

This last side of the rhetorical square is too complex to explain in a few pages — in fact, most of the rest of this text focuses on ways to construct and evaluate arguments. But before going on to those concerns, I want to conclude this chapter by considering two traditional categories of arguments and explaining some of the limitations that one encounters in working with arguments.

Logical and Nonlogical Arguments

Two categories of argument: logical and nonlogical

Aristotle and the other classical rhetoricians identified two other kinds of argument in addition to ethical appeal. They are *logical* and *nonlogical* arguments. The logical modes of argument are those that appeal to the intellect, that try to persuade by setting in motion thought processes that will culminate in the audience's reaching the desired conclusion. The chief forms of logical argument, or what Aristotle called the "appeal to reason," are deduction, induction, cause and effect, definition, arguments from comparison, and the use of evidence and testimony. The nonlogical methods most commonly used in persuasion are connotation, figurative language, tone, and diction. The classical rhetoricians classified these techniques under the "appeal to emotion."

This classification looks attractively neat, but like most pigeonholing it oversimplifies and distorts the real article. In practice, almost any rhetorical appeal combines the logical and the nonlogical;

sometimes it is nearly impossible to separate the two elements. On close analysis we usually find that the skeleton or frame of any argument will be logical; that is, it will be built on induction, evidence, definition, or some combination of logical devices. The substance or body of the argument, however, will contain substantial amounts of nonlogical material, such as figurative language or connotative adjectives.

You are most likely to make use of the rhetorical principles outlined in this chapter if, for every paper you write, you fill out the following form. Do it *before* you begin to write, check your paper against it when you have finished your first draft, and make any necessary adjustments. Making yourself follow this routine will be a nuisance at first, but gradually it will become a habit, one that will pay off.

Rhetorical Guidelines for Writing a Paper

   I.   Audience for paper: _____

          Specific characteristics of the audience to keep in mind:

          1. _____

          2. _____

          3. _____

          4. _____

  II.   Persona of writer: _____

          Important characteristics to convey to the audience:

          1. _____

          2. _____

          3. _____

          4. _____

 III.   Purpose of paper: _____

          _____

          _____

IV. Arguments to be used:

    1.   _____

    2.   _____

    3.   _____

    4.   _____

V. Chief method of appeal (check one):
    1. ethical
    2. emotional
    3. logical

Where Rhetoric Starts and Stops

If you want to be an effective writer, you need to know how to judge a rhetorical situation so you can decide when you have a good chance of explaining your ideas or convincing your readers and when you do not. In order to decide, you need to know what kinds of issues one can profitably discuss and also how to identify situations in which you would be wasting your time and energy.

Arguable Assertions

Assertions, statements that make a claim or state a position, form the framework of expository and rhetorical writing. But not all assertions can be developed into arguments. For instance, consider the following statements:

1. Pickled pigs' feet are delicious.
2. The US government should get out of the student loan business.
3. The San Francisco Forty-Niners won the 1985 Superbowl.
4. Quasars, pulsars, white dwarfs, and black holes are hypothetical concepts that modern astronomers use to explain certain phenomena they don't understand.

Strictly speaking, all four statements are what logicians call propositions: that is, they are statements that can be affirmed or denied. Only two of them, however, are *legitimate* assertions, statements of belief or judgment that can be developed and supported with evidence and rational discourse. Those two are numbers 2 and 4.

Proposition 1 is simply an expression of taste; the writer is saying, "I like pickled pigs' feet." The statement is not arguable because there is no point in debating taste, a subjective, nonrational reaction to experience. You cannot persuade people through reasoning that they like what they do not like — I cannot be persuaded that I like anchovies; I know better.

In some cases, argument is pointless

Similarly, it is pointless to try to argue people out of their phobias, such as fear of flying, or to try to prove that canoeing is a better sport than windsurfing if by *better* you mean more enjoyable. Although people do sometimes get over their fears and change their preferences, they usually do so because of experience, not because someone persuaded them with a wonderful argument. The realms of taste and emotion are not good areas for argument or explanation.

Proposition 3 is a matter of fact that can be checked in newspaper records or a sports almanac, and no amount of argument or discussion will change it. Only people who are naive or addicted to disputation would waste their time debating such a point.

Propositions 2 and 4 are legitimate assertions that can be explained, developed, and supported using a variety of rhetorical strategies. They are also on topics that would be fruitful to discuss. A writer can explain why he thinks the government should get out of the student loan business and cite figures and case studies to support his point. He may not be able to *prove* his assertion to his readers' satisfaction, but he can make a strong case. Similarly, a writer can define quasars, pulsars, white dwarfs, and black holes for her readers and present evidence to show how astronomers use these concepts to explain astronomical mysteries.

Conditions for Argument

Rhetorical situations must have two elements

The point is that engaging in rhetoric is worth your time only when the situation has these two elements: first, you have a substantive assertion that can be developed and supported; and, second, there is a possibility of enlightening readers, bringing people into closer agreement, persuading them to alter their attitudes, or getting them to take action. Under those circumstances you have a rhetorical situation.

And if you want to convince or inform your readers, remember not to overstate your assertions. Don't claim far more than you can prove in one paper or make statements that you can't possibly support. Extreme statements, such as "The prison system of this country is a total failure," or "The only way you can get ahead in business is by being ruthless," mark a writer as naive or irresponsible — or both. Both statements put an impossible burden of proof on the arguer, because if the reader thinks of even a few exceptions the assertion collapses.

When you are analyzing the rhetoric of others, you need to be equally alert to the way in which the authors' main assertions are stated. Are the assertions arguable? What kinds of claims are being made? Are their commitments more than they can support? In general, you should be skeptical of writers who overload their assertions with *most, best, worst,* and *greatest;* their arguments are likely to be as shaky as their assertions.

Assumptions

The nature of assumptions

When we read what someone has written, we see and can evaluate the assertions that the author has made. What we do not see, however, are the unstated assumptions that underlie any writing, and those are equally important. An *assumption* is a belief or proposition that is taken for granted, one that the writer considers so obvious that he or she doesn't need to mention it, much less explain or support it. For example, in writing this text, I assume that most of my readers have been reared in an American family, that they have gone to public schools, and that for the most part they share with me what are known as "American values" — traditional attitudes about individualism, free enterprise, and the role of technology in our culture. I realize that my generalizations don't fit all my readers, particularly those who grew up in another culture, but I know from surveys done by a national organization that my assumptions are warranted.[1] Most writers who go to the trouble of identifying and reflecting on their readers will not have much trouble with assumptions when they are working on this broad scale.

[1] Alexander Astin, *The American Freshman: National Norms for 1984,* published by the American Council on Education and the University of California at Los Angeles. Reprinted in *The Chronicle of Higher Education* 16 Jan. 1985.

Using Readers' Assumptions

Using shared assumptions in your arguments

However, when writers move beyond this broad area of experiences and knowledge that they share with their readers and into narrower topics and issues, they need to think more carefully about the assumptions that their readers hold and try to identify those assumptions as accurately as possible. When writers become skillful at identifying their readers' assumptions and keeping them in mind as they write, they can learn to use shared assumptions as grounds for their arguments, and they can also get their readers to participate actively in their own persuasion. Writers accomplish that by anticipating the values and beliefs readers bring with them when they begin to read. (See the section on informal logic, page 333.)

Suppose, for example, that you are a public health major and work part-time for a local hospital's patient education program. You are asked to write copy for an ad publicizing a stress-management seminar; the ad will appear in the business section of the newspaper. Before you begin to compose the ad, you identify your audience: people concerned about stress in their lives who read the business section of the paper. From this basic information, you can make several assumptions. First, they care about their health and know that uncontrolled stress is a health hazard; if they didn't, they wouldn't read the ad. Second, they are accustomed to trying to solve their problems rather than accepting them stoically; if they weren't, they wouldn't be interested in a seminar. Third, they believe in specialization and expertise; they assume that experts know about handling stress and can help people. Fourth, as business people they are accustomed to paying well for services but expect good value. You could make many other assumptions, but these are the more obvious ones.

You can use these predispositions of your readers to persuade them that they should attend the seminar. You don't have to mention any of the assumptions I have listed. You can limit yourself to telling your readers that this particular seminar can solve their problems, that the people who run it are qualified experts, and that the seminar is worth what it costs. By focusing on those points, you use the powerful strategy of tapping into strong convictions that they held before they began reading. If, however, you spend your time trying to persuade them of what they already believe, they could easily become impatient and quit reading.

But you can also damage the case you want to present by making faulty judgments about your readers' assumptions. For example, if you write a letter for your college newspaper urging all students to write their legislators and oppose building any more nuclear power plants in your state, you might take it for granted that you don't have to explain the hazards of nuclear plants or review the problems they have caused in other states. However, some of your readers may not know about those hazards; moreover, they may live in an area that needs new power sources to attract industry. You need to explain your assumptions in order to have a basis for your argument, and as soon as assumptions are explained, they cease to be assumptions and become assertions that must be supported.

De-Centering Your Writing

Learning to think about assumptions, your own as well as those of your readers, is an important part of maturing as a writer because it helps you to *de-center,* that is, distance yourself from your writing in a way that enables you to see it from another person's point of view. For instance, if you are negotiating with your union to get a day care center at the company where you work, you are assuming that it's important for the mothers of young children to be able to work, and you are also assuming that day care centers provide acceptable alternatives to a parent's staying at home full-time during a child's preschool years. Those assumptions may be so obvious to you that you don't realize they are not equally obvious to the union officials with whom you are dealing. *They* may well be men over fifty who assume that women need jobs less than men do and that all mothers should stay home and take care of their preschool children. You need to be aware of those assumptions if you want to construct an effective argument that takes them into account.

Learning to consider
other people's
assumptions

How can you learn to anticipate what your readers' assumptions are so that you can take them into account as you write? It's not easy. Mostly it requires that you try to put yourself in your readers' place and imagine what kinds of experiences and heritage have shaped their attitudes and values. Ask yourself why you hold the assumptions you do; what experiences or training have you had that make you believe, for example, that you should get a college degree? Then think about what kinds of experiences your readers have probably had and how those experiences would have shaped their assumptions. The process requires that you invest some time and energy and that you look beyond your own world, but if you develop the knack for anticipating your readers' assumptions, you will become a more effective writer.

A Priori Premises

An a priori premise is a special kind of assumption that has an even stronger emotional and cultural basis than the kinds of cultural beliefs and attitudes discussed in the previous section. The term *a priori* means "based on a hypothesis or theory rather than on experiment or evidence; made before or without examination; not supported by factual study."[2] The phrases "made *before* or *without* examination" and "not supported" are key parts of the definition. People who believe something a priori believe it at a gut level; they just *know* it is true, even though they haven't examined any evidence or seen supporting data. They don't need evidence because they believe strongly. Most patriotic, religious, and moral beliefs are a priori premises, and so are many strong cultural, social, and racial convictions.

The nature of a priori premises

It is not always possible to distinguish between common and widely held assumptions, such as "Southerners are naturally hospitable" or "City dwellers are more cautious and suspicious than people who live in the country" and a priori premises like "People are basically lazy" or "Slavery is wrong." The two categories are going to merge and overlap from time to time, and inevitably students will sometimes disagree on how a particular statement should be classified. In general, however, we can say that a priori premises are beliefs that are so deeply and fervently held that they take on the force of facts or eternal truths. By their nature they *cannot* be proved, but by their nature they cannot be *disproved* either. People can, however, usually find some evidence to support their assumptions. The evidence may be skimpy or slanted, but they can give some examples. And although the statement may surprise you, it is easier to support the contention that city dwellers are suspicious than it is the assertion that slavery is wrong. For the last statement, you would have to fall back on another a priori premise, and then another, and another.

---

[2]© 1981 by Houghton Mifflin Company. Reprinted by permission from *The American Heritage Dictionary of the English Language*.

One of the most famous a priori statements comes in the introduction to our Declaration of Independence: "We hold these truths to be self-evident: that all men are created equal, that they are endowed by their Creator with certain inalienable rights, that among these are Life, Liberty, and the Pursuit of Happiness." The crucial words here are *truths* and *self-evident*; they suggest that the authors are positive that everyone agrees with their claim about inalienable rights; they have neither the need nor the obligation to support their assertion. But are these "truths" really universal and eternal? An Indian who had been reared in a caste society would probably claim that it is self-evident that all people are *not* created equal, that a tightly stratified society is natural and right. Members of other societies, ancient and modern, would call the statement that any person has inalienable rights absolute nonsense. The state or the church, not the individual, decides what a person's rights are.

A priori premises are often cultural

So a priori premises are often cultural or national, and most of them are certainly not eternal. But that qualification does not diminish their force for the people who hold them. To nearly all Americans, the original statement still stands as an article of faith, unshaken by the most vigorous challenge. We don't have to prove it; we *know* it.

Premises About Human Nature   One of the chief classes of a priori premises consists of statements about human nature. Romanticists such as Rousseau, Emerson, and Wordsworth held that people are naturally good; the Calvinists held that they are naturally sinful. Both sides based their entire philosophical systems on a priori premises, which are unproved and unprovable. In modern times, one school of psychology argues that people behave as they do because of sexual drives and frustrations, and another claims that people are motivated chiefly by drives for power and dominance. Both schools can construct theories and cite dozens of case histories, but they cannot actually prove their premises.

They often concern human nature

Among the oldest of our a priori assumptions are those concerning the nature of women. For centuries, theologians, psychologists, and anthropologists have been claiming that there are basic and radical differences between the "natural" personalities of each sex and that certain traits are inherently "feminine," others inherently "masculine." Now, people like Betty Friedan, Germaine Greer, Gloria Steinem, and many women novelists are challenging these long-held beliefs by claiming that what is thought of as the "feminine nature" is really the product of cultural conditioning and expectations, not natural at all. As a result, a new set of a priori premises about women is emerging and gaining strength in many circles.

A priori premises often concern morality

Premises About Morality   Another important class of a priori premises includes those that deal with morality. Assertions that define what is right and wrong, good and bad, are the foundation of all ethical discussion and pronouncements. We — and all cultures — have so many moral premises that it would be impossible to list even a representative sample, but typically they deal with such matters as honesty, loyalty, trustworthiness, fairness, kindness, and so on. When we take a moral position, we inevitably base our argument on an a priori premise that we feel sure our audience shares. For example, the senator who launches an investigation into corporate bribes is saying that honesty is a virtue. The people who condemn killings by terrorists are saying that human life is valuable; those who call for an investigation of brutal practices in prisons are saying that cruelty is wrong.

Such moral feelings are so strongly rooted in us that we forget they cannot be proved or tested without falling back on other convictions that are also held a priori. Take, for example, the statement "Slavery is wrong." If someone were to ask you to prove that it is, what would you say? Perhaps, "Human liberty is a basic right." The next questions might be "Basic to whom? Did the ancient Greeks think so?" Your answer: "No, but today everybody knows that slavery is wrong." The reply might follow, "*I* don't think it's wrong — in fact I wish my family still owned slaves." And so it could go, round and round. You could not *prove* your point.

But you don't have to prove it. The fact that some or even many other people do not share our basic convictions need not in any way weaken the force of those convictions. All people have the right to say that because of training, experience, reflection, or intuition, they hold certain principles, that these principles are true and valid, and that they will serve as the basis of actions. Such an attitude is, and must be, the basis of morality.

Accommodating Your Writing to A Priori Premises   Because a priori premises are so powerful, writers need to be especially aware of their two-edged rhetorical potential.

On one hand, you strengthen your arguments when you are conscious of the fundamental a priori premises that your readers hold and tap into those premises as part of your appeal. Once more, you get your readers to participate in their own persuasion because they furnish the support for your argument. For instance, if you want to argue to a group of Iowa legislators that they should pass a bill that would help small farmers to get low-cost loans in order to survive a year of bad crops, you can be virtually sure that those legislators believe a priori that farmers are virtuous, hardworking, "salt of the earth" people whom we should all be proud of. Such attitudes about farmers go back to Thomas Jefferson, and rural-minded Iowa legislators would certainly support them. Thus you know you can claim that these farmers deserve the loans, and the legislators will provide the support for that claim out of their stock of a priori wisdom. And having them provide that support works better than giving it yourself.

On the other hand, when a writer realizes that she and her intended audience have irreconcilable a priori premises, the wise course is to back off and decide that no persuasion is possible. It's a waste of time and paper to try to change the mind of someone whose primary beliefs on an issue are so different from yours that he or she is not going to pay any attention. For example, if you believe that people are basically cooperative and peaceful, there is little point in your arguing in favor of a disarmament pact for an audience that believes people are inherently aggressive and power-hungry. You have a no-win, nonrhetorical situation. It is in order to avoid having students bog down in these emotional and intellectual morasses that most experienced teachers refuse to let them write on such controversial topics as abortion or capital punishment. The a priori premises on which the opposing positions in such issues are based are absolutely irreconcilable, and communication between the opponents is usually impossible.

Over a period of time, practical writers learn to analyze all these elements in a rhetorical situation and to make the most of them.

The benefits of using a priori premises in arguments

The hazards of using a priori premises in arguments

Exercises

1. Write sample thesis sentences or summaries that could serve as statements of purpose for the following writing assignments:

a. An essay on the benefits (or disadvantages) of living in a mobile home.

b. An essay for (or against) Zero Population Growth.

c. A report on the results of an experiment that you have recently done in your psychology class.

d. A letter to the editor of the student newspaper suggesting that study facilities be improved in the college library.

e. A letter to the board of regents asking for more subsidized housing for married students.

2. State briefly what your main purposes would be in the following writing assignments:

a. A statement of personal goals to accompany your application to law school (or to a theological seminary).

b. An application for a grant from a foundation in order that you may spend part of your sophomore year in field work doing an independent study in a subject of your choice (for example, nutrition for welfare clients, conditions in a mental hospital near your home, voting patterns within the eighteen to twenty-one-year-old age group, or racial attitudes among junior high school students in your town).

c. A letter to the dean of your college asking for reinstatement in school after you have been expelled for getting drunk and taking a midnight swim in the Memorial Fountain.

3. In the fourth century B.C. Aristotle wrote what is probably the most famous of all rhetoric texts. In it he counseled his readers to adapt their rhetoric to the character of their audience and gave them the following guidelines to help them. What do you think of his analysis? Are his assumptions about the young and the old still valid? Would you use them if you were addressing audiences in that category? What specific criticisms would you make of his generalizations?

> Young men have strong desires, and whatever they desire they are prone to do. Of the bodily desires the one they let govern them most is sexual desire; here they lack self-control. . . . The young are passionate, quick to anger, and apt to give way to

it. . . . Fond of honor, they are even fonder of victory, for youth likes to be superior, and winning evinces superiority. They love both honor and victory more than they care for money. Indeed, they care next to nothing about money, for they have not yet learned what the want of it means. . . . The young think no evil, but believe in human goodness, for as yet they have not seen many examples of vice. They are trustful, for as yet they have not often been deceived. . . . They are high-minded; first, because they have not yet been humbled by life, nor come to know the force of circumstances; and secondly, because high-mindedness means thinking oneself fitted for great things. In their actions they prefer honor to expediency; for their lives are rather lives of good impulse than of calculation. . . . They carry everything too far; they love to excess, they hate to excess — and so in all else. They think they know everything, and are positive about everything.[3]

Of the elderly, Aristotle says,

The Old have lived long, have been often deceived, have made many mistakes of their own; they see that more often than not the affairs of men turn out badly. And so they are positive about nothing; in all things they err by an extreme moderation. . . . They think evil; that is, they are disposed to put the worse construction on everything. Further, they are suspicious because they are distrustful and distrustful from sad experience. As a result, they have no strong likings or hates. . . . They are mean-souled, because they have been humbled by life. Thus they aspire to nothing great or exalted, but crave the mere necessities and comforts of existence. And they are not generous. Property, as they know, is one of the necessities, and they have learned by experience how hard it is to acquire, how easy to lose. They are cowards, apprehensive about everything . . . the old are not characterized by passion, and their actions are governed not by impulse, but by love of gain. . . . Their lives are rather lives of calculation than of moral bias. [p. 135]

[3]Lane Cooper, *The Rhetoric of Aristotle*, © 1932, renewed 1960, pp. 132–133, 134–135. Adapted by permission of Prentice-Hall, Inc., Englewood Cliffs, N.J.

4. Imagine that you have been asked to write articles for any three of these publications. Examine a copy of each of the three you choose, and in a sentence of no more than twenty-five words, specify who your audience would be in each case and what important characteristics that audience would have.

Seventeen

New York Times

Glamour

Playboy

Ebony

Time

Reader's Digest

Christian Science Monitor

U.S. News & World Report

Family Circle

Psychology Today

Vanity Fair

5. What assumptions about the audience is the writer of each of the following advertisements making?

a. *The Durable One* Our car may not be the prettiest and shiniest on the market, but it's the toughest. We built it to last. And not to cost you a fortune.

We start with a simple car that doesn't have an ounce of wasted space. Then we refuse to put on any frills. Instead, we make a tight car that doesn't rattle, doesn't rust, doesn't gobble gas.

And we test every car before it leaves the factory. No lemons allowed.

If you care more about durability than you do about decor, Bulldog is the car for you.

b. *Bahama Adventure* Guided tours you don't want — they're stuffy and dull. But how about an adventure, a real *Adventure*? A fun tour of the Bahamas with exciting nights and leisurely, sun-baked days?

Discover new people, new places, new things to do. You'll find the excitement of extraordinary places, off-the-beaten-path nightclubs and restaurants.

Only a few lucky souls find ways to put zest in their lives. You can be one of them if you join this fabulous Cruise of Adventure that only Bahamas Unlimited offers you.

c. *Mindpower: Your Key to Success!* Most people drudge along in life using only a fraction of their real capacities. They feel — know — that they have potential that has never come to the surface. Buried in them somewhere is power, the power to do the things they dreamed of once. Are you one of these unhappy ones? Do you want to find the key that will release those vital forces?

Our new, scientifically based course in *Mindpower* will show you the way. By learning ten simple rules for awakening the hidden dynamics of your brain, you can throw off that inertia that has kept you from being the man you deserve to be. Write today!

6. Clip one of the columns of a well-known journalist — for example, Russell Baker, Meg Greenfield, William F. Buckley, Ellen Goodman, Marianne Means, William Raspberry — and tape it to a sheet of paper. Under it write a short description of the persona the writer is assuming and give some evidence to support your analysis. Keep it short, not more than one hundred words in all.

7. Describe very briefly the persona you would want to adopt in each of the following rhetorical situations:

a. You are participating in Operation Outreach, a project in which students and faculty visit high schools throughout the state to encourage members of minority groups to enroll in your college.

b. You have decided to get married next semester and want to continue your education, but really need to have some continuing support from your parents. Write a letter that gives them good reasons why they should not cut off your allowance.

c. You are trying to borrow sixty dollars from your roommate so that you can impress your date by taking her to Trader Vic's for dinner.

8. Read and evaluate the following student paper written in response to an assignment that asked the writer to write an article for adults unfamiliar with rural life. Read the writer's statements of audience and purpose carefully and think about them when you are reading the paper. How well does the writer keep audience and purpose in mind? Are the topic, the word choice, and the style suitable for the audience?

Audience   Mostly an urban group probably twenty and over who may not realize the cruelty of leg hold traps (or even know they are used). I attempted to answer the following questions: (1) What are the traps and how are they used? (2) Why are they cruel? (3) Do they serve any real purpose?

Purpose   Perhaps with this audience the most important point to convey is that coyotes and predators are the victims of human injustice. I wanted to give facts along with an underlying emotional appeal. Overall, I wanted to show that compassion can be extended to wild animals and not just humans and pets.

Legholds and Limbs: A Cruel and Needless Combination

"There he is!" Joe Stinson downed his beer, cocked his 22 rifle, and headed for the struggling coyote some two hundred feet ahead of us. I followed, feeling a certain anticipation and at the same time a sense of revulsion. Joe is a trapper. And I was well acquainted with what the steel "leghold" traps he uses could do.

The leghold trap has been used since the eighteenth century to catch everything from rabbits to grizzly bears. The idea behind it is really fairly simple. Two steel "jaws" are opened into a type of rectangle which is connected to a coiled spring by a triggering plate in the middle. The set trap is buried a few inches under the soil, baited, and left overnight. If, during the night, an unsuspecting animal steps on the trigger, the jaws will snap shut on the animal's leg with enough strength to break a man's arm.

To prevent the loss of their traps, many trappers equip them with a "drag." A drag is a ten foot piece of chain attached to the trap on one end and a large three-prong hook on the other. Trappers use a drag rather than tying the trap directly to a tree or stump, to keep the caught animal moving longer. A moving animal is less likely to stop and try to pull or gnaw its foot out of the trap.

Joe's "catch" had gone more than three hundred yards before the drag's hook embedded in the base of a mesquite tree. Either the trap's initial strike or perhaps the twenty hours of trying to tug free had twisted the coyote's leg until the part caught in the trap was nothing but a mass of blood and bone. Joe was elated. "Look at that," he said. "Man, if he could escape, he would chew us up!" But when the coyote ceased struggling, turned, and stared at us, I knew the real story. Those yellow eyes held no hatred or contempt — just pain, fear, and that horrible animal misunderstanding.

Joe's coyote was hardly unique. Each year, thousands of animals are caught in the same manner. In fact, leghold traps currently comprise about 43 percent of the trapping industry. Recently, wildlife groups such as Greenpeace and the Sierra Club have called for a ban on the traps arguing that "they are the most blatant case of cruelty to animals in existence." Their argument isn't new. As far back as 1863, Charles Darwin wrote in the "Gardeners Chronicle and Agriculture Gazette": "We must fancy what it would be to have a limb crushed during a whole long night, between the iron teeth of a trap and with the agony increased by constant attempts to escape. Few men could endure to watch for five minutes, an animal struggling in a trap with a crushed and torn limb."

Stockmen, on the other hand, have historically opposed a ban. Many stockmen use the traps for predator control, claiming that predators left unchecked would put them out of business. Coyotes in particular have been charged with killing sheep, calves, and poultry and of carrying diseases such as rabies.

Using this argument, stockmen, coupled with furriers, trappers, and hunters (who fear anti-trapping legislation could lead to anti-hunting legislation) have formed a strong coalition against the banning of leghold traps. The coalition, known as the Wildlife Legislative Fund has conducted a highly successful propaganda and lobbying campaign; currently only one of fifty states in the U.S. has banned the leg holds. However, the Fund, and perhaps the state legislatures themselves, have failed to recognize some of the leghold's limitations in controlling predators.

First of all, there are no grounds to the pro-trappers claim that trapping reduces the incidence of diseases in animals. Rabies spread far more readily in bats and domestic animals than in coyotes. Also, a study done in 1975 by the President's Council on Environmental Quality actually disproved the correlation between a leghold ban and an increase in rabies. The council concluded that "the contention that rabies increases when steel leg hold traps are banned seems entirely without merit."

Furthermore, the damage actually done by predators is minimal compared to the cost of controlling them. According to an Oregon State University report, the state of Oregon alone spent more than a million dollars last year on predator control. That was nearly four times the value of reported livestock losses due to predators.

In fact, rodents and not livestock constitute the bulk of most common predators', such as the coyote's, diet. And in areas where the coyote population has declined the rodent population has risen. The resulting rodent damage to crops and grasslands in these areas outnumbers any damage the coyotes might have caused.

Finally, the leghold trap is highly nonselective. In addition to predators, thousands of "innocent" animals such as deer, elk, and turkey are caught and killed each year. A Texas study in 1974 revealed that in a predator control program aimed at bobcats and coyotes, nontarget species taken by legholds exceeded the captured predators by a ratio of 1.3 to 1.

Another question concerning the use of the leghold is — Are the traps actually inhumane? While the fractured bones and gnawed toes are evident, it is impossible to measure how much pain, if any, the animal caught in the leghold feels. Pro-trapping groups argue that, unlike humans, animals are incapable of prolonged pain, fear, and anxiety. They point out that a trapped animal, after an initial struggle, will often lie down and curl up with its foot still in the trap.

Still, the fact that it is impossible to measure the extent of animal suffering is hardly grounds to dismiss it altogether. Like humans, animals are vertebrates. Biologists have proved that vertebrates even as primitive as an earthworm have a system for registering some pain and fear. As Dr. William Fox of the Humane Society relates, subjectivity and not objectivity is the issue. "There is always going to be an element of doubt," he states. "The gap can be bridged only by ethics in the sense that we should give the animal the benefit of the doubt."

Sadly enough, a total ban on the leghold trap is for the time being, highly improbable. However, a step in the right direction would be compensating stockmen directly for losses due to predators rather than trying to control those predators in vain. Also, tax incentives could be offered to stockmen who use the more humane methods of predator control like the new "quick kill" traps and poisons.

Yet, short of a total ban, there is nothing to stop the grim death facing the thousands of animals who will be caught this year. We live in a society where the "cruel and unusual punishment" of humans has thankfully become outdated. It's time the leghold trap be outdated as well.

Sam Houston

Writing Assignments

Paper 1

The sponsor of the student newspaper at the high school from which you graduated has asked you to write an article for a column that the paper runs regularly titled "The View from College." The sponsor wants your first-hand opinion on a topic that will interest high school juniors and seniors and give them some genuinely useful advice about college. He also reminds you that the article shouldn't be preachy, full of conventional wisdom about studying hard, making a budget, and so on. He would much rather have an article giving students inside information about matters such as how to get the best room in the dorm or how to buy the right kind of T-shirt for your school. And you can't use more than 750 words.

Before you begin writing the main part of the paper, write out an analysis of your audience. What are their interests, what do they want to know, and what assumptions can you make about them? What specific questions will they want answered? Remember they will keep reading only if you hold their interest.

Also write an analysis of your purpose. What do you hope to accomplish with your readers?

Possible Topics

1. What kind of shoes (or jacket, jeans, etc.) should a freshman at your school buy? Why?
2. What kind of part-time jobs are available on campus for students who have to work? How does one go about getting one?
3. How does one learn who the best professors are in time to register for their courses?
4. What kind of help is available to students who are having trouble with their courses? Tutors, a study skills course, a writing laboratory, or what? What kinds of problems can they help and how does one use them?

Paper 2

Write an article for young readers, ages ten to twelve, on some topic about which you know a good deal and in which you are interested. Assume that your readers are bright youngsters who are curious and who are competent readers for their age. To get some idea of the kinds of things they might be interested in and the kind of writing style appropriate for them, you might want to look at something written for that age group (for example, the young readers' column in the *Smithsonian* magazine, a book about adventure that you might find in the juvenile section of the library, or a magazine like *National Geographic*). Remember that you don't have a captive audience; you have to catch and hold their attention.

Before you begin to write the main part of your paper, do the audience and purpose analysis described for paper 1. Remember that a young audience requires special consideration.

Possible Topics

1. The qualifications one must have to be accepted for training as an astronaut.

2. A biographical sketch of a woman scientist or pioneer of some kind, such as Marie Curie or Amelia Earhart.
3. How plays were presented at the Globe Theater in Shakespeare's time.
4. The Wright brothers and the first airplane
5. What happened to the dinosaurs.
6. A natural phenomenon such as the geysers of Yellowstone Park or the Grand Canyon.

4 · Revision

One of the great advantages of writing over speaking is that, in most cases, when you have written something you are not satisfied with you have a chance to revise it. Spoken words cannot be altered once they are out of your mouth, but writing is more malleable. You can add to it, change it, rearrange paragraphs or add new ones, and delete or tinker with words and sentences; you can erase the text on your computer screen or tear up your paper and start all over again.

Writing is flexible and adaptable

It is this flexible and adaptable quality of writing that makes it so powerful. Because they can revise, writers can start with incomplete ideas and awkward beginnings and develop them into polished and effective pieces of writing. They can experiment with their writing, knowing that nothing they put down has to be permanent. They don't have to get it right the first time.

In fact, you will be able to write more effectively if you don't start out with the notion that there is one "right" way to write any particular paper. Rather, there are usually several good ways to do a good job on a specific writing assignment. You need to choose one that will work for you, remembering that no one has ever before written precisely the paper that you plan to write. There is no clear prescription for it, no formula which, if followed exactly, will guarantee you an A.

Your instructor has some general criteria in mind, of course, and you will certainly want to know what those are and what he or she expects from the paper. You may also get useful suggestions from your fellow students. In addition, you have the broad guidelines for good writing discussed in the first chapter, and you will find other specific suggestions for revising in other parts of this book. You can also look at examples of what other writers have done in similar situations and perhaps learn from them. Finally, however, you have

to do your own revising, developing your paper as you work. You are *creating* a piece of writing through revision rather than simply repairing or fixing up a faulty paper. If you look at the two student papers at the end of this chapter, you can see how much the final versions differ from the first drafts. Each of the authors shaped his paper through the process of writing and revising and writing again.

You create a piece of writing through revising

You may also find it useful to remember the difference between revising and editing. To *revise* means to take a fresh look at a piece of writing you have created and consider what changes you may need to make in order to make it come closer to saying what you want to say in the way you want to say it. Doing this kind of revising usually requires that you think about your writing from both the overall perspective of content and the writing situation and the immediate perspective of style and usage. To edit a paper, on the other hand, means to correct it, tidy it up, and generally get it ready to appear in public. Obviously editing is an important step in any writing project, but it is one that should be postponed until *after* you have revised the paper. As I pointed out in Chapter 1, writers can cause major problems for themselves if they begin to edit prematurely and thus derail the process of actual revising.

Setting Priorities about Revising

Writers need to set priorities for their revising. Most of the time, both in college and in the business and professional world, writers cannot go on rewriting a paper indefinitely. They have deadlines to meet and a limited amount of time to invest, and often they must settle for the best they can do under the circumstances. Even when writers can devote considerable time to revising, many know that they burn out on a paper after three or four drafts and lose their perspective about what it needs. Given these realities, writers always need to remind themselves when they revise, DO THE BIG STUFF FIRST.

Do the important revision first

Start by reading over your draft and deciding what large-scale, or *global*, changes you need to make — that is, changes that involve content, focus, and organization. For the majority of readers, those are the elements of your writing that matter most; they want a paper to have significant content, to be tightly focused on a specific purpose, and to have a coherent pattern they can follow. When you have taken care of those concerns, you can turn your attention to small-scale, or *local,* changes, changes that primarily affect the surface features of your paper.

Surface features are important, of course, very important: you want to make a good first impression on your readers. You want them to be able to read your paper quickly and easily, without being distracted by mistakes. But because it's easier to make small-scale, local changes than to face tough decisions about content, too often writers get sidetracked into tinkering with words and sentences and don't carry through on crucial changes, such as refocusing their papers or reorganizing their arguments. They neglect the *essence* of their papers because of premature concerns about surface features. So always do global revising first.

Global Revision

The process of global revising

Doing *global revising* means reading over your whole paper after you have finished the first draft and *rethinking* it; it means looking at your draft as a whole, at the "big picture" rather than at the individual parts. You can then decide on what important changes you need to make to alter that picture. They will usually include changes in content and organization and major adjustments for audience and for purpose. They can also include expanding some parts of the paper and condensing others. The principal operations that writers engage in when they do global revising are these:

Narrowing the focus

Checking on commitment and proportion

Adjusting for audience and purpose

Restructuring or improving organization

Adding information

Revising for Focus

Questions to ask yourself:

1. Am I trying to do too much in this paper? Is the topic so broad that I really can't do it justice? Do I make a lot of broad generalizations in the paper?

2. Have I included specific details that will interest my readers? Will I have room for such details?

When writers compose a first draft, they frequently choose a topic that proves to be too broad, and in trying to write about it they find that they have far more material than they can deal with adequately in the paper. Because they are trying to cover too much ground, they write generalizations that touch only the surface of the topic; certainly they don't have the time or the space to develop all those generalizations or to give the specific examples that would make the paper interesting and persuasive. This kind of draft is often easy to write; the author simply draws on accessible material or ideas that come immediately to mind, producing a piece of writing that looks fairly good at first glance. Unfortunately, drafts produced in this manner are usually unfocused and not especially interesting; they lack the depth and details that hold a reader's attention. This kind of draft isn't "wrong," however. It can be useful as a preliminary exploration of the subject because it helps writers to explore different aspects of a topic and discover some possible subtopics they might want to write about.

The dangers of choosing a broad topic

If you read over your first draft and decide that you have tried to do too much, the next step can be to return to the topic and "tree it down" (see pp. 46–48), focusing on one particular subdivision. Another way of narrowing your topic is to read over your first draft and find one segment that you can "carve out" of the broad-scale paper, then redirect your focus to concentrate on that segment. The author of "The British Invasion" on p. 138 has taken this approach. His first draft is a broad overview about 40 years of rock and roll music, but he makes numerous general statements, any one of which might require book-length treatment. (Notice that the title of the first draft — "Talking About My Generation" — in itself suggests that this writer was taking on more than he could handle.) After conferring about his first draft and realizing that he needed to focus his paper, he picked the subtopic that most interested him: the impact of the British rock groups on this country. He titled the second draft "The British Invasion" and focused on that. Still a fairly broad topic, to be sure, but one on which he could write an interesting paper.

The first draft of "Tenzing Norgay and the First Ascent of Mount Everest" on p. 144 reveals similar problems, although they are much less severe. The author starts out to write about several mountaineers who climbed Everest and about the Sherpas of Nepal, the tribe that furnishes guides for climbers. By the second draft, however, he begins to focus mainly on Norgay and the climbing of Mt. Everest. He narrows his title and adds a map that further focuses his readers' attention. In the third draft, because his instructor and fellow students had asked questions about mountain climbing, he adds more information and shifts the focus slightly to satisfy his readers' curiosity about how mountaineers actually climb mountains.

Other problems with first drafts

Of course, not all writers have these particular kinds of problems with their first drafts. Sometimes a writer knows quite well what he or she wants to do but can't generate enough material and so produces only a skimpy first draft. Then the main problem is to add information and develop important points. At other times a writer may be writing about an issue he or she feels strongly about and may produce a first draft so emotional and biased that it would offend readers. Then the writer must think about how to modify the approach to better appeal to the audience.

Sometimes a writer may even have to write a first draft to find out that the chosen topic is really unworkable, so broad or so complex that the writer doesn't have the expertise or the space to explain everything the audience would want to know. One of my students found that out last year when he started to write a paper for young readers explaining how stars are formed. Although he knew a good deal about astronomy, after he had written the first draft he realized that in a short article he could not explain supernova explosions and gas nebulae or such abstract concepts such as luminosity and gravitational shrinkage. The paper was simply not "doable," given the constraints he was working under. But the first draft was not wasted; by writing it he gained a clearer sense of the kind of topics he could realistically write about, and he picked a workable one for his next attempt.

Revising for Commitment and Proportion

Questions to ask yourself:

1. Can my reader tell right away what I'm going to write about? Is the commitment one I'm going to be able to handle in the paper?
2. Is the paper lopsided? Have I spent too much time on one part and not enough on others?

When you're reading at the global level, probably nothing is more important than to check to see whether you have made a clear commitment to your reader early in the paper (see Chapter 6, p. 221) and have followed through on that commitment. Reread the first couple of paragraphs to see whether you have told your readers what to expect; make a note of what you are promising. Then read the rest of the draft with that promise in mind. Did you do what you said you would do? All of it? If not, at this point you need to scale down your commitment to fit what you have written or plan to expand your paper to follow through on your promise.

Notice that the author of "The British Invasion" overcommitted himself in the first draft of that paper, titled "Talking About My Generation." He indicates that he will discuss how rock and roll has influenced the lives of generations to come and the conflict it has caused in American society. In a paper of less than 1200 words he can hardly expect to fulfill that commitment. In the second draft he narrows his commitment to talk about the Beatles and their influence on American rock.

When you are reviewing your commitment, you should also check on the proportions of your paper. Some writers, particularly those who work slowly and like to make a lot of changes as they go, have a tendency to spend too much time on the first part of a paper, expanding their points with examples and polishing their early paragraphs. But then they may forget about their commitment, run out of time, or simply get tired of working on their papers. They finish by writing a hasty and skimpy conclusion that neglects the points they need to make in the second part of the paper. This early reading is a good time to check for this kind of lopsidedness and, if necessary, reapportion your paper.

Revising for Audience and Purpose

Questions to ask yourself:

1. Have I thought about who my intended readers are and why they are going to read my writing? What changes do I need to make for them?
2. Am I clear about the specific goal I have in this paper? What do I need to do to the second draft to accomplish that goal?

Although you need to start thinking about your audience even before you begin to write and, as you work, remain alert to your readers' needs, it's useful to remember that a first draft should sometimes be "writer-based," that is, written partly to help you explore your material and find an angle from which to start writing. (See p. 44, Chapter 2). At the beginning, at least, you focus on your own point of view in order to generate ideas and capture them while they are fresh. This tactic is particularly helpful when you are doing open-ended, exploratory writing. The rambling nature and abundant miscellaneous information in the first draft of "The British Invasion" suggest that its author was probably writing more to generate ideas for himself than to make his points for a specific audience. In fact, if you read the audience analysis for that first draft, you will see that he really didn't have a strong idea of who his audience was.

Thinking about your audience

When you are going over your first draft, however, you should begin thinking about how you will adapt your writing for your readers. Now you should try to switch from thinking about what *you* want to say on a topic to thinking about what your *readers* want to read. Ask yourself, "Why are they reading this?" "What do they want to know?" "How can I make my ideas and concerns interesting to them?" At this point, if you haven't already written out an audience analysis, you need to do so in order to remind yourself to keep those readers in mind. If you have written one out, you need to re-examine it to see if you need to focus it more sharply.

Thinking about your purpose

When you think about your audience you also need to think about purpose — it's hard to separate them. So also ask yourself, "Why am I writing? What do I hope to accomplish with these readers?" You could have an original draft full of information about a topic you are interested in, but it will remain no more than a memo to yourself unless you figure out why you are writing and for whom. You have to decide how much your readers already know, how much more they want to know, and why they want to know it. Consider whether you have wandered off your topic, told your readers more than they want to know, or gotten into an overly technical explanation of some operation. If so, now is the time to delete such material — there's no point in spending time revising the surface features of material you're going to discard.

For example, the man who wrote the paper about Tenzing Norgay climbing Mt. Everest was particularly interested in the subject because he was a climber himself, and he had met Norgay on a trip to Nepal. He knew a great deal about his topic, as would readers with some mountain climbing experience. But he was writing for young readers whom he assumed would be curious about that famous expedition and about mountain climbing but would know almost nothing about Norgay, the expedition itself, or how people go about climbing peaks like Everest. In thinking about those readers as he was writing, he needed both to give them basic information and to add enough drama to the account to hold their interest.

Revising for Organization

Questions to ask yourself:

1. Does this paper have a pattern that the reader can follow? What is it?
2. Does the organization of the paper seem to work? Should I arrange the sections into some other order?

Finding a pattern for your paper

As explained in Chapter 2, your writing needs a pattern, but first drafts are often poorly organized, particularly if they are exploratory drafts. Although your first draft may seem to be a jumble of ideas, you should ask yourself if there may be an underlying natural thought pattern that will help you organize it. Are you analyzing, defining, comparing, or arguing cause and effect? Are you presenting a case as a lawyer would in court by making a claim and then giving your support for it? Are you telling a story and then drawing inferences from it? Are you describing a process? If you recognize any of these possibilities in your draft, you can rough out an outline that will help you get the parts of your paper into an orderly pattern.

Also ask yourself whether you should move the sections of your paper around to make it clearer or more effective. If you have begun by explaining your thesis and then have given some examples to illustrate it, would it be better to give your examples first to dramatize your point? The author of "The British Invasion" starts his first draft with two general paragraphs about the influence of rock music. In the second draft, however, he deletes the general statements and begins with a specific, people-centered anecdote that introduces the Beatles, the group that had the greatest influence on the period he is describing. Instead of immediately introducing his main idea, he decides to lead his readers into it. Frequently that approach works better than hitting your readers with your conclusion at the start.

Revising to Add Information

Questions to ask yourself:

1. What additional information are my readers going to want about my topic?
2. What facts do I need to add to strengthen my paper?

Adding the weight of facts to your paper

When you narrow the focus of your paper for the second draft and cut out many of your general statements, you will probably find that you need to add more specific information and concrete details about your topic in order to make it interesting to your readers. At this point between the first and second drafts writers often find they must stop and spend some time on research. This is the time to get that additional information that will allow you to teach your readers something, to add the *weight of facts* to your writing.

The authors of both sample papers have done this. In "The British Invasion" we get new information about two British rock groups and about the changes they brought to popular music. The writer adds more details about the special characteristics of the kind of music the British groups played and names specific songs that affected young people. In the paper about Tenzing Norgay, the author not only gives us much more detail about the man himself but also explains in detail how climbers go about conquering a peak like Everest. He strengthens that explanation and adds an attractive visual element to the paper by drawing a map, a particularly good addition for his young readers. In both instances, the authors enhance the *ethical appeal* of their papers by incorporating new information that shows their readers they're well informed on their subjects.

Local Revision

Make small-scale changes to improve readability

To do local revising means to focus on words, phrases, and sentences — sometimes paragraphs — and make small-scale changes that do not alter the ideas of the paper or seriously affect its organization or focus. These alterations are primarily surface changes; they affect tone, style, and readability.

The principal steps writers go through when they do local revising are these, though not necessarily in this order:

The process of local revision

Making language more concrete and specific

Changing words and phrases

Reducing wordiness

Improving transitions

Rearranging sentences

Rewriting opening and closing paragraphs if necessary

Tinkering, polishing, and editing

As you compare the original and revised versions of the student paragraphs used in the following pages to illustrate these changes, you may notice that making one kind of change often leads to other improvements. For instance, when you make your language more concrete, you often also reduce wordiness; rearranging sentences can also improve transitions.

Making Language More Concrete and Specific

Questions to ask yourself:

1. Have I used mostly abstract language? (see pp. 238–46, Chapter 7)
2. Can I enliven my writing by adding people to it?

Look for places that need enlivening

Read over your paper, watching particularly for too much abstract, vague language. Look for places where you can make your writing more concrete and more visual, and where you can substitute personal sentence subjects, including personal pronouns, for impersonal subjects. For example, notice the difference in the original and revised versions of this paragraph:

Original

Although much more research is needed to disclose the effects of nonnutritious foods on body development, the very possibility that these foods can harm children is enough reason to propose banning the TV commercialization of these products. Until conclusive evidence is in, banning the products themselves is too extreme a measure to take; however, by removing the influence of commercials from children's television programs, perhaps some of the impetus to buy these products will diminish.

Revision

Although we need more research to find out how junk foods affect body development, just the chance that these foods can harm children is enough reason to propose banning TV commercials for them. Until we have more evidence, we should not ban junk food itself, but if we take junk food commercials off children's television programs, perhaps demand for such products will diminish.

Changing Words and Phrases

Questions to ask yourself:

1. Do I have long verb phrases that could be replaced with a single verb?
2. Have I used any words whose meaning I'm not sure of and should check in the dictionary?
3. Did other readers mention any words they found confusing?

Check vocabulary

Reconsider words and phrases that don't seem to sound right on second reading. Often you will have to get help from other readers to spot this kind of trouble — after all, if you had thought the word was awkward or inappropriate, you probably wouldn't have put it down in the first place, although you might have been in a hurry and careless. Check too for strung-out, flat verb phrases that could be replaced by a single verb. Here are examples of both problems in one paragraph and solutions for them in the revised version. In the original version, italics have been added to highlight problems.

Original

If you don't succeed in a particular endeavor, examine carefully the reasons why you failed. If you do succeed, don't *contribute* this success to luck. *Independence* is the key factor. On the job, let your employers know you think you're good — your own self judgment may be the only basis they have to go on. Be sure you *do not act as a hindrance* to your own advancement by being too modest.

Revision

If you don't succeed in a particular enterprise, examine carefully why you failed. If you do succeed, don't attribute this success to luck. Self-confidence is the key factor. On the job, let your employers know you think you're good — your own self-judgment may be the only basis they have to go on. Be sure you do not hinder your own advancement by being too modest.

Reducing Wordiness

Questions to ask yourself:

1. Do I have some long phrases that use six words when I could get by with one or two? (See phrases such as "There is the likely possibility" in the example that follows.)
2. Am I using repetitious phrases, such as "right and proper" or "It is obvious that . . . ?" Have I used "very" or "really" or "certainly" too often?
3. Have I overexplained, giving too many examples or repeating points?

Trim unnecessary words

Many student writers use far more words than they need. They have been conditioned by assignments that call for a specific number of words, and they have gotten in the habit of padding their writing, using unnecessary words, giving too many examples, repeating points. When you are doing local revising on a first or second draft, keep an eye out for this overgrowth and see where you can trim. One good way to spot unnecessary words is to ask yourself whether you would need them if you were paying fifty cents a word to have your paper typed. Notice how the clutter in this paragraph is eliminated in the revision:

Original

An alternative to our present system of campaign financing is to eliminate independent campaigning as we know it and replace it with a government controlled process. The simplicity of this new system is a great asset, but it is also the cause of some detrimental factors. There is the likely possibility that the party in power would favor its own candidate and make their official report appear more promising. Another aspect to consider is that Americans are so accustomed to large scale campaigns that anything short of mass media exposure would fail to bring out the vote.

Revision

One alternative to our present system of campaign financing is to eliminate independent campaigning and replace it with a government-controlled procedure. The simplicity of the new system would be an attribute but could also be detrimental. The party in power might favor its own candidate. Another problem might be that Americans are so used to large-scale campaigns that anything short of mass media exposure would fail to bring out the vote.

Improving Transitions

Questions to ask yourself:

1. Does my writing seem to jerk from one sentence to another when I read it aloud?
2. Are there places where readers said they got lost because there were no links?

Look for places that need transitions

When you work on local revision, read your paper aloud to spot places where you need to put in hooks and links (see page 64). Again, you may need help from other readers here, since we sometimes tend to supply transitions in our own work mentally. Note, for example, how the addition of more transitional words (italicized in the revision) makes this paragraph much easier to understand:

Original

The new fully automatic cameras have enabled the shutterbug to cast off most responsibility. You are no longer encumbered by the adjustments to the F-stop, shutter speed, or light meter. If you can remember to buy film, your only other job will be the development time and expense. However, without knowing the basic components of a photograph and how to adapt them to the use of your automatic camera, your pictures will not be successful. As a photographer, you must consider more than the camera itself. Think about the surrounding environment's relationship to the camera. There are many elements to take into account before snapping away.

Revision

The new fully automatic cameras now available have enabled the shutterbug to cast off most responsibility *and* no longer be encumbered by adjustments to the F-stop, shutter speed, or light meter. *Now* if you can remember to buy film, your only other responsibility is picking up the developed pictures. However, unless you know the basic components of a photograph and how to adapt them for your automatic camera, your pictures will not be successful. As a photographer, you must consider much more than the camera itself. *For instance,* you must think about the surrounding environment's relationship to the camera *and* many other elements.

Rearranging Sentences

Questions to ask yourself:

1. Do I have some sentences in which statements are tacked together with *and*? Would they be better sentences if I rearranged them to subordinate one statement to the other or make one part an introductory clause?
2. Do I have some of the same content in two or three sentences? Could I combine them into one sentence?

Check for places that can be streamlined by subordination

One of the most common local revisions is rearranging and joining sentences. This is the time to insert clauses to show subordination or modification and to streamline your writing by telescoping the content of two sentences into a single more efficient one. Five sentences become three in the following paragraph, for instance, and the use of clauses to show comparison and causation makes the writer's point much clearer.

Original

I think we should reduce the power of labor unions. Presently it is illegal for individual business firms to collude and set prices. By the same token, I suggest that the labor of different companies not be allowed to work together to set wages. Such action would reduce the bargaining power of unions to raise wages. Their power would be reduced because nationwide strikes would not be legal and therefore would not be used as a threat to employers.

Revision

I think we should reduce the power of labor unions. As it is now illegal for individual business firms to collude and set prices, it should also be illegal for the labor of different companies to work together to set wages. Such action would reduce the bargaining power of unions to raise wages because nationwide strikes would be illegal and therefore would not be used as a threat to employers.

Rewriting Opening and Closing Paragraphs if Necessary

Questions to ask yourself:

1. What am I doing in the opening paragraph? Does it lay down tracks and give the reader signals?
2. Does the last paragraph sound like a finish to the paper?

Opening Paragraph   Read your opening paragraph to see how well it does its job. Does it get your paper off to a good start, introducing your topic quickly and giving your readers strong signals about what to expect? Or does it seem to ramble and waste the readers' time while you are trying to get started? Metaphorically speaking, is the first paragraph little more than "throat clearing" or "circling to land"? If it is, and you think your reader is going to get impatient, now is the time to fix it (see pp. 220–28). Notice, in the student paragraph that follows, that the writer does no more than state the obvious, while in the revision, which was originally the second paragraph of the paper, she establishes the topic for the paper and lets the readers know what to expect.

Make sure the opening paragraph is effective

Original

Eating is one of the most enjoyable necessities we have to contend with. And when it comes to eating seafood, availability and quantity can be major factors in decisions about where to go. They certainly influence our choice of vacation spots.

Revision

Often we find ourselves in a seafood mecca such as Boston with too many places to choose from and no clue as to which is the best. We can look in newspapers, magazines, or restaurant guides to see which ads catch our eye, but chances are those glowing accounts shouldn't be taken too seriously. Actually, the safest way to find the good seafood is to ask the real experts — the locals. By checking with the friends of friends, I came up with these three places in Boston.

Closing Paragraph   Writing a good concluding paragraph can be difficult, and sometimes even if you're not satisfied with the last paragraph of your draft, it's hard to decide how to fix it (see pp. 228–29). But in general the last paragraph should give readers a sense of closure and make them feel that you have dealt with your topic adequately. They shouldn't finish reading and think, "And so?"

Make sure the final paragraph gives a feeling of closure

For example, here are two closing paragraphs of a paper on education for the deaf. The first one leaves the reader hanging (*why doesn't the general public understand?*) but the second one sums up the writer's points in a satisfying way.

Original

Communication with deaf children should be based on sign and oral language combined. When a child has oral potential he or she should receive support from everyone — teachers, parents, and other students. The general public doesn't understand that this can be done.

Revision

A deaf child needs to be surrounded by language, both oral and sign language, and that exposure to language needs to start early. When it does, the child's interactions with other people will improve, and through the cooperation of parents, teachers, and community, the deaf child will have a chance to succeed academically and socially in our culture.

Tinkering, Polishing, and Editing

Some of the problems that writers have with papers don't fall into any of the preceding neat categories, and you won't necessarily solve all your problems just by working through these suggestions for local revision. You may still want to read and reread, moving phrases around and changing words that you're not satisfied with. I call that *tinkering* — fooling with the little stuff that doesn't affect content much but can certainly affect tone and style. If you like to write and

Check spelling and punctuation

have the time to play around with your words, tinkering can be great fun and really improve your paper.

Finally, you need to edit before you make a clean copy to turn in. That means you need to check your spelling, review your punctuation and usage, and tie up all those loose ends that are so important for the impression you hope to make on your reader. Proofread your final copy before handing it in. Although your professor and your fellow students may have been tolerant of errors while you were working on your drafts, that tolerance ends with the final version.

Working on Drafts in Groups

Group work can help your writing

Some writing instructors like to have students work on drafts together in small groups, and if you are in that kind of class, you know how helpful it can be to get feedback from other students on your writing while it is still in progress. Talking to others about your writing often helps you generate fresh ideas and see possibilities for development that you might not have thought of by yourself. You can also get ideas for solving some of your own writing problems by helping other writers with theirs. So working in groups can be a productive and congenial part of your writing process.

If you are new to this method of working on drafts, however, you may encounter some problems at first, and, understandably enough, feel awkward or unsure about how you should go about helping other students with their papers and getting help with your own. On one hand, you may be reluctant to criticize your fellow students' papers, knowing that you don't like criticism yourself and feeling that you're not really qualified to make suggestions. So you may say very little in the group discussions or just limit yourself to a general comment that you liked the paper.

On the other hand, you may want to help others in the group with suggestions but you focus on editing rather than on revising and point out spelling errors, run-on sentences, fragments, or dangling modifiers. Then you realize that your comments are all negative, and you don't feel good about that.

If students working in groups go to either of these extremes, the experience can be frustrating and not very productive. With a little practice, however, and some general guidelines to follow, working on drafts in groups can be very helpful. It's important to remember that you really are qualified to comment on other people's writing — after all, you've been a reader for a long time — and that the instructor is not suggesting that you grade other students' papers, only that you join with others in your class to discuss something you're all concerned about: writing. If you think of yourself as part of a group whose members are genuinely interested in what each person is writing and in helping each other, you can both contribute to and learn from group work.

Instructors organize peer group revision sessions in different ways; some have students copy their papers and distribute them ahead of time, others have students read their papers aloud to each other. In either case, it helps to follow a systematic plan for responding to each other's papers and to make written responses on a form so that each student will have the benefit of that feedback when he or she begins to revise.

Here are guidelines that should help you to work in groups and a form that you may use for responding to other students' papers. The form can also be useful for reference when you start to revise your own papers.

- Begin by setting ground rules that no one apologizes or makes excuses for his or her own work. Everyone should understand that drafts are "works in progress" — papers to be developed and improved. Belittling one's own work or pleading lack of time serves no useful purpose.
- Always look first for what is interesting or well done about a paper. Find something you like and comment on it.
- Focus on a paper's global concerns: whether the writer is trying to do too much, whether he or she is keeping the audience in mind, whether the paper is well organized, and so on. Postpone comments about mechanical matters such as sentence structure or word choice. Because the writer is going to revise, it's not a good use of your time to suggest specific changes in a section that may be eliminated in the second draft.
- Remember that you are not grading the draft. You are a reader who is trying to give the writer some useful suggestions about what he or she could do that would make the paper more interesting and more readable.

Response Sheet for Group Conferences on Drafts

Author's Name _____

Title of Paper _____

1. What is the major strength of the paper?

    What do you like most about it?

2. Does the writer seem to have a good sense of the audience for whom he or she is writing?

    What, if anything, does the writer need to do to define the audience more accurately?

3. What do you think is the purpose of the paper?

    Does the writer state that purpose clearly?

4. Has the writer successfully focused his or her topic so that it can be adequately handled in the paper?

If not, what suggestions can you make about focusing?

5. What would you like to know that the writer doesn't tell you?

What kind of examples would you like to have?

6. What do you think is the single most important problem in the paper?

7. What two or three specific suggestions can you make that would improve the next draft?

Revising with a Word Processor

One final note on the revision process: anyone who has the opportunity to use a word processor knows how much easier it makes the whole process of writing and how wonderful it is for revising. Somehow the act of writing seems less intimidating when you know you can delete or move words or insert a whole new sentence with very little trouble. It's relaxing to feel that you're experimenting, playing around with a draft that can be redone painlessly. For this reason I strongly recommend that you learn to write with a word processor if you can. Even if you're a yellow-pad-and-pencil writer for your first draft, do the second one on the computer.

Don't start the revision process too early when using a word processor

I do, however, have one important caution about revising for those who use word processors. Try not to let yourself get preoccupied with making too many small-scale, local changes early in your writing process. The machine makes it so simple to make those changes when you are working on a first draft that you can easily spend far too much time on them and invest more in that draft than you should. You can get bogged down with details when you should be pushing yourself to produce substantive ideas that will then need to be revised. I have found this a serious hazard in my own writing since I switched to working with a word processor; if I am not careful, I lose sight of my long-range goals.

My advice is to make yourself take full advantage of the speed and ease of writing on a word processor to push out a complete first draft as quickly as you can, knowing that you have it on disk and revision will be a simple task. Once you have a printed copy, you can begin to reorganize and tinker, but try to wait until then.

The Revision Process at Work

You should find it instructive to read through the three drafts of each of the following student essays, for you will see at first hand how revision is the act of creating a piece of writing. Although you will want to pay special attention to the ways these papers reflect their authors' global revisions, note too that matters of local revision — spelling, punctuation, and word choice — are taken care of by the final draft of each paper. The first paper treats the influence of British rock music on American rock; the second, which begins on page 144, the Everest expedition of explorer Tenzing Norgay.

Student Paper I, Draft I

Audience Analysis   A class of students who are to read and analyze this paper in order to return feedback in improving it.

Purpose Analysis   I would like to inform readers of how rock and roll has influenced past and present generations.

Talking About My Generation

In the early fifties, the youth of America was attempting to define itself and to develop its own interests and tastes; trying to find something new and different. The majority of white teens listened to a type of music called "pop," which eventually fused with rhythm and blues, a music of predominantly black audiences. The result was the birth of rock and roll and the beginning of an era that would affect and influence the lives of generations to come.

The introduction of rock and roll into American society was met with much conflict. Adults expressed much disapproval, as many believed juvenile delinquency was related with rock and roll. This dispute between young and old started off a youth rebellion which is and has been a central theme in rock music. Teenagers felt that rock and roll was something they could call their own, including idols with whom they could identify with. However, there was one man who was the driving force behind the increasing popularity and recognition of this new music; Elvis Presley was responsible for getting rock and roll off the ground. It now seemed, as a new decade was beginning to unfold, that rock and roll was here to stay.

The sixties began rather quietly with much of the same sounds of the fifties, only now newer groups were playing this sound. Shortly after the death of President Kennedy, which had the nation in a state of shock, an invasion from across the Atlantic was mounting for an assault upon the United States. "The British Invasion," which was the name given to the enormous amount of

British musicians to hit the American rock scene at that time, was led by The Beatles and would change rock and roll forever. The Beatles were the innovators of this new change as they explored, experimented with and refined new musical grounds, while other British groups followed in their wake.

The youth of America was also changing, as many were becoming aware of the situation in Vietnam and not liking it. Others were experimenting with drugs, namely LSD. The music was reflecting these changes as protest songs were the voices of the youth and rock and roll was led into a psychadelic phase by The Beatles. As more and more groups entered into this period, they encouraged their fans to stand up for their beliefs and to even question authority. This was a very turbulent time as the rebelliousness of this generation was at a peak. There were many riots protesting the U.S. government for its handling of the Vietnam war, resulting in some deaths and many injuries in these demonstrations. In the end, neither side had really won and at Woodstock, the historical 3-day music festival, rock and roll said goodbye to the sixties and looked to a new beginning in the seventies.

The seventies did not get off to a good start for rock and roll. The Beatles broke up while many of rock's superstars (Jimi Hendrix, Janis Joplin and Jim Morrisson of The Doors) had died, though there was consolation in the pull-out from Vietnam. As a result, rock and roll seemed to branch out into sub-categories. Some people liked the harsher sounding groups, given the name heavy metal bands, and others liked a new sound called disco. Teenagers returned to the dance floor and the music, once again, reflected this change as disco started to take over with its dance beat and strong rhythm. Following this, the seventies ended rather uneventfully as rock and roll prepared itself for another decade.

The eighties generation is a different breed apart from the other generations. With the introduction of Music Television or MTV (a 24-hour music video channel), one can now see his or her favorite groups with the touch of a finger. This is a somewhat "hi-tech" generation as music equipment from laser-disc stereos to Sony walkmans are common. The technological advances in sound reproduction have enhanced the quality of the music itself. Rock and roll has continued to expand as disco died out and evolved into pop rock (which is a mix between disco and heavy metal). Also new wave (a more disciplined type of rock and roll, with little improvisation) became a very popular category. This expansion looks very likely to continue on for some time to come.

As for the nineties, it's anybody's guess. There will more than likely be new and different sounds being played by new and different bands that will spark yet another rock and roll sensation. Time has a way of repeating itself.

Chris Westall

Student Paper I, Draft 2

Audience Analysis A group of young people who enjoy today's rock music and may not know of its past influences.

Purpose Analysis To inform young people of a period in rock's history that influenced and shaped today's music into what it is, and how it affected the youth of that time.

The British Invasion: Rock and Roll's Second Explosion

It was the mid-sixties, actually 1964; it had been almost ten years since the initial rock explosion and rock and roll seemed to be on the decline. But wait, on Sunday night in February of that year, teenagers gathered around their television sets as they witnessed history, while four young men from Liverpool, England, dressed in matching suits and sporting bowl-type haircuts, appeared on the Ed Sullivan Show. This new English rock group, called The Beatles, and their music on that night, sparked the beginning of a turning point in rock and roll known as the British Invasion. The British Invasion refers to the enormous amount of British musicians to hit the American rock scene at this time. These new bands, with the Beatles leading the way, chartered new directions for rock and roll and has since never looked back.

This new style of rock introduced many firsts in the music business. For the first time, groups wrote their own songs, which not many groups did in the fifties because the recording labels would hire special musicians to write lyrics and set them to music for the groups to perform. This new rock and roll also introduced songs of more musical complexity, abandoning the simplistic three-chord songs of the fifties for more complex chord structures and sudden shifts in key and rhythm as a song progressed. The drummer and bassist became integral parts of this music as they supplied the steady and heavier sounding beat. Probably the biggest change was the lyrics of songs as the "let's go dancing/boy meets girl" themes of the fifties were replaced by themes of world and political dissatisfaction and an increase in sexual openess (which had a great deal to do with the embarking of the sexual revolution).

Protest songs, as they were known, were the musician's way of expressing his opinions and criticisms of political and social events and served as the voice of American youth. These songs often encouraged its young listeners to stand up for their beliefs and to even question authority.

The radical changes reflected the rebelliousness of this music as it affected young people in the same way. Guys opened eyes with their long hair and beards and girls turned heads with mini-skirts and other skimpy articles of clothing. Probably the biggest change was the way in which kids perceived the world and their situation in it. The Vietnam war had broken out and the U.S. had become involved. The draft was reinstated and young males did not at all like the idea of possibly getting killed in what they considered, someone else's war. The youth began to band together to express their anger in protests of the government, which often resulted in riots that many times became very violent and ugly.

The release of the Beatles album, Sgt. Pepper's Lonely Hearts Club Band in 1967, marked the entering into of the psychadelic phase in rock and, once again, changed its course. The innovations of new sounds and studio effects (just to name a few) of this album influenced other rock musicians to seriously experiment beyond their medium. Another landmark was the use of classical and other nonrock styles in rock and roll, known as stylistic eclecticism — the free and uninhibited switching among different styles in the same piece. And for the first time, lyrics were considered poetic which, combined with stylistic eclecticism, produced what is known as art rock. During this period, many groups surfaced who admitted to taking LSD (a.k.a. "acid") to enhance their creative processes. These groups were labeled "cult" or "acid-rock" bands and they usually had a following of faithful fans who also used LSD (among other drugs) and were referred to as "flower children" or "groupies." Most of these bands fell into the new category of art rock.

The usage of drugs was increasing among the youth as was parental concern about drug-abuse. This somewhat new topic of controversy served to further increase the tensions between young and old, which came to a peak as the sixties were winding down.

In 1969 Woodstock, the most notable rock festival ever, signaled the end of the sixties. At that time a handful of British bands from the original invasion had survived: the Beatles (who broke up a year later in 1970), the Rolling Stones, the Who and the Kinks. This demonstrated how rapidly rock and roll changes and offered notice to the second wave of British musicians who entered America; or at least to the ones who had paid attention.

Student Paper I, Draft 3 (Final Version)

Audience Analysis A group of people who enjoy rock music and would want to read this paper to learn of a very important time period in rock and roll's history.

Purpose Analysis To inform readers of the changes and innovations that occurred in rock and roll at the time of the British Invasion. Also to show how it affected the lives of the youth.

The British Invasion of Rock and Roll

It was the mid-sixties, actually 1964; it had been ten years since the initial rock explosion, and rock and roll seemed to be on the decline. But wait, one Sunday night in February of that year, teenagers gathered around their television sets and witnessed history, while four young men from Liverpool, England, dressed in matching suits and sporting bowl-type haircuts, appeared on "The Ed Sullivan Show." This new English rock group, called the Beatles, and their music on that night, sparked the beginning of a turning point in rock and roll known as the British Invasion. The British Invasion refers to the enormous number of British musicians to hit the American rock scene at this time. These new bands, with the

Beatles leading the way, charted new directions for rock and roll, which has not looked back since then.

This new style of rock introduced many firsts in the music business. For the first time, groups wrote their own songs, which not many groups did in the fifties because recording labels would hire special musicians to write lyrics and set them to music for the groups to perform. This new rock and roll also introduced songs of more musical complexity, abandoning the simplistic three-chord songs of the fifties for more complex chord structures and sudden shifts in key and rhythm as the song progressed. The drummer and bassist became integral parts of this music, for they supplied the steady and heavier-sounding beat.

The bands of this time attracted much larger audiences; thus concerts were held in large arenas, namely sports stadiums. The concerts of the sixties, as compared to the concerts of the fifties, were much louder on the musicians' and the audience's part. A British group called the Who was one of the most violent and loud acts to come out of the British Invasion. While the Beatles were very orderly onstage, the members of the Who danced and jumped around. The singer would twirl his microphone like a lasso, the drummer would throw his sticks high into the air, often missing them as well as missing a beat, and the guitarist would play by making large circular motions with his arms while striking the strings and bloodying his fingers. When they had finished the last song of the set they would smash everything up (the guitar, the amps, the drum kit, and sometimes themselves).

Probably the biggest change was from the lyrical "let's go dancing/boy meets girl" themes of the fifties to themes of political and social dissatisfaction. Protest songs, as they were known, were the musician's way of expressing his opinions and criticisms of political and social events and served as the voice of the majority of American youth. These songs often inspired young listeners to stand up for their beliefs and to even question authority. Bob Dylan is the man most identified with the protest song. Though he was not British, his anguished perception of "the politics of the day" had considerable influence on the British rock bands' political song writing. (For example, the Beatles' song "Revolution" was inspired by Bob Dylan's "Blowin' in the Wind": both contained, for the time, some very strongly stated lyrics.)

The radical social changes reflected in the rebelliousness of this music affected the behavior of many young people. Guys opened eyes with their long hair and beards, while girls turned heads with miniskirts and make-up. But the biggest change was the way in which young people perceived the world and their relationship to it. The Vietnam war became a heavy topic of discussion as the world saw the realities of war in full color. Protestors began to band together to express their anger in marches and riots against the actions the government was taking in Vietnam. Protest songs and statements, such as "Revolution," served to fuel the fire, though they were not a direct cause of this anger.

The 1967 release of the Beatles' seventh album, *Sgt. Pepper's Lonely Hearts Club Band,* marked the emergence of the psychedelic phase in rock, and once again changed its course. The innovations of new sounds and studio effects (i.e., producing distorted guitar sounds and varying tape speeds) on this album influenced other rock musicians to experiment seriously beyond their previous styles. During this period, many groups surfaced who admitted to taking LSD (a.k.a. "acid") to expand their creative processes. These groups were labeled "cult" or "acid-rock" bands, and they usually had a following of faithful fans who also used LSD (among other drugs) and were referred to as "flower children" or "groupies."

Another landmark was the use of classical and other nonrock styles in rock and roll, known as "stylistic eclecticism — the free and uninhibited switching among different styles in the same piece." This was a new concept that was conceived by the British groups, who seemed to have more of a taste for classical music than their American counterparts. Lyrics came to be recognized as poetry, which gave rock some much-needed credibility. When these lyrics were set to stylistically eclectic music, it seemed to enhance the general feeling of the music. This combination produced what is known as art rock.

Drug use was increasing among the youth, as was parental concern about drug abuse. This controversy served to increase the tensions between young and old and further widen the generation gap. If there was one song that related to this classic confrontation and represented this youth culture or "counterculture" the best, it would have to be "My Generation" by the Who, written by its lead guitarist and primary songwriter, Peter Townshend. A dramatic showpiece for their live concerts, "My Generation" warned the older generation not to try to make sense of what it heard from the young, and it was frequently accompanied by The Who's violent behavior onstage. The lyrics of the song instruct older listeners to just "f-f-f-fade away." They may not have done that, but they certainly heard, in this song and in all the music of the British invasion, that things were no longer the same — and wouldn't ever be again.

Student Paper II, Draft I

Writing Situation and Purpose   In 1972 three Sherpas from Darjeeling, India, Tenzing Norgay, Nawang Gombu and Ang Pemba, toured the United States. Tenzing, along with S. Edmund Hillary had become the first men to climb Mt. Everest on the 1953 British Expedition. Gombu in 1965 had become the first man to climb Everest twice. Pemba was a veteran of many Himalayan expeditions himself. On this tour they visited and exchanged ideas with American mountaineers as well as making public appearances at colleges and high schools.

This paper assumes the three men will make an appearance at a junior high school. The principal, anxious that his students be prepared for the visitors, does research and talks to Americans who know one or more of these men. Since his own children read National Geographic World, he writes on this pattern and later considers submitting his article for publication there.

The article seeks to explain who these men are, their cultural background, why they do what they do and their significance to the mountaineering world. This will not only give the students insight into mountaineering, but more importantly will give the students insight into the world of the Sherpa tribesmen and life in the Nepal and Indian Himalayas.

Audience Analysis   The article is written for junior High School students — generally age from 11 to 14. Although assumed to be bright and well read, it is also assumed that few will be familiar (except in the most general way) with either Sherpas, Himalayas or Mountaineering.

They will want to know who they are, why they are important

and probably be at least moderately interested and entertained while acquiring this new knowledge.

Tenzing and the Sherpas of Nepal

On May 29, 1953 at about eleven in the morning two men, Edmund Hillary and Tenzing Norgay, stood on the summit of Everest and on the verge of history. It was a clear day in the blue and blinding white world of the high Himalayas. On their high perch with the wind blowing a relatively mild 40 m.p.h., air was so thin that even breathing with the help of oxygen tank and masks they required four huge gasps of breath before taking a step. They looked around them. They could see into four countries, the brown flat plains of India to the south, the high barren Tibetan plateau to the north, the mysterious hills of the little known Himalayan kingdom of Sikkim to the east and the magnificent white spires of many of the world's highest mountains in Nepal all around them. To them though the most gripping sight was Everest itself spread below them, the mountain which had been tried so many times and not yet climbed. For 35 years well equipped expeditions featuring the best climbers in the world had been turned back; many had died, but now they were on top. They looked for signs of Mallory and Irvine. George Mallory, renowned for the now famous phrase "because it is there" answer to the question "Why do you climb mountains" was a member of the 1924 British Expedition. Along with young Andrew Irvine he had set off from high camp at 26,500 feet toward the 29,028 foot summit in the early morning. Another member of the expedition had last seen them "going hard for the top" when they disappeared into a bank of mist. They were never seen again. Did they perish on the ascent or the descent? Did they reach the summit before they died? No one will probably ever know. Not finding any trace of the two men, Hillary and Tenzing went down to their waiting friends at high camp and flashed the news by radio to the waiting world. May 29th was an extra special day for the British, the news of the Everest triumph arriving in England on the eve of the Coronation of the new queen, Elizabeth.

Tenzing, in addition to being honored by the Queen, Winston Churchill and most of the western world, became the greatest of national heroes of his home country, India. It is difficult for us to appreciate how much India thought and thinks of its hero. It is as if Babe Ruth, Abraham Lincoln and Douglas MacArthur had been rolled into one. Wherever he went he was mobbed by admiring crowds; even years later he was instantly applauded as he walked down the street of his home town, Darjeeling. After a century of colonial rule, in which Indians were subjugated to British masters, here was living proof that Indian and British side by side as equals could accomplish a great feat.

Tenzing was not born in India but in Nepal, India's neighbor to the north. He was born into the Sherpa people, the hardiest of hardy mountain people who live in the Himalayan foothills. They were farmers and animal herders who lived at the foot of massive glaciers on steeply inclined, green covered foothills. An ideal background for a future mountaineer. When he was young Tenzing's father moved to Darjeeling, India, to look for work because things were changing in the traditional Sherpa world. Modern influences were gradually creeping into Nepal. Cities were beginning to attract men away from the countryside. Tenzing grew up guiding foreign visitors up Tiger Hill, a hill above Darjeeling where on a clear day one can see Kangchenjunga, the third highest mountain in the world and, far away, Everest. Tenzing's character was summed up by the fact that most guides told visitors Kangchenjunga was Everest, because it was much closer and more spectacular. Tenzing always pointed out the true Everest. Tenzing began guiding climbers on local mountains and eventually was a much sought after member of mountaineering expeditions. He also attained the highest honor for Sherpa mountaineers. Sherpas, because they are native mountain people, have many men who work as guides on high mountains. The best of these are called "Tigers." Four years before his Everest ascent, Tenzing was made a Tiger.

After the Everest climb, Tenzing joined no more expeditions to high mountains. He has made many contributions to the mountaineering world however. He settled in Darjeeling and founded the Himalayan Mountaineering Institute. The Institute trains Sherpas in the techniques and skills of climbing high mountains. This program not only benefits the aspect of mountaineering, but even more important, trains Sherpas from Nepal and India in a skill in which they can make a good living where they might otherwise have no job. If you were to visit the Himalayan Mountaineering Institute today, you would find a very interesting Everest Museum which has photographs and equipment from Everest expeditions and a Mountaineering Museum which has all kinds of interesting exhibits explaining mountaineering all over the world. You would also find a short stocky man who is the new director of HMI after Tenzing retired two years ago. He would probably smile, shake your hand and if he was not too busy, ask you in for tea. He is Nawang Gombu, the first man to climb Everest twice and Tenzing's successor in many ways. Also born in Nepal, Gombu was a porter on the 1953 Everest expedition which put Tenzing on top. His job was to carry a load of supplies through the foothills to a camp at the base of the mountain. He so impressed the British with his strength and stamina he was invited to come on many expeditions in the 50's. His reputation spread so when the Americans arrived in 1963 to try the ascent of Everest, they invited Gombu along as a full climber. On May 1, 1963, a few days short of the 10th anniversary of Tenzing's triumph, Gombu and Jim Whittaker reached the top. Even more impressive, Gombu repeated this feat reaching the top two years later with the Indian Army Expedition. Although not as well known as Tenzing Gombu received much acclaim in India and also became well known in America when, following the American expedition he was presented with the National Geographic Society's Hubbard Medal by President Kennedy in the Rose Garden of the White House. Then, in a scene which was reported in all the newspapers the next day, Gombu presented the President with a Buddhist prayer scarf, which he hung around the President's neck. The two men beamed at each other with smiles of friendship, each very much appreciative of the honor which the other had given him.

A few years ago Tenzing returned to his Nepal homeland. He walked through the steep foothills under the high mountains. He discovered that things were fast changing in the Himalayas. On the other side of the mountains, in Tibet, the Chinese had invaded in 1959 and closed all the Buddhist monasteries, put in a Chinese socialist government and greatly transformed the society. In Nepal, foreign influences were also transforming the countryside except that the changes were not coming from China but from the West, that is America and Western Europe. The industrialization of the cities of Nepal and especially India were drawing young men out of the countryside into the cities, often leaving villages and farms short of the people required to keep them going. The beauty of the

Himalayas has attracted many many more climbers and hikers to Nepal than ever came when Tenzing was growing up. Pollution in the form of candy bar wrappers and cardboard boxes litter the trails. More and more Sherpa men are leaving the village to work for the climbers and hikers. Although this lure of work has brought Tenzing much in the world, he could not help feeling a great sadness during his trip that gradually the feeling of isolation and self-sufficiency which the Sherpas had for centuries is crumbling.

William Foster III

Student Paper II, Draft 2

Writing Situation and Purpose   In 1972 Tenzing Norgay along with two friends from Nepal and India toured the United States. Tenzing, along with Sir Edmund Hillary, had become the first man to climb Mount Everest on the 1953 British Expedition. On this tour they visited and exchanged ideas with American mountaineers as well as making public appearances at colleges and high schools.

This paper assumes Tenzing will make an appearance at a junior high school adjacent to Evergreen State College in Everett, Washington. The principal, anxious that his students be prepared for the visitors, does research and writes this introductory article for their benefit. Since his own children occasionally read National Geographic's "World," he writes the article on this pattern and later considers submitting his article for publication there.

This article seeks to explain who Tenzing is, his significance to mountaineering and his home country, India. By doing this the author also seeks to shed light on the Himalayan culture of which Tenzing and his friends are products as well as on the world of mountaineering.

Audience Analysis   The article is written for junior High School students who generally range in age from 11 to 15. Although assumed to be bright and well read it is also assumed that few will be familiar except in a very general way with Sherpas, Himalayas or Mountaineering.

These students will want to know what these things are, why they are important and probably want to be at least moderately entertained while acquiring this knowledge.

Tenzing Norgay, the Ascent of Everest and the Sherpas of Nepal

On May 29, 1953 at about eleven thirty in the morning two men stood on the top of the world. They were the first to ever stand there. They were on the summit of Mount Everest on a clear day in the blue and blinding white world of the high Himalayas. On their high perch the wind was blowing a relatively mild 40 miles per hour. The air was so thin even breathing with the help of oxygen tanks and masks they required four huge gasps of breath before taking a step. From where they were they could see into four countries, the brown, flat plains of India to the south, the high plateau of Tibet to the north (Tibet is now part of China), the mysterious hills of the little known Himalayan Kingdom of Sikkim to the east and the magnificent white spires of the world's highest mountains in Nepal all around them. To them though the most gripping sight was Everest itself spread below. The mountain that had been tried so many times and not yet climbed, was theirs.

For 35 years before well equipped expeditions featuring the best climbers in the world had been turned back, and many had died trying. They looked around for signs of Mallory and Irvine. George Mallory, famous for the answer "Because it is there" to the question "Why do you climb mountains?" was a member of the 1924 British Expedition. Along with young Andrew Irvine he had set off from the expedition's high camp at 26,500 feet toward the 29,028 foot summit in the early morning. Another member of the expedition had last seen them "going hard for the top" when they disappeared into a bank of mist. They were never seen again. Did they perish on the ascent or the descent? Did they reach the summit before they died? No one will probably ever know. Not finding any traces of the two men, Hillary and Tenzing went down to their waiting friends at high camp who had flashed the news by radio to the waiting world. May 29th was an extra special day for the British, the news of the Everest triumph arriving in England on the eve of coronation of the new Queen Elizabeth.

A mountaineering expedition to a high mountain like Everest is a huge undertaking. It took twelve other climbers a month and a half to set up the two climbers with a proper route and enough supplies for the last push to the summit. These twelve climbers set six camps up the mountain. Hillary and Tenzing left camp six at 26,100 feet and took two days to climb the last 3,000 feet to the top. Before any climbers even started 200 local porters were hired to carry all the equipment 100 miles from Kathmandu, the capital of Nepal to the base camp where the expedition started climbing. On the tortuous route to Camp Six the climbers made their way through trecherous icefalls, which are like huge frozen waterfalls requiring the climbers to climb vertical ice. They also had to cross steep glaciers roped up in case a crevasse, huge openings in the snow and ice, opened up suddenly swallowing a climber. If the climber was roped up he could be saved by his partners who would pull him up by the rope which was also attached to them. All in all the conquest of Everest was a monumental accomplishment.

Tenzing, in addition to being honored along with the rest of the expedition by the Queen, Winston Churchill and most of the western world became the greatest of national heroes in his home country, India. It is difficult for us to appreciate how much India thought and thinks of its hero. It is as if Babe Ruth, Abraham Lincoln and Douglas MacArthur had been rolled up into one. Wherever he went he was mobbed by admiring crowds; even years after the climb, he was instantly applauded as he walked down the street of his home town, Darjeeling. After a century of colonial rule, in which Indians were subjugated by British masters, here was living proof that Indian and British side by side as equals could accomplish a great feat.

Tenzing was not born in India but Nepal, India's neighbor to the north. He was born into the Sherpa people, the hardiest of hardy mountain people who live in the Himalayan foothills. They were and are farmers and animal herders who live at the foot of massive glaciers and steep green foothills that are often covered in mists and clouds. This is the land where the stories of the Abominable Snowman, known by the Sherpas as Yeti, started. In the Buddhist monastery in the tiny village where Tenzing grew up the monks keep a huge scalp from a Yeti to show visitors. Even Sir Edmund Hillary reported seeing signs of the Yeti on one of his trips to Nepal. Like Bigfoot in the United States they are supposed to be large ape-like creatures but unlike Bigfoot, Yeti is supposed to be white.

Herding animals on steep mountainsides was good training for a future mountaineer. But as Tenzing grew up the traditional Sherpa world was beginning to change. Some men from Tenzing's village had already gone to work as porters for the white men who wanted to climb the mountains. Cities were begining to attract men away from the countryside. Today this same countryside is even more changed, with more of the village people gone to the city and more of the cities' influence come to the village. Tenzing's father moved across the border to Darjeeling, India, where Tenzing made a living guiding foreign visitors up Tiger Hill outside of town where one could catch a breathtaking view of Kangchenjunga, the third highest mountain in the world and far away, Everest itself. They would make the climb in the evening and spend the night on top to see the mountains at sunrise. Western ways were new to Tenzing and one morning he arose to fix his charges' tea. As he peeked his head in the tent he saw the woman put her teeth back in her mouth. Tenzing almost fell over in disbelief. Tenzing's true character came out in these early days by the fact that even though most guides told visitors Kangchenjunga was Everest since it was closer and thus much more spectacular, Tenzing always pointed out the true Everest.

From the friends he made on these Tiger Hill climbs Tenzing's reputation spread and he was eventually invited to be a high altitude porter on mountaineering expeditions. His job was to carry supplies for the other climbers high on the mountain. He was such a strong climber the Swiss invited him to be a full climber on their Everest expedition in 1952. This climb fell just short of the summit. But the British who came the next year could not help but invite Tenzing also.

After the Everest climb, Tenzing joined no more expeditions to high mountains. He has made many contributions to the mountaineering world since then however. He settled in Darjeeling and founded the Himalayan Mountaineering Institute. The Institute trains Sherpas in the techniques and skills of climbing high mountains. This program not only benefits the sport but even more importantly trains Sherpas from Nepal and India in a skill with which they can earn a good living where they might otherwise have no job. If you were to visit HMI today you would find a very interesting Everest Museum which has photographs and equipment from many Everest expeditions and a Mountaineering Museum, which has exhibits concerning mountains all over the world. Perhaps the most impressive exhibit is a large small scale model of the entire Himalayan range which is on a table about 30 feet long.

Both the Institute and the Museum stand as a monument to a real living hero.

Student Paper II, Draft 3 (Final Version)

Writing Situation and Purpose In 1972 Tenzing Norgay, along with two friends from Nepal and India, toured the United States. Tenzing, along with Sir Edmund Hillary, had become the first man to climb Mount Everest as members of the 1953 British Expedition. On this tour they visited and exchanged ideas with American mountaineers and made public appearances at colleges and high schools.

This paper assumes Tenzing will make an appearance at a junior high school adjacent to Evergreen State College in Everett, Washington. The principal, anxious that his students be prepared for the visitors, does research and writes this introductory article for their benefit. Since his own children occasionally read National Geographic's *World,* he writes the article on this pattern and later considers submitting his article for publication there.

This article seeks to explain who Tenzing is and the nature of the event that made him famous. By doing this the author seeks to shed light on the sport of climbing high mountains, Tenzing himself, and the Sherpas of Nepal.

Audience Analysis The article is written for junior high school students, who generally range in age from 11 to 15. Although they are assumed to be bright and well read, few of them will be familiar except in a very general way with mountaineering, Tenzing, or Sherpas.

These students will want to know just exactly who is coming to speak to them and why they should be interested.

Tenzing Norgay and the First Ascent of Mount Everest

High on the Northeast Ridge of Mount Everest, at 29,028 feet the highest mountain in the world, three men awoke from a fitful sleep. Today was the day they were to try to become the first men ever to stand on top. At their altitude, about 27,000 feet, the air is so thin that even the simplest movements require great concentration. The air is thin enough to require four huge gasps of air before a climber can take a step forward, even with bulky oxygen tanks on his back to help him breathe. As the men finished their breakfast of dried beef, they peeked outside into the freezing morning. It was foggy, and they couldn't see much. Slowly, they packed the tent and sleeping bags and set out to climb the final two thousand feet. One of the men, Nigel Odell, soon felt sick and tired from the thin air and had to turn around and head back to join the other climbers at a lower camp. The two other men, George Mallory and Andrew Irvine, were watched by Odell as they climbed quickly up the ridge toward the summit. They disappeared into a bank of mist and were never seen again. Did they reach the top before they died? It is one of the great mysteries of mountaineering.

Twenty-nine years later, two men awoke hoping to do the same thing Mallory and Irvine had tried to do. They set off from 27,000 feet on the Southeast Ridge in perfectly clear weather. The appallingly high, white spires of the Himalayan mountains were visible all around them. In this dazzling blue and white world they climbed up the ridge, very slowly, the only sounds the whistle of the wind and their boots crunching in the snow. Then the two men, Edmund Hillary of New Zealand and Tenzing Norgay of Darjeeling, India, came to a vertical ice cliff. At this altitude, where even the most ordinary movements were difficult, to climb this ice would be next to impossible. Hillary took his ice axe, which is an icepick on a five-foot wooden pole, and swung it into the ice above him. With his other hand he dug a piton — a sharp metal spike used to keep tents from blowing away in the wind — into the ice. With tremendous effort he climbed hand over hand up the cliff. Tenzing did the same until both men sat, exhausted, at the top of the cliff.

They kept going up. The ridge was now a series of snow humps. They would reach the top of a hump thinking they were on the summit only to find a slightly higher hump ahead. Finally, at the top of one summit they could suddenly see the entire mountain spread below them; they had made it. From where they were they could see into four countries: the flat, brown plains of India to the south, the high plateau of Tibet to the north (Tibet is now part of China), the mysterious hills of the little-known Himalayan kingdom of Sikkim to the east, and the magnificent white mountains

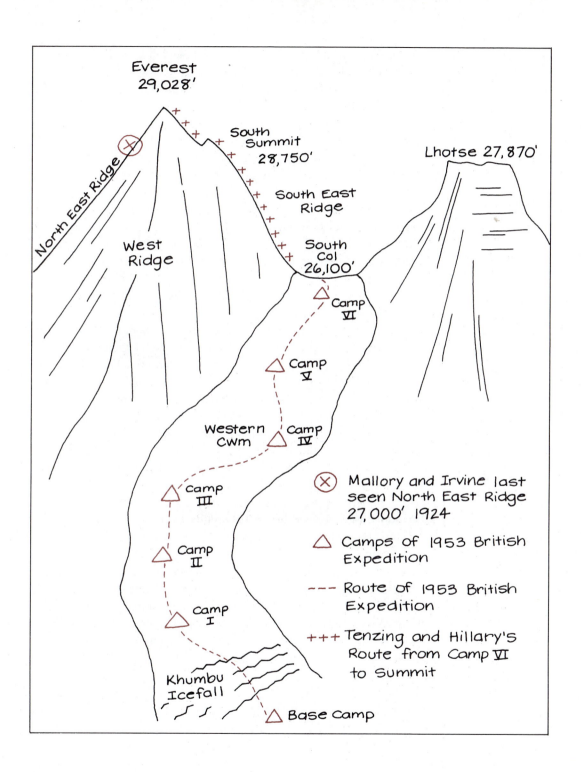

of Nepal all around them. The local people call Everest "Chomo-langma," which means "goddess, mother of the world." Mount Everest, 29,028 feet tall, half in Nepal, half in Tibet, had been climbed at last on May 29, 1953.

They looked around for signs of Mallory and Irvine but found none. They took some photographs. In the snow, Hillary buried a crucifix, and Tenzing buried the only food left in his pack, a hand-ful of lollipops, as a gift for the gods which all devout Buddhists like Tenzing believe inhabit the summit. Happily they descended. When they reached their friends at Camp VI (see map) five hours later, they radioed their Base Camp with the news. The news arrived in England (it was a British expedition) just a few hours before the coronation of the new Queen Elizabeth, a fine gift indeed.

To climb a very high mountain like Mt. Everest takes more than one day, though. In fact it takes about two months. At the nearest airport, in this case Kathmandu, the capital of Nepal, 200 porters were hired to carry all the gear and supplies the expedition would need to the Base Camp at the foot of the mountain. This included all the food, tents, small stoves, and technical climbing equipment the climbers needed. When everything was assembled at Base Camp the porters were sent home, leaving only the climbers and high-altitude porters, whose job it was to carry supplies to higher camps on the mountain.

Everest is so high it is usually not climbed "alpine style," which means that all the climbers carry all they need on their backs and climb directly up the mountain, camping along the way and de-scending only after reaching the summit. Everest had to be climbed "expedition style." This meant establishing a series of camps up the mountain.

In this kind of climbing, each camp is established and supplied in several steps. First, the trail is blazed, which means the easiest possible route is found to the site of the next camp, and the route is marked with flexible orange poles. Next, high-altitude porters and climbers supply the new camp with equipment, tents, and food. Then using the new camp as a new base, fresh climbers are brought up to blaze the trail to the next camp. The climbers and porters go up and down the mountain in a rotation. Finally, when the highest camp (in this case Camp VI) is established one or two days' climb from the summit, the "final assault" begins. Two or three fresh climbers start out from Base Camp, climbing up over the established routes and carrying very little on their backs that would tire them because all their supplies have been carried to the high camp already. From the high camp these fresh, rested climbers make a quick dash for the top. That is what Tenzing and Hillary were doing when they reached the top of Everest.

It is from the ranks of the high-altitude porters that Tenzing was chosen to be a full climber on the 1953 British expedition, the one with which he reached the top. So many previous Himalayan expeditions had been impressed by Tenzing's incredible climbing ability and stamina when carrying heavy loads up high mountains that the British naturally chose him to be a regular member of their expedition.

Tenzing and all of the other high-altitude porters were from the Sherpa people of Nepal. Living in the high foothills of the Himalayas, the Sherpas not only knew the mountains well but were used to the thin mountain air, which allowed them to be much stronger carrying loads at high altitudes than Western climbers.

It is difficult for us in the United States to appreciate how much India thinks of its hero. (Tenzing's family left Nepal when he was a boy, and he grew up in nearby Darjeeling, India. India therefore claims Tenzing as a native son.) It is as if Babe Ruth, Abraham Lincoln, and Douglas MacArthur had been rolled into one. Even years after the climb, the people on the narrow, crowded streets would part as Tenzing walked through. The crowd would break into applause and Tenzing would smile, shake hands, and pose for photographs with the endless patience which is a Sherpa trademark. After a century of colonial rule, in which Indians were subjugated by British masters, here was living proof that Indian and British side by side as equals could accomplish a great feat.

After the Everest climb, Tenzing attempted no more great mountains but founded the Himalayan Mountaineering Institute in Darjeeling, which trains young Sherpas in the skills and techniques of climbing high mountains. On the grounds of the institute there is an Everest museum, where you can discover the stories of all the Everest expeditions and see some equipment and photographs from them. Both the institute and the museum stand as monuments to Tenzing and the sport of mountaineering.

Exercises

1. Revise the following student paragraph, making the language more specific and concrete and adding people.

It is important to note that the Law School Admission Test is inherently incapable of fairly assessing the ability of minority applicants. Most sociologists concerned with the fairness of standardized tests have determined that the type of questions, if not their very wording, are biased in favor of higher income groups. The result is that those groups with culturally different backgrounds are not able to do as well on such tests. It is not because they are any less intelligent, but rather because they have not been raised in a culture which prepares them for this type of exam. Some may argue that minority quotas alleviate this problem. This may be true to an extent, but it seems to me that an evaluation of a person's achievements over a four year period is a fairer method for determining an applicant's qualifications. Also, I would argue that quotas still do not guarantee that the most qualified applicants are chosen because the number of minority applicants helped by this system is severely limited.

2. Revise the following student paragraph, changing words and phrases and using better verbs.

Many people going into college feel that they know exactly what they want to do after they get out of college. This feeling of certainty leads many people into rushing through or even missing a large portion of their lives by not taking full advantage of the college experience. College is a time for expansion of the mind, and those who restrict themselves by confining their studies to one area lose not only knowledge but a great many experiences as well. I felt this certainty when I entered college too. Luckily, I, in order to prepare for my future, enrolled in a philosophy course in Medical Ethics. It was fascinating and it convinced me of the mistake I made in wanting to focus on a strictly scientific education. It also showed me that I need to learn much more about many more things before I can begin shaping my future. A responsible decision about the rest of your life is an informed one. And by restricting yourself to any one field you deny yourself the advantage of more knowledge. You cheat yourself. The answer to such a problem is to take a wide variety of subjects.

3. Revise the following student paragraph, reducing wordiness.

The telephone is a private utility paid for by the subscriber and should not be used by companies to promote their product to customers who are not interested. Whenever anyone of these people receives a direct sales phone call, it is an invasion of their privacy. These callers are intruders in their home. Although companies have the right to sale their products over the phone and some people actually enjoy buying products over the phone, we have the right to decide whether we would like to receive such phone calls. I believe that sales phone calls should be outlawed from calling anybody who has informed the phone company that they do not want to receive these phone calls. The firms making solicitations should have to get hold of this list and not call anyone on it. With this solution nobody's rights would be invaded and both parties, the company and the uninterested customer, would be satisfied.

4. Revise the following student paragraph, improving transitions.

Through its drastic changes in design and popularity, the bicycle has emerged as an impressive machine for transportation, exercise and sport. The typical lightweight ten-speed of today is not representative of what past bikes have been, rather it is the sleek result of over a century's worth of breeding. As the ten-speed evolved so did a definite need for its existence. The typical pre-World War II bicycle was sturdy but very awkward. The bike weighed sixty to seventy pounds and was equipped with a single low gear and pedal operated coaster brake. Youngsters who weren't old enough to drive used these machines. At the end of World War II, G.I.'s returned home with a bike called an "English racer." The thinner frame and wheels, hand brakes and three speeds offered much better performance than the American bike. After its production in the United States, the younger set used the "English racer" as basic transportation because it was much lighter and its gears easily tackled hills and cruised on flat-outs. During the 50's and 60's, America's love affair with the car kept the bicycle out of the adult mind. The cheap gas and large engine cars of this era made driving the car an indispensible part of life. But as gas became expensive and the streets clogged with traffic, America rediscovered the bicycle.

5. Revise the following student paragraph by rearranging sentences.

Many women are leaving traditionally female jobs for male jobs simply for the reason that female jobs don't pay as much. Nurses in Colorado receive a starting salary of $1,064 a month, while the tree-trimmers around the hospital receive $1,164 a month. (quoted from Redbook, Nov. 1981) These women have gone through years of training to have a nursing career, they should have just picked up a hedge cutter and earn more money. Schoolteachers are wondering why they earn $12,323 a year with a college degree and two years of experience and liquor store clerks earn $12,479 a year with a high school diploma and two years of experience. Of course the jobs are different. Typically, we view women's jobs as taking care of people and men job's as taking care of machines and inanimate objects. It is a persistent characteristic of the workplace that looking after people is worth less than looking after things.

Writing Assignment

Using the response sheet on pp. 135–36, write out a full response to one of following first drafts of student papers.

Working Out!

Audience Analysis: Airline Travelers who are interested in health and fitness, but who do not have an exercise program. These people are possibly 10–15 lbs. overweight and are looking for a way to slim down and look good in that swimsuit next summer. They are middle to upper class and can afford the cost of aerobic classes at the local club.

Purpose Analysis: To let the reader know the health and emotional benefits, the basic routine or workout and how to get started with aerobics.

The scene is familiar to many. Approximately 30 to 40 men and women — mostly women, clad in leotards, leg warmers, and more torn T-shirts than in *Flashdance* and *Staying Alive* put together, jumping, clapping, and kicking to tunes like Michael Jackson's "Beat It" or Barry Manilo's "Jump Shout Boogie." At the front of the room is an energetic young girl, usually with a figure most would kill for, coaxing the slightly overweight class with phrases like "You can do it, only 50 more tummy crunchers," or "If you don't sing along, we'll add 20 more repetitions." Yes you're in an aerobics class, and in spite of the sweat, the heat, and the exhaustion, you're loving it.

Aerobic dancing began in 1971 when Jackie Sorensen started her first classes on a snowy day in March and has grown into a national rage. Everyone from Jane Fonda to the *Solid Gold* dancers has a record, book or videotape on the subject, and new studios and classes are forming across the country as the demand for physical fitness increases rapidly. Aerobic dancing combines exercise with alot of music and fun, making it one of the most enjoyable and popular ways to get in shape and stay fit. It is an excellent calorie burner, using up as much as 300 calories for a moderate 45 min. session to 500 calories for a vigorous 45 min. workout. For as long as 6 hrs. after the workout, the body continues to burn more calories (about twice as much) than at a normal resting period.

Because of its vigorous nature, aerobics workouts have many health benefits. The workout itself stresses the cardio vascular system, and the result is a stronger, healthier heart and improved circulatory system. With this overall improvement, you have more energy, and better circulation contributes to a better complexion. You can also increase your flexibility, improve your body control and rhythm, and since you're doing so much to improve your health, your self confidence goes up as well!

Filled with upbeat music and lively dancing, the workout itself is enough to give an extra boost to lunch hour or the after work blahs. The basic workout is essentially the same around the country. In her book *Aerobic Dancing* Jackie Sorensen outlines the pattern followed by most instructors. The session begins with stretching exercises geared to increase flexibility and reduce injuries. Following that is the warm-up, a slow dance combining stretches and dance steps which gradually increases the heart rate. The major part of the workout is the dance routines themselves. Usually easy, always upbeat, these steps are designed for continuous movement in order to increase your heartrate and push you to your potential. To wrap things up is the cool down, about 5 minutes of slower dancing and stretches gradually returning your heart beat to an exceptable recovery level.

In order to get started, look around for specials and advertisements in the newspapers. Ask your friends if they can recommend a good teacher or studio. *Shop around,* most places offer either free introductory classes, or classes at a much reduced rate for people shopping around, so take advantage of this! The sooner you're up on your feet, the better you'll feel.

Computers in the Classroom: Too Much, Too Soon?

Writing Situation: A freelance writer who has researched the use of computers in elementary through high school writing a short piece to inform his audience about his findings. Specifically, the writer hopes to allay some common fears and discuss some less obvious points.

Audience: A group of adults with school-age children and an active interest (or even concern) about how the computer explosion may affect their children. The audience may be thinking about home-computer purchase for their children, and this information will still apply, although to a lesser degree. The audience may not know a great deal about computers, but they are fairly educated and intelligent.

There is a commercial for a famous brand of computer that goes like this: A young man rushes to board a train for college while his parents wave goodbye. In the next scene, the parents meet their forlorn son, who (the announcer tells us) has flunked out because he lacked the computer skills to compete.

Despite such a blatant warning, the average parent should not be especially alarmed that his child may be falling behind in the race to acquire "computer skills," whatever that really means. Computer systems such as Epson's QX-10 and Apple's Macintosh serve as evidence that computers are being designed to work for people rather than people having to learn how to operate the computer. While larger, more elaborate systems do exist, few computer users other than specialists are likely to come into contact with one. Because most computer programs are designed to be relatively easy to operate — "user-friendly" — many computer users of the future will need only typing as a computer skill.

Regardless of this trend, use of computers in school is increasing. Market Data Research, Inc., of Westport, Conn., reports that as of 1983, more than half of all public schools in the U.S. had at least one microcomputer (a self-contained desktop computer system such as the Apple II or the Radio Shack TRS-80) in use, from with the percentage of computer-equipped schools increasing by level from about sixty percent of all elementary schools to well above eighty percent of junior-high and high schools. Two factors suggest that computer use will continue to increase as it has over the last three years: the sudden concern over the quality of education in public schools and the continued aggressive marketing of computer hardware and software companies.

The present public worry over the quality of public-school education will probably help push through legislation to give tax breaks to companies donating computer equipment and programs to the schools. According to one survey, the "opportunity gap" between schools with computers and those without is narrowing. However, some educators feel that the computering of schools is better for business than for students.

Advertising like the example at the beginning illustrates this problem: In order to stay in business, computer companies must sell computers and programs. Competition in the education market is especially fierce, yet support for educational-software has been poor. A survey by an independent research group reported that, of the 163 programs they tested, only about 20% had been actually developed using students for trial runs.

Currently, the average education program is a multiple-choice tutorial. A student is asked, say, to identify what part of speech a word is in a sentence. If he chooses correctly, the program lets him know and continues on to another item. If he guesses wrong, however, the program can give him anything from an unhelpful response of "WRONG" to explanatory material over the problem he missed. Picking "verb" as the part of speech for "sister" might elicit something like, "No, 'sister' is not a verb. Can you 'sister' something?" A right guess would allow the student to continue, but repeated wrong responses might lead to more specific help from the computer.

Some programs can even do such things as compiling data on how much trouble the student has with each type of problem. A very few programs even use advanced programming techniques to "guess" what the student's problem with a specific area is and to try to help him based on that analysis. Unfortunately, though, such programs are hard to write, and most software is nowhere near so sophisticated.

In fact, many programs — especially those for kindergarten and elementary-school students — are hard to tell from games. The music and colorful graphics they contain emphasize one of computer-aided instruction's best qualities: the computer can command a student's attention and, by making learning a more enjoyable experience, allow him to learn more.

But are students learning more? Perhaps: the computer seems to do well in teaching by rote, as in multiplication tables; with some simulations that emphasize planning and logic, such as spending money to run a lemonade stand; and through beginning-level programming in simple languages such as LOGO and BASIC, which teach computing logic, encourage sequential thinking, and even provide some creative outlet for more adept students who want to explore programming.

Computer-aided instruction has its critics, though. Some educators worry that students who use computers too heavily might become too reliant on the computers' instructional format, in effect becoming limited to memorizing instead of learning. Since computers are largely used to augment rather than to replace teach instruction, parents shouldn't be too alarmed: there seems little chance of their children becoming dehumanized as long as they aren't sitting at consoles six hours a day.

A great deal has been written and said about how computers

will revolutionize education, but so far the changes they have caused have been minor. As both teachers and administrators become more comfortable with computer systems, hopefully computers will be recognized as an aid to teaching rather than a substitute for it. Overall, computers in the classroom are experiencing the usual symptoms of new ideas: overenthusiasm and excessive worry.

5 · Sentences

As a native speaker of English (or a nonnative trained in the language) you already know how to put together most of the sentences you need to communicate with other people, and you use them constantly as you talk. That ability to construct oral sentences seems to be inborn. When you say sentences, you can draw on your natural ability to put words together in understandable patterns, but when you write sentences, the process gets more complicated. You lose the benefits you gain from being able to use gestures, look at your audience, and vary your tone and the inflections of your voice.

Speaking sentences is instinctive

To make up for losing those extra tools of communication, writers have to learn to construct tightly organized, carefully punctuated sentences, and they have to learn to use certain kinds of words, phrases, and patterns that help readers understand a piece of writing when they cannot ask questions about it. They need to learn to condense and edit their sentences — most of us are wordy when we talk — and occasionally to join and rearrange sentences to make them more efficient. They also need to learn how to design sentences in order to emphasize or subordinate ideas or to establish rhythms that make them more readable. In other words, good writers have to develop "sentence sense," a feeling for what makes sentences work.

Writing sentences must be learned

But having said that, I want also to urge caution. Although learning how to manipulate sentences to get the right effect is an important part of becoming a good writer, you need to remind yourself to put off intensive work with them until the second draft, if possible. During the first draft you need to concentrate on generating good content, and you should not worry if your sentences are clumsy. It's always tempting to stop and revise sentences as you are writing them, particularly if you are working on a word processor and it's easy to make changes, but try to control your tinkering instincts. If

you don't, you may wind up with eight or ten elegantly written sentences but no paper.

Kinds of Sentences

I have never known a writer who admitted that before starting to write he or she consciously thought about what kind of sentence patterns to use. I just don't think writers work that way, although some say that they often mentally rehearse a sentence before they write it. Most writers, however, simply begin writing with some sense of what they want to say and who their audience is, and they create sentences in the natural patterns that come to them as their ideas evolve. They may stop several times in the process of writing one sentence and consider how to phrase it, or they may write several sentences before stopping to reread them. Generally, however, only when they have stopped writing do they reread and check their sentence patterns. Then they may revise their work by deliberately choosing certain sentence patterns to achieve specific effects. Each of the three sentence patterns — simple, complex, and compound — has special qualities that make it work well for particular purposes.

Simple Sentences

A *simple sentence* consists of only one clause, or group of words with a subject and a predicate. It is the natural choice for plain statements of fact, simple assertions, and definitions. When you want to draw attention to characteristics or a proposal, say "This has this quality" or "That ought to be done," the simple sentence works best. For example:

Federal desegregation of schools began in 1954.

Dancing is one of the seven lively arts.

Snowmobiles ought to be prohibited.

Expansion   Simple sentences do not have to be short. They can be modified, expanded, enriched, and clarified by inserting appositives and phrases. In fact, the writer with a sense of possibilities can make a simple sentence do a great deal in relatively few words. For example, notice what can be done by starting out with a bare skeleton and fleshing it out:

San Francisco is a fascinating city.

San Francisco, a center of culture and fashion, is a fascinating city.

San Francisco, simultaneously a center of culture and fashion and a bawdy international port, is a fascinating city.

Probably this is about as far as you should go with this particular sentence; to add more modifiers just to see if it could be done — and it could — would be adding superfluous decoration that might detract from the main idea. But notice that the second and third versions of the sentence are more specific than the first and give the reader an idea of *why* San Francisco is a fascinating city.

One can also add introductory phrases to simple sentences to make them more specific, to qualify them, or to set a particular tone.

To me, San Francisco is a fascinating city.

Ironically, the size of the grain crop in Russia affects the price of bread in the United States.

In the boom years of the 1960s, every American city resounded to the din of construction.

In the last analysis, a public figure has no private life.

You can also increase the interest and concreteness of a simple sentence by adding adjectives, phrases, or other modifying terms. This process of increasing the amount of information in a sentence is sometimes called *embedding.* You should not, however, get into the habit of puffing out all your simple sentences with adjectives and phrases. The lean and direct simple sentence can be an important rhetorical tool.

Economy for Emphasis Perhaps what the short simple sentence does best is emphasize. For instance, notice how Joan Didion uses a

---

Using simple sentences for emphasis

simple sentence for stark effect in this essay about a woman who murdered her husband in California when the "hot dry Santa Ana wind" was blowing:

> There has been no rain since April. Every voice seems a scream.[1]

Because of their attention-getting qualities, simple sentences also make good openers. For example, here are two opening sentences from columns by the *Boston Globe* writer Ellen Goodman:

> They tell me apathy is in this year.[2]

> I have always been suspicious of nostalgia.[3]

You can imitate this technique by starting your papers (or paragraphs) with the plainest of assertions. For instance, "I hate shopping malls"; "Funerals are big business"; or "Money has its disadvantages." You would then go on to qualify, explain, and expand such an assertion.

When used primarily for emphasis, simple sentences like these are best kept bare. Qualifiers and modifiers will weaken rather than enrich them, and though you may incorporate more information, you will lose impact. For example, think how much would have been lost if the originators of these famous one-liners had tried to improve on them with adjectives:

> Texas is hell on women and horses.

> Make love, not war.

> We have not yet begun to fight.

Finally, clear and simple sentences are essential in most technical and business reports that stress facts and findings. One should never sacrifice accuracy and objectivity for elegance or color in that kind of writing. As a major text on technical writing puts it, "In general,

---

[1]Joan Didion, "Some Dreamers of the Golden Dream," *Slouching Towards Bethlehem* (New York: Dell, 1968) 3.
[2]Ellen Goodman, "Forgive Me for Being Gauche, But I'm Voting," *Close to Home* (New York: Simon, 1979) 110.
[3]Goodman, "Nostalgia in Small Doses, Please," *Close to Home* 122.

simple sentences should outnumber the other kinds: complex, compound, and complex-compound."[4]

Complex Sentences

The *complex sentence*, one that contains one or more dependent clauses in addition to a basic simple sentence, provides the best design for packaging complex thoughts. (A *dependent* or *subordinate clause* is a group of words that contains a subject and a verb but cannot stand as a sentence by itself.) By using complex sentences, you can show all kinds of complicated relationships between ideas. For example, you can indicate the comparative importance of statements, show that one thing happened because of or in spite of another thing, express contradictions and ironies, reservations and qualifications. And since mature people recognize how complicated good thinking must be — as some wise person said, "The truth is seldom plain and never simple" — we badly need the kind of writing tool that the complex sentence gives us.

Complex sentences show relationships

Here is a rather typical example in which a student used simple sentences when a complex one was needed. Writing on Exercise 2 at the end of Chapter 6, the student began:

> A good education is not essential for economic success in our society. Today many people believe that a good education is essential for economic success in our society.

By beginning with two contradictory statements written in such a way that they seem to be of equal value, the student confuses the reader from the start. One's first reaction is to ask, "Well, which way are we going to go?" If the student had realized the need to show the contradiction between points, he or she could have begun the first sentence with "Although . . ." and avoided the confusion; for example:

> Although many people still believe that a good education is essential for economic success in our society, it really isn't.

[4]Gordon H. Mills and John A. Walter, *Technical Writing*, 3rd ed. (New York: Holt, 1970) 48.

Or it could have been written:

> In spite of what most people believe, a good education is really not necessary for economic success in our society.

Another student writing on the same assignment got off to a bad start as a result of not knowing how to use a complex sentence to show the desired cause-and-effect relationship. The paper began like this:

> The statement "You can achieve anything you set your mind to if you work hard enough" is a product of our American heritage. The idea was formed when the country was first settled. People came here to escape the caste systems of Europe.

Redoing this with a complex sentence would not only bring out the relationship and comparative importance of the ideas, but it would also get rid of the choppiness. For example:

> Because most of the people who settled America came here to escape the caste system of Europe, they believed strongly that an individual could do anything he wanted to if he just worked hard enough. Most of us still believe this. [*Notice the prudent addition of "most" here; not all settlers came to escape the caste system.*]

Rearrangements like this really are not hard to make when a writer becomes conscious of the need to tie ideas together.

Complex sentences use signal words

Complex sentences typically employ one or more *signal words*. Among the most common are *although, in spite of, however, unless, if, when, because, as, while, during, since,* and *instead*. There are, of course, many others; whatever serves as a conjunction or relative pronoun in making a clause dependent is a subordinating signal. Such clauses are flexible and variable. They can be lengthened or shortened; put at the beginning, end, or middle; and used as introductions, explainers, or just modifiers. For example, let's take this student paragraph and see how it could be rewritten to clarify and tighten the relationship between the student's points, which are in themselves sound and pertinent to the topic.

Original

Advertising persuades people by making foods appear to be nutritionally good when they are not. Money is wasted on these foods. We should buy food that would be beneficial for us. The poor waste their food stamps frequently. Their grocery baskets are filled halfway with junk. The high cost of them is startling. Even bubble gum has gone up to two cents now. Money could also be saved from the dentist and doctor bills.

Revision

Because so many of us are influenced by advertising that makes worthless food seem nutritious, we waste a shocking proportion of our food dollars. The poor, who spend their precious cash on food stamps, waste money when they spend those stamps on expensive junk like bubble gum. What we are buying is not only worthless, it actually damages our bodies and our teeth.

This revision could have been done several different ways, all quite acceptable.

Compound Sentences

The compound sentence is so similar to the complex one in the way it works and looks that there is no need to worry a great deal about the distinction. Simply, it is this: the complex sentence contains one simple sentence and one or more dependent clauses, and the *compound sentence* combines two or more simple sentences, connected with a coordinating conjunction or semicolon. We use it to join independent statements and ideas, and the kind of joining signal we use frequently tells us what the relationship of those statements is. The section on transitions in Chapter 2 lists many of those joining words and gives their functions.

Here are some typical compound sentences:

The candidate must find new sources of money, or she will have to give up her campaign.

The combination of sedatives and alcohol is deadly; yet people looking for a thrill continue to mix them.

The first function of scientists is research; they are teachers only incidentally.

Ways of constructing compound sentences

Balanced Sentences   The balanced sentence, in which both parts have basically the same word pattern, is a particularly useful variation of the compound sentence because it provides the ideal package for emphasizing similarities or differences, usually the latter. For instance:

Weak leaders crave love; strong ones prefer respect.

Football and basketball provide recreation for the young, but tennis and golf provide recreation for a lifetime.

Minorities must first win elections, and then they can win their rights.

Winning isn't everything; it's the only thing.

Parallel Sentences   Parallel sentences are much like balanced sentences in that they achieve an effect by repeating a pattern, but they are more flexible in form. You can set up simple parallels in a rather short sentence, or you can carry a parallel structure along for several sentences; for example:

We hope to attract new students by increasing our scholarships, by improving our faculty, by expanding our course offerings, and by promoting our graduate programs.

And from President John F. Kennedy's inaugural address, which depends heavily on balance and parallelism to achieve its effects:

Let every nation know, whether it wishes us well or ill, that we shall pay any price, bear any burden, meet any hardship, support any friend, oppose any foe to assure the survival and the success of liberty.

And from a student theme:

New York City is failing. It has overextended its resources for too long, true. It has given in to pressure groups for too long, true. It has allowed itself to be taken advantage of for too long, true. But the city is failing while the president and Congress debate.

Parallel structure can be especially useful when you are writing a thesis sentence that will act as an organizing tool for your paper. For example:

The advantages of buying a mobile home are that it is comparatively inexpensive, it can be moved out of an urban area, and it can be sold quickly if necessary; the disadvantages are that it is easily damaged by wind and hail, and it is usually not attractive.

I have decided to choose a career in nursing because it is a profession that will allow me to help people, to move around the country, and to earn a decent salary.

Ways of Improving Your Sentences

Condense and Combine Sentences Occasionally

Sometimes when you reread your sentences, you realize that two or three of them focus on the same point and could be combined into a single more effective sentence, often by means of subordination. For example:

Original

When you press the shutter button on your camera, hold as still as possible. It is best to hold your breath as you slowly press the release. You will be less susceptible to sudden movements.

Revision

When you press the shutter button on your camera, keep as still as possible, holding your breath so you will be less susceptible to sudden movements.

Original

It is now illegal for individual business firms to conspire to set prices. In the same way, the labor of different companies should not be allowed to work together to set wages.

Revision

Just as individual business firms cannot conspire to set prices, labor of different companies should not be allowed to work together to set wages.

Another way to condense sentences and make them more efficient is to "telescope" them together by inserting the information from one sentence as a modifying phrase or appositive in the sentence next to it. For example:

Original

Traditionally, society has treated alcoholics as outcasts. Now more people realize that alcoholism is a disease. That disease is often made worse by social patterns.

Revision

Traditionally, society has treated alcoholics as outcasts, but today more people realize they are victims of a disease, one often made worse by social patterns.

Original

New Orleans is a distinctive city. It has good jazz, good food, and elegant old southern architecture. It has succeeded in preserving its culture in spite of growth.

Revision

New Orleans, a distinctive city with good jazz, good food, and elegant old southern architecture, has succeeded in preserving its culture in spite of its growth.

Write Agent/Action Sentences

You can make your sentences more direct and easier to read by organizing them into *agent/action* sentence patterns. To do that, ask yourself, "Who is doing what?" In other words, identify *who* or *what* is acting as the *agent* in the sentence — the person or thing carrying out the action — and make that agent the subject of the sentence. Then figure out what *action* is going on in the sentence and make the verb express that action. Notice how using this pattern improves the following sentences:

Original

Consumer habits have moved away from debt and toward saving as interest rates have increased.

If you ask yourself *who* is acting, you realize it is "consumers," not "habits"; if you ask yourself *what* is happening, you realize that the consumers are "saving," not "moving away." By rewriting in the agent/action pattern, you get a much clearer sentence.

Revision

As interest rates have increased, consumers have stopped going into debt and started saving.

Here is another example:

Original

A knowledge of computers will result for students when they are used frequently.

If you ask yourself *who* is acting, you realize it is "students," not "a knowledge of computers"; if you ask yourself *what* is happening, you realize the students are "using" the computers. Revising the sentence into an agent/action pattern makes it clearer and also gets rid of the fuzzy pronoun reference:

Revision

Students who use computers frequently will learn about them.

Here are some additional examples:

Original

The high availability of airplane glue and small containers of paint is causing an increased addiction to glue and paint sniffing among junior high students.

Revision

More junior high students are becoming addicted to glue and paint sniffing because airplane glue and small containers of paint are so easy to obtain.

Original

That these issues are important to him is evidenced by the passion of his arguments.

Revision

His passionate arguments show that the issue is important to him.

Choose Concrete Sentence Subjects

You can also make your writing clearer by choosing concrete words, those that refer to specific people, groups, or things that exist in real experience, as your sentence subjects. (That's easier to do if you use agent/action sentence patterns.) Because readers can visualize the things and people that concrete words refer to more easily than they can visualize abstractions like *loyalty* or *instability*, they grasp their meaning more quickly.

Concrete sentence subjects work better than abstract ones for other reasons as well. First, writers who start off with concrete subjects are less likely to use passive and weak verbs in their sentences because concrete subjects can act, while abstractions cannot. (More on problems with passive and weak verbs later in the chapter). Second, writers who use concrete sentence subjects are less likely to write confusing sentences because they are almost automatically more conscious of the sentence patterns they are using. For instance, the student who wrote "Cheating is attainable by someone else taking the test" wouldn't have gotten her words into such a tangle if she had started with the concrete subject *students* and written "Students can cheat by having someone else take the test for them." See Chapter 7 for techniques that will help you make your writing more concrete and specific.

Eliminate Stretcher Phrases

Check your sentences to see if you are beginning too many of them with unnecessary stretcher phrases such as "They are . . ." or "It is. . . ." If so, look for shorter and more direct ways to begin. For example:

Original
They are desirous of . . .

Revision
They want . . .

Original
The officer took cognizance of . . .

Revision
The officer recognized . . .

Original
There is no agreement among them on . . .

Revision
They do not agree on . . .

Notice that the revisions not only cut words, they substitute strong verbs for "to be" verbs.

You can also make your sentences more economical, direct, and easier to read by cutting out other strung-out phrases and making one word do the work of several. For instance:

Strung-out Phrase	*Revision*
make a selection	select
come to a decision	decide
show a preference for	prefer
in the event of	if
in regard to	about
have the capability of	can

Don't Overload the First Part of Your Sentence

Don't crowd so much into the first part of your sentence that your readers lose their way before they get to the main verb. Writers usually fall into this trap in one of two ways. First, they stretch out an opening qualifying phrase until it overpowers the main part of the sentence. For example:

> With political turmoil going on in the country, a new drought threatening in the southern regions, rising discontent from tribes in the backlands, and the rural poor flocking into the cities, the rulers of Mauretania are under severe pressure to act.

In this sentence, the reader has to hold so much in mind while waiting for the main idea that she loses her way.

Readers can also get bogged down in a sentence if its subject is a long noun clause that obscures the verb in the sentence. For instance:

> That the United States has the best medical technology in the world, yet ranks sixteenth among countries in successful births per pregnancy, results because medical costs are too high.

By the time the reader gets to the verb, he is starting to lose track of what the subject is. The problem gets particularly bad when, as often happens, the verb of the sentence is a word that could also act as a noun. That's part of the difficulty in this example.

Limit the Amount of Information in One Sentence

Generally, it's a good idea not to try to do too much in one sentence. A long and very complex sentence is not necessarily a good one. In fact, highly complex sentences often come out disastrously because inexperienced writers try to juggle too many things at one time. Frequently, they cannot handle the demands of grammar, mechanics, and structure and simultaneously cope with three or four ideas. If they try, they can turn out the kinds of confused messages illustrated by the following sentences taken from student themes (each is followed by a suggested revision):

Original

Therefore, understanding the idea that all taxpayers should be allowed to attend a state-supported institution, and all citizens are taxpayers by the mere fact that they are consumers, it is reasonable to state that all citizens should be allowed to attend the state university.

Revision

All taxpayers should have the right to use state-supported facilities. Obviously, then, anyone in the state should be able to attend the state university because everyone who buys anything pays sales taxes.

Original

Therefore, the pressure of grading should be replaced with the practice of commenting and evaluation as is necessary so as to encourage the student to learn to write well, rather than force him.

Revision

Writing teachers should put comments and evaluations on papers instead of grades. Such a system would encourage rather than force the student to learn to write.

Original

As far as the council's right to act for the people goes, however, you must understand that although representative government is a fine idea, its use to deal with specific issues is not warranted when a significant number of the governed is vocally against its use, as it is on the question of appropriations.

Revision

Although the council has the right to act for the people on many matters, it should not take actions to which a significant number of voters object. Appropriating money is that kind of action.

Sentences like the originals lose readers before they ever get to the end. Some of the difficulty, of course, comes from the excessive number of abstract words, including the subject. The last example is particularly bad on that score. But mainly these writers have confused their readers simply by trying to put too much into one package.

The best way to avoid producing such tangled sentences is to stop and check them over carefully before you write your second draft. If you are a person who writes quickly and does most of your revising as you do the second draft, you can wait until then to check over sentences to be sure you haven't packed so much into them that you have confused your reader. If you are a slow writer who frequently stops to reread as you work, check your sentences as they develop to see that they aren't getting out of control. In either case, don't hesitate to split up a long sentence if you think it will help your reader understand it more easily.

Split your sentences if necessary

Vary the Length of Your Sentences

You should be aware of the length of the sentences you are writing, whether they are simple or complex. Of course, most writers do not consciously start out by saying, "I'm going to write long sentences" or "I'm going to write short sentences" — they play it by ear according to their audience, their purpose, and the tone they want to establish. But practiced writers do realize that the trend in modern writing is toward shorter sentences, just as it is toward shorter paragraphs. By *shorter*, I mean sentences of from ten to twenty-five words. Comparatively short sentences are usually easier for a reader to follow; they also quicken the pace of the writing and help to create an informal tone. Obviously, advertising copywriters know all this and carry the practice to sometimes ridiculous extremes.

Vary sentence length according to audience

For the most part, student writers should not consciously try to write a majority of either long or short sentences. You will do much better to put your ideas down in what seems to you reasonable and normal sentence patterns, then take a look at them. When the sentences are choppy or repetitive, try combining them; when a sentence seems too long and poorly organized, try separating it. As you work, keep your audience in mind. If you think their education level is low or their attention span short, separate more sentences than you combine. If the material is difficult or rather technical, it is also better to keep your sentences short so the audience won't lose its way. If you're doing a breezy, casual article, use short sentences, perhaps even fragments (more on that later in this chapter).

When writing on an uncomplicated topic for a general audience, however, probably you would do best to try to vary the lengths of your sentences from reasonably long to medium to short and emphatic. For instance:

> You place a phone call and are put on hold. You wait. And then you wait some more. Should you hang up? Perhaps. After all, why waste another second of your valuable time? On the other hand, if you hang up, you'll only have to call again to accomplish whatever business put you on the phone in the first place. Anyway, you've already spent all this time on hold, so why give it up now? So you wait some more. At some point you finally resign yourself to the likelihood that you've been left on hold forever. Even as you hang up, though, your ear remains glued to the receiver, hoping to the bitter end that all the time spent waiting was not in vain.[5]

Notice that the writer uses very short sentences to make the most important points; they are also the sentences that especially catch the reader's attention. Working such short sentences into the text also improves the paragraph by varying the rhythm, and as a result the reader does not become bored by a repetitious, singsong effect.

Finally, you should remember that it is particularly important to limit the length and complexity of your sentences when you are writing something that will be read aloud. A listening audience will certainly have trouble following a rambling sentence that takes in several ideas, particularly if that sentence is heavy with abstractions.

Use shorter sentences for oral reports or speeches

So for speeches or oral reports, edit your prose carefully. Write mostly simple sentences or complex and compound sentences with no more than two or three clauses in them. Use sentences of no more than six or eight words from time to time as a kind of punctuation. And be particularly careful to use concrete subjects and strong verbs when possible and to illustrate your abstractions with concrete examples that help the audience's concentration by giving them visual images.

[5]Jeffrey Z. Rubin, "Psychological Traps," *Psychology Today* March 1981: 52.

Choose Effective Verbs

More than any other single sentence element, verbs give a piece of writing its color and vigor. Whether your writing drags along, perhaps boring your reader as it goes, or moves smoothly and surely toward your objective depends largely on the kinds of verbs you choose. For instance, the habitual use of *is* makes many sentences unnecessarily dull. Compare these two versions of the same idea:

Use verbs that show action

> There *is* a real need for free, tax-supported doctors and hospitals in the United States. Currently there *is* a movement toward such a program. It *is* called HMO or Health Maintenance Organizations.

> Many Americans badly need free, tax-supported doctors and hospitals. The new HMO or Health Maintenance Organization program would fill this need.

Other problems caused by the verb *to be* are discussed in "Hints for Polishing Your Writing" in the appendix.

You can also improve your writing by searching for verbs that make your readers think of actions; for example, "Inflation is *crushing* the poor" or "The candidates are *hugging* and *kissing* their way across the country." Notice for instance how skillfully Gordon Parks uses verbs to convey his admiration for Duke Ellington in this passage (italics added):

> For me, and many other black young people then, his importance as a human being *transcended* his importance as a musician. We had been assaulted by Hollywood's grinning darky types all of our young lives. It was refreshing to be a part of Duke Ellington's audience. Ellington never *grinned*. He *smiled*. Ellington never *shuffled*. He *strode*. It was "Good afternoon, ladies and gentlemen," never "How y'all doin'?" We wanted to be seen by the whites in the audience. We wanted them to know that this elegant, handsome and awe-inspiring man playing that ever-so-fine music on that golden stage dressed in those fine clothes before that big beautiful black band was black — like us.[6]

[6]Gordon Parks, "Jazz," *Esquire* Dec. 1975: 140.

Notice that Parks uses only a few strong verbs, strategically placed, to achieve his effects. Too many action words jammed into a short passage can give one the impression of reading poorly crafted fiction, which overflows with words like *exploded, hurled, slashed, careened, screeched,* and so on. And action verbs that are connotative, as so many are, have little place in technical writing or other kinds of professional reports.

Passive Verbs   For some of the same reasons that they overuse abstract subjects, student writers are frequently addicted to using passive verbs. Passive verb forms (those in which the subject does not act, but is acted upon) hamper good communication for several reasons, many of which we will take up in the section on jargon in Chapter 7. For now, I will just point out that writers who consistently use passive rather than active verbs will almost certainly produce plodding and dull prose. For example, "The change in the administration *was thought* by many people to be beneficial" drags, but "Many people *favored* the change in the administration" moves briskly to the point. "The conclusion that pigs are more intelligent than cows *was arrived* at from laboratory experiments that *had been conducted* over a period of five years" is a drab, tedious sentence. "Five years of laboratory experiments *show* that pigs are smarter than cows" says the same thing better and faster. Notice that both the longer sentences also have abstract subjects.

Avoid using passive verbs

Occasionally you must use the passive construction, and sometimes it is desirable. Technical writers, for example, use passives frequently; not only is it difficult to describe experiments or mechanical operations without them, but in most cases the technical writer wants to focus on the experiment or operation, not on the person doing it. People writing plain expository prose may sometimes want to use the passive for the same reason. For instance, "Chairs were overturned, books were thrown on the floor, and dresser drawers had been yanked out and emptied" focuses attention on the objects, not the actor; thus the passive is appropriate. Sentences like "Ralph was awarded the Navy Cross" and "Hundreds of people were turned away at the door" make good use of passive verbs because the actor is either unknown or unimportant.

But students who are trying to sound mature and judicious, or who are unconsciously imitating bad models, too frequently make a habit of using passive verbs. The results can be unfortunate; for instance:

> Three levels of interest *are considered* in developing an effective advertisement. The first level is the rational level which *is thought* of as the logical appeal of the ad. Rationality *is* easily *achieved* by using very simple topics which need little or no thought.

> Men's pride *would be injured* if women *were awarded* rights, recognition, and responsibility. The saying that men are smarter than women *would have to be recognized* as an untruth. Intelligence *is based* on the individual and not on sex. Women *would be taken* into certain fields of education that *were* previously *dominated* by men. Men would no longer *be chosen* for medical school and law school because they are men.

Dull, isn't it? Notice the improvement if we change to active verbs and more concrete subjects.

> If women *succeed* in *winning* the rights, responsibilities, and recognition they are *working* for, male pride will certainly *suffer.* Men will have to *admit* that any claim that men are smarter than women is simply not true; intelligence *varies* by individuals, not by sex. Worse, women *will begin breaking* into fields that men have traditionally *dominated.* No longer will male applicants for medical and law school have an advantage simply because they are men.

Choosing active verbs and then rearranging the sentences accordingly make the paragraph tighter and more vigorous. Such changes are fairly easy to make on the second draft, although, of course, it is better if you can choose good verbs the first time through. Like most habits, an addiction to the passive voice is hard to overcome, but it really is important that you try.

Common Grammatical Problems in Sentences

Fragments

Today's composition teachers are finding it more and more difficult to explain to their students why they should not use sentence fragments in their papers when those students encounter fragments constantly in the messages they see and hear every day. Advertising copywriters seem to be particularly fond of the sentence fragment. If you are at all conscious of the advertisements that daily assault you from all directions, you are familiar with the kind that goes:

> The Different Look! The New Look! The *You* Look! Designed for discriminating people and available only at Felix's!

Some reasons for using fragments

Presumably, people who write this way do so deliberately, and they have reasons for expressing themselves in sentence fragments rather than in traditional language units built around subjects and verbs. Usually those reasons are, first, that they want to catch the potential buyer's eye and, second, that they are really trying to convey an impression rather than an idea.

If for some reason you have those same purposes in your expository writing, you could use the kinds of fragments that Tom Wolfe does in this passage:

> Thirty-nine years old! A recluse! Bonafide! Doesn't go out, doesn't see the light of day, doesn't put his hide out in God's own unconditioned Chicago air for months on end; *years*. Right this minute, one supposes, he is somewhere there in the innards of those forty-eight rooms, under layers and layers of white wall-to-wall, Count Basie–lounge leather, muffled, baffled, swaddled, shrouded, closed in, blacked out, shielded by curtains, drapes, wall-to-wall, blond wood, screens, cords, doors, buzzers, dials, Nubians — he's down in there, the living Hugh Hefner, 150 pounds, like the tender-tympany green heart of an artichoke.[7]

In your writing you might make similar deliberate use of a fragment. For example:

> Most people believe that once a doctor or dentist has a degree in hand, he or she will break into the $100,000 a year bracket almost immediately. *Not necessarily.*

Almost no teacher is going to object to this kind of fragment. Sentence fragments *are* attention getters, and used consciously in that

[7]Tom Wolfe, "King of the Status Drop-outs," *The Pump House Gang* (New York: Farrar, 1968) 49.

way, they can be effective. But it is precisely because they are attention getters that a writer needs to be careful about using them.

Professional writers occasionally use fragments for at least two other reasons. First, they use them in dialogue or as answers to questions. Thus "Never!" or "Since noon" are workable fragments or, as some grammarians call them, minor sentences that are quite correct in context. And fragments are also useful in description, particularly when one wants to give the effect of stillness or separate, distinct impressions. Conrad uses fragments this way in his description of the Congo River in *Heart of Darkness:* "An empty stream, a great silence, an impenetrable forest."

Reasons for not using fragments

So sentence fragments are by no means always ungrammatical or unacceptable in either student or amateur writing. There are, however, good reasons why *most* writers should not use sentence fragments in *most* things they write. One practical reason is that to almost all composition teachers — and other professors as well — a sentence fragment is a glaring grammatical error that indicates a student is either extremely careless or has such a poor grasp of the fundamentals of the language as not to recognize a sentence. A second reason for avoiding fragments is that they violate traditional sentence patterns and thus may confuse the reader and disrupt communication. A third reason, and probably the most important one, is that fragments make a bad impression on almost any audience. Average-to-well-educated readers are so conditioned to think of sentence fragments as serious mistakes that if they find one in a business letter, a report, or a proposal, they will almost automatically lower their opinion of the writer. For this reason, writers should be very careful about using fragments, even intentionally. In some situations, they risk alienating their audiences.

Run-on and Fused Sentences

For some reason, most students have much less difficulty with run-on and fused sentences than they do with fragments. Nevertheless, a reminder about sentence division is probably in order.

Why to avoid run-on sentences

Run-on Sentences   A *run-on sentence* is one in which several ideas that really should be separated into independent sentences are tacked together with conjunctions. A reader is apt to get lost in one of these rambling creations, particularly because the conjunctions are not chosen carefully enough to reflect the desired relationship between the parts of the sentence. Here are some examples of run-ons and some suggested revisions:

Run-on

We came around the corner and saw that a crowd had gathered and there was some kind of trouble and the police were trying to stop it.

Revision

As we came around the corner, we saw a crowd gathered. Apparently there was some kind of trouble that the police were trying to stop.

Run-on

The person who wants to persuade an audience must remember who they are and she has to think about what kind of arguments they will respond to for if she does not they will not listen to her and she will have wasted her time.

Revision

The person who wants to persuade an audience must remember what kind of people they are and the kind of arguments they will respond to. If she does not, she will have wasted her time because they will not listen to her.

Fused Sentences   Fused sentences are very similar to run-ons. The difference is that the writer has not even used conjunctions to connect the independent clauses. Rather, they are just run together without benefit of conjunction or punctuation; for example:

Fused sentence

The great interest in professional football has inspired several football novels among them are *North Dallas Forty* and *Semi-Tough*.

Revision

Revising fused sentences

The great interest in professional football has inspired several football novels. Among them are *North Dallas Forty* and *Semi-Tough*.

Fused sentence

Some experts on nutrition accuse the American food industry of lying about health in this country by saying that we are the best-fed country in the world they are making us think we get good nutrition for our money but it isn't true.

Revision

Some nutrition experts accuse the American food industry of lying about health in this country. By saying that we are the best-fed nation in the world, they are making us think we get good nutrition for our money, but it isn't true.

Obviously, run-on and fused sentences are not only poorly constructed and thus difficult to read, but they can be confusing. Careful proofreading should eliminate them.

Comma Splices

Avoiding comma splices

Connecting sentences or independent clauses with a comma rather than separating them into two sentences or joining them with a conjunction or a semicolon is called a *comma splice,* a *comma fault,* or a *comma blunder.* Although, like sentence fragments, this kind of construction seems to be appearing more and more in advertising and popular writing, the careful expository writer should avoid it for several reasons. First, using a comma splice usually indicates indifference or uncertainty about the relationship of the ideas you are connecting. Second, when you join what should be two sentences with a comma, which should be only an *internal* mark of punctuation, you risk misinterpretation of your statements. Third, and this is important, most English teachers object to comma splices in student writing; therefore using them is definitely bad rhetoric.

Here are some typical examples of comma splices taken from student themes:

Laughter is a form of release just like anger, a good laugh often relieves tension. [*It is not clear whether the phrase "just like anger" should go with "release" or "a good laugh."*]

Congress is going to lose this battle with the president, they will win the next one if they are better prepared. [*The idea of subordi-*

*nation is lost here. The two parts could have been connected with "but,"
or the sentence could have begun "Although Congress is going to
lose . . ."*]

James Joyce seems to be detached from his characters, they reveal
themselves through their actions. [*The reader wonders what the connection between these two statements is. A good guess is that the writer
intended to show cause and effect. Suggested revision:* "Because the
characters are revealed entirely by their actions, Joyce gives the
impression of being detached from them."]

The hotel is ugly and old-fashioned, it is the fashionable place to
stay. [*The reader cannot tell if the writer means the hotel is fashionable
because it is old-fashioned and ugly or in spite of its being so. A conjunction of "but" or "because" would resolve the confusion.*]

Unfortunately, if you are in the habit of using comma splices frequently, you probably don't even realize that you are doing it. Once
the bad habit is drawn to your attention, however, you should make
a point of thinking twice about what sentences are and how you
should join them. It will help you avoid both fragments and comma
blunders.

Dangling Modifiers

Another mistake that crops up regularly in student papers year after
year is *dangling modifiers.* Usually a dangling modifier is the introductory clause in a sentence. Because English is a language in which
word order controls meaning, we read the beginning clause anticipating that the subject of the sentence is coming right after it and
expecting the clause to tell us something about that subject. When
The problem of
dangling modifiers
the clause doesn't go with the subject but dangles independently, we
are surprised, annoyed, and often amused. But most important, our
thought processes are interrupted so that we do not — at first, at
least — get the message that the writer intends us to get.

Here are some fairly typical examples of dangling modifiers from
student themes:

When leaving high school, clothes become the least important
of matters.

Watching television before lunch, a soda pop commercial encourages Sally to drink Coke with her meal instead of milk.

Notice that with both these sentences if the writers had used a personal subject for their sentences, they could scarcely have gotten into trouble. You are much less likely to attach an unsuitable modifier to a person than to a thing — although it does happen.

In these next examples, notice that the students' use of abstract subjects increases the likelihood of dangling modifiers.

Being a freshman student at the University of Texas, finances are an essential need if I am to continue my education.

When hiring employees, their appearance and attitude are an employer's main concern.

Students who have the habit of using the passive voice may also find that it leads them into dangling modifiers. For instance:

After having argued all morning, a decision was reached.

By forcing students to conform to rules, creativity is stifled and discouraged.

In each of these cases if the student had started out naming the person who was acting, she or he probably would not have gotten into the dangling modifier confusion.

Sometimes a dangling modifier appears at the end of a sentence, tacked onto an object or complement that it doesn't fit very well; for example:

The conservatives are unhappy about the vice-presidential nominee, *expecting a less controversial choice.*

The gun control laws will never make it out of Congress, *being opposed by the National Rifle Association.*

Writers need to try to clean dangling modifiers out of their writing because they make them seem careless and because the comic effect dangling modifiers sometimes create may lose them their audience's respect. The two best ways to get rid of dangling modifiers follow.

First, remember that in English, words usually modify the word or phrase that comes next to them. Be sure, then, that your opening phrase fits with your subject. Second, begin your main clause with a concrete sentence subject whenever you can. You are less apt to get phrases in the wrong place when you do this. An occasional dangling modifier is the price we all pay for trying to write more interesting and compact sentences, and it is really a small price. You can change them in the first draft without too much trouble, and usually you will have a better sentence because you have introduced a qualifying or explanatory clause into it.

One can spend a lot of time tinkering with individual sentences to produce gratifying results. Good sentences are not an end in themselves, however; actual writing requires that you combine sentences into paragraphs. In order to do this, you have to think about the relationships between sentences just as you have previously been thinking about the relationships between the parts of the sentence. The next chapter will deal with some of the ways to work out these relationships to produce good paragraphs.

Exercises

1. *Working with simple and complex sentences*
   Join the following simple sentences into one compound or complex sentence in a way that shows a relationship between the ideas being expressed. There is not any one right way to do each example. You can show different relationships by using different linking words, and several options may work for each example.

   a. The senator was forced to resign. He will probably never run for office again.

   b. Several people have applied for the job. It will not be easy to fill.

   c. Educators are alarmed about the steady decline in SAT scores. Legislators keep demanding an explanation.

   d. Parents have been crusading against violence on television for more than a decade. We now have almost no Westerns. We have detective shows instead.

e. Some physicians say that expensive yearly physical examinations are pointless. Other physicians, particularly gynecologists, think regular checkups are essential.

f. According to sociologists, even small children make class distinctions. They reflect their parents' biases.

2. *Getting rid of abstract subjects in sentences*
Try to find a concrete subject, a personal one if possible, to replace the abstract subjects in the following sentences. If necessary, you can change the word order or substitute different words.

a. Being academically prepared was the first thing I realized I lacked.

b. Choice of clothes are a combination of personal tastes, fads, and practicality.

c. A common finance concept would control all hospitals under a government system.

d. Consideration of a multitude of problems must be made by any candidate who wants to be elected.

e. The availability of openings for girls in dental school was a major factor in my decision.

f. The stopping of the encroachment of new building along the seashore has been a long-time objective of the Sierra Club.

3. *Selecting better verbs*
Try to improve these sentences by substituting a more vigorous verb for those that are italicized. There may be several good choices in some instances.

a. The danger of explosion *remains* a continuing threat in the oil fields.

b. The rating of our football team *is* at a lower level than last week.

c. Geese *are* often *present* in this neighborhood in the winter.

d. Pornographic material *has* no constructive use in our society.

e. I *am* of the opinion that the interference *is* not *warranted*.

4. *Changing passive verbs to active verbs*
Change the italicized passive verb constructions in these sentences to the active voice. You may alter the word order if you wish.

a. To make the program work, participation *was needed* by a large number of volunteers.

b. Acupuncture *is believed* to be better than drugs because it has instant effects.

c. The kinds of experiences that *are encountered* in the inner city leave a lasting impression on the young people who *are raised* there.

d. The demands that *were made* by the auto workers *were considered* excessive by the company.

e. It *is* easily *grasped* by the reader that the basis on which this opinion *was formed* is shaky.

5. *Sentence fragments*
Rewrite the following sentence fragments to make complete sentences. Join two groups of words if necessary.

a. The author criticizes Texans for the amount of money they bet on high school football. And the things that school boards do to make prospects eligible for their teams.

b. Men have been considered strong and intellectually powerful. Whereas women are considered passive and emotional.

c. When both the husband and wife are working, each feels needed. He in a financial way and she in an emotional way.

d. More people should learn about the benefits of exercise. To stay well and look better.

e. The author makes his hometown seem inviting. One reason being that the people are easygoing.

6. *Dangling modifiers*
Rewrite the following sentences to get rid of the dangling modifiers.

a. When leaving for college, a car becomes a major problem.

b. Coming from a lower-income family of five children, our bank account allows only enough for one year of college for each child.

c. When hiring employees, their appearance and attitude is an employer's main concern.

d. By learning about genetics, many children with birth defects could be avoided.

e. When given all the relevant information, problems of this kind can be solved.

7. *Comma splices or blunders*
Rewrite these sentences with correct punctuation to avoid comma splices.

a. The thought of a comedian like Bob Hope using a canned laugh track is appalling, comedians like him are good enough to be appreciated without trickery.

b. Living close to campus saves money, it is also easier to go to laboratories at night.

c. After getting my passport, the obstacles were gone, all I had to do was borrow the money to go.

d. Parents always put pressure on their children to make good grades, this is due partly to the high cost of education.

e. We will deal with the problem tomorrow, we will be better prepared then.

8. *Combining sentences*
Combine the sentences in these student paragraphs to make them read more smoothly.

a. There are only a few sports at the university that receive the honor of varsity status. Along with these eight or ten varsity sports, there are some thirty other sports at the university that are only given the status of "club sports." These club sports consist mainly of minor sports or sports that are not big crowd drawers. The university treats these sports poorly. The majority of the club sports receive little if any funding from the university. This lack of funding is one of the major hindrances to the further development of these sports.

b. Buying a used car is a tricky business. A good place to start looking is the classified section of the newspaper. Look for personal ads from individuals who want to sell a car. They are your best bet. Ads cover a wide variety of cars in all sizes and prices. If you look hard enough, you can usually find a good machine for a reasonable price. Buying from an individual instead of a dealer takes more time. Nevertheless, it is worth it.

Writing Assignments

Paper 1

One of the important ways in which we get information we need on various topics is by reading brochures. Once you become conscious of how much our society uses brochures to communicate, you will find them everywhere you look: in the grocery store, doctors' offices, banks, government bureaus, the library, the dean of students' office, the cleaners, and so on. Most of them are good examples of how to convey useful information clearly, briefly, and appropriately for a particular audience.

For this assignment, make a tour around campus and the surrounding business area and collect several brochures. Identify the audiences to whom they are addressed and the purposes their authors seemed to have had in mind. Then choose a topic you know something about and write a brochure yourself; draw on the samples you have collected for ideas about style and layout.

Before you begin your brochure, write out an analysis of your audience. Who are they, how much do they already know about your topic, why would they read your brochure, and what questions would they have when they read it? Also write out an analysis of your purpose in creating the brochure. What do you hope to accomplish?

Possible Topics

1. A brochure from the Dean of Students' office describing the services available to handicapped students on your campus.
2. A brochure from the Student Union describing their movie program: the kinds of films offered, their sponsors, schedule of showings, cost, etc.
3. A brochure describing the Al-Anon program on campus.

4. A brochure on prenatal and infant nutrition for a public health clinic.
5. A brochure for students about establishing a good credit rating.
6. A brochure advertising a service close to campus: a copying center, a tutoring service, a resumé writing service, or something similar.

Paper 2

Much of the writing that people do in the real world involves money: requests for it, justifications for spending it, complaints about overcharges or bad service, and so on. Think of a reason you have to write about money and compose a clear, well-supported letter that will accomplish your purpose in that particular situation.

Before you begin to write the letter, identify and analyze your audience. Who are they, what attitudes or concerns do they have that are important in this situation, and what information do they want to get from your letter? Also write out a purpose analysis: What do you hope to accomplish with your audience by writing the letter?

Possible Topics

1. A request for funds for a project that is important to you; for example, Recordings for the Blind, Optimists' Youth Club, American Cancer Society, Planned Parenthood, or your local humane society.
2. A letter asking your university administration to allocate $5000 from the student activity fund to a campus organization of which you are a member and explaining why your organization needs the money and how it would spend it. Some possible organizations: the college drama club, the university computer-users group, the student chess club, the student jazz orchestra, or the campus youth ministry.
3. A letter complaining to a company from which you made a major purchase about failure to honor a guarantee, misleading claims that were made about a product, or repeatedly bad service on your purchase. Some examples: a stereo, a car, scuba diving gear, a video cassette recorder, a racing bike.
4. A letter applying for a scholarship of $5000 from an organization in your home town or county that offers a stipend every year to

a student who is in a particular field of study. For example, your country medical association may offer a scholarship for a young person who wants to become a family practice physician; the Rotary Club in your town may offer a scholarship to a freshman who is majoring in business; or your local chapter of university alumni may offer a scholarship to an outstanding freshman who plans to become a teacher. If you cannot think of a specific organization that might sponsor a scholarship in your field of interest, inquire at the Student Financial Aid Office on your campus to find out what scholarships are available and what conditions a student has to meet to apply for them. You will find a surprising variety of sources willing to give money to students who can demonstrate eligibility.

6 · Paragraphs

Two ways of looking at paragraphs

Writers can look at paragraphs from two perspectives. First, they can look at them from the *outside*; that is, a writer can ask herself, "How are my paragraphs going to look to the reader? What kind of paragraph arrangement does my reader expect to find in my paper, and how long should my paragraphs be?" These are important questions because one major purpose of paragraphs is to divide a long unit of writing into smaller units so that readers can get short breaks between units and thus process and absorb more easily what they are reading.

Writers can also consider paragraphs from the *inside*; that is, a writer can ask himself, "What is the nature of a paragraph? What is a paragraph supposed to do, and what should I keep in mind as I write one?" These are also important questions because the second major purpose of a paragraph is to develop an idea.

Paragraph Unity

Looked at from the inside, a good paragraph's essential quality is unity. The well-written paragraph has one point to make, and every sentence in the paragraph relates to that point. It flows smoothly from one sentence to the next, each seeming to fit naturally with the ones that come before and after it. It doesn't sag with unnecessary detail, nor does it veer off in unexpected directions. The paragraph does what it started out to do and neither surprises nor disappoints the reader. It is under control.

Beginning with a Commitment

Probably the best way to control your writing in a paragraph is to begin by starting a commitment in an opening topic sentence and then to be sure that everything else in the paragraph relates to and develops that sentence. There are, of course, other workable approaches to paragraph writing, but the traditional method of making your assertion in the first or second sentence of a paragraph and following it immediately with expansion or supporting information seems to work best for inexperienced writers. They are less apt to wander off the track or lapse into generalities if they start off with a commitment they have to respond to. Here, for instance, is a paragraph by Larry King that is an almost perfect model of this kind of development.

Making a promise to your reader

> If I could name but one thing that beer joints provide, greater than all their many other gifts, it would be music. Jukebox music, preferably country and western. Hell, *got* to be country and western! I am not comfortable or happy in a beer joint, cannot give it a star rating, unless the guitars are jangling and the fiddles whining behind the voices of such as Ernest Tubbs, Willie Nelson, Tom T. Hall, or Merle Haggard, and they sing of walking the floor over you, blue eyes crying in the rain, old five and dimers, making it through December. Never do good-hurtin' old memories come flooding back quite as effectively, never are concerts quite so personal, as when that beer drankin' music floods the soul and the beer is cold enough to ache your teeth almost as much as the music aches your innards. It is no less — as Thomas Jefferson said of the presidency — than a splendid misery; it can almost make you glad that the Taddy Joes and the Linda Lous once took pains to break your heart.[1]

Notice that every sentence that follows King's commitment to show why music is an important attribute of beer joints vividly describes that music and its effects. He makes the general specific and the abstract concrete.

Here is another typical paragraph using the general commitment/specific response pattern.

[1] Larry L. King, "The Beer Joint," *Texas Monthly* March 1976: 80.

In the last 12 years, the Scholastic Aptitude Test scores (SATs) of high school seniors have declined. In 1962 the average score was 490; in 1974 it was below 460. A few years ago, some 54,000 seniors got verbal SATs over 650, which is outstanding; one year later, average scores had dropped eight points and only 40,000 seniors scored that high. Even at prestigious schools, such as Harvard and Brown, average verbal SAT scores are down.[2]

This opening paragraph from a student theme does the same thing:

Both animals and people respond positively to rewards. As experiments have shown, rats in a Skinner box will systematically press a lever in order to obtain food. Dogs will perform tricks in response to verbal praise. People, like those who practice and practice in order to reach the Olympics, also work for rewards. English teachers should be aware of this motivational principle and incorporate it into their teaching methods.

In contrast, here is a student paragraph that falls apart because the writer does not seem to realize that in the first sentence a commitment has been made that must be followed through on in the rest of the paragraph.

Give careful consideration to the courses you want to take in your first semester at college. Keep in mind that college is a different institution with new things to experience and new situations to adapt to. I had always been told that college isn't hard and that it's just a matter of keeping up in your classes. This is true, but I have found it to be very difficult and time consuming. My advice to the freshman is that he be sure that the number and kind of courses he takes are those he can handle. In college there is a vast number of courses one can take.

Although punctuation, grammar, and spelling are all correct, this is a wretched paragraph. One reason is that all the sentences that follow the opening assertion are hackneyed generalities — ten minutes of reading this kind of writing would put anyone to sleep. Another reason is that the paragraph has no thesis, no clear topic sentence

[2]Carol Tavris, "The End of the IQ Slump," *Psychology Today* April 1976: 69.

Sentences should not be in random patterns

that would allow the reader to get a grasp on what the writer intends to say. Instead it is made up of a series of statements that can be moved around like dominoes on a board and put together in several ways. And anytime you can do that to the sentences in a paragraph, or the paragraphs in a theme, you're in trouble. A piece of writing in which the parts can be assembled at random is poorly organized and hard to follow.

Notice too that the writer never fulfills the commitment to explain why first-semester freshmen should give careful consideration to the courses they take. Instead the writer makes three more commitments but does not meet those either; at one point the commitments even contradict one another. Another serious fault in the paragraph is the writer's failure to use specific and concrete language. The writer gives no examples and appeals to no senses but rather stays on the top level of abstraction throughout the paragraph (see Chapter 7 on abstraction levels). Now notice the change if we retain the topic sentence but expand and support it with concrete details:

New students should give careful consideration to the courses they take their first semester in college. For one thing, they should balance science and nonscience courses so they do not have too many time-consuming labs. They should also try to get a mixture between subjects they find fairly easy and those that are difficult for them. For instance, the student who does well in history but expects to have a terrible time with calculus might plan on taking both in the same semester to balance the work load. The student who does not plan carefully and takes five tough courses the first term may wind up on scholastic probation.

Downshifting   A paragraph like this not only gives several specific examples that explain the assertion of the first sentence, but it also illustrates a useful writing technique that Professor Francis Christensen calls *downshifting*. Christensen notes that one develops a paragraph by addition, just as one expands a sentence by embedding *Writing on various levels of generality* modifying words and phrases. He points out, moreover, that "when sentences are added to develop a topic or subtopic, they are usually at a lower *level of generality*."[3] Thus the term *downshifting* is used to

[3]Francis Christensen, *Notes Toward a New Rhetoric* (New York: Harper, 1967) 56.

suggest that one clarifies a point by moving down the ladder of language abstraction. The most effective paragraphs, Christensen points out, are those that have several levels of generality. Using his method of diagramming the different levels in a paragraph, we could analyze the levels in the preceding paragraph like this:

1. New students should give careful consideration to the courses they take in their first semester in college.
    2. For one thing, they should balance science and nonscience courses so they do not have too many time-consuming labs.
    2. They should also try to get a mixture between subjects they find fairly easy and those that are difficult for them.
        3. For instance, the student who does well in history but expects to have a terrible time in calculus might plan on taking both in the same semester to balance the work load.
        3. The student who does not plan carefully and takes five tough courses the first term may wind up on scholastic probation.

Employed in conjunction with other unifying devices, downshifting is effective in holding a paragraph together because it keeps reinforcing the main idea in the reader's mind. For example:

The most memorable Wyeth holiday, and the one Andrew refers to most often, was Christmas. Everyone contributed to the house decorating, a sumptuous and extravagant affair which induced particular smells and colors that still stimulate Andrew's mind with memories of the excitement and innocence of his childhood. The climactic moment in the celebration came early Christmas morning when N. C. [Wyeth], charading as Old Chris, would thump his way across the roof, crying out, ringing his sleighbells, and then quickly descend a ladder into the house to deliver presents to the ecstatic and terrified children. "I used to wet my bed, I was so excited on Christmas Eve," recalls Andrew Wyeth, — "and then move to the other side of the bed to let it dry out. Pa used to scare the hell out of me, those big feet stamping on the stairs. Old Chris was always to me a giant, plus a marvelous, magic merry spirit —

but a man who terrified me." Even N. C. would become so moved on these occasions that he cried from pleasure and excitement.[4]

In the first sentence the author makes a commitment to show the reader what was memorable about Christmas at the Wyeths' house, and she does it by downshifting to four levels, each more specific than the last.

Adding Transitions   Writers who work at giving enough examples and concrete details to develop the main idea of their paragraphs can usually turn out unified paragraphs without too much difficulty. The parts seem to fit together with natural links or hooks. Sometimes, however, the separate sentences in a paragraph can be clear and pertinent to the topic, but the reader gets the impression that there are awkward gaps or rough spots between them. In that case the writer needs to find ways to work conventional transitional words and phrases into the sentences.

Need to link sentences together

Most of the transitional hooks and signposts recommended in Chapter 2 for tying the parts of a paper together work equally well in constructing paragraphs. As you develop your main point, words like *also, moreover, therefore, however, nevertheless, consequently,* and *furthermore* will probably come to mind almost automatically as you expand or qualify your supporting material. Probably the most useful connective words you can use *within* paragraphs are the pronouns, both relative and demonstrative. By pointing back to the main topic of the paragraph, they keep the reader's attention focused on the thread of the argument. Here is an example by a professional writer that uses this technique (italics added):

> To the men who shop in *them, they* feel like private clubs. *They're* sanctuaries that spare a man's having to walk through the toy department or an acre of furniture displays when he has better things to do.
>
> If you're already known in *them,* you'll be greeted by name and engaged in conversation before being shown the items known to suit your taste. If you are a new face, chances are you'll be treated like visiting royalty. Some are equipped with a private bar where

[4]Wanda M. Corn, *The Art of Andrew Wyeth* (Boston: New York Graphic Soc., 1973) 121.

you'll be offered a complimentary drink. In none of *them* will you be greeted with that salesclerk's cliché, "Can I help you?"

What *they* are called depends on where you live or the circles you travel in. Some people call *them* boutiques. Others call *them* specialty stores. In plain, simple English, *they're* men's stores — and there are more than 21,400 of them from coast to coast.[5]

Here is a theme from a student who uses the same device:

Today's military is often managed by men *who* either cheated on exams and got away with *it,* or knew *it* was going on but ignored *it.* What the former learned at the academy was that duty and honor are pretty much optional. *They* play plenty of lip service to *these* two ideas, but *their* only uncompromisable responsibility is to *their* own welfare. These are the men *who* disobey unpleasant orders; *who* falsify records, stretch the truth in reports, or pass the blame on to someone else when convenient. *They* get away with *it* because the only ones to blow the whistle on *them* are the same men *who* refused to do *it* in the academy. *These* professional cynics have found that it's much easier to move up the ladder if *they* remain inconspicuous.

Good transitions are not noticeable

No matter how many rules and tricks one knows, achieving smooth transitions between sentences and between paragraphs never becomes automatic, even for professional writers. On the second or third draft, they still find gaps that must be bridged and loose ends that must be tied. But good transitions are so essential to effective writing that it is worth your while to work at them. You will have succeeded only when the reader is not even aware of the links in your prose.

Ways of Developing Paragraphs

Mastering the techniques of developing paragraphs is much like mastering the techniques of smoothing out connections between sentences and paragraphs. Although there are no sure-fire formulas

[5]Rita Johnson, "The Stores Behind the Man," *Esquire* Oct. 1979: 68.

or easy solutions, there are some traditional ways to approach paragraph development that seem to work for many writers. These approaches probably sound familiar: illustration and examples, comparison and contrast, cause and effect, narration, question and answer, and analogy. You can also use the six modes of argument explained in Chapter 9 just as effectively for paragraph development as for theme development.

You have many options, a variety of methods available to you. You should not, however, think that they are the only ones or even the best ones for you. You may be better off just to follow your own organizational instincts, as many writers obviously do. Certainly an analysis of the structure of paragraphs in a wide sampling of magazines reveals that there are so many good ways to put a paragraph together that we can't begin to classify them. If, however, you have trouble getting started, some of the following approaches could be helpful.

Illustration and Examples

One can handle the illustration-and-examples approach in at least three ways. The first is the straightforward one mentioned earlier in the section on topic sentences. You make an assertion, usually a generalization, in the first sentence, and then you give the concrete examples on which it is based. For example:

How to use examples

> The future lies before Russell Francis, voluptuously waiting to be had. At twenty-two, he is strong, graceful, poised, and six-and-a-half feet tall. He owns a Maserati, a condominium town house, and a Beechcraft Sierra with much of the instrumentation of an airliner. He has a quick, analytical mind, a warm, open manner, and a contract to play football with the New England Patriots that is said to be in excess of $200,000. He is a superb surfer, a first-rate student, a competition rodeo rider, and, in the words of Paul Brown, a sage of football sages, "the best tight-end prospect I've seen in the last ten years."[6]

The most common variation of this kind of generalization-with-support pattern is a simple reversal, putting the general statement at

[6]Russel Kahn, "Russell Francis, Patriot," *Esquire* Dec. 1976: 51.

the end of a list of particulars rather than at the beginning. For example:

Dressed in battered Panama hat, short-sleeved shirt, Bermuda shorts and ancient tennis shoes, he seems most in his element while pottering around the seashore inspecting biological specimens. His evenings are generally spent at home with his wife watching soap operas and sumo wrestling on TV. In conversation, he rarely ventures anything more voluble than *"Ah so desu ka* [Is that so?]?" Such are the salient features of Emperor Hirohito, born as the 124th Imperial Son of Heaven in an unbroken line stretching back 2,643 years. Schooled since birth in the remoteness and reticence that become a deity, Japan's 82-year-old monarch remains to this day as impassive and impenetrable as the stone walls of Tokyo's Imperial Palace.[7]

Another, slightly more subtle variation of the same pattern appears in this paragraph from *Newsweek:*

In Gills Rock, Wis., diving students last week knifed 45 feet into the 38-degree water of Racine Quarry to qualify for the certification card that would enable them to dive anywhere in the world. In northern California's Sierra Nevadas, underwater forty-niners are dredging river bottoms for gold. At the Florida Institute of Technology at Jensen Beach, 170 people have applied for the 100 places available next fall in a two-year-old underwater technology program that qualifies students as commercial divers. And in the unpredictable water off Cape Hatteras, one group is attempting to raise the Civil War ironclad, the U.S.S. *Monitor,* while another is trying to recover Cornwallis's fleet in Yorktown, Va. This week, Columbia Pictures will begin filming Peter Benchley's best-selling book, *The Deep,* about a honeymoon couple who discover a sunken treasure of narcotics in Bermuda.[8]

Here the writers give you the particulars, and the generalization is implied (see "Using Inductive Arguments," Chapter 10). Obviously, however, even though they don't directly state the commitment they

[7]Pico Iyer, "An Enigmatic Still Life," *Time* 1 Aug. 1983: 36.
[8]"Life Under Water," *Newsweek* 12 July 1976: 44.

have made to the reader, they are very much aware of it. Everything in the paragraph illustrates the growing popularity of underwater exploration.

Comparison/Contrast

Another kind of paragraph development that seems to come naturally to most writers is the *comparison/contrast technique.* Useful as a tool of definition (see Chapter 9), it also works well when one wants to discuss both the good and bad points of something in one paragraph; for example:

Uses of comparison and contrast

> Coronary-bypass surgery consumes more of our dollar than any other treatment or procedure. Although it is performed less frequently than the most common abdominal and gynecological operations, it is the leader in terms of equipment and personnel, hospital space, and total associated revenues. The operation is heralded by the popular press, aggrandized by the medical profession, and actively sought by the consuming public. It is the epitome of modern medical technology. Yet as it is now practiced, its net effect on the nation's health is probably negative. The operation does not cure patients, it is scandalously overused, and its high cost drains resources from other areas of need.[9]

This pattern of organization can also be used as the basis for an entire theme.

Another way this method works is by setting up a contrast in the topic sentence of a paragraph and then carrying the pattern through in the other sentences; for instance:

> For generations textbooks and readers and children's books used in our schools have depicted girls as passive observers, boys as bold achievers. Boys have been playing baseball or football while girls watched admiringly, hands clasped behind their backs. Girls were easily frightened; brave boys saved them from danger. Boys made rockets and peered through microscopes; girls played with their dolls and tea cups. Boys have been portrayed as tousled and dirty

[9]Thomas A. Preston, "Marketing an Operation," *The Atlantic* Dec. 1984: 32.

from boisterous contact with life; girls as starched and pinafored, made of sugar and spice and everything nice.[10]

Cause and Effect

Writing about cause and effect is another kind of development that seems to occur to us almost spontaneously because the urge to explain and give reasons is strong in most of us. This way of handling paragraphs is particularly appropriate for expository writing in which one is trying to analyze a situation or philosophy and speculate about consequences. For example:

> The slaves were powerless for two major reasons. Their legal status was that of chattel without rights in court and without the protection of any institution. The master was all-powerful and had the right to control every aspect of slave life from birth to death, from sex to settling disputes. His power was enhanced by additional factors. Black slaves in a predominantly white controlled land were readily identifiable. The slaves were not of a single tribe origin with a long group history and a resultant cohesive bond. They were far from home and generally unwanted except for economic exploitation. They were not able to maintain the organizational elements of their respective previous cultures — kinship ties, family organizations, religion, government, courts, etc. Thus they were not able to run away en masse; to turn in on their own culture for psychological support, or to effectively organize to attack their oppressors.[11]

Cause-and-effect paragraphs may well form the backbone of an argumentative paper. For example, a student arguing for approval of a legislative proposal to increase teachers' pay by 40 per cent based his appeal on the belief that the quality of teachers in the state was going to decline if they did not receive the raise. The opening paragraph went like this:

> If the state legislature does not pass a major pay increase for our public school teachers soon, within a few years all our best college

[10]Dan Lacy, "Men's Words; Women's Roles," *Saturday Review* 14 June 1975: 25.
[11]Hugh Davis and Ted Gurr, *The History of Violence in America* (New York: Bantam, 1969) 451.

graduates will be going into other jobs. Right now an accountant graduating from the university can start work at $20,000 a year. A dietitian working for the state will begin at $16,000. A pharmacist can make from $17,000 to $24,000, depending on where he or she is willing to live. Even technicians with only two years of training earn more in most jobs than the $11,000 that we pay our beginning school teachers. Under these circumstances we can hardly expect able young people to go into teaching.

The pattern is easily reversed; for example:

> They are often called Caspar Milquetoasts by the psychiatrists who try to treat them. They are so timid and fearful of rejection that they find it impossible to cope with many of the ordinary social situations that occur in life. They cannot send back a steak that arrives carbonized when they have ordered it rare; they lack the will to dispute an obvious overcharge on their grocery bills; some are even afraid to ask a stranger what time it is. Not surprisingly, this kind of repressive timidity takes a heavy toll in mental anguish and psychosomatic symptoms, including stomach ulcers, loss of appetite, alcohol and drug dependence, stuttering, high blood pressure and sexual impotence.[12]

Narration

Uses of narration

Writers use narrative paragraphs when they want to recount an event or an experience or when they want to tell a miniature story or an anecdote. Usually they include people in their narration, and they relate the events in straight chronological order. For example:

> Once in a long while, four times so far for me, my mother brings out the metal tube that holds her medical diploma. On the tube are gold circles crossed with seven red lines each — "joy" ideographs in abstract. There are also little flowers that look like gears for a gold machine. According to the scraps of labels with Chinese and American addresses, stamps, and postmarks, the family airmailed the can from Hong Kong in 1950. It got crushed in the

---

[12]"The Timid Souls," *Newsweek* 26 March 1973: 48.

middle, and whoever tried to peel the labels off stopped because the red and gold paint came off too, leaving silver scratches that rust. Somebody tried to pry the end off before discovering that the tube pulls apart. When I open it, the smell of China flies out, a thousand-year-old bat flying heavy-headed out of the Chinese caverns where bats are as white as dust, a smell that comes from long ago, far back in the brain. Crates from Canton, Hong Kong, Singapore, and Taiwan have that smell too, only stronger because they are more recently come from the Chinese.[13]

Here is another kind of narrative paragraph:

They lined up facing the silhouetted targets on a makeshift practice range set up at the Holiday Inn in Santa Monica. Then 50 women and three men took turns firing: ready, aim — spray. "Killed that sucker flat," shouted one woman. "Got him," yelled another. When the two-hour, $35 class at the California Tear Gas School ended, the graduates received official state permits allowing them to carry and use tear gas for self-defense. Most of them departed clutching small gas canisters. "I've had my purse snatched three times," said one middle-aged woman. "If I had this gas I would have used it. I'm getting on a bus right now — and I feel better already."[14]

This kind of paragraph can work especially well as an opening paragraph because its personal tone and concrete language help catch the reader's interest. Narrative paragraphs are also useful when you want to bring in a specific example to illustrate a theoretical point.

Question and Answer

Introducing your topic with a question

Another direct and effective way to get into a paragraph — or a paper — is to ask a question that sets up the topic to be discussed. For example, "Why is it so hard to quit smoking?" or "What is the fascination of television soap operas?" can lead you into a cause-and-effect paragraph. "What is so bad about junk foods?" or "What

[13]Maxine Hong Kingston, *The Woman Warrior: Memoirs of a Girlhood Among Ghosts* (New York: Knopf, 1975) 57.
[14]"Capitalizing on Crime," *Newsweek* 9 March 1981: 66.

kind of people are attracted to drugs?" are good ways to work into a paragraph or definition. Questions can also act as good transitions into paragraphs. For instance, you might start a paragraph of explanation by asking, "How can we meet these problems?" Or you could introduce a paragraph of support by asking, "What is the evidence for such a statement?" A question can also work well in a lead-in to the conclusion of a paper. For example, in an article on the declining popularity of history courses in college, the author introduces the last section by saying, "So what does the future hold for the field of history?"

Question-and-answer paragraphs are useful in expository writing because they allow the writer to focus the reader's attention on the specific issue and thus make it less likely that the reader will get lost. For example:

> So what's wrong with not being able to run around the block or do a dozen pull-ups? Plenty, say those sports physicians and educators who still subscribe to the ancient notion of *mens sana in corpore sana* (a healthy mind in a healthy body). "Sometimes we forget that if a child is not alert and fit, all the education in the world won't provide the benefits we want," says Ray Ciszek of the American Alliance for Health, Physical Recreation and Dance. Ciszek is in good company; no less authorities than Plato and Thomas Jefferson urged students to exercise at least one hour a day. There is also new evidence that sound bodies do help create sound minds. In one Canadian elementary school, children ran, climbed and otherwise exercised vigorously during time taken away from their basic studies. Not only did their fitness levels rise when compared to those in other schools, but so did their scores on language and math tests.[15]

Analogy

A more sophisticated but potentially very useful kind of paragraph that writers can employ for a variety of purposes is one built on an *analogy*. This device, which is covered at some length in Chapter 9, clarifies or expands on an idea or theory by comparing it to something with which the reader is familiar. Here, for example, the author

---

[15]"Failing in Fitness," *Newsweek* 1 April 1985.

of an article about freeze-dried food draws on a memory from her childhood to explain a modern process.

> Even in the dead of Missouri winter, if the day was sunny my grandmother would stand on the back porch, pin socks and shirts to a clothesline looped around a pulley, and haul them out over the snow, piece by piece. The wet clothes froze solid and blew in the wind like cardboard, but when Grandma reeled them back in, they were always dry. As a child, this disappearing act — where did the water go? — seemed magical, and today I'm equally intrigued by a technology based on the same "magic" — freeze-drying. Its scope is far greater than Grandpa's shirts: freeze-dried turkey Tetrazzini and human blood substitute, crocodile heads and largemouth bass. With its range of products both peculiar and practical, freeze-drying still seems magical — a tool that confers almost everlasting shelf life on biological tissue.[16]

Drawing analogies requires some reflection and imagination, but many of us have good material for comparison in our own experiences if we just learn how to look for it. The most ordinary events can furnish references that will help to make ideas concrete. For example, a person who has grown up on a ranch knows that fixing fences is a tedious, grueling, and never-ending job. That knowledge might be worked into a paragraph in this way:

> Anyone who is planning to go into radio and television because he thinks he will have a glamorous and exciting job that will allow him to travel and talk to interesting people should talk to a news reporter at a local station. He will find that being a TV reporter is about as exciting as being a cowboy; making the rounds of the police stations, club meetings, city council meetings, and justice of the peace courts is no more glamorous than going out every day to fix the sags and breaks in a barbed-wire fence.

Almost everyone has an area of expertise; it may be bicycling, cooking, golf, horses, anything. Students who have played football and follow professional and college ball can draw from their store of

[16]Janet Hopson, "The Freeze-drying Technique Makes for Movable Feasts," *Smithsonian* July 1983: 91.

information to set up comparisons. People who have worked in the construction business or waited on tables or helped in a political campaign or taught swimming have special knowledge to draw on for both examples and analogies. Certainly you have the same kind of knowledge about something — perhaps several things — and when you learn to use these resources to illustrate points you want to make in a paper, your writing will become more concrete and more interesting. For example:

Drawing analogies from your own experience

> The first week on a new job that you want desperately to succeed at can be terrifying. You're sure everyone in the office knows more than you do and is just waiting to laugh at you if you make a mistake. You feel ignorant and awkward and confused. But jobs really aren't that different and if you've ever waited table in a restaurant — and done it right — you can handle most other jobs the same way. Start out by listening to the orders people give you. If you're not sure what they want, ask — twice if necessary. Write it down so you won't forget anything, then check off the items as you take care of them. After you've filled the order, don't disappear, but stay close enough to get any new instructions. In a few days you'll find out that coping with the new job is a lot easier than you thought it would be.

Training yourself to think in analogies takes some practice, but if you are going to do much writing, you should try to cultivate the habit. A good analogy is invaluable for clarifying a difficult point. Remember though, that when you do suddenly think of a good comparison, write it down. You'll forget it if you don't.

The Length of Paragraphs

Now let's shift perspectives and look at paragraphs from the outside; that is, let's look at paragraphing from the reader's point of view. When we do that, the first question that arises is "How long should a paragraph be?" As with so many other questions about writing, the answer to that has to be "That depends." It depends on the purpose, the audience, and the tone you are trying to convey in your writing. And the old rule about one idea to one paragraph really doesn't help much when you get down to actual writing situations.

Nevertheless, the two basic principles of paragraphing can give us some guidance. The first of those principles is that writers break their writing into units — sentences, sections, chapters, and parts, as well as paragraphs — in order to help their readers follow their ideas more easily. The second principle — and it also applies to all of the other units except the sentence — is that the function of a paragraph is to develop an idea.

Reasons for dividing writing into paragraphs

Deciding About Paragraph Length

The first principle suggests that in informal writing for the general reader, paragraphs should not be overly long. That vague suggestion means something like not over seven or eight sentences to a paragraph unless good unity really demands extending it beyond that length. In formal, scholarly, or scientific writing, paragraphs may run much longer, but even there the trend is certainly toward the shorter paragraph. A long block of unbroken print does look rather intimidating, after all, and many of us are more inclined to read an article if we see breaks on the page.

The problem is that some newspaper editors and advertising copywriters who worry about the way print will appear in a long column have taken to breaking their articles and ads into one- or two-sentence paragraphs with almost no regard for the continuity of their material. The effect is choppy, distracting, and hard to follow. For example:

Bad effects of one-sentence paragraphs

> Thousands of people every year trade the helter-skelter pace of urban living for the more relaxed schedule of rural life in central Texas.
>
> Most have few regrets, but some find unexpected differences between the two lifestyles more than they bargained for.
>
> Big city residents who wanted to escape the crowded conditions, the rush and high taxes of urban living find they also have left behind a number of services taken for granted in the city.
>
> Lower taxes pay for a lower level of service and the relatively vast areas to be covered make it difficult, if not impossible, to provide high quality service.[17]

This kind of writing jerks the reader from one point to another without benefit of connectors or transitions to tie them together. It also

[17]Steve Hultman, "Home on the Range," *Austin American-Statesman* 18 July 1976: B1.

violates the rock-bottom fundamental of paragraphs: the ideas in them must be developed.

Since students, consciously or not, tend to model their own writing on the kind of writing they are frequently exposed to, many of them have gotten into the habit of writing one-sentence paragraphs without really thinking about what they are doing. To make matters worse, in some journalism classes students are actually being taught to write like this. Unfortunately the result is often a series of unsupported assertions, because when students construct one-sentence paragraphs they are no longer thinking in terms of developing an idea.

So one answer to the question "How long should a paragraph be?" is that it should be long enough to allow the writer to make some response to the commitment made or implied in the topic sentence. The writer who is listing evidence in order to build up to that topic sentence should collect enough data in the paragraph to warrant the conclusion. If the point is being developed by restatement and examples, the writer needs to have enough examples to strengthen the topic sentence and lead to clear rephrasing at the end. One cannot carry out that task in a single sentence and probably not in two.

Paragraphs should be long enough to meet commitment

This is not to say that one should never write a one-sentence paragraph. Occasionally you need them to emphasize a single point that you want to stand out. John F. Kennedy's inaugural address, for instance, has several one-sentence paragraphs listing the gains he expected to make in his administration. In a long narrative essay about the effects of the atom bomb that was dropped on Hiroshima, Alexander Leighton highlights the central event in this one-sentence paragraph:

One-sentence paragraphs used for emphasis

> The bomb exploded several hundred feet above their heads.

And he drives home his conclusion with two one-sentence paragraphs:

> There was one woman in Hiroshima who said, "If there are such things as ghosts, why don't they haunt the Americans?"
> Perhaps they do.[18]

[18]Alexander Leighton, "That Day at Hiroshima," *Atlantic Monthly* Oct. 1946: 90.

Inexperienced writers, however, should use the one-sentence paragraph *very* sparingly, and only when they have a clear idea of why they are using it.

Deciding Where to Break Paragraphs

Guidelines for breaking paragraphs

Finally, how does one know where to break one's writing up into paragraphs? Obviously the answer to that must be that even professionals don't know precisely where divisions should come. The old rule of thumb is to start a new paragraph when you start discussing a new idea, but often adequate development of even one idea can require several paragraphs, so we need a more specific guideline. Perhaps the only useful one is that you can break a paragraph when you are introducing a new idea or when you find a time or space separation or a slight shift in direction.

Notice, for instance, that the following paragraph could be broken at two places without violating the unity of the ideas. One break could come after the third sentence, and a new paragraph could start with "Everyone likes the way he looks, though: magnetic, exotic." Another break could come after the following five sentences, starting a new paragraph with "There is no player with faster reflexes or greater speed." In the rest of the passage, however, the sentences seem so closely tied to each other that it would be difficult to find a logical division point.

But the fans love him [Ilie Nastase] — and those who don't, love to hate him. Which is part of his draw but much of his trouble. They hooted and hollered at him during the Pohmann match like drunks at a bearbaiting; even many of the players felt sorry for him. Everyone likes the way he looks, though: magnetic, exotic. He walks like a jaguar, has the eyes of a gypsy, the body of Apollo. And his game is an amalgam of all that is spectacular in tennis. He has Manuel Santana's top-spin lob and is at times a mirror image of Rod Laver — he has a strong first serve, a good volley and two or three ground strokes to follow them up. He has, of course, all of Pancho Gonzalez' chair-throwing, ball-slamming anger. He plays closer to the net and with greater effectiveness than almost any other player on the tour; his attacks from the base line are devastating. There is no player with faster reflexes or greater speed. He has an exquisite touch with a racket, a feel for the ball that cannot be learned. It is how Gordie Howe caresses a hockey puck. He can break his wrist in ways that would fracture another player's, masking his top spin until the last instant. He plays against the movement of his opponent. He is simply breathtaking to watch.[19]

Certainly current writers are showing more and more inclination to favor the short paragraph. It seems easier to read and is probably also easier to write because one does not have to concentrate for as long at a time. But don't just arbitrarily chop your writing into little segments that may look like paragraphs but are really only groups of sentences put together without unity or development. Be sure each paragraph acts as a small unit of thought, a discernible block in the larger structure of the essay.

Opening Paragraphs

Opening paragraphs bear a heavy load because a reader expects so much from them. Most readers want the first paragraphs of an essay to do three things:

The functions of opening paragraphs

1. Catch the reader's attention.
2. Make a promise or a commitment that tells the reader what to expect from the rest of the essay.
3. Show the reader why he or she should continue to read.

As one British language expert puts it, we get started in both writing and reading by moving along tracks that have already been laid down,[20] and a key function of opening paragraphs is to lay those tracks.

But even though readers know what they want from opening paragraphs, it's hard to generalize about what kind of paragraph best meets those needs. For, once more, you can't really make intelligent decisions about what kind of opening paragraph you need until you

[19]Eric Lax, "Nasty!" *Esquire* March 1977: 98.
[20]James Britton, "The Functions of Writing," *Research in Composing*, ed. Charles Cooper and Lee Odell (Urbana: NCTE, 1978) 24.

have defined your audience and your purpose. (Later in this section there will be suggestions about adapting your introductions to your audience and your purpose.) Good opening paragraphs, however, nearly always share one characteristic: they make a commitment to the reader. They raise expectations, either directly or subtly, and establish a contract with the reader. For the rest of the essay, the writer's chief concern should be to meet that commitment, to carry out that contract.

Most opening paragraphs make commitments

Your Commitment to the Reader

The need for you as a writer to realize that you have an obligation to live up to the commitment you make to your audience is so crucial to good writing that it is worth explaining more fully. When you begin to write a paper or an article you make — or very strongly imply — a promise to the readers. Usually, but not always, you make that promise in the first sentence of a paragraph or the first paragraph of a paper. By that promise you bind yourself to explain and support a statement or to give more information on a topic. By reading your promise, readers learn what to expect. If they are not interested, they don't read any further. If they do read beyond the first sentence or paragraph, they expect you to do what you said you would do. If you disappoint them, you have not lived up to your part of the bargain.

Next time you read an article in a magazine or a newspaper, notice the opening paragraph. Almost always it — or the second paragraph — will tell you what is going to be discussed and even give you some idea of the author's attitude toward the topic. To illustrate the point, here are three short examples from magazines that usually feature good writing:

Stripped down to his protective groin guard and the smirk of triumph that flickered across his scraggly face, [boxer] Roberto Duran slumped in his dressing-room chair with the exhausted arrogance of a man fulfilled. Like some ancient Mayan king, Duran casually demanded a breeze. Aides quickly began flapping towels through the sticky air around him. Then he snapped in Spanish, "I need more room." And the well-wishers scurried from his side. Friday night in Montreal, even more than on all the other 70 sweaty nights of victory in his career, Roberto Duran got everything he wanted.[21]

Readers who begin this article instantly expect to find out what happened on the night of the big fight in Montreal. And they do.

> Jim Swain is an automotive engineer. In his files is a detailed proposal for a mid-sized car that carries four adults comfortably, is half the weight of most intermediate-sized cars, travels 80 miles or more on a gallon of gasoline, and might be sticker priced around $7500 — all with today's technology. So why doesn't anyone want to build it?[22]

The reader immediately assumes that the author of the article will explain why the person who conceived this apparently great idea hasn't developed it. And he does.

> Mexico City has its faults; its residents live under the constant threat of earthquakes, and the city regularly experiences tremors and occasional minor quakes. But it is the man-made disasters, rather than the natural ones, that threaten to destroy the city which has been called the Paris of the Western Hemisphere.[23]

The readers who start this article expect to learn how Mexico City has deteriorated in the past years. And they do.

Although these writers have the professional polish that no one expects from a student, it is the method, not the style, that is crucial here. And it is as important for you to let your reader know what you are going to do, and then do it, as it is for professional journalists. Well, almost as important — if they don't do it, they will soon be out of a job.

Making a commitment to your audience and then following through on that commitment with explanation and details are so basic to day-to-day communication that usually we don't even think about the process. When we open a conversation with "San Francisco is a great city" or "Inflation will be a crucial issue in the next

[21]Pete Axthelm, "The Big Brawl in Montreal," *Newsweek* 30 June 1980: 40.
[22]Ben Daviss, "Battelle Has a Better Idea," *Science 85* April 1985: 40.
[23]George Natanson, "Mexico City Is the Most Uninhabitable City in the World," *Texas Monthly* Sept. 1975: 79.

election," our audience expects us to follow through with supporting details, and ordinarily we have no trouble doing so because we already know what our reasons are for making the assertion. And if we forget to give our reasons, our audience will remind us of the lapse by saying, "Why do you say that?" or "What do you mean?" In writing, however, we often have to remind ourselves that we need to follow up on our commitment.

Varieties of Opening Paragraphs

The Straightforward Announcement   Anyone writing a technical or business report should begin with a direct, clear, carefully organized statement that lets the reader know exactly what to expect: no tricks, gimmicks, anecdotes, or unnecessary preliminaries. And in general this rule applies to letters of application for scholarships and fellowships, grant proposals, reports of experiments or surveys, and autobiographies or statements of goals written to send with applications. The audience for these kinds of documents wants facts, stated quickly and economically; it does not want opinions or generalities. So with any writing that is strictly informative, the best introduction is one that goes straight to the point. For example:

> I am writing to apply for the position of shop foreman that you advertised in Sunday's *Times-Herald*.

> I would like to be considered for the four-year scholarship in tax law and accounting that your firm offers to an Illinois high school graduate every year.

> My name is Joanna Benson. As a native Georgian and recent honors graduate of Emory University, I meet the requirements for a graduate fellowship.

> This paper is a preliminary report of the findings of the Minnesota Council on Child Abuse, appointed by the governor in 1975 to do a two-year study of child abuse in the Minneapolis–St. Paul area.

> This report will be an analysis of the data collected in twenty-four experiments conducted with rats from September 10 through September 17, 1976, in Skinner boxes in the psychology laboratories of Purdue University.

Notice that there are no colorful adjectives in any of these sentences. The sentences that make up the rest of these opening paragraphs should follow the same pattern of giving pertinent information in an objective tone, and each should carry out the commitment to give supporting information that the opening sentence implies.

There is nothing wrong with using a direct and simple introductory paragraph for nontechnical papers written for a variety of audiences and purposes. It can frequently do well the two things that any opening paragraph should do: get the readers' attention and give them a reason to continue reading. For example:

Last year there were fifty million unwanted dogs and cats in the United States and despite the efforts of humane societies to dispose of strays and persuade people to neuter their pets, this animal population continues to grow. The results are pathetic and sometimes frightening. In many cities, one often sees big dogs wandering in packs searching for food. Bought for protection but abandoned when they proved too costly or troublesome to keep, they pose a menace to tame animals and even to small children.

The cheating scandal that erupted at West Point in the spring of 1976 raised once more the question of whether the United States service academies can continue to hold their cadets to strict honor codes. Lawyers for the West Point cadets who have been charged allege that cheating is far more widespread than the academy authorities will admit. They maintain that up to half of the graduating class is involved and that all of them should be dismissed from the service if that penalty is imposed on those who have admitted their guilt.

Explicit, no-nonsense opening paragraphs like these get the reader's attention by pointing out a problem; anyone who is interested in that problem will continue reading for more information and suggestions about ways to solve it. Not only are such introductions courteous to the reader in that they don't waste time, but also they are fairly easy to write. Once you have made up your mind to just say it like it is, you can usually break through that barrier of inertia that stymies all efforts to get started.

The Anecdote or Narrative   Often you can catch your reader's interest and establish a commitment to hold it by starting with a narrative paragraph that creates a picture or sketches out a situation. For example:

Early on a crisp October morning, pilot Dan Kettle and I clattered across the high desert country of central Idaho in a small, turbocharged helicopter with a big Plexiglas bubble. We were searching for wild horses, and soon two bands of them materialized directly below us. With their long shadows, they looked like small ships sailing on a sage-green sea. We dropped toward them with a nauseating lurch and they began to run. I picked out our target, a sorrel stud with stocking legs and a telltale white patch on his side, and when he broke clear of the others we stayed right behind him. I leaned out of the bubble, aimed my gun at his left flank, and squeezed the trigger. *Pop!* A brilliant orange splotch exploded harmlessly on the animal's hide just before he disappeared into a stand of timber, another pony painted for science.[24]

This skillful writer has created a vivid action picture for his readers to arouse their interest in the wild horses, even adding a little suspense and drama to the paragraph.

Another example is from a student paper:

You have donned all of your equipment and are ready to go overboard. Taking a few short puffs of air from your regulator to make sure your equipment is working properly, you enter the sea by taking a giant stride off the boat. As the bubbles clear you find yourself suspended weightlessly above a beautiful tropical reef. Below, you might see basket sponges as large as an oil drum and a sea fan as wide as you are tall. Brightly colored corals are everywhere. From under a coral head a spiny lobster waves his long antennae at you much like a swordsman might threaten his opponent. And all around you are multicolored fish moving about totally undisturbed by your presence in their watery realm.

This writer draws his reader into his essay on scuba diving by beginning with a colorful narrative of descending into the water.

[24]John Turner, Jr., "Given a Free Rein, Prolific Mustangs Gallop into Trouble," *Smithsonian* Feb. 1984: 88.

Other Kinds of Openers   Another standard way of leading into an expository or persuasive essay is to ask a question in your first paragraph. For example:

> Is public broadcasting nearly dead? The casual PBS viewer, who has seen the quality and variety of public TV programs improve over the years, may be stunned to learn that right now this is an urgent question. In the corridors of local public stations everywhere and in the system's seats of power in Washington, there's talk of a rapidly approaching doomsday for public television. The suddenly looming villain: cable TV.[25]

Notice that this opener focuses the reader's attention on the issue to be discussed, and it also makes a strong commitment to explain how cable TV is threatening public television.

Another frequently used opener is the appropriate quotation or reference to a news item, but for a student, unless you happen to know where to lay your hand on the news item or actually know the quotation well enough so that you only have to check the source, it is probably not worth taking the time to dig something out. Searching for a reference to fit your idea usually isn't practical.

Poor Opening Paragraphs

Two problems often mark opening paragraphs that don't work well. One is that the writer strings together a series of generalities that do little more than state the obvious. The reader quickly becomes bored and impatient; if possible, he or she probably quits reading. Here is a student paragraph that illustrates this problem:

> There are many things about college which are much different than high school. It is really hard to put in words. You would need to be part of it to really know what I am talking about exactly. There is so much difference between such things as study habits, clothes, people, athletics, and other things also.

A second major fault of opening paragraphs is that they fail to make a commitment, fail to let the reader know what to expect. Here

[25]Peter Caranicas, "Can PBS Survive Cable?" *Saturday Review* Jan. 1981: 36.

is a fairly typical example of such a failure, which also incorporates the first fault, rambling generalities:

America is the best-fed nation in the world. Our country is, after all, a very prosperous nation. Our food supply is sufficient, even abundant. Our farmers utilize the most modern, efficient techniques to increase harvests. Our educators and physicians are top-notch, and our technology is superior. Our dilemma is that the advanced techniques that furnish us with quick, convenient, time-saving, instant foods also allow nutrients to be lost and discarded during this food processing. The refining and processing of almost every food cause the loss of much or all of its nutritive value. However, highly refined foods keep better than do natural foods; they are easier to store and to ship. On the other hand, being fed with refined foods does not make a nation "best-fed."

These paragraphs have much in common: both are repetitious and vague; they give the reader no facts or concrete details; and they don't tell the reader what to expect from the rest of the paper. The authors are really just warming up, getting ready for the real thing, like golfers practicing their swings or a football team doing jumping jacks and knee bends before the first play is called. This kind of writing might also be likened to a dog turning round and round several times getting ready to lie down. Such exercises may be useful as part of prewriting — they are at least preferable to staring at a piece of blank paper — but they should be cut out of the final paper. They bore the reader, and they contribute nothing to the development of the main idea.

Two other kinds of introductions that students would do well to avoid are the overworked leadoff with a dictionary definition or obvious fact — "Lyndon Johnson was the thirty-seventh president of the United States" — and starting off with a summary of background material that is either trivial or irrelevant. For example, avoid an autobiography that begins like this:

My birth took place in St. Paul's Hospital in Dallas, Texas. I have been told that I was a happy, healthy baby whose greatest feats were walking at seven months old and talking at an early age. The childhood memories I still retain are mostly happy. They consist mainly of my family and the carefree moments of play I enjoyed with my younger brothers and sisters as well as with the other children of the neighborhood.

It is painful to think how an admissions board would react to this application.

Finally, remember that there is not a thing wrong with writing your introduction last. Professional writers frequently work that way, because after they have finished an article they know better how they want to introduce it. An added bonus of waiting until last to write the introductory paragraph is that you may find you really don't need one. Rereading may show that you have said everything you want to say and the paper doesn't need any opening ruffles and flourishes. This is particularly true of short papers. For them, beginning with a single sentence that gives your main assertion often does the job quite well. Don't feel compelled to add any trimmings.

Concluding Paragraphs

After reading through scores of closing paragraphs in a wide variety of essays, both amateur and professional, I can only conclude that one cannot safely generalize about what makes a good conclusion. Again, it depends on whom you are writing for and what your purpose is. If you are doing a report, particularly a long one for a business group or a class, you should summarize your main points in the conclusion. If you are trying to persuade your audience to accept an idea or an opinion, you should probably restate your thesis at the end, just as a trial lawyer would sum up a case for a jury. Sometimes signal transition phrases such as *"Finally,"* *"Thus,"* *"In conclusion,"* or *We can then"* are good openers for a last paragraph. And remember that for short papers, you may not even need a last paragraph. One sentence that seems to tie up loose ends will frequently do the job.

Although it is difficult to give any positive guidelines for writing those painful last paragraphs, two warnings about what *not* to do in conclusions may be useful. First, don't keep on writing after you have actually finished what you have to say. When you are through, stop. It is better to be a little abrupt than to risk boring your audience with mere repetition or a statement of the obvious. Remember how many times you have thought, "If the speaker had just quit ten minutes earlier, it would have been a much better speech." So stop while you still have your audience's attention.

Second, resist the temptation to indulge in platitudes or nice-sounding generalities at the end. For some reason — perhaps because conclusions *are* hard to write or because theme outlines always call for conclusions — inexperienced writers often end up with what might be called *pious-platitude* or *noble-sentiment endings*. They don't really have any more to say, but they want to add something that sounds good. Feeling reasonably sure that no one could object to what is obviously "right thinking," they tack on paragraphs like these, the first written for an assignment about the generation gap.

> Today the generation gap still goes on; there will probably always be one. Nevertheless, steps have been taken to bridge that gap. If we cannot close it, we must work harder, both young and old, to make the gap as small as possible. Only in that way can we make this a better world to live in.

This closing paragraph came at the end of a paper about the role of the American business person abroad:

> The American businessman must realize that he can protect our American heritage. He is the only one who can preserve capitalism and free enterprise. America possesses a great society and economic woes must not destroy it. By having a government of the people and for the people, America can remain a world power and not fall in to being a second rate country.

Conclusions like these, which sound as if they could have been manufactured by a computer stocked with clichés, make their authors sound embarrassingly naive.

Finally, all one can really say about concluding paragraphs, whether for essays, stories, or books, is that they should give the reader a sense of closure, a feeling that the writer has finished saying what he or she started out to say. The best conclusions, like the best transitions, grow out of the structure of the writing, and ideally you shouldn't have to point out to the reader that you are stopping. But ideals are hard to achieve, and conclusions remain hard to write. My only advice is to keep tinkering until they look right.

Exercises

1. What kind of commitment are the authors of these opening paragraphs from magazine articles making to their readers?

a. Shrimping in the Gulf has never been a calling men pursued for the fun of it — or for the easy money. Oh, there was plenty of money to be made once: the lowliest deckhand could return from a fifteen-day trip with $3000 in his pocket. But the work was brutal and, most of all, lonely: two or four or six weeks on a pitching boat in the middle of the hostile ocean. Shrimp are elusive creatures, apt to change their feeding grounds from year to year, and some years the shrimpers never quite figured out where they were. Those were the years of frustrating summers and lean winters. And then in the good years the crew could work themselves near to death, hauling up the writhing beasts by the ton, working around the clock to get them decapitated and iced down before the sun had a chance to make them spoil.[26]

b. Despite all the current fuss and bother about the extraordinary number of ordinary illiterates who overpopulate our schools, small attention has been given to another kind of illiterate, an illiterate whose plight is, in many ways, more important, because he is more influential. This illiterate may, as often as not, be a university president, but he is typically a Ph.D., a successful professor and textbook author. The person to whom I refer is the straight-A illiterate, and the following is written in an attempt to give him equal time with his widely publicized counterparts.[27]

c. Many observers have concluded from the news coverage of the past year — the Reagan sweep, the disarray of political liberalism, the tighter constraints of our economy, the emergence of fundamentalist groups opposed to the ERA, abortion, and sex education — that the United States is swinging back to the disciplined, self-sacrificing habits that ruled American life before the heyday of affluence. But that inference is incorrect. Tomorrow is not going to look like yesterday. In fact, tomorrow — to the extent that research data can yield clues about it — is being shaped by a cultural revolution that is transforming the rules of American life and moving us into a wholly uncharted territory, not

[26]Victoria Loe, "Shrimpers," *Texas Monthly* April 1981: 128–29.
[27]James P. Degnan, "Masters of Babble," *Harper's* Sept. 1976: 37.

back into the lifestyles of the past. Irreversible in its effects, this cultural revolution is as fateful to our future as any changes in the economy or politics.[28]

2. Write from three to five sentences that would adequately fulfill the commitment made in one of these opening sentences for paragraphs:

a. Swimming is a particularly good form of exercise.

b. Television commercials seem to be at their worst during the evening news programs.

c. In my opinion, we must defeat the incumbent senator.

d. Some critics feel that a college education is not necessarily a good investment.

3. Rewrite the following two paragraphs to make them smoother and more coherent. Begin each one with a topic sentence that will serve as a guideline for developing the rest of the paragraph.

a. All too often young people enter into the bond of marriage without considering the future financial situations that can arise. One such problem is self-supported education. College educations are expensive, and one or both partners may have to work. This results in separation of the couple. Further separation is caused by the many hours that have to be spent studying and doing homework. Working eight hours a day, going to school, and studying leave very little time for the couple to spend together. Most jobs require the student to devote his full attention to the work being done. Little time is left, therefore, for his studies.

b. "I did not know I was eligible to enter the university." This is what Eddie Jones said to his high school counselor when he was told his grades met the university entrance requirements. Eddie is an average student who believed the myth that our university is only for smart people. Many students fail to apply simply because they are uninformed about its requirements. Minority students are the most uninformed about their opportunities. I think

[28]Daniel Yankelovich, "New Rules in American Life: Searching for Self-Fulfillment in a World Turned Upside Down," *Psychology Today* April 1981: 35–36.

all minority students would be able to attend the university. At other colleges drives to enlarge enrollments always succeed in increasing the number of students. Therefore, concerted drives should be made to bring more minority students to this university.

4. Evaluate the following opening paragraphs from student themes. What are your reasons for thinking they are successful or not successful?

a. You have hardly stepped out of your building, and what do you see? Runners. Spread a picnic in the park and there they are again. Their races are televised, their faces sell credit cards and cereal. Can you even cross the street without being trampled? Maybe you once thought running was all a quirky fad that would pack its bags and fade away one night. But now that over 25 million Americans run regularly, how much longer can you ignore the tiny little voice inside that nags, "Shouldn't I join them?"

b. Pornography should not be banned because people are basically curious. Almost every animal is curious, and people are not any exception. A child that has recently reached puberty will be increasingly curious about the opposite sex. Curiosity is the basis for human progression. Humans must be curious in order to search into the truth of the unknown.

c. In the United States, education is considered a right and thus is tax supported so that all children in this country can have the opportunity to go to school. Our children's education is not neglected because parents do not have enough money. Education is even more than a right, for children are required by law to attend school to a certain age. But is health care a right? No, good health care is the privilege of those who have the money to pay the bills.

d. Nearly 250 years ago on the green and brown slopes of a volcano, Vesuvius, on the west coast of Italy, a young peasant farmer plowed in his field. The sun's early morning rays cast his long shadow on the dark, moist soil, and white clouds covered the dark, wide mouth of Vesuvius. Below, the blue sea sparkled and shivered in the Bay of Naples. The peasant was plodding along in his usual morning routine, when suddenly his plow scraped against a solid object. He bent to remove what he thought was only a rock and jumped in surprise when he saw bright and vivid colors glaring at him through the black, fertile dirt. Brushing aside the soil, he pulled from the ground a beautiful vase of very fine quality. He stared in amazement and awe at the scene he saw painted so delicately on the vase.

5. Analyze the commitment the writer has made in the opening paragraph of this student paper. What is it, and how does she meet it? Then analyze the way the writer develops her paragraphs, paying particular attention to the strategy of *downshifting*.

Responsible Drinking Tips for the College-Bound

You're entering college; no parents in sight. You're making your own decisions now, and one of your first will invariably concern drinking. According to the National Institute on Alcohol Abuse and Alcoholism, nearly 90 per cent of college women drink alcohol. Yet, a haze of uncertainty may cloud your decisions. How does alcohol affect your body? Will you react differently to alcohol than a man? Answering such questions requires a working knowledge of alcohol that you may lack. Knowing the facts on alcohol and how you differ as a woman will enhance your college drinking and make you not only a more mature drinker but also a healthier one.

College abounds in opportunities to socialize, and students often use alcohol to enhance these times. You may not realize, though, that alcohol is a depressant drug similar to barbiturates and ether in effect, suppressing the nervous system and affecting every body organ. Alcohol bypasses digestion and directly enters the bloodstream from the stomach and small intestine. Rising percentages of alcohol in your bloodstream affect your reason and reaction time, your speech and vision, and finally, if you consume it in large quantities, your involuntary functions of breathing and heart rate. In short, drinking can temporarily render you physically and mentally incompetent. Drinkers rarely consider this, though, because when they drink, oftentimes they feel falsely confident, especially habitual drinkers. The Texas Commission on Alcoholism reports that in tests measuring speed of motor response, auditory and visual discrimination, object preparation, and finger coordination, habitual drinkers "proved as impaired as inexperienced drinkers even though the former appeared almost completely sober." You might feel "normal" after you've had a few drinks, but chances are your body's more affected than you realize.

Many people drink to escape their problems or when they're lonely and depressed, hoping that the alcohol will lift their spirits and give them a lightened feeling of euphoria. Alcohol does produce a temporary euphoria, often causing people to feel less inhibited, but because it's a sedative or "downer," the unhappy person frequently feels worse after he or she drinks. Your body's ability to tolerate alcohol, too, fluctuates depending on your mood, attitude, and past drinking experience. If you're tired and upset, alcohol will affect you more than at times when you're happy and relaxed.

More than emotions, though, how fast you drink those couple of beers determines their effect. The body processes approximately one-half ounce of alcohol per hour, so if you stick to a drink an hour, you'll give your body time to metabolize or process the alcohol, and you'll feel few effects from drinking. Once alcohol enters the bloodstream, though, only time can offset its effects. Women take longer than men to process alcohol because their bodies have less body fluid and more body fat. Alcohol can't diffuse as rapidly into body fat, so the concentration of alcohol in your blood stays higher longer. Moreover, alcohol may affect you more right before your period, so pay particular attention then to know when your body's had enough.

You may have heard that you won't get as drunk on beer as on hard liquor like gin — don't believe it. That certain types of alcohol are less potent than others remains a prevalent drinking myth. Generally speaking, drinking one beer (12 ounces) is the same as drinking a glass of wine (5 ounces) or one drink of liquor (1 ounce). Each contains about a half ounce of ethanol. What it means to "be drunk" is equally misunderstood. Legally, you are drunk when your blood alcohol concentration reaches .10 per cent or 1 part alcohol per 1000 parts blood. For a 120-pound woman, that's three to four drinks in a relatively short time. Vitamins, cold showers, and stimulants (like the caffeine in coffee) can't cure your intoxication, no matter what some people say. You may feel more awake, but you'll still be drunk.

Even though you can't regulate how quickly your body processes alcohol once it's in the bloodstream, you *can* alter the rate at which the bloodstream absorbs it. If you're drinking, plan on eating, too. Choose high-protein, high-fat foods such as meats, cheeses, and nuts. A midnight pizza goes great with a late-night beer, but if you haven't the bucks for a pizza, peanuts from the local machine work equally well. Food slows the absorption of alcohol into your circulatory system and helps buffer its impact on the body. Have you ever heard, too, that when you drink too much you'll get a headache? That's because alcohol robs body cells of water. Though you feel like you're consuming lots of liquids, your body actually is dehydrating. To avoid this, try drinking a glass of water along with your beer, alternating after finishing one or the other. Choose water or fruit mixers, too, over carbonated drinks like Cokes because carbonation speeds absorption while water and orange juice dilute the alcohol and slow its entry into the bloodstream.

A large percentage of college students drink, and drinking may be something you want to experience on your own, but responsible drinking only heightens the pleasures of alcohol and makes the times you do decide to drink more enjoyable. Remembering that alcohol is a drug best used slowly and in combination with food and other drink will make you not only a smarter drinker but also a safer and healthier one.

Lynn Favour

Writing Assignments

Paper 1

A good way to find out more about the career you might want to pursue is to write about it. Suppose that the director of the career placement center on your campus is putting together a collection of short papers that explain various careers and will pay fifty dollars for the best paper on each career. She plans to publish the papers in a loose-leaf notebook that will be available to any student who comes to the center hoping to find out about a specific profession. You have been asked to submit a paper of no more than 750 words on a career in which you are especially interested.

Your paper should be quite specific, covering at least these points: the primary activities of the career, the personal qualities that are important in this kind of career, the type and length of training required, salary ranges, long-range opportunities in the field, and the advantages and disadvantages of the profession.

Your audience will be other students who want to know more about the career, but it will also be the director of the career placement center. She wants interesting and informative papers that are well written, accurate, and filled with effective and engaging personal examples. So it is important that you invest some time in your topic and do research if necessary; several personal interviews could be useful. And if you know someone who is active in the career you are writing about, you can cite that person as an example.

Before you start your paper, write out an analysis of your audience, specifying what they hope to get from reading your paper and what questions they would have when they began to read. Also write out a purpose analysis: what do you hope to accomplish with this paper?

Possible Topics

1. An obstetrician or surgeon
2. A civil engineer
3. A television camera person
4. A marine biologist
5. A newspaper or magazine editor
6. A landscape architect
7. A paralegal aid
8. A psychologist
9. An economist
10. A sports announcer

Paper 2

Your campus newspaper puts out a weekend supplement section that features articles submitted by students on issues or problems of special interest at your school. The articles can be no more than 750 words long, must be on fairly serious topics, and must show that the writer has some first-hand knowledge or immediate concern about the issue or problem discussed. It is helpful, although not absolutely necessary, for the writer to make some specific suggestions about how the issue or problem might be dealt with.

This kind of paper gives you the chance to begin your paper with a personal anecdote or short dramatic opening paragraph that will catch your readers' attention and set the context for your paper. (See some of the sample opening paragraphs in this chapter.)

Before you begin the main part of your paper, write out an analysis of your audience. What information do they already have about the issue or problem, why are they interested in it, and what questions do they hope to have answered by your paper? Also write out a statement of purpose: what do you hope to accomplish with the paper?

Possible Topics

1. Poor on-campus study and meeting facilities for students who live at home and commute to campus every day.
2. The problems that exist because many freshman classes at your school are taught by part-time instructors who do not have offices or access to departmental services; or the problems caused by many departments' using graders or teaching assistants who speak and write English poorly.
3. The problem caused because recent cuts in funding have forced the Bible study center on campus to discontinue its free Sunday night suppers and discussion groups for students.
4. The issue of bicycle theft on campus.
5. The problem of frequent automobile accidents among students returning to campus after attending off-campus clubs and fraternity parties where beer is served illegally.

CHAPTER 4

7 · Concrete Words, Jargon, and Sexist Language

CHAPTER

How do writers choose words that best convey their meaning and achieve the effect they want on their readers? No one can give a simple answer to that question because there are no sure-fire formulas for creativity, but we do have some knowledge about how people respond to language, knowledge that can help writers choose the combinations of words that will make their writing clear, strong, and effective.

Abstract/Concrete and General/Specific Language

It's useful for any writer to learn to distinguish between concrete and abstract language and to develop a sense about when one should use concrete words and when one needs abstract ones.

Distinguishing between abstract and concrete words

Abstract words are those that refer to ideas, qualities, attitudes, and characteristics. They refer to concepts we know only intellectually, not through our senses. The term *loyalty* is abstract; so are *tolerance, accountability, existentialism, victory, patriotism,* and any other word that stands for something we cannot see or experience. *Concrete* words, in contrast, refer to objects, living creatures, and physical characteristics and activities. *Swimming* and *bicycling* are concrete words; so are *parrot, shuttle bus, pink, rough, tree, ice,* and other words that make us think of something we can see, taste, feel, smell, or hear. In general, we *conceive* the abstract through our minds; we *perceive* the concrete through our senses.

Definitions like these are useful, but they are also oversimplified. We cannot just call a word "abstract" or "concrete" and be finished with it; we must also recognize degrees and levels within each category. For example, *house* is a concrete term, but it is much less concrete than *two-story red-brick Colonial home; illness* is a concrete word,

but it is not as concrete as *typhoid fever* or *pneumonia. Philosophy* is more abstract than *existentialism,* and *literature* is more abstract than *poetry* or *drama.* In his book *Language in Thought and Action* the semanticist S. I. Hayakawa illustrates the concept of word levels by setting up a ladder of abstraction with steps moving from the most concrete to the least concrete and simultaneously from the least specific to the most specific. Such a ladder looks like this:

6. ethical philosophies
5. religion
4. Christianity
3. Protestantism
2. the Baptist Church
1. the First Baptist Church of Canton, Ohio

Distinguishing between general and specific words

In talking about language, it is also important to distinguish between *general* and *specific* words. General words refer to large groups or broad categories; for example, *people* and *country* are general words. Specific words refer to individuals, items, particular groups, or particular cases; for example, Maya Angelou refers to a specific individual, and Guatemala refers to a specific country. And just as there are levels of abstraction, there are levels of generality, and words can be arranged on a scale. For instance:

7. Creative people
6. Artists
5. Authors
4. English writers
3. Sixteenth-century dramatists
2. Elizabethan playwrights
1. William Shakespeare

"Creative people" represents the broadest class, and as we move down the scale of generality, we encounter words that represent smaller and more specific groups. At the bottom is a single individual of the class.

Using Abstract and General Words

Although writers are constantly told to "be concrete" and "use specific examples," all of us must frequently use abstract and general language if we are to talk about anything more significant than the price of gasoline and who did what to whom. In order to discuss values, beliefs, and theories we have to use conceptual, abstract language. Thus, sentences like "An unshakable belief that private enterprise leads to the exploitation of the working classes is fundamental to Marxist theory" and "Some ethical philosophers hold that all moral values are merely expressions of cultural preferences" are necessary kinds of statements. Furthermore, it is broadly true that the more knowledge we have and the more complex our thinking becomes, the more we have to depend on abstract words to express ourselves. We must expect, therefore, that much of our communication about ideas will use words taken from the upper levels of the abstraction ladder.

Highly abstract writing makes dull reading

Too often, however, inexperienced writers — and sometimes even experienced ones — fall into the trap of identifying abstract language with intellectual achievement and the pursuit of knowledge. As a result, they think that in order to make their writing sound "academic" and impress their readers, they must use abstract words. But writing that is overloaded with abstractions is apt to be dull and difficult to read. Thus, writers need to remember that in order to hold their readers' attention, they also need to use concrete and specific language so their readers can *see* and *feel* the force of their words.

The Advantages of Concrete and Specific Words

Adding a visual element to your writing

Successful professional writers have learned to give their writing this visual, concrete quality by using specific examples that help their readers form images in their minds as they read. For instance, if they start an article or a paragraph with an abstract statement, often they downshift immediately into concrete and specific illustrations, as James Trefil does here:

> Like all scientific theories, the theories about the Big Bang have to be tested. How do you prove that something was hot many billions of years ago? Well, how can you tell if there has been a fire in a fireplace recently? If you came into a room and saw coals glowing red hot, you would conclude that there had been a fire not too long ago. If the coals were dull orange, you would still know that there had been a fire, but that more time had elapsed since the flames died down. The duller the glow, the longer the

time interval. Even if the coals were not glowing, you could hold your hand over them and see if you felt any heat.[1]

The Concept of Presence in Writing

Trefil uses concrete and visual language to give *presence* or immediacy to his subject matter. By appealing to his readers' senses, he brings it to life for them. To illustrate how presence works, one communications expert cites an example from an ancient Chinese tale:

> A king sees an ox on its way to sacrifice. He is moved to pity for it and orders that a sheep be used in its place. He confesses he did so because he could see the ox, but not the sheep.[2]

Giving presence to your writing

This tale illustrates a powerful truth: we become more concerned about animals and people when we can see them because they become real to us. That is why television programs about starving children cause a great surge in donations for food programs. And that is why writers who want to catch and hold their readers' attention should at least occasionally use concrete, visual examples.

The author of the following paragraph about conditions in underdeveloped countries missed an opportunity to add presence to his writing by giving concrete examples of conditions in those countries. Instead, he has written a totally abstract paragraph:

> There may be no realistic hope of the present underdeveloped countries reaching the standard of living demonstrated by the present industrialized nations. . . . Noting the destruction that has already occurred on land, in the air, and especially in the oceans, capability appears not to exist for handling such a rise in standard of living. In fact, the present disparity between the developed and underdeveloped nations may be equalized as much by a decline in the developed countries as by an improvement in the underdeveloped countries. A society with a high level of industrialization may be nonsustainable.[3]

[1]James S. Trefil, "Closing in on Creation," *Smithsonian* May 1983: 33.
[2]Quoted in Chaim Perelman, *The Realm of Rhetoric* (Notre Dame: U of Notre Dame P, 1982) 35.
[3]Jay W. Forrester, *World Dynamics* (Cambridge, MA: Wright-Allen, 1971) 12. Quoted in Arthur Herzog, *The B. S. Factor* (New York: Simon, 1973) 44.

Concrete Words, Jargon, and Sexist Language

The paragraph is by no means incomprehensible to an intelligent reader who is willing to work at it, but it is difficult and dull, primarily because there are no concrete examples in it. As you read it, your mind wanders because nothing in the passage appeals to the senses or calls up an image. Writing like this is not merely dull, it is literally lifeless.

Fortunately, student writing seldom reaches an extreme level of impersonality and dryness. Too many students, however, succumb to the notion that college writers should use stiff, abstract language. Thus, in their effort to be formal and rise to new expectations, they produce sentences like these:

It is required that regular school attendance be observed by everyone.

Compulsory school attendance is a general law that is nationally observed.

The concept of compulsory school attendance is accepted throughout the educational system.

Grammatically, the sentences are acceptable; rhetorically, they are a flop. They are lifeless; they bring to mind no images, not even a school. Moreover, there is no point in their being written so abstractly, since the idea expressed in them is not complex or difficult. To say, "In most states everyone has to go to school until he or she is seventeen" would do the job simply and effectively.

Putting People in Your Writing

Adding people to enliven your writing

Adding people to your writing may do more to make it concrete and readable than any other rhetorical device. When a writer actually names or describes people, readers find it easier to visualize what is happening, and they grasp the meaning more quickly. For example, compare the sentences in these pairs:

Original
In federally financed hospitals the abilities and facilities of all could be easily brought together to conquer the problems in medicine.

Revision

In federally financed hospitals, doctors and scientists could come together in laboratories to solve medical problems.

Original

Achievement in sports trains a person to be able to work hard and under pressure.

Revision

The young boy or girl athlete who competes in sports events learns to work hard under pressure.

Original

The corruption of youth appears to be a more common topic of discussion with adults than the assets of youth.

Revision

Adults seem to enjoy talking about what's wrong with youth more than they do discussing what's right about them.

As you can see, in each case the revision creates a more compelling sentence — one you can actually read without feeling a vague sense of boredom overtaking you at the third or fourth word.

Combining the Abstract and the Concrete

Incorporating abstract and concrete language in outlines

Since all writers must deal with abstract concepts from time to time, they all face the problem of finding ways to use concrete language to clarify their writing. One good way to approach the problem is to begin the execution stage of your writing process by roughing out an outline or summary in which you use general statements to express the main points and then make notes about concrete examples to use as second- or third-level supporting material. Suppose you are going to write a paper to argue that your college should give full scholarships to students who excel in the sciences, as well as those who excel in athletics. Your main points will be value statements that you must express in abstract terms; your supporting evidence,

Concrete Words, Jargon, and Sexist Language

however, should be concrete, vivid, and specific. An outline for your paper might be:

I. The present practice discriminates among students on the basis of physical ability and sex.
   A. Thousands of high school athletes receive full scholarships.
   B. Few women athletes receive scholarships.
   C. Bright science students must compete for only a few National Science Foundation grants, which are often quite small.
   D. College athletes get extras: tutoring, fraternity dues, summer jobs.
II. The present practice discourages scholastic achievement among high school students.
   A. High school athletes work hard to develop talents because rewards are substantial.
   B. Science students have little incentive to spend extra hours and effort on developing abilities because there is no tangible reward.
   C. Scholarships reinforce the high school value system: worship of athletes, indifference to studies.
III. Over a long period of time the present practices will prove shortsighted.
   A. Subsidized college athletes usually become professional football players. Earning years are relatively short; contribution to society relatively minor.
   B. Subsidized students in science would become doctors, biologists, research scientists, or teachers. Earning years long; contributions to society potentially great.

When you have an outline like this, you are not likely to write a theme that is simply a collection of generalities. Moreover, in the process of writing, you will probably think of actual incidents that illustrate your points and thus can add a personal note to the paper.

Guidelines for using concrete language

To summarize: in order to make your writing as clear and as forceful as possible, keep in mind these four guidelines.

1. Use abstract language to express ideas, but whenever possible reinforce and clarify it with concrete and specific examples.

2. When you are writing try to avoid those vague and overworked adjectives I call *fuzzy intensifiers*, words like *fantastic, horrible, incredible, marvelous, unbelievable, wonderful,* and *awful,* to name just a few. Although such words can add emphasis in casual conversation, in writing they are so trite and imprecise that they really tell the reader nothing. They only take up space without creating images or adding to information. Rather than cluttering your writing with such nonwords, you are better off to leave out the modifier altogether.

3. Try to avoid using abstractions as sentence subjects, particularly those overworked words *aspect, factor, element,* and *concept.*

4. Keep in mind the excellent advice Hayakawa gives in his book: "The interesting writer, the informative speaker, the accurate thinker, and the sane individual operate on all levels of the abstraction ladder, moving quickly and gracefully in orderly fashion from higher to lower, from lower to higher, with minds as lithe and deft and beautiful as monkeys in a tree."

Jargon

Definition of jargon

Jargon is a style of writing characterized by wordiness, a preponderance of abstract terms, excessive and irresponsible use of the passive voice, euphemisms, weak verbs, pretentious diction, clichés, excessive caution, and the absence of strong words and statements. A piece of writing does not have to have all these qualities to be labeled as jargon, but even a few jargon phrases, if overused, can turn decent prose into gobbledygook. Writing that is weighted down with jargon is, at its best, dull and confusing. At its worst, it is pretentious, evasive, and incomprehensible. Any level of jargon is a nuisance to the reader, who must unwrap a cocoon of words to extract the meaning. Take, for example, this paragraph from a student theme:

One factor which may account for the conservatism of this generation of students is the realization that there is a growing possibility that the common American assumption that a minimum amount of expended effort will yield a standard of living higher than one's parents may no longer hold true. There is a finitude of resources available to be consumed, and the end of these resources is regarded as a definite possibility. The origin of this fear of lack of availability can be found in the 1973 oil embargo, which forced Americans to realize their vulnerability. Their realization, and the fear which it raised, are in large part responsible for the new conservatism among college students.

Although the paragraph is technically correct, it is so overloaded with abstract nouns — words like *vulnerability, finitude, realization, availability,* and *conservatism* — passive verbs, and pretentious diction that the reader's first impulse is to skim right over it because it is hard to read. There are no concrete words or details and nothing visual.

Here are some examples taken from published writing:

Once politics is defined negatively as an enterprise for drawing a protective circle around the individual's sphere of self-interested action, then public concerns are by definition distinct from, and secondary to, private concerns. Regardless of democratic forms, when people are taught by philosophy (and the social climate) that they need not govern their actions by calculations of public good, they will come to blame all social shortcomings on the agency of collective considerations, the government, and will absolve themselves.[4]

Members of the faculty or staff of component institutions should not be discouraged from accepting appointments of a consultative or advisory capacity with governmental agencies, industry, or other educational institutions. The consideration to the System of such activity is the improvement of the individual by virtue of his continuing contact with nonacademic problems in the nonacademic world.[5]

The entropic perspective . . . poses a fundamental challenge to the materialistic assumptions that define and justify civilization as an illimitable program of technological expansionism. In that sense, entropy casts a pall over the progressivist values on which civilization relies to vindicate what it extols as the worthiest of contemporary projects, the pervasive extension of modernization

[4]George Will, *Statecraft as Soulcraft,* quoted in the *Austin American Statesman* 5 May 1983: E1.
[5]*Handbook of Operating Procedures,* University of Texas.

(mechanization by another name), and the drastic exploitation, production, and consumption of energy.[6]

Notice that these paragraphs exemplify the characteristics of jargon: abstract terms, pretentious diction, weak and colorless verbs, impersonal style, and an absence of direct or strong statements. They are so intimidating to read that one's mind just "hydroplanes" right over them without absorbing the meaning.

Why Do People Write Jargon?

As anyone knows who habitually pays attention to the writing he or she encounters daily, there is a lot of jargon around. Why do people who presumably want to communicate clutter their writing with so many long, dull sentences and so many abstract, confusing terms? Why is it nearly impossible to read insurance forms or government regulations or many scholarly articles?

Certainly a major reason is that most people find it easier to write badly than to write well, and some writers, even professionals, are either too lazy to work at writing clearly or don't care enough about *Writers use jargon* their readers to make the effort. But writers also have other rea- *for a variety of* sons, particularly in the realms of government, business, and the *reasons* professions.

First, sometimes writers deliberately use language to exclude and intimidate. By writing something in a language that seems to be English but is so full of difficult terms and abstract concepts that almost no one can understand it, writers can sometimes make their readers feel inferior and ignorant, shut out of the inner circle of those in the know. That's an old and shabby trick, and you shouldn't let yourself be taken in by it.

Second, writers sometimes use language to conceal rather than clarify meaning. They don't want their readers to understand what is going on, so they try to disguise it by using language that is as fuzzy and abstract as possible, language that evokes no images and uses no specific details. Why do writers seek to conceal meaning? George Orwell provides a reason in his essay "Politics and the English Language":

[6]Michael Vannoy Adams, book review in *The Lone Star Review*, May 7, 1981: 1.

In our time, political speech and writing are largely the defense of the indefensible. Things like the continuance of British rule in India, the Russian purges and deportations, the dropping of the atom bombs on Japan, can indeed be defended, but only by arguments which are too brutal for most people to face, and which do not square with the professed aims of political parties. Thus political language has to consist largely of euphemism, question-begging, and sheer cloudy vagueness. Defenseless villages are bombarded from the air, the inhabitants driven into the country, the cattle machine-gunned, the huts set on fire with incendiary bullets; this is called *pacification*. . . .

People are imprisoned for years without trial, or shot in the back of the neck, or sent to die of scurvy in Arctic labor camps; this is called *elimination of unreliable elements*. Such phraseology is needed if one wants to name things without calling up mental images of them.[7]

Third, writers sometimes use jargon to confuse. They really don't want their readers to understand what they are saying about the conditions in a contract or the directions for filling out a form.

But probably the main reason that writers use jargon is that they want to impress their readers. They think that if they write impersonal, wordy prose loaded with important-sounding terms, they will convince their readers that they are intelligent and highly educated. And they also think that jargon-laden language sounds very serious, scholarly, and businesslike. They assume that serious readers expect that kind of writing.

When students write jargon, they most often do so for this last reason. They equate academic writing with abstract, hard-to-read writing, and they think their professors expect them to produce that kind of prose. But such assumptions are almost never justified. Professors — perhaps more than other people because they must read so many papers — want their students to write clear, straightforward, and economical prose that explains their ideas as effectively as possible. And certainly readers outside of college deserve no less. They want to be able to understand what they read without having to wade through writing that is unnecessarily difficult or dense.

Readers dislike confusing jargon

[7]George Orwell, "Politics and the English Language," *Shooting an Elephant and Other Essays* (New York: Harcourt, 1950).

Getting Rid of Jargon in Your Writing

To eliminate jargon from your writing completely would be as difficult as always staying on a diet or never wasting time when you study. All of us lapse occasionally; we get careless or lazy or in a hurry and let phrases slip into our writing that we know we should revise or eliminate. So don't expect perfection of yourself or get discouraged because clichés and euphemisms keep popping into your mind as you write. Just keep crossing out the jargon, and gradually your writing will become clearer and stronger.

Many jargon problems will disappear if you observe the general rules for improving your writing: try to be concrete and specific; use active verbs whenever possible; remember that writing simply is a virtue, not a defect; be as brief as you can be and still cover your topic adequately. More specific guidelines to keep in mind are these:

Guidelines for getting rid of jargon

1. Be wary of overloading your writing with abstractions; you will need some, of course, but they should be reinforced and clarified with concrete language.
2. Whenever you use the passive voice, ask yourself if it conceals the agent that is acting, slows down the sentence, or makes the sentence stiff and flat. If it does, replace it with an active verb.
3. Use straightforward (though not vulgar) diction instead of genteel expressions or euphemisms. *Under the influence of alcohol* instead of *drunk, relieved of the position* instead of *fired,* or *passed away* instead of *died* weaken your writing and irritate your reader.
4. Try to find simple substitutes for pretentious words. *Student* is better than *scholastic* and *building* is better than *edifice*. There is seldom a real need for foreign words and phrases such as *vis-à-vis* or *Zeitgeist,* and business terms like *finalize* and *maximize* are not appropriate for most writing.
5. Avoid inflated expressions such as *at this point in time* instead of *now,* or *it is not without a certain amount of hesitation that* instead of *I hesitate.* Plain prepositions are better than stretched-out phrases; for example, use *about* instead of *in regard to* or *on the subject of.*
6. Keep in mind the distinction between using needless qualifiers and making sensible reservations. Phrases such as *most students* or *many people* and words such as *often, usually,* and *frequently* put limits on what otherwise would be sweeping generalizations.

Concrete Words, Jargon, and Sexist Language

Somewhat, to a great extent, rather, and *to a certain degree* are phrases that usually hedge rather than clarify.

Coping with Jargon in Your Reading

Inevitably you will find that as you work to get rid of jargon in your own writing, you will become more aware of and more annoyed by the jargon you run into in your reading. It's maddening to be confronted with dense, overblown writing in an article or textbook that you must read, whether you like it or not, and you will probably face that situation often in your college courses. The only way to cope with it is to read slowly, try to translate it into plain English, and make marginal notes that summarize the ideas.

Learning to deal with jargon in your reading

As you become sensitive to jargon, you will also become more critical of authors who are trying to deceive you, intimidate you, or confuse you, and that reaction is a bonus. Learning to spot phony and pretentious writing is a significant part of everyone's education. And the more you learn about good writing, the more secure you will become about refusing to be impressed by overblown writing and authors who seek to overwhelm you with their erudition.

You should remember, however, that it's not fair to assume that just because you are having trouble reading an essay or text, the author is necessarily at fault. He or she may not be writing jargon. It may be that the concepts in the text are complicated and the author has to use abstract language and terms that are unfamiliar to you. Many articles, for example the kind that appear in *Scientific American,* are inherently difficult for the average reader, and books by Artistotle or Kant often require that you invest substantial attention and effort.

Sexist Language

The effects of sexist language on readers

In the past two decades, an increasing number of people have become concerned about sexist language — that is, language that discriminates against women by consistently using masculine pronouns to refer to both men and women, by using the word *man* as a general term for *people,* and by perpetuating stereotypes of male and female roles through the images it creates of men and women. Because language is such a powerful molder of attitudes, critics of sexist language believe we must eliminate sex bias from our language if we

---

are to make real changes in the status of women and in society's attitude toward women. And indeed, it is difficult to remember that women played an active and significant role in the early days of our country when one reads passages like this in a book by historian Henry Steele Commager about our American culture. Italics have been added to highlight the sexist language:

> Circumstances opened the way to talent or to luck, and the American had no use for caste or class. *He* was democratic and equalitarian, but *his* democracy was social and political rather than economic, and as *he himself* expected economic success next year or the year after, *he* had little envy of those who achieved it this year. Where shrewdness in speculation had been elevated to a public service, *he* was not inclined to look too critically at the means whereby success was achieved. *He* tolerated with mere ceremonial protests the looting of the public domain or the evasion of taxes or the corruption of legislatures, so long as these things brought visible profits, and resented government interference with private enterprise far more than private interference with government enterprise. The self-made *man*, not the *heir*, was the *hero*, and by "made" the American meant enriched.[8]

Commager's style is typical of almost any book or article written more than twenty-five years ago. Probably he didn't think of himself as sexist; he would have claimed that when he used *he*, it was generic and referred to all people. But readers are not going to say to themselves constantly, "Yes, I know he is talking about women, too." The language makes it difficult to remember that women were also part of the colonial experience in America. That is why it is important for modern writers to make an effort to write in a way that doesn't cast this sexist haze over their work.

Many writers protest, of course, particularly those who want to keep the language pure and don't like to see the old rules change. They say that it inhibits a writer's style to have to worry about finding ways to avoid using *he* and *man* in a general sense, and that substituting *he or she* and *him and her* or even occasionally using *she* instead of *he* produces a clumsy style that intrudes on the reader.

[8]Henry Steele Commager, *The American Mind* (New Haven, Yale UP, 1954) 13.

Perhaps. Making a change is always difficult at first, but we can quickly get used to it if we think it's worthwhile.

It *is* worthwhile to try to eliminate sexist language, for several reasons. Probably the most important reason is the one already mentioned: language shapes our attitudes and the way we view the world. As long as we have a male-centered language, it's going to be hard to break other male-centered patterns in our culture.

Why writers should avoid sexist language

But there are also other good reasons for getting rid of sexist language. One is economic. The editors of most major newspapers, magazines, and books — particularly textbooks — are now very sensitive to sexist language and go to considerable trouble to get rid of it in the nonfiction that they publish. They consider it good business to do so because they don't want to offend their millions of women readers. People who produce brochures and pamphlets or advertising are also very conscious about sexist language or implications in what they print. For example, an advertisement for business machines must not fall into traditional stereotypes by showing all the managers as male and all the clerical workers as female, or the company that makes the machines may lose orders from women executives.

Other writers try to avoid sexist language for legal reasons. Because federal and state regulations prohibit sex discrimination, any official document must be careful not to indicate or even hint that certain jobs are open only to women or to men or that there are different rules governing the sexes. Anyone who writes or administers grants, loan programs, scholarship applications, and so on must also be careful about discriminatory language.

Finally, writers are more accurate when they are careful to avoid consistently writing *he* or *him* or *man*. We no longer live in a world in which almost all doctors, engineers, police, judges, and pilots are men, or one in which all telephone operators, nurses, and teachers are women, and in order to describe our present-day world accurately, writers have to use language carefully. If they don't, they are likely to offend, and therefore lose, many of their readers.

Guidelines for Getting Rid of Sexist Language

Fortunately, eliminating sexist implications from your writing is not difficult to do. Mainly, you just have to become conscious of the problem; once you do, you will find that, with a little thought, you can usually write clear and nondiscriminatory prose. Here are some guidelines for doing so.

Guidelines for avoiding sexist language

1. When you can, use plural forms. Often this is the simplest way to solve the problem. For example, change "A speaker who hopes to be taken seriously must do his homework and get his facts straight" to "Speakers who hope to be taken seriously must do their homework and get their facts straight." Change "The driver who gets three speeding tickets will lose his license for a month" to "Drivers who get three speeding tickets lose their licenses for a month."

2. When you cannot use plural pronouns in a sentence, you have three options for solving your problem. First, you can write *he or she* and *him or her* when you need to use a pronoun. Second, you can write *he/she* or *him/her* when you need to use a pronoun. Third, you can alternate between using *he* and *she* or *him* and *her*; that is, for some examples use *he* and for other examples use *she*.

3. If you can, substitute *person* or *people* for *man* or *men*. You can also just leave out *man* or *men* in some phrases. For instance, instead of writing, "The man who chooses to go into politics must be prepared to compromise," write "The person who goes into politics must be prepared to compromise." Instead of using *policeman*, use *police*; instead of using *Frenchmen*, use *the French*.

4. Sometimes you can substitute *one* or *anyone* for *he* or *she* or *man* or *woman*. For example, instead of writing "If a man is enterprising and lucky, he can become a millionaire," write "If one is enterprising and lucky, one can become a millionaire." Or instead of writing "The woman who doesn't smoke usually has fewer wrinkles," write "Anyone who doesn't smoke usually has fewer wrinkles."

5. When you can, instead of identifying people by their gender, identify them by their roles or their actions. Instead of using *mailman*, use *mail carrier*; instead of using *fireman*, use *firefighter*. Instead of writing "Housewives who buy groceries in supermarkets should consider food co-ops," write "Shoppers who buy groceries in supermarkets should consider food co-ops." Instead of writing "Men who invest in real estate must know their tax laws," write "Real estate investors must know their tax laws."

6. Avoid using language that stereotypes certain professions or jobs as male or female. For instance, don't automatically use *he* and *him* as pronouns when referring to engineers, judges, surgeons, or legislators and use *she* and *her* as pronouns when referring to teachers, secretaries, or nurses. Avoid classifying people into traditional roles by writing sentences like this: "Even when they are in junior high school, girls can earn money baby-sitting and boys can earn money mowing lawns."

7. Avoid special female designations if you can. For example, it isn't necessary to use *poetess* or *songstress*; *poet* and *singer* are better.

8. Avoid stereotyping people by supposedly sex-linked traits; for example, describing women as frivolous, emotional, or intuitive and men as stalwart, rugged, or logical. Also avoid mentioning a woman's appearance unless in the same circumstances you would mention a man's appearance.

9. Refer to women by their own names, such as Mary Scott Webster or Julia Martin, rather than as Mrs. John Webster or Mrs. James Martin. Mention their marital status only if that information is important to your readers and only if you also refer to men's marital status; that is, don't say Ruth Collins is divorced unless under the same circumstances you would mention that Jack Collins is divorced.

10. Be consistent when you refer to people by their last names; that is, if you write *Faulkner* and *Capote,* also write *Didion,* not *Joan Didion*; if you write *Reagan,* also write *Thatcher,* not *Margaret Thatcher.*

Exercises

1. Which of the following words are abstract and which concrete? Notice that you may have to settle on a limited definition for some of these words before you can classify them accurately.

science	duty	treaty	son-in-law
machine	expressway	yellow	deed
identity	safety	tone	abortion
dormitory	recognition	barrier	integrity
condominium	character		

2. Arrange the following three lists of words into ladders of abstraction:

gasoline-propelled conveyance	three-month-old Great Dane	the poems of T. S. Eliot
product of the Ford Motor Company	dog	academic subjects
mode of transportation	domesticated animal	twentieth-century literature
two-door automobile	canine species	English
Mustang	mammal	"The Love Song of J. Alfred Prufrock"
Mach II fastback	puppy	

3. Write short paragraphs that develop concretely these two opening sentences:

a. A brief tour of the campus reveals an urgent need for modernization.

b. The candidate's record on ecology issues will hurt her with young voters.

4. Bring to class a paragraph from an essay or magazine article that you think is particularly well written. What parts of the writing are concrete and what parts abstract?

5. Study the following sentences from student themes; then rewrite them to make them more concrete and effective. Use different words if necessary.

a. The behavior of the residents is also a factor of annoyance.

b. The author tends to have a negative attitude toward the values of youth.

c. Social and economic conflicts will arise if the student takes any involvement in college affairs.

d. The author's words produce feelings of unfavorable reaction in the reader.

e. The writer uses phrases that negate the idea of sexual freedom in our culture.

f. The first consideration that should be taken is what particular interests the person has in the areas of job preference.

6. In "Politics and the English Language," George Orwell rewrote a famous passage from Ecclesiastes 9:11 as a modern author might have phrased it. Here are the original and Orwell's jargon version:

> I returned, and saw under the sun, that the race is not to the swift, nor the battle to the strong, neither yet bread to the wise, nor riches to men of understanding, nor yet favor to men of skill; but time and chance happeneth to them all.

> Objective consideration of contemporary phenomena compels the conclusion that success or failure in competitive activities exhibits no tendency to be commensurate with innate capacity, but that a considerable element of the unpredictable must invariably be taken into account.[9]

What particular qualities of the original passage make it good writing? What specific characteristics of jargon has Orwell incorporated into his version? The first version has more words than the second, but the second one seems much longer. Why? If you read the two versions aloud, what striking differences do you notice in the way they sound?

7. Analyze the language of the following paragraph for sexist features.

> A fairly common sexual pattern is for a writer to have many affairs in his youth, to marry a woman older than himself, to watch the marriage break up in quarrels resulting from a conflict of standards — or from professional jealousy, if the wife is a writer too, or simply because she drinks too much — then to

[9]Orwell 84.

marry a woman his own age and stay married, perhaps with minor infidelities. If the second marriage is a failure he either makes the best of it or else tries again, for he can't get along without a wife. In a writer's household the wife discharges a whole group of functions besides the simple one of being his mate. She not only acts as housekeeper, nursemaid, chauffeur, and hostess — like most American wives of the business classes — but also serves, on occasion, as secretary, receptionist, office manager, business consultant, first audience for the writer's work, guardian of his reputation, and partner in what has become a family enterprise. That phrase at the end of the forewords of many scholarly books, ". . . deepest thanks to my wife, without whose devoted patience . . ." is funny because it recurs so often, but also funny because it is innocently true.[10]

8. Revise the following sentences to get rid of sexist language or implications.

a. A driver who wants to keep his insurance rates low must be careful that he doesn't get traffic tickets for moving violations.

b. If a professor wants his students to respect him, he will always come to class prepared.

c. Men who choose to go into politics in this country need tremendous stamina and a talent for communication.

d. A woman can prevent premature aging by always protecting her skin from the sun.

e. Statistics show that policemen who receive training in interpersonal communication and stress management have less job burnout.

f. Engineers who work abroad must often be separated from their wives for long periods of time.

g. Faculty wives are a traditional source of cheap labor in many colleges.

h. President Reagan and Mrs. Thatcher conferred about economic problems frequently last year.

i. The chief witness for the defense was a pretty blonde divorcée.

[10]Malcolm Cowley, *The Literary Situation* (New York: Viking, 1955) 197.

Writing Assignments

Some of the advice that writing instructors give most often is "Be concrete and specific. Your readers wants facts, details, examples." Instructors also continually recommend "*Show* your readers; don't tell them. They want to see somebody *doing* something." The chief purpose for the writing assignments for this chapter is to give you practice in adding the weight of facts and examples to your writing and to encourage you to add visual details.

Paper 1

At your campus book store or a local magazine stand, locate an interesting magazine that is aimed toward a specialized group of readers such as runners, skiers, photographers, gardeners, writers, policemen and women, working women, and so on. Check to see what kinds of short personal-experience or advice articles the magazine publishes, the kind that might be written by amateur writers. For example, a student of mine had an article published in *Motor Home Magazine* on her experiences as the only women in a community college course on auto repair.

Write a short article of no more than 1000 words about an experience you have had in connection with one of your hobbies that might be interesting to the readers of that magazine or about something you have learned about your hobby that might be of interest to other readers of the magazine. Give the specific and concrete details of your experience, using visual description. You might even add sketches or pictures to illustrate your point.

Before you begin your paper write out an audience analysis. What kind of people read the magazine, why would they be interested in an article such as yours, and what questions would they want answered in the article? Also write out a purpose analysis; what do you hope to accomplish in the article?

Possible Topics

1. Pointers for taking pictures of animals.
2. Exploring an unusual cave.
3. For a magazine for working women, an article relating a signifi-

cant incident that happened while you were working as a nurse's aide, a traffic dispatcher, an airline hostess, or a model.

4. For a magazine such as *Woman's Day*, hints for the student/wife/mother on organizing meal planning, shopping, and cooking around a class schedule.

5. An article on the benefits of stretching exercises for runners.

Paper 2

Two professors on the faculty of your college, one in the English department and one in the psychology department, are doing a survey of student attitudes toward writing. You are among 100 freshman they have asked to write a personal account of an experience or experiences you have had that significantly affected, either positively or negatively, the way you feel about writing. They want specific details; how old were you, under what circumstances did the incident occur, who was involved, what was your feeling then and later, and why do you think that experience or those experiences had such an effect? You have a good opportunity to use anecdote and visual detail here.

Before you begin the main part of your paper, write out an audience analysis. What qualities do you think these professors have that are important in this situation, why are they asking you for this account, and what questions do you think they hope to have answered? Also write out your purpose: what do you want to convey to the professors who are doing the survey?

Paper 3

One of the best ways to add *presence* to your writing (see page 242) is to give a concrete description that engages your readers' attention, or to begin a paper with a narrative or anecdote that has visual appeal. This assignment asks you to describe an object (for example, a pickup truck or a sailboat), an event (for example, a sporting event or an accident), or a place (for example, a self-service laundry/bar or a hard-rock night club) in such a way that readers can *feel* the essential quality of the thing about which you are writing. You can choose an event or place that typifies your hometown or city. For instance, in some rural Texas communities, a big event of the year is the tractor-pulling contest; in other Texas towns, the big event is the spring rattlesnake hunt; in others, it is the fall rodeo. In your city, you may have more sophisticated events such as the annual water-skiing contest or a charity soccer game. An object that you might find interesting could be a memorial to the war dead or a particularly ugly stretch of a highway through your town. Whatever you choose, find a visual angle that will make your paper memorable.

Choose as your audience the readers of your student newspaper or the newspaper in your hometown. You are writing to give them a fresh view of whatever you are describing and to convey to them the pleasure or amusement you feel about your topic. Before you start writing, do a full analysis of your audience: Why might they be interested, and what would they want to know? Also write out your specific purpose for the paper.

8 · Connotation, Metaphor, and Tone

CHAPTER

When writers want to persuade their readers, they frequently use language to appeal to their emotions. Some of the most common kinds of appeal are made through connotation, metaphor, and tone.

Connotation

Definition of connotation

The *connotation* of a word is the emotional baggage it carries with it in addition to its denotative, or strictly dictionary, definition. That emotional baggage makes readers or listeners react to the word in ways that go beyond simply recognizing and understanding its meaning. Connotation triggers powerful responses, either positive or negative, because of attitudes, beliefs, or feelings that the audience already holds. An old story illustrates how connotation works.

A legislator was asked how he felt about whiskey. He replied, "If, when you say whiskey, you mean the Devil's brew, the poison scourge, the bloody monster that defiles innocence, dethrones reason, creates misery and poverty — yes, literally takes the bread from the mouths of little children; if you mean the drink that topples Christian man and woman from the pinnacle of righteous, gracious living into the bottomless pit of degradation, despair, shame and helplessness, then certainly I am against it with all my power.

But if, when you say whiskey, you mean the oil of conversation, the philosophic wine, the ale that is consumed when good fellows get together, that puts a song in their hearts and the warm glow of contentment in their eyes; if you mean Christmas cheer; if you mean the stimulating drink that puts the spring in an old gentle-

man's step on a frosty morning; if you mean that drink, the sale of which pours into our treasury untold millions of dollars which are used to provide tender care for our crippled children, our blind, our deaf, our dumb, pitiful, aged and infirm, to build highways, hospitals, and schools, then certainly I am in favor of it.

That is my stand, and I will not compromise.[1]

The example is humorous, of course, but it illustrates a sound principle. Connotation can enhance almost any argument by tapping into the readers' or listeners' sympathies and biases. That's not necessarily bad; language stripped of all color and emotion is fit only for programming a computer. But if, as writers, we want to use connotation effectively and responsibly, and if, as readers, we want to minimize the extent to which we are unwittingly controlled by the connotative language of others, we need to understand how it works.

How Connotation Works

Appeals to the Senses   Connotation functions by the process of association. At the simplest level, it does little more than trigger sensuous reactions. We hear or see the word *silky,* and without actually thinking about it, we remember the sensation of feeling silk. For most people, the memory is pleasant, and the good feeling transfers to whatever the word *silky* is describing. This is the kind of response an advertisement tries to elicit by saying, "Your hair will turn out silkier, more lustrous, glossier than it was when you started." All direct appeals to our senses work in this way. In the following passage, for example, the author conveys an impression of exotic luxury by the way he describes a restaurant and its food:

Connotation triggers associations

Vincent Alberici, a graduate of the Culinary Institute of America in Hyde Park, New York, was appointed executive chef of the Bellevue Stratford Hotel four years ago when he was but twenty-seven and spends his time overseeing the hotel's lovely, softly lighted, chocolate-brown Versailles Room. From his kitchen come such creations as medallions of pork in a *coulis* of fresh figs, sau-

[1]Retold by William Raspberry, "Any Candidate Will Drink to That," *Austin American Statesman* 11 May 1984: A10.

Connotation, Metaphor, and Tone

sages blending sweetbreads, veal, and spinach, a wonderfully pungent red snapper in a sauce of red peppers and saffron, and roast breast of pheasant stuffed with red cabbage.[2]

Connotation appeals to biases

Appeals to Prejudice   Other kinds of connotation work in a more complex way by reminding us of the stereotypes that we all carry around in our heads, images that include racial types, policemen, DAR matrons, small-town girls, politicians, pot parties, admirals, professors, the Mafia, and dozens of others. A single reference to one of these stereotypes can evoke a mass of associations, both positive and negative. Writers depend on this kind of nonlogical reaction when they use terms like *punk, hard-hat, cop, Communist, bureaucrat,* or other loaded labels.

Connotation appeals to cherished beliefs

Appeals to Beliefs and Attitudes   Because most of us believe in the traditional virtues of honesty, courage, loyalty, self-reliance, hard work, and fair play, there is little doubt about the way we will respond to words such as *indolent, shifty, craven,* or *freeloader.* We Americans conventionally believe in independence and individualism, in freedom and dignity, in progress and prosperity (all concepts we have absorbed with our education), and we nod our approval to any term that reminds us of them. We prefer — or think we do — the natural to the artificial, and so *real, genuine, original,* and *authentic* are good words; *synthetic, imitation, substitute,* and *pseudo* are bad ones.

Connotation appeals to weaknesses

Appeals to Insecurity   We have other attitudes that we are not quite so proud of but that influence us as much as, or more than, our traditional beliefs. We crave approval. We want to be thought of as young, sexually attractive, intelligent, and successful. No one wants to be classified as a mediocre person: dull, conventional, and timid. Notice how a magazine ad can play on these apprehensions in a positive way.

> Are you the kind of person who wants *more* from life? Wants that new adventure, that special kind of vacation that others don't know about? Do you want to set the pace, not follow? If you're a leader, have that special knack for taking charge, our magazine is

[2]Fred Ferretti, "A Philadelphia Story," *Gourmet* May 1985: 44.

for you. Read *Paladin* to find out where to go for the best and the brightest. The last word in life-styles is at your nearest newsstand.

In the same way, our desire for status makes us susceptible to snob-appeal ads, which encourage us to buy expensive cars that will make our neighbors envious. Brewers play to our continual pursuit of happiness by coining such slogans as, "You only live once — why not enjoy the finest beer brewed?"

Appeals to Fear   Probably the most insidious kind of connotation is that which attempts to sway us by touching our deepest, instinctive fears. Phrases such as "Communist conspiracy" and "Fascist plot," with their innuendoes of secrecy and mysterious machinations, may immediately put us on our guard. Labels such as "outside agitators," "alien influences," and "foreign elements" appeal to the distrust and suspicion of outsiders that are difficult for even open-minded people to overcome. An inclination to panic at the prospect of injury or death assures a response to mottoes like "Insure your safety" or "Protect your loved ones," phrases that can serve equally well to sell burglar alarms, insurance, a politician's position on law and order, or an intercontinental missile system.

Using Connotation

General Connotation   The kinds of connotation discussed so far — and the examples are intended to be representative, not exhaustive — are broadly based and general; that is, their emotional appeal rests on warranted assumptions about the majority of the people in our society. The sum of generally shared attitudes is the conventional wisdom of our society, the prevailing opinion of that mythical person in the street. Writers at both ends of the political spectrum depend, and with good reason, on their audience's responding to words that have general connotation.

Strengths and weaknesses of general connotation

But a broad, unfocused emotional appeal has serious weaknesses. For one thing, many words and phrases have been used so often that they have lost their impact and deteriorated into clichés. We are so used to hearing about "good government," "individual freedom," "democratic processes," and "human potential," for example, that the phrases simply roll off our minds. At best, they evoke only mild approval; at worst, cynicism. Another problem is that perceptive readers dismiss broad connotation as little more than the glittering generalities of propaganda, push-button devices aimed at people who are totally governed by their emotions.

Uses of selective connotation

Selective Connotation Thus, connotative language works best when it is selective, chosen with a specific audience in mind. Writers who decide to tailor their appeals to particular groups are taking a risk, of course; they must make assumptions about their audiences that may be wrong. But for the person who makes a careful and rational analysis of an audience, using the methods discussed in Chapter 3, the gamble will probably pay off. For instance, a candidate who is promoting tax-supported day care centers for preschool children might speak of more freedom for mothers and equal opportunity for career women if she were addressing a group of young women. If she were advocating the same measure to a men's club, she would avoid those phrases and instead talk about the ways in which day care centers could improve the efficiency of women workers and about the advantages to the children of being in the care of licensed, professional people. By varying her approach, the speaker is not compromising her principles; since both her arguments are legitimate, neither contradicts the other, and both promote the same purpose. Rather, she is showing sensitivity to the concerns of her audiences and adapting her diction to the rhetorical situation.

Risks of Connotation

Dangers of overusing connotation

Rhetoricians risk defeating their own purpose when they overuse connotation. The writer or speaker who expects to persuade mainly through slanted language is assuming that the audience, like a laboratory animal, is totally conditioned and has no critical faculties. Such tactics may work when the audience is already in full agreement with the speaker; in that case the speaker is doing little more than leading a cheering section anyway. In a genuine rhetorical situation, however, the audience is likely to be more insulted than convinced by a barrage of connotative words and phrases, whether the phrases are political slogans or advertising clichés. Except on those few occasions that are unabashedly emotional, connotation is most effective when it is used with restraint.

Metaphor

How Metaphor Works

Like connotation, metaphor works by setting up associations, but it operates more directly and specifically. The key to creating metaphors is to find a well-known process or object to use as one part of your metaphorical equation and then to show how the concept you want to clarify resembles what is already familiar. For example, a book written in 1893 by the American novelist Frank Norris has as its theme the railroad's exploitation of the people and land of the western United States in the late nineteenth century; the title of the book is *The Octopus.* For most readers the word *octopus* raises an unpleasant image; they see a frightening creature with tentacles that stretch out to grab anything within its reach and strangle it to death. Because Norris has equated the railroad with the octopus, readers transfer their impressions of the creature to the railroad and think of it as a grasping and destructive live thing that preys upon people.

Metaphor works by drawing comparisons

A passage from the literary critic Alfred Kazin's autobiography, *A Walker in the City,* provides another example. He writes, "When I passed the school, I went sick with all my old fear of it. . . . It looks like a factory over which has been imposed the facade of a castle." Here Kazin wants his readers to attribute the characteristics of a factory to the school. When the readers envision a school that operates this way, they react in a surge of pity for students caught in such a system. Notice too the phrase "the facade of a castle," another metaphor that illustrates the school administration's pretensions about the institution. The method employed by Norris and Kazin is simple: A = B; therefore, B has the characteristics of A. The effect is illumination; the readers see a thing that is ordinary and familiar to them in a new light. For convenience, we shall call this kind of comparison straight metaphor, a simple equation of unlike objects. We need also to consider three other categories: the submerged metaphor, the extended metaphor, and allusion.

Submerged Metaphor   The *submerged metaphor* consists of implied comparisons made in one or two words, usually verbs, nouns, or adjectives. These metaphors give the language much of its vigor and color. Take the sentence "The vice president of the firm had clawed his way to the top." The word *clawed* is metaphorical, not literal;

people do not have claws. The verb implies the ruthlessness and ferocity associated with a wild animal; the writer had gotten a lot of mileage (notice the submerged metaphor in the noun *mileage*) out of a single word. The sentences "He cut down the opposition's case" and "She tortured her hair into the latest style" use the same verbal technique. Reading just a few pages of a newspaper or a magazine like *Time* or *Newsweek* reveals how heavily reporters depend on figurative language. "The company recently *launched* a new advertising campaign"; "The movie has *spawned* a host of imitations"; "Today the police chief said they had *dealt a knock-out blow* to drug pushers in the city." Of course, the device can get out of hand. Tabloid writers' efforts to find a sensational adjective become comic at times, and many authors of mystery and adventure stories overload their fiction with fast-action verbs and shocking metaphors.

Hidden metaphors

If you are adventuresome enough to try a metaphor now and then, either straight or submerged, you can put some life into your prose. Instead of writing "It is my opinion that drastic changes must be made if we are to solve this problem," try "The problem calls for a full-scale overhaul of the system." Whenever possible use verbs that call to mind some kind of physical action. Occasionally, your imaginative efforts may misfire, but with practice you will learn to write with a livelier style. The gamble is worth it.

Elaborate metaphors

Extended Metaphor   Working with *extended metaphor,* one that carries a comparison through several sentences or even paragraphs, is a little tricky; a writer has to be wary of overdoing it. Here is an example of an effective extended metaphor by a person known for colorful language:

> "I figured when my legislative program passed the Congress," Johnson said in 1971, "that the Great Society had a real chance to grow into a beautiful woman. And I figured her growth and development would be as natural and inevitable as any small child's. In the first year, as we got the law on the books, she'd begin to crawl. Then in the second year, as we got more laws on the books, she'd begin to walk, and the year after that, she'd be off and running, all the time growing bigger and healthier and fatter. And when she grew up, I figured she'd be so big and beautiful that the American people couldn't help but fall in love with her, and once they did, they'd want to keep her around forever, making her a

permanent part of American life, more permanent even than the New Deal. . . . It's a terrible thing for me to sit by and watch someone else starve my Great Society to death. She's getting thinner and thinner and uglier and uglier all the time; now her bones are beginning to stick out and her wrinkles are beginning to show. Soon she'll be so ugly that the American people will refuse to look at her; they'll stick her in a closet to hide her away and there she'll die. And when she dies, I too will die."[3]

Allusion   A final kind of metaphor is *allusion,* a reference to events or characters from an outside source, usually literary or historical. This device acts as a rhetorical shorthand; it enables writers to compress extra meaning into a few words by using short phrases that bring certain associations to mind. For example, the phrases *sour grapes* and *cry wolf* describe certain kinds of human behavior with a minimum of words because we know the Aesop's fables to which the writer refers. The terms *Good Samaritan* and *kiss of death* describe by evoking our memories of Bible stories, and references like *Achilles' heel* and *Trojan horse* say a great deal in a few words if we have read *The Iliad.*

How allusion works

Although myth, legend, classical literature, and the Bible are the most common sources of allusion, a writer can also use contemporary references with good effect. You might characterize a wisecracking student as another Eddie Murphy or a crusading reformer as a Ralph Nader. When you use such allusions, you not only make your writing more vigorous and concrete, but you strengthen your ties to your audience by drawing on a stock of shared experiences and common knowledge. Sports, television, movies, popular songs, books, current events, politics — almost everything around us furnishes material for allusions that help us to communicate.

When you are using allusions, however, remember to ask yourself if your audience is going to be able to understand them. Allusions can be so specialized that only a few people grasp them, and they also go out of date quickly. You'll alienate your readers if you use too many that they don't recognize. It's also good to remember that an important part of getting a good education is increasing your stock of general knowledge so that you recognize the allusions you

[3]Quoted by Doris Kearns, "Who *Was* Lyndon Baines Johnson?" *The Atlantic* June 1976: 73.

encounter. Readers who know nothing of Greek myths, Arthurian legend, Shakespeare, or Biblical history are handicapped whether they are reading the Great Books or *Newsweek.*

The Purposes of Metaphor

The varieties of metaphor serve several rhetorical purposes. First, as already discussed, they give color and vigor to writing, bring it to life, make it move. That result alone helps to win your audience. Second, using metaphor is one way to make the abstract concrete. Philosophers and psychologists frequently employ metaphor to help their readers grasp difficult concepts. In one of the most dramatic passages in philosophy, Plato illustrates the function of the soul by saying that it is like a team of two horses with its charioteer; the charioteer is the guiding force for the horses, one of which represents good instincts and the other, bad instincts.

Use metaphors
1. To add vigor
2. To add concreteness

> The horse that holds the nobler position is upright and clean-limbed; it carries its head high, its nose is aquiline, its color white, its eyes dark; it is a lover of honor . . . temperance, and decency. . . . It needs no whip, but is driven by word of command alone. The other horse, however, is huge, but crooked, a great jumble of a creature with a short, thick neck, a flat nose, dark color, grey bloodshot eyes, the mate of insolence and knavery, shaggy-eared and deaf, hardly heeding whip or spur.[4]

Plato extends the figure of speech for several paragraphs, vividly dramatizing the struggle that reason, the charioteer, has in finally bringing the dark horse, or the soul's sensual desires, under control.

3. To clarify a theory

Third, writers often use metaphor to clarify or explain a theory. The sociologist David Riesman elucidates his classification of people as "inner-directed" and "other-directed" by saying that inner-directed people have what he calls a "psychological gyroscope." "This instrument, once it is set by the parents and other authorities, keeps the inner-directed person . . . 'on course' even when tradition . . . no longer dictates his moves." In contrast, other-directed people pattern their behavior according to the responses they receive from those

---

[4]Plato, *Phaedrus,* trans. W. C. Helmbold and W. B. Rabinowitz (Indianapolis: Bobbs, 1956) 38.

around them. "What [is] internalized is not a code of behavior but the elaborate equipment needed to attend to . . . messages. . . . This control equipment, instead of being like a gyroscope, is like a radar."[5] This kind of vivid clarification we find too seldom in the writing of social scientists. When we do encounter such striking figures, they stick in our memories.

Another example of a metaphorical explanation is one used by a psychologist to make a normal person comprehend the agony felt by a person who is the victim of irrational fears. The psychologist dramatized the psychotic's fears of the most routine things, such as sleep, by comparing the psychotic's feelings to those a normal person would have toward sleeping in a bed located at the edge of a precipice.

4. To persuade and convince

A final rhetorical function of metaphor is that of persuasion. By drawing comparisons, not only can writers make you see things more clearly, but also very often they can influence you to see them their way. Some persuasive metaphors are obvious: "Television is a giant wasteland" or "Lake Michigan is the sewer of Chicago." Others, however, are so subtle that readers may not realize they are being influenced. Let us take an example from James Baldwin's *Notes of a Native Son*.

> That year in New Jersey lives in my mind as though it were the year during which, having an unsuspected predilection for it, I first contracted some dread, chronic disease, the unfailing symptom of which is a kind of blind fever, a pounding in the skull, a fire in the bowels. Once this disease is contracted, one can never be really carefree again, for the fever, without an instant's warning, can recur at any moment. It can wreck more important things than race relations. There is not a Negro alive who does not have this rage in his blood — one has the choice, merely, of living with it consciously or surrendering to it. As for me this fever has recurred in me, and does, and will until the day I die.[6]

Baldwin equates his resentment and anger and hatred with a disease. Think for a minute of the characteristics of a disease. First, it infects a person without the person knowing it; one does not delib-

[5]David Riesman, *The Lonely Crowd* (New Haven: Yale UP, 1950) 31–32, 37.
[6]James Baldwin, *Notes of a Native Son* (Boston: Beacon, 1955) 94.

erately choose to have a disease. Thus, Baldwin cannot be held responsible for his "rage in the blood." Second, a disease, and particularly a fever (notice that he repeats the word three times) affects a person's ability to act rationally. Again, we cannot hold Baldwin responsible for what he does while he is in its grip. Third, a disease is painful ("a pounding in the skull, a fire in the bowels"), and so we feel sympathy, not anger, for the person afflicted with it. If we make the transfer of characteristics that Baldwin wants us to make, we will view some of the problems of black people from a new perspective.

Effects of metaphor on thinking

You may protest that the power of metaphor is exaggerated, that you do not make all these associations when you read and therefore are not particularly affected by an author's clever comparisons. It is true, of course, that because few of us pause in our reading to make a close analysis of figurative language, many of the author's nuances escape us; nevertheless, if we accept the metaphors an author creates, we also, without really thinking about it, are inclined to accept his or her point of view. A particularly apt comparison, such as Kazin's identification of the elementary school with a factory, can be more persuasive than an elaborate explanation.

Tone

Tone conveys attitude

The *tone* of a piece of writing is the frame of mind and mood that it conveys to readers. Analogous to a speaker's tone of voice, it reveals the writer's attitude toward audience and material. It is an extension of the persona, an essential part of the image of oneself that is projected to the audience. For this reason, writers who want to make a favorable impression on their audiences will carefully edit their writing and take out any words that might jar the tone they want.

The list of words for describing the kinds of tones or attitudes that writers can project includes almost all the words we use to talk about our emotions: angry, proud, ironic, amused, sorrowful, disgusted, indignant, pitying, bitter, amused — the list could go on for half a page. We also need to be thinking about what kinds of people the writers seem to be. What do we think we can tell about the character of writers from the tone of their writing?

A passage from Benjamin Franklin's *Autobiography* illustrates how important one's manner of speaking or writing is. As a young man,

Franklin worked out a plan of self-improvement; he made a list of twelve character traits that he wanted to acquire and outlined a plan for achieving them. In writing about his program, he comments:

My list of virtues contain'd at first but twelve; but a Quaker friend having kindly informed me that I was generally thought proud; that my pride show'd itself frequently in conversation; that I was not content with being in the right when discussing any point, but was overbearing, and rather insolent, of which he convinc'd me by mentioning several instances; I determined endeavouring to cure myself, if I could, of this vice or folly among the rest, and I added *Humility* to my list. . . .

I cannot boast of much success in acquiring the *reality* of this virtue, but I had a good deal with regard to the *appearance* of it. I made it a rule to forbear all direct contradiction to the sentiments of others, and all positive assertion of my own. I even forbid myself . . . the use of every word or expression in the language that imported a fix'd opinion; such as *certainly, undoubtedly,* etc., and I adopted, instead of them, *I conceive, I apprehend,* or *I imagine* a thing to be so or so; it so *appears to me at the present.* When another asserted something that I thought an error, I deny'd myself the pleasure of contradicting him abruptly, and of showing him immediately some absurdity in his proposition; and in answering I began by observing that in certain cases or circumstance his opinion would be right, but in the present case there *appear'd* or *seem'd* to me some difference, etc. I soon found the advantage of this change in my manner; the conversations I engag'd in went on more pleasantly. The modest way in which I propos'd my opinions procur'd them a readier reception and less contradiction; I had less mortification when I was found to be in the wrong, and I more easily prevail'd with others to give up their mistakes and join me when I happened to be in the right.

And this mode, which I first put on with some violence to natural inclination, became at length easy, and so habitual to me, that perhaps for fifty years past no one has ever heard a dogmatical expression escape me. And to this habit (after my character of integrity) I think it principally owing that I had early so much weight with my fellow-citizens when I proposed new institutions, or alterations in the old, and so much influence in public councils when I became a member; for I was but a bad speaker, never eloquent, subject to much hesitation in my choice of words, hardly correct in language, and yet I generally carried my points.[7]

What Franklin changed, of course, was his tone. By doing so he induced his audience to accept him as a reasonable and moderate man. Hypocritical? Not at all. He gave up no principles and did nothing dishonest. He simply adjusted his diction and delivery to show respect rather than contempt for his audience.

Some writing is toneless

There is, of course, much writing that is essentially "toneless" because the author has no purpose other than to convey information as accurately and objectively as possible. For example, in the following passage Isaac Asimov explains acceleration to the layperson:

> When something moves, it has kinetic energy. The quantity of kinetic energy possessed by a moving object depends upon its velocity and its mass. Velocity is a straightforward property that is easy to grasp. To be told something is moving at a high or low velocity brings a clear picture to mind. Mass, however, is a little more subtle.[8]

You are no more aware of tone in this writing than you would be of tone of voice in a weather report or the stock market quotations. Writing that is strictly informational — and that includes newspaper reports — should have a neutral and unemotional tone; if writers allow their biases to show, they are violating their persona of the objective and impersonal observer.

Casual Tone

Characteristics of casual tone

Writers achieve a casual, easygoing, conversational style and tone by using language suited to talking intimately with a few people. They make free use of contractions such as *it's, don't, wouldn't,* and *can't.* They may inject a few slang words and phrases such as *awesome* or *wicked* and occasionally lapse into one of the minor grammatical errors that people often make in conversation: *It's me* or *It runs good.* The pronouns *I, you, we,* and *our* appear frequently, and bits of conversations are quoted directly. Most of the words are concrete rather

[7]Benjamin Franklin, *The Works of Benjamin Franklin,* ed. and comp. John Bigelow (New York: Putnam's, 1904): 78–79.
[8]Isaac Asimov, "The Ultimate Speed Limit," *Saturday Review of Science* 8 July 1972: 53.

than abstract, and the sentences are comparatively short and simple. In writing with this kind of tone there is virtually no distance between writer and reader; it is as if two or three people were chatting over a cup of coffee or a beer.

Some writing assignments may warrant your using this casual, colloquial tone, but they are apt to be few. Unless you are writing a personal narrative or doing a satiric description of a person or a group, extreme casualness is inappropriate. One problem is that advertisers have so overused the casual tone that it often sounds insincere. The fake friendliness of many ads has made it difficult for the amateur writer to write in a colloquial tone without running the risk of sounding cute, coy, and phony.

Informal Tone

Characteristics of informal tone

The style and tone that will best meet most of your writing needs is that of informality. The term *informal tone* is about as broad and inclusive as the phrase *informal clothing,* and there are parallels between the two classifications. The notation *informal attire* on an invitation, loosely interpreted, means "Don't wear a nightgown or a swimsuit, and don't wear a tuxedo or white tie and tails, but almost anything else will do." Similarly, informal tone excludes the intimate or the ceremonial, but almost any other kind of writing qualifies.

Writers who use an informal tone establish a comfortable distance between themselves and their readers, one at which speakers do not have to raise their voices or use a public address system. The writer's imaginary setting might be a classroom, a club meeting, or a gathering of colleagues at a dinner. Authors who are writing for this kind of situation often make free use of the personal pronouns *I* and *you,* assuming that they and the audience have mutual concerns and interests. They write carefully and employ standard English usage although they might use a few contractions; if they bring in a slang term, they probably put it in quotation marks. Their vocabulary is that of educated people, and their language is a mixture of the abstract and concrete.

Formal Tone

Using a formal style and tone establishes a greater degree of distance between writers and their readers. People who write in a consistently formal tone give the impression of addressing a large audience they do not know. The imaginary scene could be one in which they are addressing a crowd from a speaker's podium; the occasion would be dignified, the topic serious. In formal writing, writers use an elevated vocabulary and an abundance of abstract terms; their sentences are relatively long, probably complex. They may use the pronoun *I* but do not address their audiences as *you*. The grammar is meticulously correct, and there is no slang or use of popular idiom.

In our time, so few people speak or write formally that it is almost impossible to find examples. John F. Kennedy's inaugural address comes close to it:

> We dare not forget today that we are the heirs of that first revolution. Let the word go forth from this time and place, to friend and foe alike, that the torch has been passed to a new generation of Americans — born in this century, tempered by war, disciplined by a hard and bitter peace, proud of our ancient heritage — and unwilling to witness or permit the slow undoing of those human rights to which this nation has always been committed, and to which we are committed today at home and around the world.

The balanced and complex sentence structure, the abstract language, and the lofty sentiments expressed qualify the passage as formal writing, although Kennedy does not seem completely remote from his audience.

In earlier, less hurried times, there was an abundance of formal writing. You will encounter it now mainly in reading nineteenth-century writers like Matthew Arnold or John Stuart Mill or in our own Federalist papers. It can be eloquent and elegant, but neither statesmen nor the public seem any longer to have the temperament or the patience for it.

Although students should learn to read formal writing and to appreciate its dignity, they should avoid it in their own writing. On the few occasions when your topic might seem weighty and lofty enough to call for it, it would be better to stay with serious informal writing. If not handled with great skill, formal writing can be dull, pretentious, and difficult to follow. At its worst, it degenerates into jargon.

Exercises on Connotation

1. Analyze the connotations of the terms in each of these groups. Are the words negative, positive, or neutral?

   club woman, joiner, civic leader

   moralistic, straight-laced, ethical

   athlete, sportsman, jock

   nonconformist, individualist, eccentric

   playboy, hedonist, good-time Charlie

   do-gooder, crusader, volunteer worker

   pious, sanctimonious, devout

   reactionary, conservative, prudent

2. What associations do you think automobile manufacturers wanted to establish when they chose these names for their cars?

Cougar	Mustang	Toronado	Jaguar
Skylark	Charger	Tempest	Firebird
Cutlass	Imperial		

3. What stereotypes do these labels evoke?

redneck	bleeding heart	cowboy	banker
freak	frat rat	quack	homemaker
brass hat	bureaucrat	egghead	women's libber

4. Rewrite the following paragraph, first with unfavorable connotation, then with favorable connotation. Which rewriting do you find easier to do? Why?

   In 1970 the President's Commission on Obscenity and Pornography concluded that the sale and distribution of pornographic material to adults in the United States should not be restricted. The report asserts that no one has established a connection between exposure to pornography and sexual offenses, that legislation to ban pornography is ambiguous, unenforceable, and potentially repressive, and that a nationwide sex education program would do more to solve sex-related problems than the banning of pornography would.

5. Identify the connotative words in the following passage, then rewrite the passage without them. Is the meaning of the rewritten passage substantially different from the original?

> "McDonald's Hamburger Stand is right in your neighborhood," says the company's annual report. It is no idle boast, for the firm has some 3,000 stores located almost everywhere. This $1.5 billion giant has a greater impact than merely intruding into America's diverse neighborhoods with its neon uniformity and trash-strewn presence. Its unerring sameness alters our perception of food. Mimi Sheraton, writing for *New York* magazine, reported that the fish caught for McDonald's Filet O'Fish sandwiches is treated on factory ships to stay white and be odorless and tasteless. It is then frozen and shipped to a central plant, where it is cut into shape, thawed, breaded, refrozen, and shipped to golden arches throughout the world. . . .
> The McDonald's standard is conformity. Their buildings look the same, their food tastes the same, their people act the same. They even operate a training center in Illinois, called Hamburger University, to make sure that their management and hamburgers in Toledo *are* the same as those in Phoenix. It is that conformity that they are selling — wherever you are, you can be sure that a meal at McDonald's will be uniformly clean. There is not much chance of your getting food poisoning at these places, but neither will you get excited.[9]

Exercises on Metaphor

1. Identify the submerged metaphors in the following sentences.

a. The lobbyists carefully cultivate members of Congress with favors and reap their rewards when the votes are taken.

b. Trapped in a white-dominated world, blacks have learned to live with trouble.

c. The methods of psychoanalysis remain shrouded in half truths.

d. Professionals steeped in jargon are bound to ooze it out in their writing.

[9]Jim Hightower, *Eat Your Heart Out* (New York: Vintage, 1975) 291–92.

e. Contemporary people are free, but often rudderless.

f. Office holders are besieged by requests for special favors.

g. He is a hard-boiled character.

h. Marxism carries the seeds of its own destruction.

i. One of the main planks of their platform is a pledge to close tax loopholes.

j. The program has too many strings attached to it.

2. Study the front-page stories and the editorials in your daily news-paper to find examples of metaphorical language. Which ones seem to be chosen deliberately, and which are little more than clichés? In your opinion, do those that appear to be chosen de-liberately help the writer's persuasive purpose? How?

3. Write out the meaning suggested by each of the following allu-sions. For example, you might explain the phrase "the Midas touch" as the ability to make money from any business ven-ture. If necessary, consult an unabridged dictionary or a desk encyclopedia.

Procrustean bed	Machiavellian tactics	Pyrrhic victory
Achilles' heel	Rabelaisian humor	Gordian knot
Socratic method	Panglossian optimism	

4. Think of ways in which these contemporary references could be used as allusions in your writing.

Ralph Nader	Disneyland
Hugh Hefner	Chris Evert Lloyd
Madonna	Charlie Brown

Exercises on Tone

1. Analyze the tone of the following passages. Ask yourself these questions: What reactions do the authors seek to evoke from their audience? How do the authors present themselves? What word or words describe the tone? What specific elements in the passages contribute to that tone?

a. Main Street is the climax of civilization. That this Ford car might stand in front of the Bon Ton Store, Hannibal invaded Rome and Erasmus wrote in Oxford cloisters. What Ole Jenson the grocer says to Ezra Stowbody the banker is the new law for London, Prague, and the unprofitable isles of the sea; whatsoever Ezra does not know and sanction, that thing is heresy, worthless for knowing and wicked to consider.

Our railway station is the final aspiration of architecture. Sam Clark's annual hardware turnover is the envy of the four counties which constitute God's Country. In the sensitive art of the Rosebud Movie Palace there is a Message, and humor strictly moral.

Such is our comfortable tradition and sure faith. Would he not betray himself an alien cynic who should otherwise portray Main Street, or distress the citizens by speculating whether there may not be other faiths?[10]

b. The Winnebago or Camper Crowd tends to be dedicated family types, somewhat overweight, extremely fertile, and usually middle-aged, regardless of their chronological age. They read the *Reader's Digest, Field & Stream, The American Legion Monthly, TV Guide*, and can be heard any time of the day or night endlessly blabbing back and forth over their beloved CB radios, using such terms as "Coed Seven," "Ten-Four," etc., picked up by watching "Adam 12" in reruns, one of their all-time, favorite TV shows.

On the other hand, the Van People tend to be heavily bearded, dedicated lifetime subscribers to *Rolling Stone*, compulsive consumers of granola, and they often pride themselves on making their own yoghurt. Their social habits tend to a distinct aversion to marriage unless it is performed by a guru or a Navaho shaman standing knee-deep in the waters of Gitchee-Goomie while the assembled company bays in concert to the moon, evoking the Great Wolf God, which is guaranteed to bestow eternal happiness and good vibes forever.[11]

2. Bring to class two advertisements with contrasting tone. Some pairs of magazines that could be useful are *The New Yorker* and

[10]Sinclair Lewis, *Main Street* (New York: Harcourt, 1920), preface.
[11]Jean Shepherd, "The Van Culture and the Camper Crowd," *A Fistful of Fig Newtons* (New York: Doubleday, 1981),

---

Seventeen, Playboy and *Ebony, Cosmopolitan* and *Reader's Digest,* or *Psychology Today* and *Ladies' Home Journal.*

3. Analyze the tone of one of these student papers. What elements in the paper create the tone?

American Business Interests Kill Cupid

What has America made of Valentine's Day? Business profits. Valentine's Day is defined as one day in which a sweetheart is "chosen or complimented." Well, a compliment is one thing, but an inundation of candies, cards, and carnations is something else! American business interests have brainwashed us into feeling obligated to buy our friends', family's, and lovers' love annually on February 14th with such products as candy, greeting cards, and flowers. Instead of a day complimenting our loved ones, Valentine's Day has become a profit-making occasion for certain money-hungry American business interests.

Red Hots. Sugar Hearts. Heart-shaped boxes of chocolate. Who needs a bunch of red-mouthed Americans running around? And what about those silly little sugar hearts you buy in little boxes? Have you ever read the sayings on them? "Hot Shot" "O.U. Kid." "Red Hot Mama." These outdated slogans are written on candies that don't even taste that good. And, aah, the infamous heart-shaped boxes of chocolate by Whitman's, Pangburns, and Russell Stover, to name a few of the designer candy companies. These are the epitome of the valentine clichés. So many thousands of them are packaged each year, they can hardly be considered a special compliment. And did you ever wonder how long the chocolates have been sitting in those pink- and red-cellophaned parcels? Since we know how overweight America is, it would only do us good to forgo all of this valentine candy.

Rack after rack of cards, cards, and more cards. The greeting card industry further exemplifies how American business interests have blown Valentine's Day way out of proportion. You know that Hallmark and the others have stretched the limit when they begin to print Valentine's cards for moms, dads, sisters, brothers, and Toto, too. Sure a card complimenting your sweetheart is appropriate, but a "Grandma and Grandpa, Be My Valentine card" is a little ridiculous.

Carnations. Red roses. The American flower industry definitely makes a killing on February 14th each year. That golden man must really wear out his little wings making all those deliveries. And poor (literally) boyfriends. They either buy their sweethearts a dozen long-stemmed red roses or their name is mud. And if it's not enough that the guys feel obligated to buy flowers in the first place, the florists also hike up their prices in honor of this one-day occasion. Thus, Valentine's Day is not only a day in which we are made to feel coerced and guilty by American business interests, it is also a giant rip-off!

Candy, cards, carnations. All have been used by American business interests to make Valentine's Day one of the most commercial holidays. Instead of expressing our love and affection 365 days a year, we have been taught that February 14th is *the* day set aside each year to show our love with material, store-bought goods. Romanticists unite. Let us kill the commercial features of Valentine's Day and enable Cupid to live!

Elizabeth Ann Black

That Quality Called "Drive"

To play Little League baseball, all boys must endure three hours of torture — a tryout. Tryouts test players' abilities in fielding, hitting, and pitching, as the coach looks on like a Roman emperor, with thumbs-up power of life or death over the young gladiators on the diamond. Parents bribe, cajole, coax, threaten and hound coaches into picking their boys. Mothers' bodies have been sold for a starting shortstop position. But ability and parental influence aren't the only ways to achieve baseball greatness. There is also that dogged quality which enhances mediocrity and transforms average players into vital parts of a team — drive.

I once had a coach who'd stand in front of the dugout, scrutinizing each player as if he were buying a used car.

"Men," he would bark, as 20 sets of braces disappeared behind 20 sets of lips, "to be on my team, you gotta have drive. Today's tryouts are designed to find out who does. Only 12 of you will make my team — those who have the drive."

Then we'd scatter onto the field like litter in a windstorm, each player taking his position, each player wondering whether he had the drive.

Standing at home plate, his voice echoing throughout the ball-park like the crack of a bat, the coach would loudly inform us that only eight fielders would be chosen, then pitchers would take the mound while the rest took turns in the batter's box. The speech usually ended with, "May the best men earn what they deserve."

The coach would then systematically swat the ball to different areas of the field, working the infielders and outfielders with the precision of a batting machine. He preyed on our weaknesses, trying to hit the holes, trying to find the boy to fill that hole. With a nose like an anteater, the coach would sniff the drive in a boy even if he was out in right field. He watched for players who didn't shy away from bad hops, and for those who didn't throw their gloves after the ball in disgust when they lost a fly in the sun. These were the "men" with enough drive to make the coach's team.

After about three hours of fielding, throwing and hitting a grueling barrage of baseballs, the coach would call time and barricade himself inside a dugout to make his final choices. Players stood around in groups, spitting in the palms of their gloves, smacking record-breaking gobs of Super Bubble, chewing the cleats off their shoes. Each minute lasted nine innings; time seemed to stop, as it does when you're waiting at the warning track for a long drive to come back into orbit.

Emerging from his meditation, the coach looked like the man who says, "May I have the envelope please," but who already knows what's inside. He enjoyed driving us crazy, he thrived on the suspense he held us in, he liked having us by the baseballs.

"Men," (he started every sentence as if he were Vince Lombardi) "I've decided to sleep on this. It's a tough decision, so I'll go home tonight and reassess the situation. A list will be posted tomorrow morning on the dugout wall with the names of my team on it." He pretended not to hear the groans and grumbles as he walked to his car, then turned as if stricken by another gem of baseball wisdom.

"Men," he intoned with reverence, "drive has nothing to do with cars, but it has everything to do with making them take you where you want to go." He smiled serenely, as if mentally comparing himself to coaching greats down through the ages, leaving a gaping group of bubble-blowers to bask in his wisdom.

That night, 20 ballplayers slept with baseball gloves under their pillows, praying something magical would rub off as they slept.

The next morning, 20 ballplayers arrived at the field before the sun, starting a vigil which lasted until the coach arrived with the List.

Finally, after tedium had evolved into a frantic desire to kill, the coach would drive up in his blue El Camino, equipment bags stacked neatly in the back, and slowly walk towards the dugout, the List in his hand.

The coach knew he held a captive audience, and he could never resist a chance to make a speech.

"Men," he said, as if addressing a plumbers' union, "there are no winners or losers, only those with drive and those without." He would then post the List and drive off in a cloud of El Camino dust.

We would crowd around, elbowing and pushing, trying to glimpse our names on the Holy Document, keeping fingers, legs and toes crossed. My name was never on the list, but I knew I'd be back next year, having the drive to endure another tryout.

Steve Bennett

Writing Assignments

In order to achieve the results they want with different audiences and for different purposes, all writers need to learn to control the tone of their writing. One accomplishes that goal by becoming sensitive to connotation, to various kinds of examples and anecdotes, and to the different shades of meaning that a change in language can convey. These writing assignments ask you to think about connotation from two different approaches: one asks you to analyze how two authors writing about similar topics achieve different tones through their choice of examples, their language, their expressed attitudes, and their distance from their material. The other asks you to write two versions of a paper with essentially the same content in ways that will change the tone of your writing.

Your audience for this paper is your instructor and your classmates who have also been studying connotation, metaphor, and tone. Before you begin to write the main part of either paper, write out a brief analysis of your readers. What assumptions can you make about them that will control how much specialized language you can use and how much explanation you have to give? What do your readers expect to get from reading your paper and what questions are they likely to have? Also write out your purpose in your paper.

Paper 1

Read these two examples about mother-daughter relationships by different authors and write a paper on how they differ in tone and in author's persona.

The mother who considers femininity her "blessing" from God may have a daughter who curses its name. "Being a good house-wife and mother is a most fulfilling role which God planned for all womankind and for which He especially equipped her with such assets as the ability to be all-loving, self-sacrificing, gentle, femi-nine," says a New Jersey housewife. "It is reward enough for me to see my husband busy but happy, my children leaders in their schools, because I am at home each day making beds, cooking good meals, and ready to listen each day with a full heart and ear to problems, sorrows, and joys."

But the daughter of a "buried woman" writes, "After my father's death, my mother, who had entirely given up her identity as an individual, then gave herself 'unselfishly' to us. She was afraid to walk on the street by herself. The children did the marketing 'be-cause you are so smart,' she used to say, while she stayed at home, mended our clothes, and wheedled finances from the rest of her family. She never could and never will feel like a whole person without us. At fifty-seven, my mother expects the children she raised to reap beautiful rewards for her. But believe me, I will have to be paralyzed, deaf, dumb, and blind before I become a preying, bigoted 'femininity-ist.' " (Betty Friedan, *It Changed My Life*)

As daughters we need mothers who want their own freedom and ours. We need not be the vessels of another woman's self-denial and frustration. The quality of the mother's life — however embattled and unprotected — is her primary bequest to her daugh-ter, because a woman who can believe in herself, who is a fighter, and who continues to struggle to create livable space around her, is demonstrating to her daughter that these possibilities exist. . . .

Many woman have been caught — have split themselves — be-tween two mothers: one, usually the biological one, who repre-sents the culture of domesticity, of male-centeredness, of con-ventional expectations, and another, perhaps a woman artist or teacher, who becomes the countervailing figure. Often this "counter-mother" is an athletics teacher who exemplifies strength and pride in her body, a freer way of being in the world; or an unmarried woman professor, alive with ideas, who represents the choice of a vigorous work life, of "living alone and liking it." This splitting may allow the young woman to fantasize alternately living as one or the other "mother," to test out two different identifications. But it can also lead to a life in which she never consciously resolves the choices, in which she alternately tries to play the hostess and please her husband as her mother did, and to write her novel or doctoral thesis. (Adrienne Rich, *Of Woman Born*)

What seem to you to be the main differences in tone and persona in these two pieces? How do the authors achieve those tones? What writing strategies do they use? Which passage do you find more effective, and why?

Paper 2

Write two short pieces of about 250 to 300 words each in which you treat the same topic using a different persona and a different tone. For example, you might write one essay from the point of view of an 18-year-old young man describing his new (actually secondhand) car to his older brother, and the other essay from the point of view of a 50-year-old successful stock broker describing his new car to his former college roommate, now president of a corporation. You create the characters and the situation, writing out their descriptions as part of the assignment.

Possible Topics
1. Two accounts of a person getting arrested for driving while intoxicated.
2. Two accounts of a street person who lives out of a backpack and a shopping bag on the streets of a major city.
3. Two descriptions of a currently popular music star.
4. Two commentaries on an exhibit of art, technology, architecture, or something similar that is currently on display on your campus or in your city.
5. Two commentaries on a controversial issue currently being debated at your school or in your city: for example, a teachers' strike, an incident of alleged police brutality, or a proposal to increase taxes or fees.

9 · Modes of Argument

*Definition of
argument*

In this book the term *argument* means more than a controversial or persuasive piece of writing; it also means writing that explains or informs. So one might say, "Weinberg's argument for the Big Bang theory of creation is based on evidence that the universe is expanding." Anytime a writer sets out to defend his or her ideas or to make a case for beliefs or opinions, he or she must construct arguments that support those ideas or opinions. The purpose of this chapter is to help you find or build those arguments and to suggest how they may be used.

The modes, or methods, of argument discussed in this chapter work particularly well when you already know most of your content before you start writing; that is, when you are writing self-contained prose of the kind described in Chapter 1. Suppose, for example, that you are a member of the board of directors of the student union and are asked to write a brochure to inform students about it. You have virtually all your information before you start — what kind of facilities the student union has, what activities it sponsors, what its hours are, what its fees are — and you have made a list of benefits students will get from using it. Now, as is so often the case with writers, your main job is to find an effective way of presenting what you already know to your audience.

*Ways of using the
modes of argument*

When faced with this kind of writing task, in which you are really trying to decide how you are going to structure your argument rather than what you are going to say, you will find the modes of argument particularly useful. You can ask yourself questions like these:

How can I describe to my audience what the student union is like? (*definition*)

How can I explain to them how they will benefit from using the student union? (*cause and effect*)

What specific examples of student union activity can I use? (*evidence*)

What other places that they enjoy are like the student union? (*comparison*)

The following discussion of these and other modes of argument may suggest some useful strategies for developing your arguments and for helping you to find new ones.

The Argument from Definition

Writers who want to argue intelligently and effectively must learn how to construct good definitions because often the first thing readers demand of a writer is that he or she explain key terms and define the issues to be discussed. And if readers don't understand those definitions, they are likely to quit in disgust. Thus the competent writer should understand what kinds of definitions he or she can use, which kind works best for specific situations, and how one goes about constructing them.

Traditionally, definitions fall into three categories: logical definitions, figurative definitions, and extended definitions.

Categories of Definitions

Logical Definition   Logical definition works by describing the thing to be defined briefly, explicitly, and objectively. For example, "A slave is a person who belongs to another"; "A book is a collection of printed pages bound together"; "Education is the training of the mind." Introducing a logical definition that sets precise limits to a word is often helpful in avoiding confusion in expository writing. For instance, in writing about the problems of narcotics, you would need to know the exact definition of *narcotic*. You look in the dictionary and find it defined as a drug that, taken moderately, dulls the senses, relieves pain, and induces profound sleep but that in excessive doses causes stupor, coma, or convulsions. Given these specifics, you would not be justified in calling tobacco a narcotic, but you might well classify alcohol as one. Similarly, you should know

Logical definition sets precise limits to a word

precisely what terms such as *capital crime* and *corporal punishment* mean when you use them in a paper.

Usually you will be able to find a clear, logical definition by going to the dictionary, but it is well to remember that logical definitions must meet two standards. First, they must be reversible; that is, the order of the word being defined and its definition can be reversed without affecting the meaning. Second, they must not be circular. A reversible definition of *narcotic* is: "a drug that dulls the senses, produces sleep, and with prolonged use becomes addictive."[1] It would not, however, be reversible if it defined *narcotic* as "anything that induces sleep." That description could fit an anesthetic, warm milk, or even a dull teacher. The circular definition that describes a narcotic as something that induces narcosis has little value because it simply repeats the key word in another form. Not quite so obvious but equally circular is a definition that defines feminine traits as characteristics typical of women.

Figurative Definition   Figurative definitions are those that define by using a figure of speech, principally metaphor. A figurative definition may be striking and colorful, but because its purpose is usually to persuade rather than to clarify, it should not be used when you are primarily trying to explain or identify. Here are some famous figurative definitions.

Figurative definition defines through metaphor

> Religion is the opiate of the people. (Karl Marx)
>
> A cauliflower is only a cabbage with a college education. (Mark Twain)
>
> War is hell. (General Sherman)
>
> Man is but a reed, the weakest in nature, but he is a thinking reed. (Pascal)

Notice that the real purpose of all these definitions is to express an opinion. Used as a nonlogical rhetorical device, the figurative definition may be effective, but it is an inadequate reply to someone who asks you to define your terms.

---

[1] © 1981 by Houghton Mifflin Company. Reprinted by permission of *The American Heritage Dictionary of the English Language.*

Extended Definition   An extended definition is, in a sense, an expanded logical definition that gives more information or details about a particular term or phrase. It can range in length from a paragraph to an entire essay or even a whole book. A literary handbook, for example, could define *satire* in one paragraph, but a teacher giving a course in satirical literature might take two or three lectures and many examples to give an adequate definition.

Extended definitions explain and persuade

Frequently, writers who are making extended definitions are trying to persuade as well as enlighten. By writing at length to show how they would define a term, they are really trying to convince their audience to share their beliefs. So Cardinal Newman wrote *The Idea of a University* to promote his beliefs about education, Thoreau wrote *Walden* to promote the simple life, and Sartre wrote *Existentialism and Human Emotions* to promote the philosophy of existentialism. And many writers have defined their ideal society in books: Plato's *Republic*, More's *Utopia*, and Skinner's *Walden II* are famous examples of such utopian literature.

How to Define

Ways of defining

Writers define by using a variety of techniques, singly or in combination. The most common ones are: attributing characteristics, analyzing or enumerating parts, comparing and contrasting, giving examples, and stating functions. These categories overlap, or even merge occasionally, but it does not matter if the categories cannot always be identified distinctly. Knowing how a process works is more important than giving it exactly the right name.

Attributing Characteristics   Defining by attributing characteristics requires that you concentrate on characteristics distinctive to the thing being defined. For example, if you were listing the characteristics of democracy, it would not be sufficient to say that in a democracy the rulers have the support of the majority of the people and are responsive to their will, because other kinds of government, monarchies or dictatorships, can also have those characteristics. The necessary and distinguishing characteristic of a democracy is that the rulers are chosen by the people in free and regular elections.

Giving distinctive characteristics

Similarly, if you were giving the defining characteristics of alcoholics, you would have to do more than say that they are people who drink too much. Alcoholics have other distinctive characteristics, such as drinking secretly and drinking compulsively. Notice that in the following passage Susan Sontag defines woman (or the role that she thinks our culture has assigned women) by listing what she identifies as uniquely feminine characteristics:

> To be a woman is to be an actress. Being feminine is a kind of theater, with its appropriate costumes, decor, lighting, and stylized gestures. From early childhood on, girls are trained to care in a pathologically exaggerated way about their appearance and are profoundly mutilated (to the extent of being unfitted for first-class adulthood) by the extent of the stress put on presenting themselves as physically attractive objects. Women look in the mirror more frequently than men do. It is, virtually, their duty to look at themselves — to look often. Indeed, a woman who is not narcissistic is considered unfeminine. And a woman who spends literally *most* of her time caring for, and making purchases to flatter, her physical appearance is not regarded in this society as what she is: a kind of moral idiot.[2]

Listing essential characteristics

Analyzing Parts   Defining by analysis or enumeration of parts is a similar device in that it lists features that are peculiar to and typical of the thing being defined. For example, the definition of *jargon* on page 246 gives a list of the various writing defects that typically appear in jargon. A definition of *beef stroganoff* would list the ingredients: strips of beef, onions, mushrooms, beef bouillon, and sour cream. A person who is defining the term *inner city* needs to specify the particular conditions that make an area qualify for that term. Some of them are traffic congestion, dilapidated housing units, a comparatively high rate of unemployment, a relatively high proportion of residents with low income or on welfare, substandard schools, few recreation areas, and inadequate public services, such as garbage collection and maintenance of streets.

In the following passage an author defines by analyzing the component parts of the topic:

> The Seventies were a time when planned outrage was in fashion, and Alice Cooper was taking full advantage of it. He was a forerunner of today's fascination with violence, harsh sexuality, and androgyny; his stage show featured simulated bloodletting, raw,

[2]Susan Sontag, "The Double Standard of Aging," *Saturday Review of the Society* Oct. 1972: 34.

---

suggestive song lyrics, and leering incitements of his young audiences. Alice appeared onstage every night wearing grotesque facial makeup and outlandish costumes; his show was the epitome of calculated tastelessness.[3]

Comparing and Contrasting   One of the most popular defining techniques is that of comparison and contrast. For example, you can define good writing by comparing it with bad writing. Good writing is clear, vigorous, precise, and original; bad writing is confusing, dull, vague, and hackneyed. The comparison/contrast technique is particularly useful in writing extended definitions of concepts or beliefs — for example, Riesman's "inner-direction" and "other-direction" mentioned on page 271; the literary movements of "realism" and "romanticism"; the notions of what is "masculine" and what is "feminine."

Showing likenesses and differences

The device can also be useful for defining personalities. For example:

> Tom Heggen and Ross Lockridge were similar in that neither had any previous notoriety, and they came from obscure, middle-class, Midwest backgrounds. Yet as men they could not have been more different.
>
> Ross was an oak of prudence and industry. He rarely drank and he never smoked. He excelled at everything he did. He had married his hometown sweetheart, was proudly faithful to her and produced four fine children. After a sampling of success on both coasts he had gone home to the Indiana of his parents and childhood friends.
>
> Tom Heggen had a taste for low life. He had been divorced, had no children and shared bachelor quarters with an ex-actor and screenwriter, Dorothy Parker's estranged husband, Alan Campbell. Tom was a drinker and a pill addict. He turned up regularly at the fashionable restaurant "21," usually bringing along a new girl, a dancer or an actress.[4]

Giving Examples   Probably the simplest and most concrete way to define is by giving examples. At the most elementary level, this tech-

---

[3]Bob Greene, "Alice Doesn't Live There Anymore," *Esquire* April 1985: 35.
[4]John Leggett, *Ross and Tom* (New York: Simon, 1974)

nique amounts to pointing to an object that a word stands for; for instance, the easiest way for an architect to define a mansard roof would be to show you one. In writing, however, we usually use examples to supplement and expand other kinds of definitions. If you were defining *antiutopian writing,* you would probably first specify that in this kind of literature authors depict planned and controlled societies that they want readers to reject. To support and expand the definition, you could then give Aldous Huxley's *Brave New World* and George Orwell's *1984* as examples of this kind of writing. Such examples are often invaluable in clarifying a definition. The term *natural sciences,* for example, can be defined as studies that deal with physical matter and phenomena. This definition seems vague, but your reader will understand the meaning immediately if you list physics, chemistry, biology, and geology as natural sciences. Defining with examples is one of the chief ways in which you can put into practice a cardinal rule of explanation: whenever possible, refer to the concrete and familiar to explain the abstract and unfamiliar.

Stating the Function   Finally, we sometimes define by giving the function of a person or object; that is, we answer that key question, "What is it for?" Sometimes specifying function may be the most important part of a definition. For example, a psychiatrist is a doctor who is trained to treat mental disorders; the purpose of sociology is to study patterns and processes in society; a thesaurus is a book that lists synonyms. At other times, listing the function of something may be of secondary importance, or it may be inapplicable or even impossible. You might, for instance, define a commune as an experiment in a new style of living and extend your definition by listing features typical of communes, analyzing the economic and domestic arrangements, and giving examples. Saying precisely what the purpose of a commune is would be more difficult. For some residents it might be saving money; for others, it might be expressing protest, seeking friends, or just trying something new. And when it comes to defining certain abstractions such as loyalty, liberalism, wealth, or existentialism, the question of function simply does not arise.

Using the Argument from Definition

The argument from definition usually takes at least one of the following forms:

---

1. It creates a yardstick or standard of measurement and then evaluates something according to that measurement.
2. It describes an ideal and seeks to persuade the audience to adopt that ideal.
3. It gives the bad feature or features of a person, institution, or theory and states or implies that the thing being defined ought *not* to be as it is.

Using definition to evaluate

A writer following the first form might outline the criteria for a good college athletic program and, by applying those criteria to the program at his or her own college, argue that officials need to make major changes. One could use the same method to argue that *Crime and Punishment* is a great novel, that Anthropology 302 is a bad course, or that the prison system in this country is a failure. The process is simple: create a yardstick, apply it, and make a judgment.

Martin Luther King provides an example of the second form in this excerpt from his famous "Letter from Birmingham Jail":

One may well ask: "How can you advocate breaking some laws and obeying others?" The answer lies in the fact that there are two types of laws: just and unjust. I would be the first to advocate obeying just laws. One has not only a legal but a moral responsibility to obey just laws. Conversely, one has a moral responsibility to disobey unjust laws. I would agree with St. Augustine that "an unjust law is no law at all."

Now, what is the difference between the two? How does one determine whether a law is just or unjust? A just law is a man-made code that squares with the moral law or the law of God. An unjust law is a code that is out of harmony with the moral law. To put it in the terms of St. Thomas Aquinas: An unjust law is a human law that is not rooted in eternal and natural law. Any law that uplifts human personality is just. Any law that degrades human personality is unjust. All segregation statutes are unjust because segregation distorts the soul and damages the personality. It gives the segregator a false sense of superiority and the segregated a false sense of inferiority. Segregation, to use the terminology of the Jewish philosopher Martin Buber, substitutes an "I-it" relationship for an "I-thou" relationship and ends up relegating persons to the status of things. Hence segregation is not only politically, economically and sociologically unsound, it is morally wrong and sinful. Paul Tillich has said that sin is separation. Is not segregation an existential expression of man's tragic separation, his awful estrangement, his terrible sinfulness? Thus it is that I can urge men to obey the 1954 decision of the Supreme Court, for it is morally right; and I can urge them to disobey segregation ordinances, for they are morally wrong.[5]

The next example, taken from an article urging radical changes in reform schools, illustrates the third form of the argument from definition, negative definition. By showing what reform schools are, the author argues for their abolition.

(1) They are expensive. Officials in a number of states have pointed out that it costs as much to keep one juvenile in an institution for one year as it would cost to send him to the most prestigious and costly prep school. . . .

(2) They are populated by children of the poor, generally blacks and Puerto Ricans in the East and blacks and Chicanos in the West . . . 89 per cent of the inmates came from homes where parents were on, or eligible for, public assistance. . . .

(3) They cannot be institutions of learning. The so-called industrial or training schools teach skills, not subjects, and the skills are generally those that are obsolete or designed to anchor the juvenile securely to the bottom of the social and financial scale.

(4) Their professional personnel are generally of low caliber. . . .

(5) Study after study has shown that the recidivism rate of young people is directly proportionate to the amount of time they spend in institutions. . . . A youth who spends several years in an institution is almost certain to spend most of his life behind bars.

(6) Finally, and perhaps most important, reform schools are prime devourers of the lard doled from the political pork barrel. Jobs in the school from top to bottom are political appointments, and local politicians are fighting tenaciously to retain this power to make appointments.[6]

[5]Martin Luther King, Jr., "Letter from Birmingham Jail — April 16, 1963" from *Why We Can't Wait* by Martin Luther King, Jr. Copyright © 1963 by Martin Luther King, Jr. Reprinted by permission of Harper & Row Publishers, Inc. and Joan Daves.
[6]Brian Vachon, "Hey, Man, What Did You Learn in Reform School?" *Saturday Review of Education* Oct. 1972: 72.

The Argument from Cause and Effect

The power of cause and effect arguments

Causal argument, the attempt to persuade an audience that one event caused another or that certain consequences will follow from certain actions, must be among the oldest patterns of human reasoning — and, in fact, of animal reasoning. People are naturally curious. They want to understand causes and be able to predict consequences, partly because if they can, they have some chance to control their lives. For this reason, cause-and-effect arguments can be particularly powerful.

Guidelines:
1. Don't overstate your case

As a writer you can construct good causal arguments and evaluate those of others if you keep in mind a few guidelines. First, when making a cause-and-effect argument, be willing to settle for establishing reasonable probability; don't overstate your case and force yourself into an indefensible position. You cannot really prove that the Supreme Court's abolishment of the death penalty will cause an increase in major crimes or that rising medical costs are going to bring about socialized medicine in this country. At best, you can only hypothesize and say that under the circumstances such results seem highly probable. And after you have made such a hypothesis, you have an obligation to support it by explaining how you arrived at your conclusion and by giving examples that reinforce your reasoning.

2. Don't oversimplify

Second, avoid simplistic thinking about cause and effect. One kind of oversimplification entails assuming that an event is the result of a single cause; for example, claiming that a decline in verbal scores on the Scholastic Aptitude Test has been caused by young people's watching too much television or that the changing status of women in the United States has caused a shortage of teachers. Both theories are attractively neat and simple, but they do not take into account the many complex factors that contribute to each of these effects. If you do want to argue a hypothesis like one of these — and it is certainly possible that each claim has an element of truth in it — protect your own credibility by saying, "One of the major causes of the teacher shortage in the United States is the changing status of women." You have a good chance of supporting that limited claim.

3. Don't confuse sequence with cause

Third, avoid confusing simple sequence with cause and effect. To do so is to commit the false cause fallacy, which is discussed in the section on fallacies in Chapter 11. Such confusion can be as simple and primitive as claiming that you had bad luck because you broke a mirror — in other words, superstition — or as sophisticated as the claim made by the philosopher Bertrand Russell when he asserted that conventional living destroys creativity. He based that claim on his belief that the quality of Wordsworth's poetry declined after he left his mistress in France and married a respectable young English-woman. The poet's work might have deteriorated for several reasons that had nothing to do with his love life.

4. Don't confuse correlation with cause

Fourth, be careful not to confuse *correlation,* or correspondence, with cause and effect. Sometimes when one reads about a correlation between two events, it's tempting to conclude that one caused the other when, in fact, one only parallels the other. For instance, one can show a correlation between people's credit rating and the amount they exercise. That doesn't show, however, that exercise *causes* a good credit rating. What it does show is that if people have the energy, motivation, and self-discipline to exercise regularly, they are also likely to have the energy, motivation, and self-discipline to make money and manage it wisely. When officials promote wearing seat belts by showing that people who wear seat belts live longer, they imply that wearing a seat belt *causes* you to live longer. Of course it doesn't, unless you are in an accident — then it certainly does. What the statistics do show is a high correlation between wearing seat belts and living longer, because people whose temperament and concern for safety makes them wear seat belts are likely to be the same kind of people who don't smoke or drink excessively and who eat carefully.

5. Don't give easy explanations for complex problems

Finally, be suspicious of cause-and-effect reasoning that brings in scapegoats or conjures up conspiracies to explain misfortune, and avoid it in your writing. Complex social problems have complex causes, and trying to solve them or to rationalize them away by blaming one group is naive or deceitful. A classic example of this tactic is Hitler's propaganda campaign against the Jews. By blaming them for the economic and social problems that followed World War I, he was able to divert the attention of the German people from their dissatisfactions and concentrate their hostility on a scapegoat. The same thing occurs in our country when people try to explain riots and demonstrations by blaming them on "foreign elements" and "outside agitators." Such simplistic rationalization prevents us from looking for the real causes of social unrest and postpones solutions. The critical thinker avoids this kind of thinking and rejects it in the writings of others.

The Argument from Circumstance

Characteristic phrases

The argument from circumstance is a special kind of cause-and-effect argument in which the speaker or writer seeks to persuade the audience to approve or at least accept a certain course of action on the grounds that no other course is practical or possible. Certain phrases recur so frequently in the argument from circumstance that they signal it. Typical ones are: "It is inevitable"; "We have no choice but to"; "Under the circumstances, our only option is"; "We are forced to"; and "Whether we like it or not, we must." Sometimes the argument contains the appeal "Our backs are to the wall" or "We are trapped by forces beyond our control." At other times it takes the fatalistic approach of "We might as well accept the inevitable." In any case, the task of the rhetorician is to convince the audience that the circumstances described as a cause are so pressing, so serious, that certain effects must follow. This is usually done by giving a detailed analysis and description of the circumstances.

The rhetoric of the Declaration of Independence fits the pattern of the argument from circumstance well. To explain why they advocated revolution, the writers used these words (italics added):

> But when a long train of abuses and usurpations pursuing invariably the same object, evinces a design to reduce them [the people] under absolute despotism, it is their right, it is their *duty,* to throw off such government, and to provide new guards for their future security. Such has been the patient sufferance of these colonies; and such is now the *necessity* which *constrains* them to alter their former systems of government. The history of the present king of Great Britain is a history of repeated injuries and usurpations, all having in direct order the establishment of an absolute tyranny over these states. To prove this, let facts be submitted to a candid world.

Fourteen paragraphs follow detailing the oppressive acts of George III. Apparently, the colonists agreed that the circumstances described were indeed intolerable and accepted revolution as the only solution.

In our own time, Martin Luther King's "Letter from Birmingham Jail" furnishes another example of the argument from circumstance (italics added):

> You deplore the demonstrations taking place in Birmingham. But your statement, I am sorry to say, fails to express a similar concern for the conditions that brought about the demonstrations. I am sure that none of you would want to rest content with the superficial kind of social analysis that deals merely with effects and does not grapple with underlying causes. It is unfortunate that demonstrations are taking place in Birmingham, but it is even more unfortunate that the city's white power structure left the Negro community *with no alternative.*
>
> . . . .
>
> As the weeks and months unfolded we realized that we were the victims of a broken promise. The signs remained. As in so many experiences of the past we were confronted with blasted hopes, and the dark shadow of a deep disappointment settled upon us. *So we had no alternative* except that of preparing for direct action, whereby we would present our very bodies as a means of laying our case before the conscience of the local and national community.[7]

Fictional arguments from circumstance

Arguments that explain human behavior solely in terms of environment constitute another kind of circumstantial argument. To claim that a person became a criminal because of growing up in a slum is really saying that "under the circumstances, crime was inevitable." Novelists often use this kind of argument by creating a set of circumstances to account for their characters' behavior. In *The Grapes of Wrath,* for example, Steinbeck carefully sets up natural and economic events that drove the Joads to become migrants. By portraying them as a poverty-stricken tenant farm family in Oklahoma during a prolonged era of drought, he makes the reader feel that their trek to California is inevitable.

Typical arguments from circumstance

We encounter less dramatic forms of the argument from circumstance in our everyday lives. For instance, when someone uses that

[7]King 79–80.

old cliché "If you can't lick 'em, join 'em," argument from circumstance is being used. People who reason that if they do not take advantage of an opportunity, someone else will, or who justify an action by saying that everyone else does it, are also arguing from circumstance. Anyone who argues that people can't help being the way they are is using the same reasoning.

Strengths of the argument from circumstance

The argument from circumstance can be extremely persuasive and difficult to refute. If a rhetorician can convince the audience that the circumstances are indeed compelling, so overwhelming that they lead to only one logical conclusion, probably she or he will win the point. In 1975, for instance, New York City authorities persuaded the administrators of City College of New York that students attending the college were finally going to have to start paying tuition even though such a move violated the traditions on which the college was based. They did so by simply pointing to the New York City budget and saying, "We can no longer pay the bills to run the college as it is." That claim was reinforced when the college closed its doors for several weeks and the faculty did not receive their paychecks. That kind of argument from circumstance is irrefutable. The crucial task in presenting a circumstantial argument is giving enough evidence to make a strong case for your side; merely hypothesizing about what *might* happen under certain circumstances will probably not convince a skeptical reader.

Weaknesses of the argument from circumstance

The weakness of the argument from circumstance is that often it is distorted into a justification for immoral or self-serving acts. People who are going to do something unethical, something that they are ashamed of, usually want to divert blame from themselves. Thus, they may try to avoid taking responsibility for their acts by pleading that they are victims of forces over which they have no control. For example, a scholarship athlete may justify his poor grades by pointing out that the four hours a day he has to devote to football practice make it impossible for him to study as much as he should; a politician may excuse broken campaign promises by saying that he had to make them in order to get elected; the owner of a business may claim that if she spends money to install pollution control devices, she will be forced out of business by her competitors. The argument from circumstance can easily degenerate into the argument from expediency. In evaluating both your own circumstantial arguments and those of others, you need to make careful distinctions between the inevitable and the merely probable, between consequences that are disastrous and those that are only inconvenient or unpleasant.

The Argument from Comparison

The Argument from Analogy

How analogies work

The person who argues from analogy tries to persuade by suggesting to an audience that things that are alike in some respects are probably alike in other respects. The logical process on which this kind of argument is based goes like this: if A and B share the qualities of X and Y, which we can observe, then they are likely to share the quality of Z, which we cannot observe.

Analogy can clarify but cannot prove

The argument from analogy is often striking and dramatic and for those reasons, it is frequently persuasive. You should remember, however, that at best it only enlightens and clarifies. Used as a reinforcement for other kinds of arguments, analogy can be very effective, but it never *proves* anything. The reason it does not is that rarely do you find two things that are alike in every major respect. Also, if the concepts or situations being compared are alike in one or two important ways, but not at all alike in other significant ways, the analogy will break down.

Take for example the "lifeboat" analogy proposed in this article by Garrett Hardin:

> If we divide the world crudely into rich nations and poor nations, two-thirds of them are desperately poor, and only one-third comparatively rich, with the United States the wealthiest of all. Metaphorically, each rich nation can be seen as a lifeboat full of comparatively rich people. In the ocean outside each lifeboat swim the poor of the world, who would like to get in, or at least share some of the wealth. What should the lifeboat passengers do?
>
> First, we must recognize the limited capacity of any lifeboat. For example, a nation's land has a limited capacity to support a population, and as the current energy crisis has shown, in some ways we have already exceeded the carrying capacity of our land.
>
> *Adrift in a Moral Sea.* So here we sit, say 50 people in our lifeboat. To be generous, let us say it has room for 10 more, making a total capacity of 60. Suppose the 50 of us in the lifeboat see 100 others

swimming in the water outside, begging for admission to our boat, or for handouts. We have several options: we may be tempted to try to live by the Christian rule of being "our brother's keeper," or by the Marxist ideal of "to each according to his needs." Since the needs of all in the water are the same, and since they can all be seen as "our brothers," we could take them all into our boat making the total of 150 in a boat designed for 60. The boat swamps, everyone drowns. Complete justice, complete catastrophe.

Since the boat has an unused capacity of 10 more passengers, we could admit just 10 more to it. But which 10 do we let in? How do we choose? Do we pick the best 10, the neediest 10, "first come, first served"? And what do we say to the 90 we exclude? If we do let an extra 10 into our lifeboat, we will have lost our "safety factor," an engineering principle of critical importance. For example, if we don't leave room for excess capacity as a safety factor in our country's agriculture, a new plant disease or a bad change in the weather could have disastrous results.[8]

The analogy Hardin draws is appealingly simple and, as he intends it to be, alarming. But it is also weak. The prosperous countries of the world do not really have much in common with lifeboats filled with wealthy people afloat in a sea in which other struggling and hostile people are swimming. For one thing, there are no more resources to be found or developed in a lifeboat; everything that can be used is already there. This is not true in the world, especially not in vast areas like Russia, China, and Brazil. Also, for the population of the world the choice is not simply float and survive, or sink and die. The people of the underdeveloped countries are, in most cases, surviving although sometimes not very well. And some of the countries, such as India, are taking drastic measures to see that they don't sink. There are also other major flaws in the analogy that any thoughtful person who questioned it would quickly see.

The following is an example of a more cogent and thought-provoking argument from analogy:

Public education is the nation's largest consumer industry. . . . In cases where quality of education is demonstrably poor, there is rea-

[8]Garrett Hardin, "Lifeboat Ethics: The Case Against Helping the Poor." Copyright © 1974 by Ziff-Davis Publishing Company. Reprinted from *Psychology Today*.

son to believe that consumers may legitimately take action in the courts. Students, parents, taxpayers, and, for that matter, Ralph Nader may well claim that the principles of law that govern business, industry, and some professions extend to education.

Do they? Here are some parallels that suggest possible lines of attack:

When a doctor or lawyer performs negligently, ignoring proper practice, he bears legal responsibility. When school boards, administrators, or teachers behave negligently in their instructional duties, do they bear major responsibility? Do they bear *any* responsibility?

When consumer products fail to work, the manufacturer or producer bears some legal responsibility for the failure. When teachers fail to teach, do the schools of education that produced those teachers bear responsibility for their failure? Similarly, when students fail to learn, are those responsbile for their learning — schools, teachers, and publishers and purchasers of educational materials — legally responsible for student failure?

When a consumer purchases a car, there is an "implied warranty" from the manufacturer and his agent to the purchaser that the car will perform certain minimal functions; for example it will start, propel itself, turn, stop, give a warning signal. Is there an implied warranty to the customer of educational services from the state and its local agents that, as a result of schooling, graduates will perform certain minimal functions?[9]

Don't stretch analogies too far

The authors of this article prudently frame their analogies as questions, inviting the reader to consider whether the reasoning is indeed valid. Such an approach actually strengthens their argument because, instead of annoying their audience by claiming more than they can prove, they simply say: Here is a new way to look at the responsibility of educators that has some profound implications. What do you think?

The A Fortiori Argument

This Latin term (which is pronounced "ah-for-shee-ór-ee") literally means "all the stronger." It is used to describe a mode of argument

[9]Gary Saretsky and James Mecklenburger, "See You in Court?" *Saturday Review of Education* Nov. 1972: 50.

A special kind of argument by comparison

that is based on probability. The argument works like this: you hypothesize about two possibilities, the second of which can happen more easily than the first; then, if you can show that the first possibility became a reality, you conclude that the second one should also materialize. In practice, this process is not nearly as complicated as this abstract description makes it sound; you have probably encountered it frequently and occasionally used it yourself. In its complete form the a fortiori argument looks like this:

> If we have the technology to put a shuttle into space, we should be able to figure out how to feed the hungry people in the United States.

> We have the technology to put a shuttle into space. Therefore, we ought to utilize our technology to feed the hungry people in the United States.

Presumably, launching a space shuttle is a much more complicated and difficult task than finding ways to feed people; the implication, then, is that it is ridiculous for us to be able to do the first and not be able, or at least willing, to do the second. Reduced to the form in which we usually find it, this argument reads, "If we can launch a space shuttle, we ought to be able to feed people in this country."

A fortiori arguments based on reason

Some a fortiori arguments are effective because they appeal to our sense of what seems logical. The argument that if an eighteen-year-old boy is old enough to fight for his country, he is old enough to be allowed to buy a beer is this kind of argument. An a fortiori argument that is sometimes advanced in favor of socialized medicine is this: if the state builds public schools and pays teachers in order that everyone may have the right to an education, why should it not build public hospitals and pay doctors in order that everyone might have the right to good health? It is a line of argument that is not easy to refute.

A fortiori arguments based on beliefs

Another form of the a fortiori argument appeals to our conviction that people are consistent and predictable. Arguments based on that assumption might run like this: if a woman will cheat a member of her family, she will certainly cheat a stranger; if a student will turn in a plagiarized paper, it is likely that he or she will cheat on an examination; if an army cadet panics in war games, he will go to pieces under enemy fire; the person who does well in difficult subjects like calculus ought to do well in comparatively easy ones such as Spanish. This kind of argument, which involves speculation about human behavior, is not as solidly grounded as those based on reason, but it can be forceful nevertheless.

The Argument from Evidence

Reinforcing opinions with facts

People who teach writing constantly remind writers to be concrete, give examples, use supporting evidence. Such advice is little more than a reminder to do in writing what most of us do almost automatically when we speak. In an oral argument we try to add the "weight of facts" to our claims, knowing instinctively that just our opinions are not going to persuade our listeners. So we turn to what we have seen, what we have read, what we know from direct experience, and what we have learned from others. All information of this kind comes under the general category of *evidence*. The principal kinds of evidence that the term covers are reports, statistics, personal testimony, factual references and history, and the appeal to authority from our experience or reading.

Reports

Using reports

In our mass-media culture, we have an unprecedented number of reports; television, radio, books, newspapers, and magazines keep us informed about a multitude of events and topics. The person who keeps up with current events through these channels has an impressive stock of resources with which to reinforce rhetoric. If you want to argue that this country should subsidize public hospitals, you can quote from an article in *Newsweek* that reveals what happens to the quality and cost of health care when business begins building hospitals for profit. You can bolster arguments on defense spending, migrant labor, or political propaganda by quoting television documentaries on those topics. Both the news columns and feature articles in newspapers can furnish you with supporting evidence for papers on topics such as conditions in the local jails, the cheating problem in colleges, or the need for more medical schools in your state. When you are writing on almost any controversial topic, you can find reports that will give you usable information.

Two questions to ask about reports:
1. Is the source reliable?
2. Is the reporter biased?

Reports are valuable when you are relying on evidence as one of your chief modes of argument, but they do present a problem because obviously all reports are not of equal value. How, then, do you evaluate them? There is no easy answer, but a good rule of thumb is to ask two questions about every report: (1) Is the source reliable? and (2) What is the bias of the person or group doing the reporting? In general, we can assume that major newspapers, national television and radio networks, and magazines of established reputation tell the truth. They may use loaded language and they may leave out certain important details, but what they print or broadcast is reasonably accurate. They cannot afford to have it otherwise. Less well-known newspapers and magazines that specialize in sensationalism or cater to an uncritical and poorly informed audience are less apt to be reliable.

Answering the question about bias involves determining whose interest the report might serve. Often the answer is that it serves no special interest, and you should not be so suspicious or cynical that you assume most reports are distorted in favor of a particular group or party. But only a naive person would fail to realize that a report on the condition of the beef industry put out by the Cattlemen's Association is going to differ in tone and emphasis from one put out by the Consumers' Protection League, just as a report on the quality of health care in this country that is made by the American Medical Association is going to differ from one made by the World Health Organization. It is not that the people who make reports deliberately lie; it is rather that someone who has an investment, emotional or financial, in a particular area — education, business, defense, medicine — can scarcely avoid stressing some points and playing down others. The persons who receive and use those reports should at least be alert to possible bias.

Statistics

The use of statistics can pose the same problem of bias. After all, whose statistics are they? A good rule here is to trust statistics and data that come from research organizations such as the Brookings Institution, from government bureaus and agencies, from national survey organizations such as the Gallup poll, from a nationally known encyclopedia or publications such as the *World Almanac*, and from research groups funded by universities or nonprofit foundations. But you should be at least slightly skeptical of polls financed by candidates or a lobby and about reports sponsored by individual companies, and very skeptical of any statistical data from unspecified sources. Phrases such as "reports show," "an independent research organization has found," and "statistics prove" do not constitute good evidence.

Bias in statistics

Personal Testimony

Your own experience is valuable

Personal testimony, their own and that of others, provides student writers with an easy and effective way to support many kinds of arguments. If you are working with a topic about which you have firsthand knowledge, you can use no better source of evidence than your own concrete experiences. What you have learned about race problems from incidents in your high school or what you have found out about graft in the construction business by helping to build an apartment house in which shoddy materials were used is impressive testimony, as good as an incident reported in the *New York Times* or *Playboy* magazine. When you recall the variety of experiences you have had in your life or know about in other people's lives, you will find that you have a surprising amount of testimony on which to draw. You should be careful, of course, not to overgeneralize from one or two incidents because the personal experiences of one individual are not enough to *prove* a general theory, but used as reinforcement and illustration, they add interest and concreteness to your papers.

Citing the experience of others

Using the personal testimony of others can also be effective, but here you may encounter problems regarding reliability. When you cite the experience of another person as evidence to support your point, be sure that you have direct knowledge about that experience or know the person well enough to vouch for his or her credibility. Anecdotes that you hear in casual conversation, particularly those for which no source is given, may be enlightening, but they do not provide substantial evidence with which to support a serious assertion. A critical audience will dismiss that kind of testimony as no more than "hearsay evidence," not admissible in any court and therefore not to be taken seriously.

Factual References

The weight of facts

The careful writer supplies the reader with solid evidence. For instance, in a column arguing that the United States is not a healthy country, Michael Killian compares the life expectancy in the United States with that of Iceland:

> The world's healthiest country is the one that would be my favorite even if it was the world's least healthy — Iceland. Life expectancy at birth in Iceland is now 73 years for men and 79.2 years for women — the highest expectancy on the planet. This compares with an American life expectancy of 68.7 years for men and 76.5 for women.[10]

A student writing a paper arguing for nationally subsidized day care centers used these facts:

> The Soviet Union has poured over one billion dollars into a new day care system in the past two years, and the system now serves more than 13 million children. The French have an extensive nursery system, a free kindergarten network for children over the age of three, state-licensed agencies that place children with volunteer sitters, and some 200,000 professional nannies. The Swedish government not only provides a day care center for children through the ninth grade, but will also pay 90 per cent of one parent's salary for a year so one parent can stay home.

Draw on references familiar to your readers

The supporting evidence used by both these authors is effective because it employs references that are familiar to a reasonably well-informed person. If you search your memory when you are writing a paper, you will probably find that you have a stock of similar material readily available. You can draw on historical as well as contemporary material, or you can use what you are learning in other courses. If you are writing a paper in which you try to show that harsh repression of unpopular opinions is not only cruel but also shortsighted, you might cite the examples of the Romans' persecution of the Christians, the Catholic church's persecution of Galileo, and the British government's treatment of Mahatma Gandhi. In a

---

[10]Michael Killian, "No Work to Longevity," *Austin American Statesman* 1 Dec. 1978: 14.

Modes of Argument

paper arguing for tighter controls on television advertising, you could support your claim that commercials are often misleading by bringing in two facts you learned in your nutrition course: rats fed for three weeks solely on so-called enriched bread died of starvation, and some cereals advertised as "nutritious and full of energy" really furnish the body nothing but calories. Once you develop the habit of looking for rhetorical material in your own experience, you will be surprised at how much information you have stored in your head.

The Appeal to Authority

Ways to argue from authority

The final kind of evidence that you can draw on in order to support your rhetoric or exposition is the appeal to authority. In an argument to support your assertion that there should be unity among the various factions on campus, you might quote Lincoln's warning: "A house divided against itself cannot stand." If you are trying to prove that riots and demonstrations are not phenomena of the twentieth century only, you could quote from the report of the presidential commission on the causes and prevention of violence. You could support a proposal to abolish the grading system by pointing out that low or failing grades have bad psychological effects on children, citing as your authority the famous behavioral psychologist B. F. Skinner, who claims that people learn best when they receive positive, not negative, reinforcement.

If you argue against smoking, you would be making an appeal to authority by quoting the inscription on all cigarette packages, "Warning: The Surgeon General has determined that cigarette smoking is dangerous to your health." You are also using authority when you cite a dictionary definition; for example, "Prejudice is an adverse judgment or opinion formed beforehand or without knowledge or examination of the facts; a preconceived preference or idea; bias."[11] References to the Constitution, the Bible, or any other revered document to emphasize or strengthen a point constitute another kind of appeal to authority. You can see that the stock of authoritative sources available to you is vast and varied. Usually the difficulty is not finding an authority to quote, but deciding which one best suits your purposes.

[11]© 1981 by Houghton Mifflin Company. Reprinted by permission of *The American Heritage Dictionary of the English Language.*

Problems With the Appeal to Authority   Because most of us are awed by experts, especially those with advanced degrees, titles, and several impressive awards, the argument from authority can be a powerful one. It does, however, pose certain problems. First, does the authority cited have credentials that will command the respect of your audience? You are more likely to win assent to your claims if you give the title, position, and qualifications of the authority you quote. For example, if you want to cite evidence on the problems of college faculties, you may say, "Dr. Reece McGee, professor of sociology at Purdue University and the author of *The Academic Marketplace* and *Academic Janus,* says that . . ."; in an argument against cutting defense spending, you could quote an opinion from the chief of naval operations. In both cases, you show that your authorities have the position, the qualifications, and the experience to make their testimony worth listening to. To rely on unverifiable and vague references such as "a well-known economist" or "the president of one of America's major universities" is an evasion of responsibility. And just as you should not rely on such devices yourself, you should not be impressed by them in the rhetoric of others. Remember also that you should not give much weight to the evidence of an authority who is operating outside his or her field of expertise. If a Nobel Prize–winning geneticist criticizes the space program, she should be listened to as a private citizen, not as an authority; when Paul Newman endorses a political candidate or O. J. Simpson recommends a car rental agency, their opinions should be regarded as those of private citizens because their expertise in show business or professional football does not carry over to politics or rental cars.

The other problem with using the argument from authority is that one can, without too much trouble, often find two qualified, reliable authorities who take opposite views on the same topic. Certainly you have heard biblical quotations brought in as support for both sides of an argument: "An eye for an eye, a tooth for a tooth" opposed to "Father, forgive them; they know not what they do." On the question of disarmament, you may find Senator William Proxmire on one side and Senator Phil Gramm on the other, both experienced, knowledgeable men, but with radically differing opinions. Two well-known, highly trained, and well-thought-of psychologists, Carl Rogers and B. F. Skinner, disagree emphatically on the best ways to influence human behavior. And so it goes. In situations like these, you can conclude only that intelligent authorities of good will

Cite your authority's credentials

The problem of authorities who disagree

often view matters differently and that there may be no single right answer available. For your rhetorical purposes, it is perfectly legitimate to try to find qualified authorities who support your point of view. If you give their credentials and quote them both accurately and in context, you are arguing fairly.

Combining Arguments

In practice, of course, any rhetorician combines several modes of argument (including some we have not yet discussed) and a variety of persuasive techniques in order to make her or his arguments convincing. You will be doing the same. It should be easier now that you realize how many places there are where you can look for ways to develop and support your assertions. As an illustration of how many means are available to the arguer, let us analyze the kinds of arguments that one writer put together in a short, persuasive essay.

Does the Devil Make Us Do It?

From evidence: personal testimony

New York — I was passing a sex shop on 42nd Street recently when the police were conducting a raid. The cops went in and the patrons came out. One customer, trying to duck the television cameras, exited quickly and then pretended he was merely a passer-by. He sidled up to me, to blend into the crowd, and watched.

"What's happening?" I asked him.

"A raid."

"What for?"

"Because," the man said, indignant now, "they got all that filth in there."

From definition: attributing characteristics; giving examples

The incident says a lot about the confusing American view of pornography. That view has always been a hypocritical one. As a nation we have never made up our mind, when handed a dirty picture on the corner, to smile, to call the cops, or both.

I vote we just smile. What's all the big sweat, anyway?

From definition: attributing characteristics

From definition: stating function

We are a people titillated by sex. Increasingly so. Where once the smut business in this country was largely manufactured in France or at least made in Japan, it is now fully an American industry. It is big, big business. New York City has two dozen weekly sex newspapers selling from 50 cents to $1 an issue. Forty-second

Street hawkers sell everything from phony stimulants to pathetic photos of "genuine schoolteachers from Ohio."

Silicone-breasted go-go dancers perform in the shadow of Washington's capitol, not rarely for nightclub-touring government officials. X-rated movies have become so common many drive-ins have begun offering them, along with customer anonymity. . . .

Indeed, pornography has gone socko. Why? Because the nation wants it (although the nation won't admit it). People now spend as much as $2 billion annually, by some industry estimates, to further the phenomenon.

Undeniably, much of what has happened has been unfortunate. Manhattan's 42nd Street, which used to be a tourist attraction, is now, with its bosom-boosting, a mean tourist trap. The sex clubs along Washington's 14th Street are, late at night, overly aggressive, with their loud music, their nude window photographs and their pimps at the door begging customers. Many people are genuinely offended that newspapers now advertise X-rated movies with their drippy titles ("The Midnight Plowboy"). This kind of aggressiveness is, perhaps, open to legislative restriction — if only because it foists pornography on that part of the population which is definitely not interested.

But beyond this protection of the innocent (including children), there seems to be no logical or even moral reason to call the cops on smut. You look or you don't look. You buy or you don't. If nobody forces you, what really is the crime? . . .

Two years ago, the President's Commission on Pornography and Obscenity released the results of a thorough, three-year, extremely objective study of smut in America. It was a blanket admission that the nation, the John Birchers, the J. Edgar Hoovers, had been worrying for naught for generations. The commission says that exposure to sexual material does not cause crime, emotional problems or lead to character deterioration. It said that it is "extremely unwise" for governments to attempt the legislation of morality beyond behavior. It said that all laws prohibiting or limiting sale or showings of sexual material should be repealed. And it said, moreover, that most Americans believe in sexual propaganda.

The commission's report, predictably, was buried under a blanket of condemnation. But its findings are, two years later, no less relevant and revealing. The First Amendment of the Constitution (free speech, free press) applies to all or it does not really apply to any. If we allow this newspaper to print, we have to also, consti-tutionally, even though we personally object, allow the beady-eyed peddlers to go to press too.

So smile. Smile! Is sex really so decadent?

O.K. So you don't like pornography. Stout fellow. But others do, a good many others, and hypocritical though some of them are, they are remarkably human. The fellow outside the 42nd Street shop, for example. When he started cheering the police raid, I told him to can it, that I had seen him slink out of the door, that even then he had a dirty book in his pocket.

"Oh," he said, turning colors, ending up in green, "well, ah, that is," he took out the book and grinned, "the devil made me do it."[12]

Exercises

1. Identify the mode or modes of argument appearing in the follow-ing examples.

   a. Running a university is like running a business, and therefore it is a good idea to have business people for regents. The purpose of a university, after all, is to turn out a reliable product.

   b. If a person can find time to jog and play handball every day to keep in shape, you would think that he or she could find time now and then to read a book to keep the mind in shape.

   c. I see nothing wrong with selling dirty books at the college bookstore. If it doesn't do it, the store next door will.

   d. "A State which dwarfs its men in order that they may be more docile instruments in its hands even for beneficial purposes — will find that with small men no great thing can really be accom-plished; and that the perfection of machinery to which it has sac-rificed everything, will in the end avail it nothing." (John Stuart Mill)

   e. The head of the psychology department at our university says that this country is on the brink of a sexual and social revolution.

   f. "In all things that are purely social we [the black and white

---

[12]Tom Tiede, "Does the Devil Make Us Do It?" *Taylor (Texas) Daily Press* 24 Nov. 1972. Reprinted by permission. © 1972 NEA, Inc.

races] can be as separate as the fingers, yet one as the hand in all things essential to mutual progress." (Booker T. Washington)

g. A true liberal is one who believes in progress and is willing to listen to new ideas. Senator John Kerry's voting record has convinced me that he fits the description.

h. Henry cannot really be blamed for stealing the car. His home life, the pressures of poverty, and our culture's stress on the automobile as a status symbol made it impossible for him to resist.

i. The Department of Labor recently put out a bulletin showing that there would be a 26 per cent increase in the demand for nurses and other health workers in the next decade. Obviously these professions provide the ideal choice for an ambitious young person.

j. Professional football is now the king of sports in this country. When I try to visit my friends on Sunday afternoon or Monday night from August through December, I find them sprawled in their living rooms with their eyes glued to the television. Half the sports section each week is taken up with analyses of games past and games to come. Like well-paid gladiators who cannot last in the arena more than a few seasons, the battered but arrogant pros endure their weekly agony so that the citizenry may be entertained. Our new national heroes are violent and brutal men, and the effect on our young people is bound to be degrading.

2. Using at least three of the standard methods of defining, write an extended definition of one of the following:

   a. A slum
   b. An unscrupulous politician
   c. A successful athlete
   d. A bad environment for a child
   e. A foolish parent
   f. A racist
   g. A conservative

3. Analyze the various methods of defining that the author uses in the following selection.

"Ghetto" was the name for the Jewish quarter in sixteenth-century Venice. Later, it came to mean any section of a city to which Jews are confined. America has contributed to the concept of the ghetto restriction of persons to a special area and the limiting of their freedom of choice on the basis of skin color. The dark ghetto's invisible walls have been erected by the white society, by those who have power, both to confine those who have *no* power and to confine their powerlessness. The dark ghettos are social, political, educational, and — above all — economic colonies. Their inhabitants are subject peoples, victims of the greed, cruelty, insensitivity, guilt, and fear of their masters. . . .

The ghetto is ferment, paradox, conflict, and dilemma. Yet within its pervasive pathology exists a surprising human resilience. The ghetto is hope, it is despair, it is churches and bars. It is aspiration for change, and it is apathy. It is vibrancy, it is stagnation. It is courage, and it is defeatism. It is cooperation and concern, and it is suspicion, competitiveness and rejection. It is the surge toward assimilation, and it is alienation and withdrawal within the protective walls of the ghetto.[13]

4. How good are the following analogies?

a. The House version of the bill gave the President the right arbitrarily to cut back [congressional] spending in any area at all — including, theoretically, social security, or veterans' pensions, or interest on the national debt. . . . There is plenty of resistance in Congress, in part for the same reason that an extravagant wife resists when her husband proposes to take over sole control of a joint checking account. Senate Majority Leader Mike Mansfield has even said that if the House bill became law, "you might as well abolish Congress," which is the kind of exaggeration to which extravagant wives are prone.[14]

b. What could become of such a child of the seventeenth and eighteenth centuries, when he should wake up to find himself

[13]Kenneth Clark, *Dark Ghetto: Dilemmas of Social Power* (New York: Torchbooks, 1967) 11–12.
[14]Stewart Alsop, "What Nixon Hears the Voters Saying," *Newsweek* 23 Oct. 1972: 120.

required to play the game of the twentieth? Had he been consulted, would he have cared to play the game at all, holding such cards as he held, and suspecting that the game was to be one of which neither he nor anyone else back to the beginning of time knew the rules or the risks or the stakes? . . . Probably no child born in the year held better cards than he. Whether life was an honest game of chance or whether the cards were marked and forced, he could not refuse to play his excellent hand. . . .

As it happened, he never got to the point of playing the game at all; he lost himself in the study of it, watching the errors of the players.[15]

5. Carefully examine the analogies that are drawn in the passage from the article "See You in Court?" on pages 304–305. What likenesses are the authors suggesting between the processes and products of an educational system and those of a corporation? What likenesses are there between the professional obligations of a doctor, lawyer, or engineer and those of a teacher? What major similarities do you see? What major differences do you see? What strengths and what weaknesses do you find in the analogies? If, as the authors imply by their title, the charge of the schools' turning out substandard products were taken into court, what do you think the decision would be?

6. Which of the following cause-and-effect arguments and arguments from circumstance do you find convincing? Why?

a. The high standard of living in the United States has brought about our energy crisis.

b. We must grant the Department of Justice the privilege of tapping phones and installing listening devices in homes or offices because if criminals make use of this modern technology, law enforcement agencies cannot afford to do without it.

c. Doing away with the grading system in college would put a stop to students' cheating.

d. Television advertising is responsible for the "revolution of rising expectations" in this country.

[15]Henry Adams, *The Education of Henry Adams* (New York: Modern Library, 1931) 4.

e. The power of the farm bloc in Congress has declined in the last twenty-five years because the number of people living on and making a living from farms has dropped from 15 per cent to 7 per cent.

Writing Assignments

Cause and effect and circumstantial arguments, arguments from comparison, and arguments from evidence and testimony can be particularly useful for organizing and developing papers in which you want to explain something to your audience or convince them about a particular issue. Use some of the strategies for argument discussed in this chapter to develop one of the following papers.

Paper 1

Your mother is a graduate of the same college that you attend and in charge of the twenty-fifth reunion for her college class. Before it is held next fall, she would like the alumni who are going to attend to have the chance to read about some of the major changes on campus since they graduated. She is asking you and your classmates to contribute short essays of no more than 150 words on various topics, and she and an editor will pick ten to publish in the alumni magazines. (They will be what editors call "blind submissions"; that is, the authors will be identified only by number and the person who chooses the essays will not know who wrote them.) You can write about anything you think the alumni will find interesting: anything from the change in living styles or dress to the change from working with sliderules and typewriters to working with pocket calculators and word processors. If you look around your campus and talk to your mother about her college days you should find an abundance of possible topics.

Before you begin the main part of your paper, write out an analysis of your readers, stating why they would want to read, what they would hope to get from reading your paper, and what questions they would like to have answered. Also write out your specific purpose in the paper: what do you hope to accomplish with you readers?

Possible Topics

1. The change from old-style, closely restricted dormitories to contemporary coeducational dormitories.
2. The change from slide rules to calculators.
3. Major new buildings on campus in the past ten years.
4. A new major field of study that didn't exist ten years ago.
5. Comparison of the cost of education today and twenty-five years ago: tuition, dormitories, fees, etc.

Paper 2

In a short article of no more than one thousand words, also written for the alumni magazine of your college, discuss the reasons for a current problem on your campus that is causing college administrators serious concern. Analyze the elements of the problem, suggest some of the reasons it has developed, and suggest a possible solution or solutions.

Before you write do an audience and purpose analysis that includes the points suggested in the directions for Paper 1.

Possible Topics

1. Excessive drinking on campus, leading to serious accidents and a high failure rate.
2. Outdated and inadequate housing facilities on campus.
3. Decrease in student aid funds that is causing some students to leave school.
4. Excessive focus on athletics.
5. Poor teaching in certain courses.

Paper 3

You may have heard some of the professors at your college or university or some of the college alumni blaming the high schools for not giving students adequate preparation for college. (Professors and alumni have always made this complaint, by the way, but each generation seems to think it must repeat it.) In a short article of no more than a thousand words, written for your college's alumni magazine, use the evidence of your own experience in high school to argue for or against the allegation that high schools don't do a good job. For instance, you may write about a wonderful high school math teacher who gave you excellent preparation for your college calculus course, or you might write about a language teacher who made learning French or Spanish or Latin a fascinating adventure. You might also write about an English teacher who used ingenious gimmicks for encouraging his or her students to write. Or you might conclude that for your high school, at least, the complaints are true, and give examples from your own experience to support your points. This assignment gives you an excellent chance to put people in your writing and to write about something on which you are certainly a qualified authority.

Before you write, do the same kind of audience and purpose analysis suggested for Paper 1.

10 · Three Approaches to Argument

CHAPTER

In addition to using the modes of argument described in the previous chapter, writers who want to persuade with an appeal to reason frequently use *induction* and *informal logic.* This chapter will examine those two reasoning processes and suggest ways in which we can use them most effectively. The chapter also describes *Rogerian argument,* a nontraditional method of rational appeal that has been gaining popularity in recent years.

Induction

Induction moves from the specific to the general

The person who argues inductively is using a variation of the argument from evidence; that is, he or she gathers and examines data, reports, testimony, and other evidence and arrives at a conclusion. This kind of reasoning is sometimes called the *scientific method* because scientists frequently arrive at their theories and findings by observing evidence, analyzing it, and drawing conclusions that account for what they have observed. But whether we call it induction or the scientific method, we are describing a process of reasoning by which one moves from observations about specific, individual cases to a generalization that applies to all of those cases.

All of us use inductive reasoning, but too often we do not even stop to think about whether we are being careful about the kinds of conclusions we draw or whether we are generalizing from too little evidence or from evidence that is biased or poorly chosen. Unfortunately, many people form strong opinions from inaccurate and inadequate data and, by doing so, brand themselves as sloppy thinkers. For example, suppose you are trying to convince your parents that you should change your major from business to psychology because

you have decided you want to become a family and marriage counselor. They refuse even to talk about it because they once went to a counselor who had so many personal problems of her own that she finally committed suicide. They insist that all counselors are crazy themselves. You would be furious and frustrated because they were basing decisions about your career on just one example.

Yet an astounding number of people are too lazy or too attached to their biases to go to the trouble of looking at a number of samples before they make up their minds. As the logician Lionel Ruby points out:

Pitfalls of induction

Hasty generalization is perhaps the most important of popular vices in thinking. It is interesting to speculate on some of the reasons for this kind of bad thinking. One important factor is prejudice. If we are already prejudiced against unions, or businessmen, or lawyers, or doctors, or Jews, or Negroes, then one or two instances of bad conduct by members of these groups will give us the unshakable conviction that "They're all like that." It is very difficult for a prejudiced person to say, "Some are, and some aren't." A prejudice is a judgment formed *before* examining the evidence.[1]

Generalizations are necessary

Nevertheless, as Ruby goes on to say, in spite of our knowing that generalizations are dangerous, we must generalize. If we did not, we could not learn from our experiences or make any inferences from information that we gather. What we must do, then, is to find guidelines for the legitimate use of the inductive method, guidelines to follow in constructing our own arguments and to use as a check in evaluating the inductive arguments of others.

Criteria for Valid Induction

We cannot expect perfection in any argument, but we can set up and apply reasonable criteria. The criteria for the proper use of evidence in an inductive argument are, briefly, as follows:

1. The evidence should be of sufficient quantity.
2. The evidence should be randomly selected.

[1]Lionel Ruby, *The Art of Making Sense* (Philadelphia: Lippincott, 1954) 259.

3. The evidence should be accurate and objectively presented.
4. The evidence should be relevant to the conclusion drawn.

Choosing a large enough sample

Sufficient Evidence　When you construct an inductive argument, the first question you should ask yourself is "How big should the sample be?" The answer, of course, depends on the size of the whole about which you are going to generalize. Although there are no hard and fast rules about proportion, common sense tells you that the larger the population (group being investigated), the larger your sample should be. Thus, if you are going to generalize about a student body of ten thousand, you should probably gather data on at least five hundred individuals in that body; to use fewer would be to run the risk of missing important evidence. Note, however, that in generalizing about a comparatively small group, you have to use a proportionately larger sample. It stands to reason that if you have an assortment of cards bearing ten different designs, you will not get a representative cross section of those designs by turning up only five cards out of one hundred; if you were to turn up five hundred cards out of a total of ten thousand, however, your chances of getting a fair sample are much better. Similarly, if you were polling a class of one hundred, you could not come to any supportable conclusions by interviewing only five people from that class.

In practice, few writers specify exactly how many individual items their sample includes or mention the size of the total population about which they are generalizing. Rather, they give several examples, and the reader must decide whether the examples are sufficient. The reader must also estimate the size of the total group, but in most cases that is not too difficult to do. Usually a reader can tell whether a writer is generalizing about a whole population or a comparatively small subgroup, such as factory workers, professors, or housewives. Since there are, after all, time and space limitations when presenting an argument, readers should not be too critical or always ready to reject an argument because the sample may not be as large as, ideally, it ought to be. They must be satisfied with what seems like a reasonable number of examples.

Random Samples　When you are gathering evidence for an inductive argument, the amount of evidence you collect may be less important than the variety of evidence. For valid inductive arguments, you must have a *random sample.* Investigators can get a random sample in two ways: first, they can choose data strictly by chance, or second, they can choose data that reveal a true cross section or representative picture of the whole population.

This second kind of sample is exemplified by the voter profile analysis method the major television networks use in order to predict final results very early in the evening on election night. You may have been surprised (and a little irritated by the apparent wisdom of computers) to hear the news reporter say, "On the basis of 2 per cent of the vote now in in our sample precincts, we predict that Senator Lugar will win by a landslide in Indiana." And usually he turns out to be right, not because he or the computers possess any supernatural wisdom, but because the sample precincts have been carefully chosen to be as representative as possible of the state as a whole.

If Indiana has 39 per cent Protestants, 13 per cent Jews, 38 percent Catholics, and 10 per cent other, so do the precincts; if the state has 12 per cent of the population earning above $30,000, 25 percent earning between $20,000 and $29,000, 38 per cent earning between $10,000 and $19,000, 22 per cent earning between $5,000 and $9,000, and the remainder below $5,000, so do the precincts. Other relevant data, such as level of education, occupation, percentage of eligible voters going to the polls, and political party registration, also enter into the calculations. The tremendously complex process is made possible by sophisticated computers that can retain and analyze huge amounts of diverse information. The result is a nearly perfect piece of inductive reasoning.

In ordinary rhetoric you have neither the need nor the means to do such detailed and meticulous sampling, but you can learn much from the voter profile method. If you are generalizing about a group, you must have evidence from a representative cross section of that group; if you do not, your sample will be warped or skewed. For instance, if you want to find out what the dominant political opinions are on your campus, you will need to get evidence from students in a variety of departments: engineering, business, fine arts, languages, English, pharmacy, and physics might make a representative sample. You will also need to include students from different income levels. The accurate distribution of your sample will be as important, or more important, as the number of students you poll, for people in certain occupations and income levels have a predisposition to think alike. If you take your sample from only one group

— the group easiest to reach — you will not get a true cross section.

If you do not have enough information about the subdivisions of your total population to construct a "sample precinct," you can use the other technique that will insure a random sample: selecting your evidence solely by chance. One way to do this would be to pick every tenth name out of the student directory; another would be to pick every tenth student who goes into the university bookstore at textbook-buying time or every twenty-fifth student who comes through the line to pay registration fees. If your sample is large enough it will be a reasonably accurate cross section. Professional pollsters like Gallup or Roper use both the representative and chance methods to insure an unbiased, truly random sample of public opinion. They are also careful to frame their questions in neutral terms because loaded questions produce biased evidence. Asking people "Are you opposed to forced busing to achieve integrated schools?" will evoke quite different answers from "Are you in favor of busing as a tool to achieve racial balance in schools?"

Examples of biased samples

A few examples will illustrate the dangers of generalizing from a skewed sample. The classic instance is the 1936 presidential poll conducted by the now defunct magazine *Literary Digest.* On the basis of responses from people chosen by chance from the telephone books of several cities, the editors predicted that Landon would defeat Roosevelt. They couldn't have been more wrong. What they failed to consider was that in 1936, when the depression was still severe, only the relatively prosperous segment of the total electorate had telephones.

Another example of a biased sample occurred in 1980 in a report that suggested that a high-fat and cholesterol diet may not be as harmful as earlier studies had indicated. The report drew angry criticism when it was revealed that "half of the 15 members of the nutrition panel have acknowledged that they have financial ties to the food industry."[2]

We all should keep in mind how easy it is to fall into the habit of basing conclusions on biased evidence. Most people prefer to spend their time with others who think as they do: business people talk to other business people, professors talk to professors, doctors to doctors, and students to other students. Occasionally, we may have a

[2]Anne Roard, "Science Academy's Nutrition Report Arouses Congressional Ire," *Chronicle of Higher Education* 30 June 1980: 14.

serious conversation with someone whose views differ from ours, but usually we seek out individuals whose opinions reinforce our own. It's more comfortable that way. The danger is, however, that we will take the small part of the world that we know best as representative of the larger whole. So doctors may find it difficult to believe that any substantial number of people are in favor of socialized medicine, and business people tend to think that everyone is satisfied with our economic system. Because we tend to believe what we want to believe, it is all too easy to interpret agreement from others like ourselves as broad-based support. Politicians, pollsters, and research scientists are among the few classes of people who make a conscious, consistent effort to take a truly random sample before they draw conclusions. The rest of us could learn from their methods.

How to judge the integrity of the source

Accurate Evidence   Judging the accuracy of inductive evidence may pose problems. In this age of specialization and experts, many of us feel we are not qualified to decide which data are genuine and which spurious. Most of the time we have to rely on the integrity of the speaker or writer; we must assume that most people tell the truth and that they do not falsify reports that could easily be checked. If, for example, a government official says, in arguing for a continuation of our Intercontinental Ballistic Missile program, that the Soviet Union has 1,712 intercontinental missiles, that person may be exaggerating but probably is not. The senator who opposes the program also has access to such information and would be quick to attack a false statement.

Use your common sense to test evidence. If you read a statement in some magazine or paper you suspect is biased, don't accept it unless the writer has included supporting statistics or facts and given the source of those facts. And be suspicious of the writer who makes extravagant claims on the basis of a small number of data.

The student writer also has an obligation to identify sources when quoting material or opinions. If you use statistics, you should be sure they are reliable, and you should let the reader know where you found them. If you make a positive statement about a matter on which there are conflicting views, show in some way that you have significant information to back up your statement; you could, for example, quote a professor from whom you took a course, or you could cite a documentary film you saw.

Relevant Evidence, Relevant Conclusions   Finally, we must ask whether the conclusion drawn from the evidence is relevant and whether the facts given actually do point to the conclusion that we or a writer or speaker have drawn. Although it is true, for example, that Americans spend more of their personal income for medical care than the people of any other nation, we are not justified in concluding that consequently we get the best health care. Doctors' fees, drug prices, and hospital charges are significantly higher in the United States than in other countries, but there is no provable correlation between cost and quality. Similarly, concluding that today's farmers are lazy because most of them no longer keep a milk cow or raise chickens would not be warranted, for it ignores the fact that they are simply devoting their energies to other, more profitable work.

Evidence must fit the conclusion

In his article on the American use of convenience foods, "Science Has Spoiled My Supper," Philip Wylie commits the error of drawing an irrelevant conclusion from the evidence given:

> Without thinking, we are making an important confession about ourselves as a nation. We are abandoning quality — even, to some extent, the quality of people. The "best" is becoming too good for us. We are suckling ourselves on machine-made mediocrity. It is bad for our souls, our minds, and our digestions. It is the way our wiser and calmer forebears fed, not people, but hogs; as much as possible and as fast as possible, with no standard of quality.
>
> The Germans say *"Mann ist was er isst* — Man is what he eats."* If this be true, the people of the U.S.A. are well on their way to becoming a faceless mob of mediocrities, or robots. And if we apply to other attributes the criteria we apply these days to appetite, that is what would happen! We would not want bright children any more; we'd merely want them to look bright — and get through school fast. We wouldn't be interested in beautiful women — just a good paint job. And we'd be opposed to the most precious quality of man: his individuality, his differentness from the mob.[3]

Although Wylie may make a good case that the frozen and packaged foods described in the essay are inferior, he establishes no necessary or even probable link between Americans' eating processed food and

[3]Philip Wylie, "Science Has Spoiled My Supper," *Atlantic Monthly* April 1954: Reprinted by permission of Harold Ober Associates Incorporated. Copyright © 1954 by the Atlantic Monthly Company, Boston, Massachusetts.

their loss of individuality and good taste — qualities that, by the way, he does not prove they had before they started eating convenience foods.

Consequences of invalid induction

Drawing an irrelevant conclusion about convenience foods does no great harm, but misusing the inductive method can have more serious consequences. Probably you know of instances in which unthinking people have made rash and sometimes harmful judgments on the basis of wholly inadequate evidence. Beliefs many people share about welfare furnish one example. An individual may know or hear of one or two families on welfare who have color television sets. When driving through the poorer areas of a city, this person may also see expensive cars parked along the curb and several apparently able-bodied men standing around talking and laughing with each other. On the basis of these observations, none of which have been investigated — it isn't known, for instance, if the family won the television in a supermarket promotion contest, who actually owns the cars, or whether the observed men are on the night shift or are construction workers not currently employed — this person may conclude that all people on welfare are freeloaders who are defrauding the state. Moreover, this person may not hesitate to use this so-called evidence to justify strong opposition to all welfare programs.

Equally faulty inductive reasoning led many nineteenth-century defenders of slavery in this country to assert confidently that a slave was really happier and better off living as a slave than as a free person competing in the mainstream of society. Because most slaves did not dare express their discontent, such defenders were hardly getting either an accurate or random sample of the slave population as a whole. Furthermore, the relatively few slaves an average Southerner knew well scarcely constituted an adequate sample from which to generalize. Yet many of the people who took a proslavery stand genuinely thought that they were making valid arguments based on solid evidence.

These kinds of conclusions illustrate one of the major pitfalls of inductive reasoning: selecting and interpreting evidence in such a way that it will confirm a bias already held. Individuals who do this may honestly believe that they have solid grounds for their opinions; what they do not realize is that they are reasoning from a priori premises, premises formed before the evidence was examined. Consequently, if they are called upon to defend those opinions, they select evidence that reinforces their premises and reject or ignore that which does not. This process cannot be called valid induction.

Forming a hypothesis There is, of course, nothing inherently wrong with forming a hypothesis before examining the evidence. Much scientific research begins in just this way because if investigators do not have some idea of what they are looking for, they don't know where to start gathering data. Nevertheless, the person using the inductive method should hold a hypothesis only tentatively and be willing to alter or modify it when conflicting evidence is found. The person who is committed to a theory before beginning research must be particularly scrupulous both in selecting and evaluating evidence in order not to succumb to the temptation to find what is desired.

Using Inductive Arguments

Judging the Arguments of Others By now, this analysis of the ways in which inductive arguments can go wrong may have you ready to challenge any that you encounter and even a little dubious about the wisdom of trying to use the method yourself. A challenging attitude is healthy if you don't carry it to extremes. If writers or speakers give you a reasonable number of examples that seem to be accurate and randomly selected and their conclusions are statements *Give writers the benefit of the doubt* of probability rather than sweeping generalizations, give them the benefit of the doubt. After all, we can scarcely expect rhetoricians to present *all* the relevant data on an issue; if they were to attempt to do so, the audience would become so bored it would never hear the argument to the finish. Furthermore, we must accept generalizations and hypotheses from qualified, reliable people if we are to learn anything. Your best approach to the inductive arguments of others is, then, to be receptive but not gullible, open-minded but not naive. Be alert to possible bias, omission, or distortion but don't assume that everyone seeks to deceive.

Constructing Your Own Arguments You should not assume, either, *Trust your ability to use evidence* that the task of constructing a respectable inductive argument is too complex and difficult for you to master. It is not. You have access to perfectly good evidence on a variety of topics, and you now have some guidelines for shaping it into an effective argument.

For example, you could write a paper demonstrating that the people in your hometown or city are or are not serious about conserving energy by using what you already know about the city and supplementing it with data gathered in a survey that wouldn't take more than a few hours. For instance, if you know that your city has one or more enclosed shopping malls that are heated in winter and cooled in summer — one of them may even operate a skating rink all year round — you have one strong piece of evidence that energy is being wasted. You can also observe how many stores leave their show windows lighted all night, and how many lighted billboards or other lighted displays you have seen late at night. You could go into several public buildings chosen at random and check to see how warm or cold they are being kept. You could sit on a bench and count the number of passengers in the first fifty cars that pass. If most cars have only a driver, again you can conclude that a lot of energy is being wasted. You could get more data by asking several friends if the heat or air conditioning is kept on over the weekends in their schools or office buildings.

All this kind of evidence is specific and relevant to the topic, and you can draw a legitimate conclusion on the basis of it. The same kind of investigative techniques could furnish data for papers on study conditions in the library, living facilities for married students, or even broader topics, such as public transportation in your city or low-cost child-care facilities for student mothers.

Making the "Inductive Leap"   As long as we are working from a sample, rather than examining every single unit of the whole that we are generalizing from, the inductive method cannot yield perfect results. For instance, we cannot prove beyond any doubt that attending college in the North or East is always more expensive than attending college in the South unless we have data on every single school. The possibility of error is always present when we are projecting from a sample — even the voter profile analysis is wrong sometimes. Nevertheless, we can, by careful sampling, establish high probability: a survey of representative institutions in the North, South, and East would show that going to college in New York or Minnesota is very likely to cost more than going to a school in Alabama or Louisiana. Moving from an examination of some of the available evidence to a generalization about the whole population from which that evidence is drawn is known as the "inductive leap." If our sample is sufficient, random, accurate, and relevant, we can be confident that the leap is warranted. If the sample does not meet these criteria, we are not reasoning, but jumping to conclusions.

Moving from evidence to conclusion

Informal Logic or Toulmin Argument

How Informal Logic Works

How we use informal logic

All of us also use another kind of reasoning besides induction, one that employs patterns of argument similar to those that lawyers use in court. The philosopher Stephen Toulmin calls this kind of reasoning *informal logic* because he believes it resembles the kind of thinking we all engage in when we feel called upon to justify our ideas or assertions to others in our day-to-day lives. Typically, writers or speakers who use it start out with a *claim,* just as a lawyer's case would be based on a claim; for example, the claim that someone's property had been damaged or that a contract had been broken. The lawyer would then build a case to support that claim, using whatever evidence and reasons he or she felt were needed to present a convincing argument. Speakers and writers can build their cases in a similar manner, and Toulmin has devised a system to describe how this can be done. The key terms in his system are:

Key terms of Toulmin's system of argument

Claim: the statement that is put forth for the approval of others, the conclusion to the argument. The claim may be actually stated, or it may be implied; it may be a universal statement or a qualified statement.

Data: the evidence brought in to support a claim.

Warrant: a statement of general principle used to justify the claim by showing its relation to the data that have been cited.

Support: any material provided to strengthen the force of the data, the warrant, or the claim.

Qualifier: a qualification that limits the scope of the claim; typically, words such as *probably, in most cases,* or *usually.*

Reservation: a statement giving circumstances under which the claim would not be valid.[4]

The only one of these terms that may need additional explanation is warrant. It is helpful to think of a warrant as the *bridge* that connects the data and the claim; it is also the *tie* that links data and claim

---

[4]Adapted from Richard D. Reike and Malcolm Sillars, *Argumentation and the Decision-Making Process,* 2nd ed. (New York: Wiley, 1975) 77–78.

together, that enables the reader or audience to get from effect to cause or cause to effect. What is tricky about analyzing the Toulmin diagrams to find the warrants is that often they are unstated or invisible. The writer is assuming that the link he or she implies between the data and the claim can be supplied from the readers' own knowledge, that it is so obvious it would be insulting to state it. That assumption that the reader can supply the link can be both the strength and weakness of Toulmin argument, as I will show in the next section.

This concept of the warrant in an argument is most easily explained through examples. For instance, suppose that a nutritionist were trying to persuade a group of people who want to lose weight that they should forget their mothers' admonitions during their childhood to clean their plates at every meal. Her argument would be that they do not need to feel they are wasting food if they don't eat all of it because it is no more wasteful to throw food away than it is to eat it when one's body doesn't need it. The parts of the nutritionist's argument would look like this.

Claim: Dieters should not feel guilty about leaving food on their plates.

Data: It is no more wasteful to throw food out than it is to eat it if one's body doesn't need it.

Unstated warrant or link: It is hard to lose weight if you eat everything someone puts on your plate.

Most people who were trying to lose weight would know the warrant without having it stated, but it is, nevertheless, a necessary link between the data and the claim even if it seems too obvious to mention. Note that it would not be obvious to someone who knew nothing about nutrition.

Let's look at an example in which the warrant needs to be stated. In several recent studies of people who have been torturers for an official regime or authority, psychologists have concluded that torturers are not usually psychopaths but apparently ordinary people who have two qualities: they are totally obedient to authority, and they see the world in black/white terms and separate people into two groups — us and them. Those making the studies concluded that the reason these ordinary people are able to become torturers is that they feel no identity with the "them" they are torturing, and they feel no responsibility for their acts because they are obeying orders.[5]

The data here are the studies done by psychologists and other groups such as Amnesty International. The claim is that torturers are ordinary people with two particular character traits. The warrant — that torturers do not identify with their victims and feel no responsibility — is the explanation that links the data and the claim, and it is really the link that makes the studies significant.

Taking another example, suppose that you receive a bill from a department store demanding the first payment on a microwave oven that you did not buy. You call the store manager to complain, telling him that you are not liable for the money because you did not buy the oven and have not signed a charge slip or a contract authorizing the store to bill you for the oven. Here are the parts of your argument:

Claim: You are not liable for the amount that has been charged to your account.

Data: You did not sign a contract or a charge slip for the oven.

Warrant: Stores cannot charge a customer for purchases for which they can show no contract or charge slip.

In this case, you would not have to state the warrant because your audience already knows it, but if you were angry enough you might remind the manager of it for emphasis.

Not all elements need be present in every argument

So people who are arguing do not necessarily use all six elements of informal logic in their arguments, nor do they always explain all the elements that they do use. Sometimes they just make a claim and give their data, assuming it is so strong they don't need to support it further. Sometimes they don't qualify their claim or mention any reservations. Sometimes they don't actually state their warrant but leave the audience to infer it.

But in spite of the various ways in which informal arguments are constructed, one can usually identify three or four of the major elements in any argument. For example, take the following paragraph:

Stupidity is not related to type of regime; monarchy, oligarchy, and democracy produce it equally. Nor is it peculiar to nation or

[5]Reported by Daniel Goleman in *The New York Times,* May 14, 1985.

class. The working class as represented by the Communist governments functions no more rationally or effectively in power than the aristocracy or the bourgeoisie, as has notably been demonstrated in recent history. Mao Tse-tung may be admired for many things, but the Great Leap Forward, with a steel plant in every backyard, and the Cultural Revolution were exercises in unwisdom that greatly damaged China's progress and stability, not to mention the chairman's reputation. The record of the Russian proletariat in power can hardly be called enlightened, although after sixty years of control it must be accorded a kind of brutal success. If the majority of Russians are better off now than before, the cost in cruelty and tyranny has been no less and probably greater than under the czars.[6]

Tuchman states her claim at the beginning of the paragraph: Stupidity is not related to one type of regime or to nation or class. Her implied warrant is that the disastrous consequences of policy demonstrate stupidity in government. The data that support that warrant are the examples she gives from Mao Tse-tung's regime in China and the Communist regime in Russia. The qualification she makes to her claim is the statement that the Russian regime "must be accorded a kind of brutal success."

Toulmin has devised a pattern for diagramming these informal arguments that helps one to understand how they are constructed. Here are some examples:

Argument: By 1995, medical doctors' income may drop substantially because statisticians predict a surplus of at least 100,000 doctors.

Diagram:

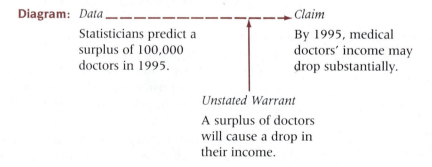

Data ————————————→ *Claim*

Statisticians predict a surplus of 100,000 doctors in 1995.

By 1995, medical doctors' income may drop substantially.

Unstated Warrant

A surplus of doctors will cause a drop in their income.

[6]Barbara Tuchman, "An Inquiry into the Persistence of Unwisdom in Government," *Esquire* May 1980: 25.

Argument: Consumers often have no way of knowing whether the fish or meat they eat contains cancer-causing substances because they don't know where the fish were caught or under what conditions cattle or sheep were raised. Some fish live in dangerously polluted waters, and many ranchers inject their cattle with stilbestrol or other hormones.

Diagram:

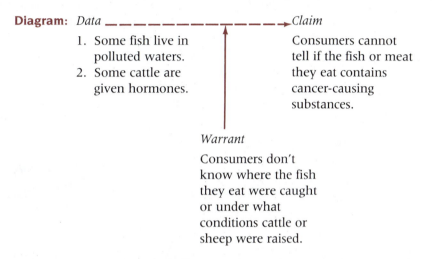

Data

1. Some fish live in polluted waters.
2. Some cattle are given hormones.

Claim

Consumers cannot tell if the fish or meat they eat contains cancer-causing substances.

Warrant

Consumers don't know where the fish they eat were caught or under what conditions cattle or sheep were raised.

Notice that a writer who wanted to have readers supply their own connections between claims and data here could leave the warrant unstated. The force of the argument would be even stronger for readers who prefer not to have everything spelled out for them.

Argument: At the present time, over a million cars a day clog the streets of Mexico City, most of them burning leaded gas. If officials do not begin immediately to reduce that flow of traffic drastically, in ten years the air will be so polluted that infants and old people with lung problems will not be able to live in the city.

Diagram:

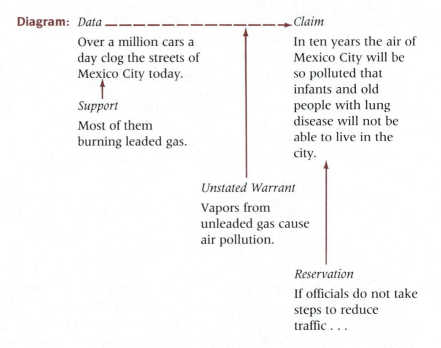

One could even point out a second unstated warrant here: Extreme air pollution causes lung disease. For many readers, that fact is too obvious to mention; for others, however, it might have to be stated.

Argument: According to author David McCullough, powerful men are often "Mama's Boys"; that is, devoted sons of strong women who have either lost or rejected their husbands and focused their energy, love, and ambition on their sons. He cites as examples the case histories of Douglas MacArthur, Harry Truman, Franklin D. Roosevelt, Frank Lloyd Wright, and Lyndon Johnson.

Diagram:

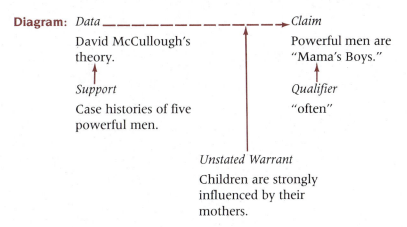

Data — — — — — — — — — → *Claim*

David McCullough's theory.

Powerful men are "Mama's Boys."

Support

Case histories of five powerful men.

Qualifier

"often"

Unstated Warrant

Children are strongly influenced by their mothers.

Using Informal Logic in Your Writing

When you understand how the elements of informal logic work, you can use that knowledge to help frame your own arguments. Since the claim is the center of almost every argument, a good place to start building your case is to do as a lawyer does and ask yourself, "What is my claim? Do I need to qualify it?" When you determine that, you can once more imitate the lawyer by asking, "What data or evidence do I need to support my case?"

Finding your claim in an argument

For example, suppose you wanted to argue that the United States should either get out of the Olympics or start paying their athletes because the games are no longer really for amateurs. They have turned into semiprofessional events that are open only to athletes who are wealthy or heavily subsidized. That is your claim. What is your evidence? You will have to find articles and newspaper accounts that give you data about how long athletes have to train, who pays for their training, how some countries subsidize their athletes totally, and how much American businesses invested in the last Olympic Games. Your warrant would be that no matter how talented they are, amateurs who cannot afford trainers or who must work to support themselves can really not compete in the Olympic Games.

Diagrammed, your argument would look like this:

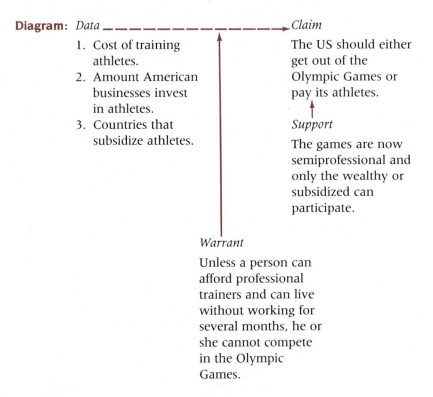

Diagram: *Data* ────────────────➤*Claim*

1. Cost of training athletes.
2. Amount American businesses invest in athletes.
3. Countries that subsidize athletes.

The US should either get out of the Olympic Games or pay its athletes.

Support

The games are now semiprofessional and only the wealthy or subsidized can participate.

Warrant

Unless a person can afford professional trainers and can live without working for several months, he or she cannot compete in the Olympic Games.

Different Kinds of Support for Different Audiences

Notice that informal logic requires that you use different kinds of support for different audiences. Using the data cited in the Olympic Games example would work well if you were writing a newspaper editorial to persuade the general public, because they would need considerable evidence or data just to help them understand the problem. Thus, information about how long it takes for an athlete to train, how much money East Germany invests in its athletes, and the cost of professional trainers is useful.

If, however, you were arguing to a group of college athletes who already knew a good deal about what is involved in becoming a world-class athlete, you would have a more effective argument if you looked for supporting data that show how difficult it is to solicit funds to support amateurs in the early rounds of training for the Olympics and how many college athletes are eliminated because they must work during the summer.

The Strength of Informal Logic: Involving Your Audience

One of the major strengths of informal logic is its flexibility, which allows writers and speakers to adapt their arguments to specific audiences and specific situations. You do not have to follow a set of formal rules to prove your case, but, like a lawyer, can construct your argument based on what the particular situation demands and on the needs of your audience. You also have the advantage of being able to tap into what your audience already knows or believes, and you can use that knowledge or those beliefs as part of your argument. Thus, the audience actually contributes to its own persuasion.

Advantages of drawing on what your audience knows

Suppose, for example, the personnel manager of a major national corporation visits your campus to talk to business majors about what kind of traits young people should try to develop if they want to succeed in the corporate world. She claims business students need to study psychology and literature as well as business subjects because in order to succeed in corporations, new employees not only need to know their specialties but also must be perceptive and intuitive. She says it may be more important to understand the myths and unwritten rules of the corporation than to be the bright new whiz kid. For evidence, she cites cases she has observed in her own company, and she quotes from the best-selling Peters and Waterman book *In Search of Excellence,* a study of some of the top corporations in America. (The unstated warrant in the argument is that studying psychology and literature will help students develop intuition and perception.)

In this case the personnel manager draws on what she knows about her audience to get them to provide the supporting data for her argument. First, she knows that many in her audience have read or at least heard about *In Search of Excellence* because it was at the top of the best-seller list on college campuses for over a year. Thus, they can actually provide the specific cases that make up her data from their own knowledge. Second, she knows that her audience realizes she has years of experience in watching who succeeds and who fails in one of the country's most prestigious companies; the audience's respect for that company becomes one of the elements that she can count on to help persuade them.

Getting your audience to furnish the warrant

Frequently, writers can also depend on their audience to provide the warrants that link data and claims. For example, suppose you wanted to argue in a letter to your legislative representative that the state should not raise university and college tuition because doing so would make it difficult for low-income families to send their children to school. Your claim is that the state should not raise tuition: your data are the effects it would have on low-income families. Because you can reasonably assume a state legislator believes that it's important for the children of low-income families to be able to attend college, you can depend on him or her mentally to provide the warrant for your argument: the state has an obligation to help its citizens get an education.

Here is another example in which the audience would provide its own warrant.

You want to persuade your father to buy you a microcomputer, arguing that if you don't have one, you're not going to do well in your accounting and finance courses because you'll be competing against many students who use computers to work the problems in the course. You assume your father will supply the obvious warrant: it's important for you to do well in your business courses.

When you give your audience the opportunity to furnish part of the evidence for an argument out of its own knowledge or to provide the causal link between data and claim out of its own opinions, your argument will carry more force than it would if you had to provide all the support and warrants yourself.

Using Informal Logic for Writing College Papers

Informal logic works particularly well for many kinds of writing assignments in college because frequently those assignments, either papers or essay exams, call for you to state your claim and support it. If you begin such an assignment by sketching out a Toulmin diagram of the kind shown earlier, you will be able to see the parts of your argument and what you need to do in order to develop it. You will be able to see if you need to qualify your claim, what kind of data you need for support, whether you should find backing for the data, and whether you need to state your warrant or can leave it to be inferred.

Suppose, for instance, your history of science professor asks you to write a paper on the person you consider the most important scientific figure in the sixteenth or seventeenth century. You need to ask yourself three questions:

What is my claim?

Why do I make it; that is, what is my warrant?

How can I support it; that is, what are my data?

Let's assume that you choose Galileo, a scientist whose life and work spanned both centuries, and claim that he is the most important figure of both centuries. Here's how you might plan your argument:

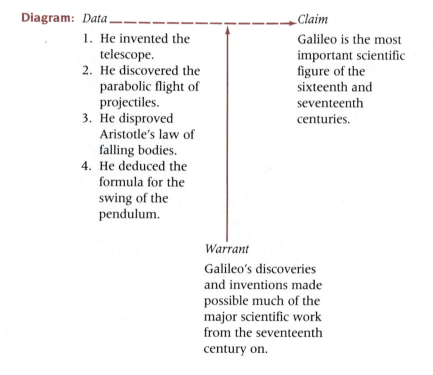

Diagram: *Data* _____→ *Claim*

1. He invented the telescope.
2. He discovered the parabolic flight of projectiles.
3. He disproved Aristotle's law of falling bodies.
4. He deduced the formula for the swing of the pendulum.

Galileo is the most important scientific figure of the sixteenth and seventeenth centuries.

Warrant

Galileo's discoveries and inventions made possible much of the major scientific work from the seventeenth century on.

Here are two other representative college writing assignments for which you could use informal logic and Toulmin diagrams:

Question: What style of architecture dominates the government buildings in Washington, D.C.? Why?

Diagram: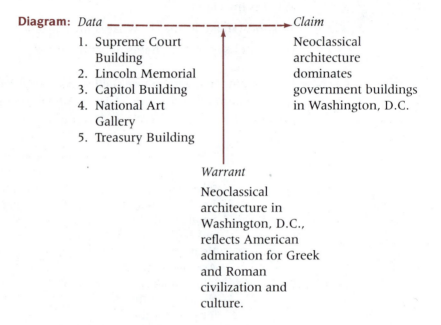

Data ⟶ *Claim*

1. Supreme Court Building
2. Lincoln Memorial
3. Capitol Building
4. National Art Gallery
5. Treasury Building

Neoclassical architecture dominates government buildings in Washington, D.C.

Warrant

Neoclassical architecture in Washington, D.C., reflects American admiration for Greek and Roman civilization and culture.

For this paper your main task would be to find material to expand on and support the warrant "Americans admire Greek and Roman civilization and culture." In the following assignment, however, you would probably have to spend most of your effort giving examples to strengthen your data.

Question: What are some of the advantages Japanese manufacturers have over American manufacturers?

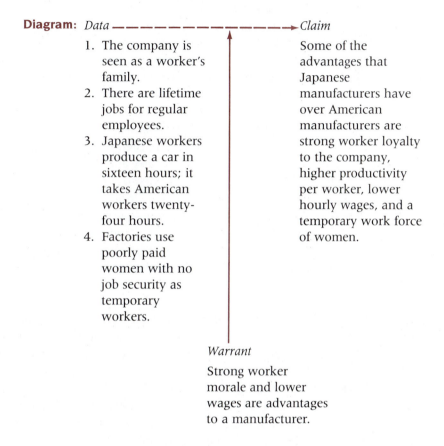

Diagram: *Data* ——————————→ *Claim*

1. The company is seen as a worker's family.
2. There are lifetime jobs for regular employees.
3. Japanese workers produce a car in sixteen hours; it takes American workers twenty-four hours.
4. Factories use poorly paid women with no job security as temporary workers.

Some of the advantages that Japanese manufacturers have over American manufacturers are strong worker loyalty to the company, higher productivity per worker, lower hourly wages, and a temporary work force of women.

Warrant

Strong worker morale and lower wages are advantages to a manufacturer.

So this data, claim, warrant pattern works well in a wide variety of writing situations. Its great advantage is that you can adjust its elements according to the demands of the task.

The Rogerian or Nonthreatening Argument

For centuries writers and speakers have been using and studying the traditional kinds of argument we have just been considering: definition, cause and effect, circumstance, induction, claims and warrants, and so on. And these rhetorical strategies often succeed because people frequently do respond to reasoned, carefully supported, and skillfully constructed arguments. Yet we all are aware that sometimes logic doesn't work, that sometimes apparently rational people simply refuse to listen to reason. Ironically, such breakdowns in rational communication seem to occur most often when the arguments concern issues about which we care a great deal — issues involving questions of morality, fairness, or personal or professional standards. Because such issues involve a person's basic values, arguments about them can challenge that person's a priori premises (see page 102). When that happens, a reader or listener is likely to stop reading or listening, and the person who is arguing fails because she has lost her audience.

But the noted psychotherapist Carl Rogers thinks we do not have to admit defeat in such situations. He believes that people can communicate about sensitive issues in a rational manner and move beyond controversy to understand and perhaps accept what another person is saying if they will learn how to engage in *nonthreatening argument*. In order to do that, they need to grasp these principles of communication:

Rogers's principles of
communication

1. Threat hinders communication. When a person feels threatened by what another person is saying (or writing), he or she is apt to stop listening (or reading) in order to protect the ego and reduce anxiety.
2. Making strong statements of opinion stimulates an audience to respond with strong opinions. Once people have expressed these opinions, they are more likely to be interested in defending them than in discussing them.
3. Biased language increases threat; neutral language reduces it.
4. One reduces threat and increases the chance of communicating with someone by demonstrating that one understands that person's point of view.
5. One improves communication by establishing an atmosphere of trust.[7]

In his discussion of communication blocks, Rogers shows how these principles work:

[7]Condensed from Carl R. Rogers, "Communication: Its Blocking and Its Facilitation," *On Becoming a Person* (Boston: Houghton, 1961) 329–37. Used by permission.

Although the tendency to make evaluations is common in almost all interchange of language, it is very much heightened in those situations where feelings and emotions are deeply involved. So the stronger our feelings, the more likely it is that there will be no mutual element in the communication. There will be just two ideas, two feelings, two judgments, missing each other in psychological space. . . . This tendency to react to any emotionally meaningful statement by forming an evaluation of it from our own point of view, is, I repeat, the major barrier to interpersonal communication.[8]

Probably you can easily find in your own experience an example of the kind of situation Rogers refers to. For example, if someone says to you, "I thought *The Purple Rose of Cairo* was a wonderful movie," your first impulse is probably not to ask why the other person liked it, but to give your own opinion: either "So did I" or "I didn't like it at all." Almost inevitably, once two people have committed themselves to opposing opinions on an issue, even one so trivial as the merits of a movie, they are not likely to keep an open mind on the question. Probably both parties will hasten to justify their opinions instead of listening to what the other person wants to say.

Using the nonthreatening argument

If we unthinkingly throw up this kind of barrier to communication on relatively unimportant matters, how much more likely we are to trigger strong reactions from our audience when we are writing or speaking about controversial ethical, political, or social issues. Suppose, for example, that you are a scientist doing research on lung diseases and you must write a letter to persuade members of the Humane Society not to work for the passage in the state legislature of a bill that would prohibit the use of dogs in laboratory experiments. You have a very tough rhetorical problem on your hands, one that logic alone will not solve. If you simply list the medical advances that have been made possible by laboratory experiments on dogs and suggest, rationally, that animals' lives are less important than people's lives, you are not likely to make much impression on your audience because you are ignoring the real source of their opposition, their feelings. If you angrily attack your audience as sentimental and impractical meddlers whose proposals will interfere with important scientific research, you will make matters even worse

[8]Rogers 331.

because you will be threatening your audience. Its members will refuse even to consider what you are saying and stiffen their opposition. The communication breakdown will be total, and you will have done more to promote the unwanted bill than to stop it.

What can be done about such an impasse? Very little, if you insist that your position is the only rational one and that intelligent people ought to accept it. If, however, you are genuinely interested in solving the communication problem, Rogers suggests that there is much you can do. First, and most important, you can start by looking at the issue from the other person's point of view — that is, by trying to *empathize* with the audience you want to communicate with. As Rogers point out,

Try to empathize with your audience

> Real communication occurs, and this evaluative tendency is avoided, when we listen with understanding. What does that mean? It means *to see the expressed idea and attitude from the other person's point of view, to sense how it feels to him, to achieve his frame of reference in regard to the thing he is talking about.*[9]

To try to understand the viewpoint of the Humane Society's members, you would probably need to talk to one or two and ask them what their goals are. You would ask them to explain specifically what it is they object to about using dogs in laboratory experiments. You would also ask what they hope to achieve with the legislation and what incidents led them to propose it. During the whole conversation you would have to force yourself to stay calm and really listen instead of getting defensive or pointing out flaws and misconceptions in their statements. Maintaining such calm would probably be the hardest part of the conversation because few people *really* want to listen to opposing views; our instinct is to attack them.

Once you fully understand the other person's point of view and can genuinely appreciate how he or she feels, even if you don't agree, you are ready to start trying to construct a nonthreatening argument. Remember, though, that the purpose of such an argument should not necessarily be to win. Rather, your first goal should be to increase understanding and improve communication between you and the other party, thus making it more likely that you may agree on some points. If you can establish some common ground and be-

[9]Rogers 331–32.

gin to create an atmosphere of trust, it's possible that you may be able to resolve some of your differences.

Keep an open mind about issues

Since the Rogerian approach to argument is heavily exploratory and requires that you keep an open mind about the issues, you shouldn't start writing with a detailed plan in mind. Rather, you should first write down the other side's main concerns; then you can jot down some of the key points you want to make and perhaps also list some of the problems you anticipate. Finally, think about what points you can probably agree on. When you have accumulated this information, you can start writing a first draft and see what develops.

Your notes for the letter to the members of the Humane Society might look like this:

Their Concerns

cruelty to animals

lack of restrictions on experiments

insufficient supervision of experiments

dogs sometimes ill treated

many experiments unnecessary

laboratories sometimes buy stolen pets — encourage black-market operation in laboratory animals

Your Points

large animals necessary for testing experimental drugs

dogs used are unwanted strays who often starve

sufficient human volunteers not available

horror stories exaggerated

animals well taken care of in most labs

animals humanely disposed of after experiments

Problems

convincing society members that animals are not abused

convincing them that animals are absolutely necessary to medical research

convincing them that scientists are not callous and cruel

Common Ground

concern for animals' welfare

concern for advancements in medical science

agreement that animals are neglected and mistreated in some labs

agreement that profession needs to establish strict regulations about how animals can be used

agreement that state should supervise labs more carefully

When you have accumulated this information, you can start writing a first draft of your letter or paper. Certainly there is no prescribed form for nonthreatening argument — the best approach is to let it develop from the material. You should, however, make sure it contains these elements:

Elements of the nonthreatening argument

1. A brief and objectively phrased statement that defines the issue.
2. A complete and neutrally worded analysis of the other side's position. This should demonstrate that you understand their position and their reasons for holding it.
3. A complete and neutrally worded analysis of the position you hold. You should carefully avoid any suggestion that you are more moral or sensitive than your audience.
4. An analysis of what your positions have in common and what goals and values you share.
5. A proposal for resolving the issue in a way that recognizes the interests of both parties.

If you can write an argument that does all these things, you will significantly reduce the threat to your readers and greatly increase the chances that they will read and consider your argument.

Obviously this nontraditional approach to argument requires extraordinary patience and effort, and to undertake it you would have to care deeply about coming to an understanding with a person or group. The approach also requires courage, for as Rogers points out,

> If you really understand another person in this way, if you are willing to enter his private world and see the way life appears to him, without any attempt to make evaluative judgments, you run the risk of being changed yourself. You might see it his way, you might find yourself influenced in your attitudes or your personality.[10]

No one would claim that this approach is easy to work out or even that one can use it consistently in emotionally tense situations. When both you and your audience have serious disagreement and, in some cases, basically different a priori premises, it is difficult to sustain the control and open-mindedness that Rogerian argument

[10]Rogers 333.

requires. Most of us are not good enough — in both senses of the word — to construct a careful but nonthreatening argument very often. And it will not work at all if one party uses the strategy as a trick to win agreement from the other party, then twists that agreement into a point for his or her side.

Advantages of the Rogerian approach

But the Rogerian approach to rhetoric can be effective if you are really more concerned about increasing understanding and communication than you are about scoring a triumph. You may be able to "win an argument" by showing an audience that the person on the other side is foolish and biased and ill informed, but you do *not* convince the person you are criticizing. Threatening and hostile comments only put people on the defensive; you do not persuade people by making them angry. The mature person who realizes this should be ready to try Carl Rogers's approach.

Exercises on Inductive Reasoning

1. The following paragraphs illustrate some patterns of inductive reasoning. From the evidence given or suggested in each one, what judgment would you make about the conclusion that is drawn?

    a. Both this summer and last, I taught a section of freshman English with an enrollment of twenty students. In each of those sections I had a student who was an active member of the Socialist party. This leads me to believe that 5 per cent of the students in summer school are Socialists.

    b. At a recent meeting the leaders of our local parent-teacher association expressed concern because the afternoon meetings held on the first Monday of every month do not attract enough parents, particularly fathers. Someone suggested holding the meetings at night, but the president rejected that idea because those present decided, two to one, that night meetings would be inconvenient.

    c. The Cuban refugees who came to this country after Castro's rise to power have done quite well. A survey by the United States Bureau of Immigration shows that 48 per cent of the refugees have entered the professions they were in in Cuba, 35 per cent have gone into other businesses, 10 per cent are in college or technical training and only 7 per cent are receiving aid from a government source or relatives.

d. Our student newspaper recently conducted an experiment that demonstrates rather conclusively that the landlords in the university area are not abiding by the no-discrimination clause required in all leases. The reporters called one hundred apartment houses chosen at random from the Yellow Pages of the telephone directory asking if they had vacancies and if they rented to students. The supervisors of sixty-seven of those called said they did. Yet when a black couple applied to rent those apartments, in fifty-four instances they were told that there were no vacancies and none was expected.

e. A survey of members of the United States Chamber of Commerce, people who represent the outstanding achievers in our country's free enterprise system, supports this committee's belief that new corporate taxes would seriously impede industrial expansion and new investment in the next fiscal year.

f. A recent grand jury investigation of conditions in the county jail indicates a drastic need for reforms. They found three and four prisoners confined in two-person cells, inadequate lighting and ventilation, no recreational facilities for prisoners, two suicides and nineteen instances of assaults by inmates on other inmates in the past month, and sanitary conditions that one juror described as "simply unbelievable in an institution that is under government supervision."

g. Obviously influence counts more than brains when they're deciding who gets into the service academies. Admiral Crosby's nephew was accepted at Annapolis this year, and his grades weren't as good as those of a friend of mine who was turned down.

2. What kind of evidence would you need to support the following generalizations? Which ones would you phrase in more moderate terms?

a. The college students of the eighties are not interested in protest and social reform.

b. English 101 is a flunk-out course on this campus.

c. The student who graduates from a German high school is

much better educated than the average high school graduate in the United States.

d. People who have taken a defensive driving course are much safer drivers than those who have not.

e. Professional football has replaced baseball as the national American pastime.

f. We are living in the most corrupt era this country has ever seen.

g. Television advertising is a major cause of the economic discontent of low-income groups in America.

h. The automobile has caused radical changes in the American way of life in the last forty years.

i. The decline in verbal scores on the Scholastic Aptitude Test may be at least partially due to the fact that we now have a whole generation of students who have been reared on television.

j. Raising and showing Arabian horses is a rich person's hobby.

Below are three generalizations, followed by evidence that might be used to support them. For each generalization decide which pieces of evidence constitute good support and which are of dubious value. Give your reasons.

a. Football is a character-building sport.

    1. The successful football player must practice self-discipline.

    2. Football is the most popular of all high school sports.

    3. A good football player learns that teamwork is the key to winning.

    4. Learning plays develops the memory, and drills improve the player's physical coordination.

    5. A high percentage of football players have been chosen as Rhodes scholars.

b. In the fifty years following the Civil War in this country, a series of scandals occurred that caused many people to feel that the American dream had succumbed to greed and corruption.

    1. In 1905 six United States senators were under indictment for fraud.

2. Mark Twain wrote "The Man That Corrupted Hadleyburg."

3. Under the Grant administration cabinet officers sold positions in the Bureau of Indian Affairs.

4. Upton Sinclair's book *The Jungle* revealed that in the meat-packing industry the owners exploited the workers and sold meat from animals that were diseased and condemned as unfit for human consumption.

5. Andrew Carnegie used his fortune to establish free public libraries across the country.

c. Over the past decade the make-up of the college population in this country has begun to change significantly.

1. Because of the increasing number of community colleges that make it possible for students to go to school at night, more and more adults are entering college.

2. The open admission policies that are being adopted by many publicly financed colleges make a college education available to those who were not previously qualified.

3. More and more adults are returning to school as automation makes many present jobs obsolete.

4. More women want college degrees in order to become independent.

4. Analyze and evaluate this student paper as an inductive argument:

The Fast Food Employee Blues

Over the past twenty years America has gone fast food crazy. With an explosion of spontaneous growth, mammoth chains like Kentucky Fried Chicken, Jack-in-the-Box, Burger King, and of course, McDonald's, have changed the eating habits of the nation. Today, any town of appreciable size, probably including yours, has its "strip" of fast food eateries, each one in keen competition with its neighbors. The competition, naturally enough, breeds a desire among chain owners for cheap, hardworking labor. That's important — especially for you teenagers. Because believe it or not, the giant fast food industry could not exist without you. That's right — McDonald's doesn't do it all for you, you do it for them. By your need for flexible working hours, by your willingness to work hard for minimum wage, and by your inexperience concerning management tactics, you allow your local hamburger joints to operate at a profit. So if you're thinking about going to work for one of these establishments, you'd be wise to read the following.

Like ten million other teen-agers every year, when I was fifteen I went to work for a fast food chain. (The manager who interviewed me kindly promoted me to legal working age with a slash of his pencil.) Like everyone else, I took the job because it was easy to get and no experience was necessary. It fit in well with my school hours, and who cared if I was only making $1.60 an hour? That was $1.60 more than I'd ever made before. I figured I had it made.

But I didn't, and it took me six years to realize why not. It's simple really, so obvious it's hard to convince yourself it's really happening. In the fast food business, company policy dictates the continued exploitation of its own employees until they get smart and quit. Like strip miners ruining a landscape, the industry methodically uses its workers until they are used up.

Don't get me wrong, I'm not going to tell you any horror stories of sweatshop-type forced labor; that simply isn't so. Although the pay is ridiculous, the jobs themselves aren't *that* bad, as far as they go. In fact, they aren't very demanding at all at the nonmanagement level. And all those reasons I gave for taking the job do apply. If they didn't nobody would work there at all. No, the fast food industry exploits young people in ways much more subtle, but almost as damaging. They are successful because, frankly, most teen-agers haven't experience enough to realize they are being taken advantage of. They don't have unions to bargain for them, they don't have previous job experience to draw upon, and in most cases, they don't value their own work highly enough. They are anxious to please. High-level management knows this only too well, and predictably enough, manipulates it.

They do this by fostering a cheery, bustling, all-business atmosphere designed to make the uninitiated youngster feel he is a vital part of a larger whole. Unskilled teen-agers are hired, given a uniform and an hourly wage. Most are so thankful for the job they don't care what they make. Inevitably, the new employee is given a set of rules to abide by. If the rules are followed, a gracious dime raise is meted out every six months or so. If they are broken, pay is docked or the employee is fired. By this weeding-out process, all remaining employees become cogs in a machine. Each day they perform their particular function in an assembly line of meal construction. Some draw soft drinks, some build sandwiches, some stuff French fry bags. Usually everyone does the same job every day. The advantages of teamwork are highly stressed — motivational posters abound and are changed every month. It's really a very smoothly run machine, and the atmosphere is infectious. As a fast food employee, you're happy to be there, to be a part of it. You've got job security for the first time in your life. You may not make as much money as others your age, but you're comfortable where you are.

Now some fit into the machine better than others, that's to be expected. The ones who do are usually offered a promotion to crew leader or assistant manager. Here is where the screw is really turned tight. Store-level managers are the most important people in the fast food business because they are the ones who actually set the production rate. In spite of this, they are also the most exploited.

Most assistant store managers are seventeen to twenty years old. People this age are dazzled by the opportunity to tell others what to do. I know this because it happened to me and those around me. I was filled with warmth by the thought that the company trusted me enough to run the store. I received a key to the front door, held complete responsibility for operations during my shift, and to top it off I was equipped with a brand-new weekly salary — no more punching the time clock for me. This was all pretty heady stuff; I would have done it for nothing. Oh sure, I knew I'd have to work a lot more (six days a week), and that I'd be on call when I wasn't working, and that I'd have to forgo much social life. I might have even figured out that my new salary didn't amount to much more than my old hourly wage. But I didn't care, because while my peers were mowing lawns or sacking groceries, I was a *manager.* I figured the advantages outweighed the disadvantages.

I was wrong. To be brief, my working life the next few years was a constant stream of frustrations and letdowns. I couldn't understand why, after working so hard, I never made much more money and never received another promotion. I thought for a while my problems were due to personality conflicts with my supervisors. Later, much later, I caught on. *Nobody* got promoted; nobody got raises. Management vacancies were created solely by firings or resignations. In six years I saw only one store manager get kicked upstairs to the district office, and that was the supervisor's nephew. At that point, at age twenty-one, after delaying my college education for three years because I thought I was doing so well, I walked out and never went back.

My experience is not atypical, nor is it of a type confined to one particular company. Every large fast food chain in the country operates this way, simply because it is the most profitable legal method available. Teen-agers are lulled by labor-savvy businessmen into accepting jobs with the lowest possible wage and the least chance for significant advancement. Should employees tire of these conditions and quit, fine. High turnover rates are no big problem; job training is quick, and easy. To make it perfectly clear, it is just not worth these companies' effort to care much about the people who work for them. They know that the profit margin in fast food is relatively low, about twenty per cent. Any kind of incentive programs, or insurance benefits, or profit-sharing arrangements would cut into that twenty per cent, so they don't even consider it.

But *you* should consider it. You can avoid the frustrations encountered by millions of young people caught in the fast food trap every year. As one who's been there, I can offer you some valuable advice about working for a fast food chain. Don't. In the long run, and the short run, you'll be better off mowing lawns or sacking groceries.

Paul Geilich

Exercises on Toulmin Logic

1. Label the statements in each of these arguments as claim, data, warrant, qualifier, support, or reservation.

a. (1) Shards and tools found at the site of a Mayan city (2) lead archaeologists to believe that a culture earlier than the Mayans must have existed in central Mexico (3) since experts agree that such shards and tools are good indicators of chronology. (4) Unless new evidence puts the Mayans at an earlier date than is now accepted, (5) the find will be a breakthrough.

b. (1) The prosecution maintains that the officers of the company conspired to defraud the public; (2) the records found last week are solid evidence of deliberate intent. (3) Given that no such records would have existed if the officers were not involved, (4) we can expect a grand jury indictment next week (5) if the corporation does not enter a *nolo contendere* plea before then.

c. (1) Men like Lee Iacocca and Ross Perot who have succeeded brilliantly in business (2) seldom run for public office (3) because by the time they reach the top of their companies, they are so used to power and command that they are unwilling to make the compromises necessary to be successful politicians.

2. Using the Toulmin model of argument, analyze and diagram the arguments being used in the following student paper to support the belief that Noah's ark existed and was wrecked on Mt. Ararat.

Noah's Ark: A Matter of Fact or Faith?

Audience: This article would probably be published in a magazine like R-A-D-A-R, which is a magazine for children in Christian Sunday schools.

Purpose: To suggest to young kids with a curious wonder of the world that Noah's Ark may have existed. I would like to express however that although it would be exciting to find the Ark, its existence really should have no bearing on our faith. Faith should come from trust and should not have to be proven.

If you asked someone on the street, "Do you know the story of Noah's Ark?," he would probably say yes because it is one of the most universally known tales of all time. But if you asked that same person if he believes the story of Noah's Ark is true, there's no telling what he might say. He might take all Bible stories literally and consider them word for word the truth, or he might just treat Old Testament stories as fables or legends, all depending on the amount of faith he has in God and in the Bible.

Many people measure the truth of stories like Noah's Ark not only by the amount of faith they have, but also by the amount of cold, hard evidence they can find to support them. They feel that the more evidence they can see and touch, the stronger their faith will become. And so, throughout history there have been many attempts to find the Ark, which some people believe is preserved under layers of ice, on top of a high mountain where the Ark supposedly landed after the Great Flood. As a result of these attempts, several very convincing reports have been made of sightings of what is very possibly the real Noah's Ark. Before we examine the evidence that tends to prove the Ark exists, it is important to understand the location in question and the physical characteristics of the Ark itself.

In Genesis 8:4 the Ark is said to have landed after the flood on the "Mountains of Ararat." The problem is that there are hundreds of peaks included in this mountain chain which stretches across the four modern-day countries of Turkey, Iran, Iraq, and the Soviet Union. There is however, one peak called Mt. Ararat in Eastern Turkey. Skeptics doubt that this is the Ark's landing place, but the Armenians who have lived in the region for thousands of years, and explorers who claim to have seen the ship embedded in ice in a cleft near the top of that mountain, are convinced that it is the place.

Genesis 6:15 describes how God specified that Noah was to build the Ark 450 feet long, 75 feet wide, and 45 feet high out of "Gopher Wood" which is more commonly known as Cypress wood. It was to have a skylight all the way around the ship 18 inches below the roof, and there were to be three decks inside the boat, and a door in the side like a gangplank. After he built it, he was to coat the Ark inside and out with pitch, a resin from trees. Now these are pretty strict specifications, but amazingly, each of the following reports parallel the description closely, which makes it hard to write off the reports as purely coincidental.

One of the first known sightings was several hundred years ago when a series of earthquakes caused huge blocks of ice to fall from

Mt. Ararat and destroy a village below. Turkish officials went up the mountain to help the village people and noticed a giant ship sticking out of the ice in a gully near the mountain top. When they investigated the Ark, they found it in pretty good condition and were able to enter three of the large compartments inside that were not full of ice. Unfortunately, extremely severe blizzard conditions chased the group away from their discovery and they never again had the chance to return.

An equally convincing account was one told in 1920 by an American born in Armenia, right before he died. He told his friends about a time in 1856 when he was living near Mt. Ararat and three foreigners hired him and his father to be their guides up the mountain. The foreigners intended to prove by making the climb that the Ark was not there, but to their dismay, it was. They were angry and tried without success to destroy the Ark. Then they swore never to tell anyone about the discovery and threatened to kill their guides if they ever said anything. Curiously, a post-World War I newspaper article verified the man's story. It told the exact same account from a different point of view, that of a British scientist who confessed on his deathbed to being one of the three who found the Ark. It does seem a bit amazing that two unrelated men could come up with the exact same story about finding Noah's Ark, if all it was was a story.

By 1916 there were not only Armenians, Americans and British interested in the treasure of Mt. Ararat but Russians were getting into the act too. A Russian pilot told his countrymen of having flown over the Ark and of having brought back measurements which paralleled the description in the Bible as proof that it was actually Noah's Ark. The Tsar was very impressed and sent a team of men to take accurate measurements and pictures of the craft. They did, but unfortunately their detailed report was destroyed on its way to Moscow during the Russian Revolution.

Most recently, in 1953, an oil-pipeline worker named George Jefferson Greene said he was flying a helicopter over Ararat when he spotted a big dark object on the mountain top. He hovered about 100 feet away from it and snapped a series of six photographs which were shown around the Southwestern United States. Today there is no trace of his pictures, although at least 30 reliable witnesses confirm having seen them. One man even drew a sketch of one of the pictures in which he showed a large kind of square object on the edge of a cliff, embedded in ice. In detail there were parallel lines on the hull where the planking joined. Shortly after this report the Turkish officials closed the area to explorers due to unfriendly conditions on the Soviet border.

I think it is significant to note one common element which all these reports share: Mysteriously, in each instance, the cold, hard evidence (like the photographs or the detailed Russian report) was lost somehow. Could it be possible that even if the Ark is there, that God doesn't want us to find it? Maybe He would rather us trust Him because of what we feel in our hearts, not because of what we see with our eyes. After all, isn't that what religion is all about? . . . Faith not fact.

Ellen Volkert

Writing Assignments

Paper 1

The columnists and authors who write for newspapers and magazines frequently use statistics and data as the basis for their opinion pieces and articles. For example, using statistics about teenage pregnancy as a starting point, Ellen Goodman wrote a column about the possible bad effects of publicity about unmarried movie stars having children. Citing figures on high rates of unemployment among blacks, William Raspberry wrote a column suggesting that middle-class black professionals should assume more responsibility for creating jobs for young black people. This assignment suggests that you use the same approach to write an editorial for a paper or journal that you read regularly; perhaps a paper put out by your church, the student newspaper, or a magazine such as *Mademoiselle* or *Ebony*. Before you begin the main part of your paper, write out an audience analysis specifying where your article would be published, what interests that audience would have that would make them want to read the article, and what questions they would have. Also write out a purpose analysis stating what you would hope to accomplish with your article.

Here are two sets of statistics on which you can draw for an argument; you may be able to find others in recent newspapers or in magazines like *U.S. News and World Report* or *Time*.

1. The Bureau of Labor Statistics reports these figures on working women in 1985:
   - 55 per cent of the nation's estimated 32.2 million women with children 18 and younger hold jobs outside the home.
   - 47.7 per cent of an estimated 9,248,000 women with children age three and under were either working or looking for work in March, 1985.
2. Nielsen Report figures on television viewing as of January, 1985, indicate:
   - 84,900,000 households have at least one TV set.
   - During the 1983–84 season, TV households watched TV an average of seven hours and eight minutes a day.
   - In November, 1984, TV owners viewed the box more than 52 hours a week — more than most people spend on their jobs.
   - In general, women watch more TV than men watch.

Using this evidence in any way that you wish, construct a thesis and develop an argument. Think about some of the less obvious implications of the figures that you use and write an argument that goes beyond conventional conclusions that will be no news to your readers.

Paper 2

You have been elected the representative from your neighborhood to appear before the city council at a zoning hearing. Using Toulmin argument as your strategy, write a ten-minute speech (no more than four double-spaced pages) arguing for or against one of the following propositions that is before the city council. At the end of the paper, diagram your argument according to the Toulmin model so that you will be able to explain it to a lawyer who asks.

Before you begin the main part of your paper, write out an audience analysis. What are the city council's main concerns? What do they need to know from you? What questions will they want your speech to answer? Also write out a statement of your purpose. What do you hope to achieve with the city council by making the speech?

Possible Topics for a Zoning Hearing

1. A change in zoning to allow a sixteen-unit condominium apartment building to be built on a two-acre tract at the intersection of two narrow streets in your neighborhood.

2. A change in zoning to allow the Salvation Army to put up a shelter for transients on a tract where there is now an elementary school that is no longer used. The vacant school is in the middle of a residential district in one of the older parts of town.

3. A change in zoning to permit a commercial operator to convert an old apartment house into a combination laundromat and bar that will be open from 6:00 A.M. until 12:00 P.M. It will be in a small center now occupied by a public library, two doctors' offices, and a Montessori school.

4. A change in zoning to allow a sheltered house for mildly retarded adults to be established in a neighborhood of your city that so far has prohibited any buildings other than single-family dwellings. The neighborhood borders a recently constructed, busy expressway, and as a result, property values have been declining. The mental-health agency that wants to establish the home for retarded adults is negotiating to buy a large, once-elegant home with four acres of walled property and a swimming pool. From the agency's point of view, the property is ideal, but some of the neighbors are fiercely opposing the zoning change that would make it possible. The retarded adults who would live in the home are able look after themselves and are not considered dangerous in any way; they are not, however, either emotionally or financially able to maintain their own homes.

5. Your town has an old zoning law that prohibits any store that is open seven days a week from being located within a half mile of a public school. The original purpose of the zoning was to keep out convenience stores that stock sexually explicit magazines and comic books. Now, however, a national chain of convenience stores has bought lots near the city's two major high schools and is going to challenge the zoning. The management of the stores claims that the advantages to the high school students and the faculties of the schools more than offset the possible problems caused by the students' access to certain magazines and that the store has a firmly enforced policy of keeping magazines such as

Penthouse out of sight and selling them only to customers who can prove they are over 18.

Paper 3

Write a paper in which you put yourself in one of the situations described below and try to persuade your audience to consider your point of view by using Rogerian argument. Before you begin to write the main part of the paper, write out a comprehensive audience analysis in which you analyze why your readers might be threatened by the proposal you are making and analyze what concerns and values you and they share that would give you a basis for constructing the case you want to present. Write out an analysis of both points of view like the one shown on p. 349.

1. You are a young man of 30 who makes about $27,500 a year as an auto salesman, but after seven years at it, you detest your work and want to go back to college to become an engineer. As a veteran you will receive about $400 a month while you are going to school; your wife has a job that pays $780 a month. You have no children. You want to convince your wife that in the long run you will both be happier if you make this change, but she is skeptical.

2. You are a young psychologist who has just bought a home in one of the old, established neighborhoods in your city. You cannot afford to rent a separate office in a medical complex, and you want to establish your counseling practice in your home. You will be able to do this only if every home owner on your block will sign a statement agreeing that you can open a professional office in that block. Write a letter to these homeowners that might persuade them to sign such a statement.

3. You work in an office with twenty other people, all of you in a large open room where desks are fairly close together. Four of your co-workers smoke and so far have refused to abstain from smoking during working hours. You have protested to the supervisor, but she maintains that they have as much right to smoke as you do not to smoke and that she will not interfere. If you want to regulate smoking in the office, it's up to you to get everyone to agree. It's important that you get along with all of your fellow workers and that you have a harmonious atmosphere in

the office since many of your projects must be joint efforts. If you alienate these particular four workers, all of whom are important to the functioning of the office, you will have a hard time fulfilling your own obligations on the job.

Construct a Rogerian argument to try to persuade the smokers who work with you to join you in finding a constructive solution to the problem.

11 · Fallacies and Propaganda: How Not to Argue and What Not to Believe

Fallacies, ideas based on mistaken logic, are sometimes called *counterfeit arguments.* That's an apt figurative description because, like bogus money, fallacious arguments superficially resemble sound, rational arguments, but they have flaws that cancel their value as effective rhetoric. Fallacies are usually classified as *formal* if those flaws lie in form or structure and as *material* if the flaws lie in content.

The chief flaws in inductive reasoning — generalizing from an insufficient sample and using data that are biased or not randomly selected — were discussed in Chapter 10. Those might be called the formal fallacies of induction. The formal fallacies of informal logic are failing to support a claim and omitting a necessary part of the argument, such as the data.

Another kind of formal fallacy is the *circular argument.* This kind of reasoning appears to move from a premise to a conclusion, but in reality it does no more than move in a circle. Such a pseudoargument might go like this: "The proposed gun control legislation is a left-wing plot because only Communists would scheme to take guns away from citizens." "Jones cannot be trusted because she is an unreliable person" is just as circular. The main assertion is not supported but simply repeated.

Informal Fallacies

Faulty Analogy

Two major informal fallacies, *faulty analogy* and *false cause,* have already been touched on in Chapter 9, but they are important enough

to warrant a brief review. Prudent writers seldom use analogy as a main rhetorical device because, although a good analogy can clarify and reinforce an argument, it cannot actually furnish proof. And most analogies break down if they are pushed too far. For instance, proponents of our multibillion-dollar space program have sometimes drawn an analogy between that program and the opening of our American frontier to justify the expenditure and human resources that we have invested in space exploration. The comparison is a faulty one, however, because there are far more differences than similarities between the two enterprises. Each may introduce people to an unknown territory, but people cannot journey to space on their own, and they cannot settle and cultivate the area after they get there. The comparison of trips to the moon to Columbus's voyages has the same weaknesses. Analogies of this kind have more emotional than rational force. Because Americans are likely to respond favorably to words such as *exploration, pioneer,* and *frontier,* too often they do not carefully examine the validity of the arguments in which they are used.

Weak analogies hurt arguments

As a precaution against being misled by such easy comparisons, when you use or encounter an analogy you should ask yourself, "Are there enough important similarities between the two things being compared really to support the conclusions that are being drawn?" If a comparison is far-fetched, as it would be if drawn between the president of the United States and the captain of the football team, or if it is trivial, as it would be if it were drawn between learning to fly a plane and learning to ride a bicycle, you should reject it.

False Cause

The informal fallacy of *false cause* (Latin term: *post hoc, ergo propter hoc*) is another form of simplistic reasoning. Human laziness or the desire to see dependable patterns in a complex world tempts us to solve problems by setting up neat cause-and-effect relationships. It is much easier to say, "Permissive child rearing causes juvenile delinquency," "The Vietnam War caused our economic problems," or "Pornography causes sex crimes" than it is to try to trace and understand the complicated chain of circumstances that underlies most problems or events.

In the 1950s, shortly after the United States government had conducted a series of hydrogen bomb tests in the Pacific, the country was hit by an unusually severe winter. Despite the meteorologists' protestations that the weather was the predictable result of a change in the Gulf Stream, some people insisted that the bomb tests had caused it. *The New Yorker* magazine satirized this kind of thinking in a cartoon showing two Neanderthal men peering out of a cave at a torrential rain. The caption was, "We never used to have this kind of weather before they started using bows and arrows."

False-cause arguments are common in political rhetoric

Understandably perhaps, people who are running for office rely heavily on the "after this, therefore because of this" strategy. First, most campaigners who are trying to discredit the current officeholders suggest that they are directly responsible for all the bad things that happened while they were in office. If taxes or unemployment or the crime rate or the cost of living went up during an administration, the challenger always blames the incumbent just because he or she was there. The incumbent, of course, oversimplifies in the same way by taking credit for all the good things that happened during the administration. And the "ins" and the "outs" both project their false cause fallacies into the future by predicting with great certainty that certain effects will follow the election: good effects if "we" are elected, bad effects if "they" are elected.

Now not all such reasoning is faulty. We base our votes on the premise that electing particular candidates will at least help cause or prevent certain effects. And if such predictions are backed with reason and evidence, we are justified in believing them. But one should always be careful about claiming that any one person or act caused something complex to happen.

This same technique is used extensively by advertisers, who rely on it heavily to convince their customers that delightful effects will follow their purchase of a certain product. "Drive our car and the girls will swarm all over you"; "Bleach your hair and rekindle your husband's lagging affection"; "Take our correspondence course and earn $20,000 a year"; "Use Endocreme and look young again." What deceptively simple cause-and-effect arguments!

Begging the Question

Another informal fallacy that crops up as often as weeds in a garden is *begging the question.* The term describes the process of assuming in the premises of an argument what you ought to be establishing by proof; another name for it might be *loading the assertion.* It resembles circular reasoning in that the writer does not construct a legitimate argument but merely asserts that something is because it is. For example, the statement "Henry Miller's filthy books should not be allowed in our library," which neither proves that the books are filthy nor shows why they should be taken out of the library, is a loaded assertion masquerading as an argument. So are the following sentences: "Useless courses such as Greek and Hebrew are a waste of time"; "This fine public servant deserves our support"; and "This corrupt official should be thrown out of office." A reader would probably agree that useless courses are a waste of time, fine public servants deserve support, and corrupt officials should be gotten rid of; such statements are almost redundant. But in each case the writer has not proved the allegation.

The fallacy of begging the question creeps into writing in subtler ways as well. A common form is the question-begging epithet — that is, a favorable or unfavorable label attached to the subject of the assertion, for example, "John's *disgraceful* conduct ought to be censured" or "This *treasonable* act must not go unpunished." Such statements substitute connotation for argument. Other expressions that appear frequently in question-begging arguments are "It is common knowledge," "Everybody knows," "Everyone would agree," "It is obvious," and "The fact is." When these are followed by no more than statements of opinion, the chances are that the writer is trying to evade the burden of proof. Statements like "Everyone knows that socialized medicine has been a failure in England" and "It is common knowledge that the Syndicate controls the numbers racket" prove nothing unless they are followed by supporting evidence.

Argument to the Person

Argument to the person (Latin term: *argumentum ad hominem*) focuses on an individual's character or personal life rather than on the issues involved. If a person is running for office, the debate should center on qualifications, experience, and the kind of program advocated, not on religious beliefs, military record, or marital status. The campaigner who overemphasizes a war record and church affiliation and keeps appearing on television with his or her family, but who says little about taxes or legislation, may reasonably be accused of evading the real issues. That person is trying to appeal to the audience's emotions rather than to its reason. Unfortunately, such tactics often work. Until recent years, a divorced person stood little chance of being elected to public office, and John F. Kennedy was the first successful Catholic presidential candidate. But the thinking person tries to look beyond personalities and personal biases when making a judgment about an individual's qualifications or achievements. To condemn an author's works becaue she or he is reputed to be a heavy drinker or to say that a person ought not to be elected to Congress because he or she does not belong to a church shows a poor grasp of the real issues involved.

People who want to make thoughtful and rational judgments will pay little attention to mudslinging, gossip, or unsupported accusations against office seekers or other public figures. They will try to focus on matters that affect a person's work and official behavior. For this reason you should be wary of anyone who tries to sell you a program or platform not by stressing issues and proposals but by relying on patriotic clichés, such as "He fought for our country" and "She is a devoted wife and mother."

There are times, however, when habits or beliefs can become legitimate concerns. If a person who is running for office actually is an alcoholic, that person may not be able to handle the responsibilities of the office. Or if you want very much for the next legislature to legalize gambling in your state, a candidate's religious affiliation may indeed be pertinent. But everyone should try to distinguish between personal attacks and information that bears on the issue. The following kind of political advertisement illustrates the problem:

Vote for Honesty and Decency

John Q. Candidate stands foursquare on his record of thirty scandal-free years as county treasurer. You *know* he's honest. On the other hand, his opponent is a man who declared bankruptcy in 1968, has been married three times, and last year was brought into court twice on charges of reckless driving.

Is it an *argument to the person* fallacy or a justified release of relevant information?

Argument to the People

Argument to the people (Latin term: *argumentum ad populum*) is similar to the previous one. It takes the form of impassioned emotional appeals "to the people," that is, to the deep biases people have for institutions such as God, motherhood, country, family, and may have against fascism, communism, atheism, or other such abstract concepts. This fallacy too seeks to arouse emotions rather than confront issues. In Albert Camus' *The Stranger,* the state prosecutor pleads to the jury to send the protagonist, Meursault, to the guillotine not so much because he killed a man in a moment of irrationality, but because he did not cry at his mother's funeral and was unmoved when the prosecutor showed him a crucifix. And the jury convicted. As we shall see, propaganda relies heavily on the argument to the people.

You're Another

This fallacy (Latin term: *tu quoque*) takes the form of evading the issue or deflecting a hostile charge or question by making a similar charge against the opponent. For example, a person who had been charged with cheating on an expense account might counter the accusation with, "Who are you to criticize me for padding my expense account when I know you cheat on your income tax?" Lionel Ruby quotes a typical *you're another* argument on the issue of the draft. A younger man might say to an older one, "You're in favor of the draft because you're too old to go." The older one might reply, "Maybe so, but you're against it because you're afraid you'll have to go."[1] The so-called argument is entirely beside the point; neither has mentioned the merits or defects of the draft law.

Exchanges on a low personal level are not difficult to spot for the counterfeits they are, but these kinds of arguments sometimes become rather sophisticated — in fact, one finds them in surprising company. Take, for example, this paragraph from a Jean-Paul Sartre essay on existentialism:

> As is generally known, the basic charge against us [existentialists] is that we put the emphasis on the dark side of human life. Someone recently told me of a lady who, when she let slip a vulgar word in a moment of irritation, excused herself by saying, "I guess I'm becoming an existentialist." Consequently, existentialism is regarded as something ugly; that is why we are said to be naturalists; and if we are, it is rather surprising that in this day and age we cause so much more alarm and scandal than does naturalism,

[1]Lionel Ruby, *The Art of Making Sense* (Philadelphia: Lippincott, 1954) 89.

properly so called. The kind of person who can take in his stride such a novel as Zola's *The Earth* is disgusted as soon as he starts reading an existentialist novel; the kind of person who is resigned to the wisdom of the ages — which is pretty sad — finds us even sadder. Yet, what can be more disillusioning than saying "true charity begins at home" or "a scoundrel will always return evil for good"?[2]

Sartre has not at all refuted the charge that existentialism is a gloomy philosophy that focuses "on the dark side of human life." He has only deflected the criticism by saying, in effect, "You call us gloomy! You're just as gloomy with your cynical slogans and admiration for naturalistic novels."

Black/White Fallacy

Either/or options often oversimplify

This fallacy may also be called the *fallacy of insufficient options* or the *either/or fallacy.* Writers or speakers who use it are trying to force their audience into choosing between two conflicting alternatives by suggesting that there are no other options. In fact, there may be several options or even the option of making no choice. This kind of oversimplification is attractive to people who have what the psychologists call "two-valued orientations"; that is, they see the world in terms of black and white, right and wrong, good and bad. As you can imagine, they don't have many philosophical problems. A typical example of their outlook on life is illustrated by the bumper sticker "America — Love It or Leave It." This kind of attitude is as prevalent on the left as it is on the right. "Either you believe in socialism or you're a dirty Fascist pig" is as bad as "If you're not an advocate of free enterprise, you're a Communist sympathizer."

Rational thinkers neither rely on this tactic nor allow themselves to be intimidated by it. For example, if they are concerned about industrial air pollution in this country, they do not argue that we have to choose between factories and clean air. They know there are other options: filtering devices and other controls that will give us clean air if we are willing to pay for it, relocating factories to reduce the concentration of pollutants, and so on. They do not subscribe to the simplistic view that the solution to our technological problems is

[2]Jean-Paul Sartre, "The Humanism of Existentialism," *The Philosophy of Existentialism* (New York: Philosophical Library, 1965) 32.

a return to nature. Moreover, they see the flaws in arguments such as the following by Hugh Kenner:

> Johnny goes by the official title of "student." Yet Johnny is the face every professor would prefer to see anywhere but in the classroom where it blocks with its dreary smile, or its stoical yawn, the educational process on which we are proud to spend annually billions of dollars. By his sheer inert numbers he is making the common pursuit of professors and students — real students — impossible.[3]

Kenner goes on to define the "real student" as one who insists on knowing:

> . . . What it does not know it will encounter with pleasure. And it *must* learn, as a cat must eat. . . . [I]ts tireless curiosity is unmistakable. In time, if all goes well, it will accept training, and the lifelong responsibilities of keeping itself trained.
>
> But Johnny has no such appetite, no such momentum. When Johnny applies his brand-new ball-point to his first blue book, each sentence comes out smudged with his unmistakable pawprint.

Throughout the essay Kenner recognizes only two kinds of students: Johnnies and real students. The real student is always described in favorable terms — "tireless curiosity," "a mind that insists on knowing," "encounters knowledge with pleasure" — while Johnny is defined by his "dreary smile," "stoical yawn," and the smudge of "his unmistakable pawprint." The argument is totally black and white; Kenner does not acknowledge the possibility that there may be students who do not fit into one of his categories. As a result his argument, although cleverly written, falls to the ground.

Misuse of rhetorical questions

The loaded rhetorical question that allows for only one acceptable answer is a form of the black/white argument:

> Are we going to take steps to maintain law and order in our community, or are we going to allow the thugs and dope addicts to take over this town and ruin our homes and families?

[3]Hugh Kenner, "Don't Send Johnny to College," *Saturday Evening Post* 14 Nov. 1964: 12–16.

Shall we vote against this bill for increased welfare payments, or shall we abandon our fight to stop creeping socialism in our society?

The Complex Question

The *complex question* is fallacious because it sets up a question in such a way that a direct answer can only support the questioner's assumption. The classic example is "Have you stopped beating your wife?" To answer either "yes" or "no" is incriminating. The deceptive part about this fallacy is that the questioner is apparently asking only one question, but in reality is asking two: "Did you ever beat your wife?" and "Do you now beat your wife?" Other variations of this fallacy might take these forms:

Does everyone in your town still get drunk and raise hell on Saturday night?

How long have you been consorting with known criminals and other Syndicate types?

What made you think you could get away with plagiarizing that paper?

When did you start cheating on your income tax?

Questions like these are designed to trick an audience and therefore do not deserve a direct answer. You can cope with them only by insisting that the questioner break the question down into two distinct parts to be answered separately and independently.

Red Herring

Bringing in irrelevant issues

This term, which refers to smoked herring, a particularly strong-smelling fish, is a figurative phrase that describes the tactic of bringing in an irrelevant point to divert the audience's attention from the main issue. It refers to the old belief that dragging a red herring across a trail would divert the attention of hunting dogs from the scent they were expected to follow and send them off in another direction. There are many kinds of diversionary tricks used in arguments, but we usually reserve the term *red herring* for the digression a speaker or writer uses to sidetrack an argument.

For example, if a labor leader were arguing that unions ought to be exempt from antitrust laws but spent much of the speech describing the hardships union people endured in the early part of this century, he or she would be employing a red herring fallacy. Labor's fight for the right to bargain collectively is important historically but has nothing to do with the present issue. The fallacy also crops up when a speaker interrupts a debate on a specific issue to bring in matters that are not under discussion. For instance, a college faculty member who tried to sidetrack a discussion about faculty salaries into an attack on the school's publish-or-perish rules would be using a red herring fallacy. The latter problem may be worth discussing, but it is not the issue under consideration.

The Genetic Fallacy

Misleading references to origins

People who argue from the *genetic fallacy* assert that we can predict a person's nature and character if we know that person's origins. They would hold that the same is true for institutions, works of art, or ideas. We often find this fallacy expressed as an enthymeme:

He wouldn't do that because he's from a good family.

Jane must be a racist since she spent her life in South Africa.

The Reivers must be a Gothic novel since Faulkner wrote it.

Acupuncture cannot be an acceptable technique for modern doctors since it was developed in ancient China.

Jack is bound to be exceptionally bright because his father is a professor.

That radio won't last very long if it came from Japan.

Some of these conclusions *may* be true, but proving them requires evidence, not simply speculation about origins.

Special Pleading

This term describes a totally one-sided argument that is presented as the whole truth. The points that the arguer makes for or against the issue may be quite true, or at least supported with reasonable evidence, but the position is so biased that it cannot be considered valid. Mark Twain used this kind of argument against the church and Christianity in his novel *The Mysterious Stranger.* He focused on the crimes that have been committed in the name of the church, on the misery and injustice that God allows to exist in the world, and on the suffering of good Christians and the triumph of those who flout God's laws. Bertrand Russell took the same approach in his book *Why I Am Not a Christian.* Neither man conceded any good to Christianity. Even those people who are inclined to share the writers' prejudices should realize that their arguments, although supported with examples, are completely unfair. Any argument that concentrates solely on the merits or defects of an institution or system and ignores whatever points may be made on the other side is open to the same charge.

Biased use of evidence

The Appeal to Ignorance

Persons who use the *appeal to ignorance* (Latin term: *argumentum ad ignorantiam*) typically assert that a claim or theory must be right because no one can prove that it is wrong. Thus they try to evade their own responsibility for supporting or proving a point by simply shifting that obligation to their opponents. Frequently, people who argue in this way will make highly dubious cause-and-effect statements and defy their challenger to show that the relationship is impossible. If the challenger cannot, the arguer interprets the response as agreement.

Putting burden of disproof on opponent

For example, someone might claim that wearing a copper bracelet will bring about improvement in people who suffer from arthritis. Although medical specialists have repeatedly pointed out that there is no scientific basis for the claim, the promoters of copper bracelets can say that neither has anyone proved that they *don't* help. Therefore, they claim, they have a right to say they do help.

Recognizing Fallacies

This catalogue of common fallacies by no means includes all the ways in which an argument can go wrong. Studying it, however, should alert you to the more obvious weaknesses in the arguments of others and help you avoid such pitfalls in your own rhetoric. If, while you are constructing an argument, you can spot those places at which an opponent might justly say, "Oh, but you're not being logical" or "Ah ha! Your conclusion does not follow from the evidence you have given," you can strengthen your own writing. But we also have to remember that almost no rhetoric is totally free of fallacy — even Plato or John Stuart Mill produced arguments that might be justifiably criticized.

We cannot demand perfection and unswerving consistency from any speaker or writer; such a demand is in itself a kind of fallacy. What we must do, then, is make a balanced and charitable judgment of other people's arguments. An occasional question-begging epithet or genetic fallacy does not constitute sufficient grounds for rejecting an entire editorial, essay, or speech. If, however, an argument contains blatant false cause fallacies or personal attacks and the author twists the evidence, you have every right to say that it is not a sound or just argument. Finally, you should remember that your opponents are not the only ones who indulge in fallacies. You must be honest enough to search out the fallacies in arguments you agree with, as well as in those to which you are hostile.

Why Not Use Fallacies?

Ethical Considerations   Students often ask, "Well, what's the matter with using fallacies in an argument if they help you to win?" There are two answers to that question, one ethical, one practical. The first involves definition. Using dishonest means — and that is what fallacies amount to if a person is using them consciously — to attain an end brands you as a dishonest person. A fallacy is a swindle, a counterfeit argument, an evasion of your responsibility to support your beliefs with logical and legitimate methods. Viewed from an ethical standpoint, this question is on the same level as "What is the matter with cheating if it gets you a good grade?" or "Why shouldn't I lie if it's to my advantage?"

Practical Considerations   Viewed from a practical standpoint, fallacies in your argument may contribute to defeating your purpose. If you use fallacies deliberately and cynically, you are assuming that your audience is not very bright and cannot detect twisted reasoning. Even people with untrained minds are not necessarily gullible; they can recognize loaded statements and spurious appeals to their emotions, and they will realize you are insulting them. People with trained minds will immediately dismiss a fallacious argument as not worth bothering with. If you cannot construct a rational defense for your ideas, they will label you as a sloppy thinker. If they think you are capable of putting together a reasonable and careful argument but prefer to make an irrational one in the hope of winning, you will lose their respect and support.

Propaganda

All rhetoric seeks to persuade, but *propaganda,* as we shall use the term here, seeks to persuade principally by appeals to the emotional, irrational side of our nature. As Lionel Ruby put it:

> A propagandist, in the strict sense, is not interested in the truth for its own sake, or in spreading it. His purpose is different. He wants a certain kind of action from us. He doesn't want people to think for themselves. He seeks to mold their minds so that they will think as he wants them to think, and act as he wants them to act. He prefers that they should *not* think for themselves. If the knowledge of certain facts will cast doubts in the minds of his hearers, he will conceal those facts.[4]

Propagandists rely on fallacies

Given these goals, we might expect propagandists to rely heavily on fallacies to achieve their ends. And so they do. Whether they are promoting a product, an ideology, a frame of mind, or a person, they employ counterfeit arguments designed to short-circuit the reasoning process and go straight to the emotions. Sometimes this technique is employed to achieve useful, even admirable, goals; nevertheless, propagandists quite often reveal a real contempt for their audience. They operate from the assumption that the audience is irrational, shallow-minded, more swayed by myths than by facts, and incapable of abstract or logical thinking. Propagandists who have contempt for their audience agree, in effect, with Adolf Hitler that "the people in their overwhelming majority are so feminine by nature and attitude that sober reasoning determines their thoughts and actions far less than emotion and feeling."[5] These propagandists

[4]Ruby 76.
[5]Adolf Hitler, *Mein Kampf,* trans. Ralph Mannheim (Boston: Houghton, 1933) 183.

are confident that they, with their superior intellect and knowledge of human weaknesses, can manipulate and condition the masses into buying what they have to sell.

Commercial Propaganda

Advertisers rely on fallacies

In recent years the advertising industry has learned so many ways to use fallacies and to manipulate the language that commercial persuasion has become almost a special branch of communication. As a former adman, Carl P. Wrighter, puts it in his book, *I Can Sell You Anything:*

> You see advertising is really a science, and it is mostly a science of human motivation and behavior. When we get ready to pitch a new soap to you, we know more about what you do in your bathroom than your own wife or husband. Not only that, we know why you do it, how you do it, and what makes you do it. We know what kind of appeals you will respond to, what kind of emotions you will fall prey to, even the very words which will strike a chord on your heart strings. In short, persuasion in advertising is done not so much by dispensing information publicly as by attacking your weak spots emotionally, and having our products soothe your savage ego.[6]

Ads appeal to the emotions

Ad agencies learn to play on your emotions and ego by spending large chunks of their budgets on motivational research, the systematic study of people's needs, fears, anxieties, hopes, and desires. They hire sociologists to advise them about patterns of behavior and the attitudes of various economic groups. They hire psychologists to tell them what stimuli will trigger favorable responses toward a product and what symbols they can use to set up good associations with their products in the minds of the consumers. And using these insights, they assault each of us, one student of our culture claims, with a minimum of five hundred messages a day.[7]

Arguments to the people, red herrings, and question-begging fallacies abound in advertising; so, of course, does the false cause fallacy that suggests that using a product will cause certain wonderful

---

[6]Carl P. Wrighter, *I Can Sell You Anything.* Copyright © 1972 by Ballantine Books, a Division of Random House, Inc. Reprinted by permission of the publisher.
[7]Alvin Toffler, *Future Shock* (New York: Bantam, 1970) 167.

results. And what almost all advertisements have in common is their heavy load of emotional appeal. Carl Wrighter analyzes it like this:

> Emotionalism is always present in advertising. It is used in two ways: First, as a hook, leading up to the factual message or claim; and second, as a sale all by itself, when no fact, claim or demonstration is available. Generally it relies on buzz words, which trigger emotional responses, and usually occurs in unnecessary products. There are nine basic approaches.[8]

Nine kinds of advertising appeals

Wrighter goes on to summarize the nine categories of emotional gimmicks that advertisers rely on:

1. The family environment. Showing a warm family scene that suggests that the product will give you this kind of life.
2. Motherhood. Appealing to the customer's need for understanding and love; she'll make everything all right.
3. Feeling good. Suggesting that using the product will make the customer happy.
4. Sympathy. Implying that the people who make this product know and sympathize with the client's problems.
5. Identity. Using references and language that make the buyer feel comfortable and at home.
6. Music. Getting the buyer to respond to rhythm and melody and thus feel good about the product.
7. Borrowed interest. Getting the buyer to transfer good feelings about something to the manufacturer's product. The four most common interests used here are babies, animals, sex, and status.
8. Scare tactics. Making customers think something bad is going to happen to them if they don't use the product.
9. People to people. Trying to get the customer to take someone else's recommendation. There are two variations of this: first, bringing in the common, everyday person, who must be telling the truth; second, getting the endorsement and implied wisdom of someone famous.

Wrighter also warns about the deceptive use of authority figures (ads showing the person in the white coat) and about the *weasel*

---

[8]Wrighter, 117.

words of advertising: *fortified, special, different, new, best, helps prevent,* and *lasts up to,* and a multitude of equally slippery terms.

Armed with these tools, the advertisers mount their campaign to persuade the great buying public to part with its dollars. In return for these dollars, buyers get the manufacturer's product, which to them may represent some of the good things in life: pleasure, love, security, popularity, prestige, new images of themselves. What appeal do you think the following hypothetical ads might have for what types of audiences?

The Jupiter is *the* auto! Built by true craftsmen for those few who demand the finest. And those few who can afford the finest. Its sleek styling, its understated elegance, its unmistakable *éclat* says — but ever so subtly — that you've arrived!

You Can't Afford to Wait! You feel young doing those fun things you love — swimming, skiing, riding. But the sun, the wind, the water are the enemies of that fresh complexion. Don't wait for them to dry out those precious oils your skin must have. Be young! Keep that dewy look your man loves so much! Start today to use Ponce de Leon Essence of Youth. Smoothed over your skin twice a day, it will help to erase those tiny wrinkles that steal away your youth! Only $15 for a half-ounce jar.

Mother McCrea's bread is as good as that wonderful bread your mother used to make. You could make it too, if you had time. But because we know you don't have those hours and hours it takes to make really delicious bread, we want to help you. Just take a Mother McCrea's ready-to-brown loaf, brush a little butter on the top, pop it in the oven, and you'll have that delicious, golden-crusted bread you remember. Your family will love it! And you! Because you've taken time to bake for them. *(According to Vance Packard, author of* The Hidden Persuaders, *advertisers use this kind of copy to overcome the guilt women feel about using prepared foods. Notice the emphasis on "you" and "your.")*

VIXEN! It's not for the timid. Only a *real* woman would dare to wear it, dare to hint at that exciting, provocative you that simmers just beneath the surface. But if you're not afraid, VIXEN is your perfume. And you'll find a *real* man.

Do you want to serve a wine to those special guests but are afraid to? Afraid you'll reveal your ignorance when you bring out the bottle? Want to cover up the label for fear it might not be the right kind? Don't be. You'll never be gauche if you choose our *vin extraordinaire*. White or red, it's superb. Serve it proudly — it says all the right things about your taste. And may even get you that promotion.

Not all or even most advertisements are deceptive or contrived wholly to appeal to the emotions. In fact, many advertisers stress information about their product and try to appeal to their audience's reason. Even though words are often connotative and the accompanying pictures may fall into one of the categories that Wrighter mentions, the tone is partially rational. Such ads cannot be called propaganda in the bad sense because at least part of their purpose is informative.

Commercial appeals like the ones illustrated earlier, however, and the kinds of television ads that play on viewers' fears by showing people who are old or sick or unpopular or alone, must be classified as attempts to sell a product by manipulating the audience's insecurities and anxieties. Such ads sell hope and illusions, and perhaps there is nothing wrong with that. The rational woman should know, however, that when she pays fifteen dollars for a half-ounce jar of face cream to make her look ten years younger, she is buying an illusion — nothing more.

Political Propaganda

Political propaganda usually appeals to lazy thinkers

Political progadandists also sell illusions, but of a potentially more dangerous kind. One of the chief illusions they promote is that there are simple solutions to complex problems. They want people to believe that if they will just put their faith in one party or one candidate or one creed, all their troubles will disappear. By employing almost every kind of fallacy and emotional appeal, they try to short-circuit the voters' intellects and go straight to their biases, sentiments, prejudices, and basic physical drives. They depend on people being so mentally lazy that they are ready to substitute slogans and clichés for thinking.

Although modern propagandists have more sophisticated techniques and technology at their command than did their colleagues of the preelectronic era, their basic methods have changed very little since 1939, the year the Institute for Propaganda Analysis published the definitive analysis of propaganda techniques. Notice how apt the following categories and descriptions still are:

Seven kinds of propaganda

Name Calling — giving an idea a bad label — is used to make us reject and condemn the idea without examining the evidence.

Glittering Generality — associating something with a "virtue word" — is used to make us accept and approve the thing without examining the evidence.

Transfer carries the authority, sanction, and prestige of something respected and revered over to something else in order to make the latter acceptable; or it carries authority, sanction, and disapproval to cause us to reject and disapprove something the propagandist would have us reject and disapprove.

Testimonial consists in having some respected or hated person say that a given idea or program or product or person is good or bad.

Plain Folks is the method by which a speaker attempts to convince his audience that he and his ideas are good because they are "of the people," the "plain folks."

Card Stacking involves the selection and use of facts or false-hoods, illustrations or distractions, and logical or illogical statements in order to give the best or the worst possible case for an idea, program, person, or product.

Band Wagon has as its theme, "Everybody — at least all of *us* — is doing it"; with it, the propagandist attempts to convince us that all members of a group to which we belong are accepting his program and that we *must therefore* follow our crowd and "jump on the band wagon."[9]

Notice how many of the fallacies go hand-in-hand with propaganda devices; argument to the person, argument to the people, and begging the question with "name calling," "glittering generalities," and "plain folks"; special pleading, red herring, black/white, you're another, and false cause with "card stacking" and "band wagon."

Fortunately, in this country no single power group has ever totally monopolized the media so that it can pour out a constant stream of

---

[9]Alfred McClung Lee and Elizabeth Briant Lee, *The Fine Art of Propaganda* (New York: Harcourt and the Institute for Propaganda Analysis, 1939, and Octagon, 1972; San Francisco: Institute for General Semantics, 1979) 23–24, by permission of the authors, who are the copyright owners. Copyright renewed 1967.

fallacies and propaganda that gives us a one-sided, simplistic view of politics and effectively prevents criticism or opposition. We also, for the most part, seem to have a tradition of fair play and restraint that keeps all but the most extreme groups and individuals from indulging in the completely irrational, hate-filled propaganda that totalitarian states make use of. But we should not be complacent about our comparative freedom; to retain it, we need to be always alert to the propaganda surrounding us, to have an internal warning system that goes off when adviser, politician, or all-purpose swindler starts using one of the familiar devices. We should analyze the actual meaning of the words and make our decisions based on what we think is right or best and not what others are doing.

Merging of political and commercial propaganda

Unfortunately, in the last decade resisting and analyzing propaganda has become more difficult — but also more important — because the commercial and political propagandists have joined forces. The merger is particularly obvious in that most pervasive branch of all the media, television. Joe McGinniss describes the alliance in his book, *The Selling of the President, 1968:*

> Politics, in a sense, has always been a con game. . . .
> Advertising, in many ways, is a con game too. Human beings do not need a new automobile every third year; a color television set brings little enrichment of the human experience; a higher or lower hemline no expansion of consciousness, no increase in the capacity to love.
> It is not surprising, then, that politicians and advertising men should have discovered one another. And, once they recognized that the citizen did not so much vote for a candidate as make a psychological purchase of him, it is not surprising that they began to work together.[10]

McGinniss's book is a detailed, documented account of how the professional writers and advertising people who were hired to help with the 1968 presidential campaign "marketed" Richard Nixon to the public through television. Our concern here is not with the merits of the candidate himself — presumably the "salespeople" would have handled Abraham Lincoln or Franklin Roosevelt the same way

[10]Joe McGinniss, *The Selling of the President, 1968,* pp. 19, 20. Copyright © 1969 by JoeMac, Incorporated. Reprinted by permission of Simon & Schuster, a division of Gulf & Western Corporation, and the Sterling Lord Agency, Inc.

if they had run those campaigns. Our concern is, rather, with the professional propagandists and their methods. McGinniss quotes one of them as writing,

> "Voters are basically lazy, basically uninterested in making an *effort* to understand what we're talking about. . . . Reason requires a high degree of discipline, of concentration; impression is easier. Reason pushes the viewer back; it assaults him, it demands that he agree or disagree; impression can envelop him, invite him in, without making an intellectual demand. . . . When we argue with him we demand that he make the effort of replying. We seek to engage his intellect, and for most people this is the most difficult work of all. The emotions are more easily roused, closer to the surface, more malleable. . . .
>
> "[Nixon] has to come across as a person larger than life, the stuff of legend. People are stirred by the legend, including the living legend, not by the man himself. It's the aura that surrounds the charismatic figure more than it is the figure itself, that draws the followers. Our task is to build that aura. . . .
>
> "So let's not be afraid of television gimmicks . . . get the voters to like the guy and the battle's two-thirds won."[11]

The promoters built their campaign on this philosophy. They assumed that voters didn't want to think about the issues, that they wanted to feel, to be impressed, to be swept along in a warm swell of emotions.

The advertising people created a new slogan: "This time vote like your whole world depended on it" — ambiguous, vague, but catchy. Their marketing masterpiece, however, was a series of sixty-second television commercials based on still pictures. McGinniss describes them this way:

> Treleaven could use Nixon's voice to accompany the stills but his face would not be on the screen. Instead there would be pictures, and hopefully, the pictures would prevent people from paying too much attention to the words.
>
> The words would be the same ones Nixon always used — the words of the acceptance speech. But they would all seem fresh and

[11]McGinniss 32–33.

lively because a series of still pictures would flash on the screen while Nixon spoke. If it were done right, it would permit Treleaven to create a Nixon image that was entirely independent of the words. Nixon would say his same old tiresome things but no one would have to listen. The words would become Muzak. Something pleasant and lulling in the background. The flashing pictures would be carefully selected to create the impression that somehow Nixon represented competence, respect for tradition, serenity, faith that the American people were better than people anywhere else, and that all these problems others shouted about meant nothing in a land blessed with the tallest buildings, strongest armies, biggest factories, cutest children, and rosiest sunsets in the world. Even better: through association with the pictures, Richard Nixon could *become* these very things.[12]

Eighteen of those sixty-second commercials were produced, each carefully edited to remove anything controversial. They became one of the major propaganda devices used in the last weeks of the campaign. McGinniss reports the comment of one of the people who helped make them:

"You know, . . . what we're really seeing is a genesis. We're moving into a period where a man is going to be merchandised on television more and more. It upsets you and me, maybe, but we're not typical Americans. The public sits home and watches *Gunsmoke* and when they're fed this pap about Nixon they think they're getting something worthwhile."[13]

Did the professional propagandists con the American public? No one knows the answer to that question. Richard Nixon did win in 1968, to be sure, but by a very narrow margin. He did not even receive a majority of all the votes cast, so the propagandists' success was certainly not overwhelming. Moreover, he might well have received all his votes entirely on his own merits, or because of a number of events quite beyond his or anyone else's control. It would be foolish to overestimate the power of the Big Sell. But it would be foolish also to be unaware of the new techniques of propaganda that

[12]McGinniss 83.
[13]McGinniss 117.

technology has made possible. Your only weapon against them is reason and critical thinking — and being more perceptive and better informed than some manipulators give you credit for being.

Exercises

1. Identify and analyze the following fallacies. Although you should be able to identify each by name (sometimes more than one designation could apply), the most important thing is that you be able to tell why the reasoning is faulty.

a. You see, the priests were right. After we threw those virgins into the volcano, it quit erupting.

b. This campaign to legalize filthy and corrupting movies is the irresponsible work of a few perverted individuals.

c. We ought to elect Bill Duncan to the Senate because he was a Medal of Honor winner in World War II.

d. Are all the people in your hometown still rednecks and bigots?

e. It is common knowledge that socialized medicine has not been successful in England.

f. Are we going to vote a pay increase for our teachers, or are we going to let our schools deteriorate into substandard custodial institutions?

g. The people of Rome lost their vitality and desire for freedom when their emperors decided that the way to keep them happy was to provide them with bread and circuses. What can we expect of our own country now that the government gives people free food and there is a constant round of entertainment provided by television?

h. Of course, Madame, since you loved your husband so dearly you will want to buy this $2,800 casket, our very finest.

i. The policy that Jones is proposing is unsound because it won't work.

j. Jack must be a very tough young man. He just got out of the marines.

k. Two kinds of young women go to college: those who want an education and those who want a husband. If a girl drops out without graduating, it is a sure sign that she wasn't really interested in an education.

l. Vote for Burns. She'll make a good governor — honestly.

m. My opponent for the state legislature, Mrs. Jenkins, may be a capable woman, but in my opinion, and I think yours, capable women should be using their talents to provide a good home for their husbands and children. If they have extra time after doing that, they should devote their energies to volunteer work in the community.

n. The question before us today is how we can raise the money to provide this state with a new medical school. I am for a medical school; the citizens of this state need it if we are to have adequate care. But I shall refuse to vote for the appropriation as long as the doctors of this state continue to charge such excessive fees for their services.

o. Women should not be allowed to go to stag parties because they are for men only.

2. Analyze the fallacies in the following paragraphs:

a. Now, in the 1980s, every intelligent person would agree that marijuana ought to be legalized. Only a few puritanical types who think that anything that is fun must be bad for people still want to keep our ridiculous laws on the books. They claim that getting stoned on marijuana now and then is harmful, but they think nothing of tossing off a couple of martinis before dinner every night. As for the argument that smoking marijuana leads to experimenting with hard drugs, I know for a fact that that is not true. I know several people who have smoked pot but as far as I know none of them is on heroin. And studies have demonstrated that there is no necessary connection between the two.

b. There is no doubt that the present deplorable state of morals among our young people is due to the increasing popularity of sex education in the schools. Showing films on sex to youngsters and then expecting them not to experiment with it is like putting them in a room full of food and expecting them not to eat. And statistics prove that one out of every three high school students who has been enrolled in a sex education course has gone on to have intercourse at some time within the next two years. We should realize that one of the avowed aims of the Communists is to weaken the moral fiber of our young people. We must choose: either we return to the old Christian way of chastity and continence before marriage, or we let our society degenerate into a shameless hedonism of the kind that destroyed ancient Rome.

c. The people I heard talking at the Symphony luncheon yesterday convinced me that Marietta McFarlane should not be elected to the City Council this year, and I am certainly not going to vote for her. She's got a divorce from one of the nicest men in town two years ago and has since been seen dating a handsome foreign-looking man who must be from out of town and is at least ten years younger than she is. If she is going to run our city, she shouldn't be fooling around like that. The young people of this city need a model of family stability before them.

d. The history of the labor movement in this country is a history of heroic workers fighting against powerful and ruthless companies who mostly thought only of their own profits and cared nothing about the people who toiled in their factories. Books like Upton Sinclair's *The Jungle* and Frank Norris's *The Octopus* documented the injustices and the defeats of labor. And the owners never hesitated to use violence to break strikes — they were determined to prevent collective bargaining at all costs. The workers won their rights only after prolonged struggles, led by men like Big Bill Thompson and John L. Lewis who were willing to go to jail for their beliefs if necessary. Anyone who talks about the faults of today's labor unions and points to abuses by some of their members should remember their history and think about how hard it has been for them to get where they are.

3. For several days read your daily newspaper carefully, particularly the editorials, syndicated columns, letters to the editor, and news stories in which public officials are quoted. Clip and bring to class any fallacies that you may find. Be prepared to say specifically what you think those fallacies are and to make a judgment about whether they seriously damage the effect of the article.

Fallacies and Propaganda

4. Carefully examine the advertisements in two magazines, prefer-
ably two with very different audiences. Clip or photocopy advertisements that you think are based on fallacious reasoning or that
represent commercial propaganda.

12 · Writing the Research Paper

What Is Research?

Most college composition courses try to help students develop research skills and strategies by assigning a research paper along with other types of writing. However useful such an assignment may be as an introduction to the resources of the library and to forms of documentation, it is important to remember that research itself is not just a mechanical process that results in the required paper. Research of any sort is an activity fundamental to education and, in fact, to all learning, whether it occurs inside or outside of school. Research, in short, is the process of *finding out,* an activity that ideally is motivated by personal interest and genuine curiosity, by a desire to discover answers to questions and solutions to problems, or simply to learn more about some subject that holds special interest for the researcher. Writing a research paper is a formal way of sharing what you have learned from your investigation of a subject with other similarly interested people.

Research is fundamental to education

A Case Study

Ideally, a researcher's special interest stems from some personal connection with the topic, some vested interest. To illustrate, let's suppose that a man named Steve Palmer develops a bad back. He may want to find out what he can do to minimize pain or prevent a worsening of the problem; he may be interested in learning about diets or exercises or other treatments that could bring about an improvement in his condition. So he may begin to research his problem.

In this particular instance, the first reference Palmer consults may be a doctor or chiropractor. But he may not be satisfied with the

This chapter was written by Mary Trachsel of the University of Texas.

recommendations of a single medical expert, and he may decide to seek a second, third, and fourth opinion from other qualified people. At the same time, Palmer might seek the knowledge and advice of another sort of expert, namely, other individuals like himself who suffer from back pain. He may ask this second group of experts some of the same questions about his symptoms, treatment, and prognosis that he poses to the trained professionals. In addition, however, he may ask this second group for advice and information that will help him better understand and evaluate the statements and recommendations of the medical professionals. From these lay experts, for instance, he might seek answers to his questions about the reputations of individual doctors and chiropractors, about the reliability of various medical procedures to cure the problem, or about the relative merits of conventional medical treatments on the one hand and chiropractic treatments on the other.

A third group of sources Palmer could consult consists of printed materials on the subject of back pain. This category of reference works covers a broad range, from books and articles by various experts to pamphlets published by professional groups and public health agencies to articles Palmer might stumble upon while reading general-interest magazines such as *Redbook* or *Esquire*. Some of these printed sources might be recommended to Palmer by the medical experts or the veteran back pain sufferers he has consulted. And others may be discovered through his own efforts — for instance, he may make a trip to the library to check on health care books, or he may examine selections from the brochures displayed at the doctor's office and peruse the section on back pain in the *Family Guide to Health Care* on his own bookshelves. Television and radio, too, may be sources from which Palmer gathers information to help him decide how to deal with his problem.

Yet another step that Palmer might consider in his research is to gather background information — for instance, to try to increase his understanding of anatomy in order to better understand the information and evaluate the advice he receives from medical professionals, either those with whom he consults in person or whom he encounters in print. One likely source of information for Palmer's research into anatomy would be books and articles on human anatomy, once again produced by such experts as medical researchers and other health care specialists.

As he does his research, Palmer should not overlook a different sort of expert on the subject — namely, himself. Admittedly, he is not a trained expert in the same sense as the various professionals he has consulted. Nonetheless, he brings to his investigation a store of common sense, an ability to judge people's credibility, and an intimate knowledge of his own body's performance capabilities, its response to certain types of treatment in the past, its tolerance of pain, and so forth. He may use all these types of knowledge, consciously or otherwise, in shaping his decisions about whose advice to follow and what variations or combinations of recommended treatments to try.

Thus, Palmer does not passively and unquestioningly accept any and all information he is given; rather, his own mind is actively involved in the search for a solution to his problem, sorting out and evaluating the information he receives from his various sources. He may, for instance, somehow have to reconcile to his own satisfaction conflicting advice about the cause or treatment of his condition. In short, as researcher, Steve Palmer must interact intellectually with his sources, accepting or rejecting their advice as it seems justifiable to him to do so and tailoring their recommendations to match his own needs. He does not allow his sources to solve his problem *for him*; rather, he uses them to help him arrive at a solution himself.

Academic Research

Research in college is a major learning activity

Palmer's search for a solution to his health problem does not occur in an academic setting, and Palmer is not going to write up his findings in a formal research paper or report, as you will probably be asked to do in your college classes. His example nevertheless illustrates some basic principles that hold true even for more formal, academic research projects. In many ways, of course, writing assigned research papers for college courses is undeniably an academic exercise that requires you to practice some of the skills and become familiar with some of the conventions of an important educational activity. But the exercise need not be an empty one that merely demonstrates mechanical skills. Remember that true research is a learning activity, one that exposes you to viewpoints and factual information that may be new to you. Proper research demands that you think critically about your material in order to formulate a well-informed answer to the question that initiated your research efforts.

Topic Selection

Steve Palmer, in essence, had his research topic chosen for him. Nonetheless, clearly it was a subject of deep personal interest. His own involvement with the problem of chronic back pain created a need for him to find a solution, and this same need dictated the kind and number of sources he would consult and the particular information he would seek from those sources.

As a student you may have to put much more conscious effort into topic selection than Palmer did before you embark upon your research projects, but you can apply the same principle. If you have some freedom to choose your own topic for research, you would be wise to select a subject with which you have some personal involvement or some special interest. Certainly you will have little motivation for conducting a thorough and worthwhile investigation of a topic that bores you or that is so unfamiliar you have no idea where or how to begin researching it.

Guidelines for choosing a topic

Ideally, like Steve Palmer, you will be motivated to pursue your investigation by a genuine curiosity — by a need or desire to find out the answer to a question or the solution to a problem. For this reason topics formulated as questions to be answered or problems to be solved are good starting points for the research you do in your college courses. Moreover, these questions or problems should be ones for which you do not have answers or solutions at the outset of your investigation. After all, doing research provides you with an opportunity to learn new information from a variety of sources. It would be a waste of this opportunity — and of a good deal of time and energy as well — to search for information and answers you already have.

There are, of course, many situations in which people turn to outside sources in order to bolster preconceived theories or positions. Consider, for example, campaign workers who must produce political flyers to persuade people to vote for their candidate or advertising writers who cite expert opinions and scientific studies to boost the sales of certain products. In both these instances, research efforts are likely to be very selective. From the beginning the writers intend to gather only those testimonies and data that support a predetermined conclusion — "This candidate deserves your vote" or "This product is the best on the market."

The same cannot be said of academic research, however. As a genuine search for answers and solutions, academic research is an impartial activity — in essence, a search for truth. This being the case, researchers in college courses who set out with preconceived notions about their topics must be prepared to revise or even to change dramatically their positions if their findings indicate that their ideas are faulty or inadequate.

Suppose that you are asked to research and report on the social benefits and/or disadvantages of the use of minority quotas under the Equal Opportunity Employment Act. You must avoid the temptation to focus your investigation, even subconsciously, with questions such as "Why is the quota system necessary to insure equal opportunity for all?" or "How is the quota system unfair to white males?" Both of these questions presuppose certain conclusions — on the one hand, that the quota system is necessary and beneficial, and on the other hand, that the system is unfair. You could, of course, marshal evidence and testimony in support of either side of the issue; that is precisely why the issue is a controversial one in the first place. But if you approach your research in this way, you will prevent yourself from learning anything that might help you resolve the conflict. As an academic researcher, searching for truth, you investigate controversies or problems in order to help settle them, not to intensify or prolong them by unthinkingly supporting one side or the other.

Avoid topics that are too emotional

Of course, it is difficult to be completely objective about all topics, particularly controversial ones or ones with which you have too much personal involvement. For this reason, issues in which you find yourself emotionally embroiled do not usually make good topics for research papers in your college courses. Emotionally charged issues such as abortion or euthanasia or matters of religious doctrine often invite a type of pseudoresearch that aims at proving or defending a position rather than discovering truthful answers and practical solutions.

Sources

Once Steve Palmer identified his problem and recognized a need to solve it, his next step was to gather information to help him decide upon the best solution. One of the most obvious sources of such information is a medical expert, and so Palmer consulted first with a doctor or a chiropractor. But realizing that there may be more than one approach to his problem, Palmer did not end his research efforts once he had consulted a single source. His questioning attitude led him to seek advice and information from a variety of places and experts in order to obtain a fuller understanding of his problem and thus to be in a better position to decide how it should be solved.

Various sources of information

For student writers such as yourself, thorough research may entail a good deal of time in the library, scanning card catalogues, bibliographies, and indexes and tracking down books and articles on your subject. But you should also keep in mind that sources of information exist outside of the library. Much of Palmer's research, for example, involved personal interviews with different types of experts, and even some of the printed material he consulted, such as the pamphlets on back pain he found in the doctor's waiting room, did not come from the library.

Your topic will determine your sources

As always, you should select your sources according to the particular research questions you want to answer. Some topics can be adequately researched with the services of a good library alone. For other topics, however, you need to consider possible alternative sources of information. If you are researching the quota system for hiring at a university campus, for instance, you may find it useful to contact professors in the sociology, political science, and business departments, as well as at the law school, to get their insights into the issue. You may also want to write to your congressional representative to obtain transcripts of congressional proceedings concerning equal opportunity legislation or arrange for personal interviews with employers and employees in the community. Possibly, too, you may discover special interest or public service organizations that publish their own informational pamphlets and periodicals not readily available through libraries. In any case, be resourceful in seeking out the information available to you. Don't ignore television, radio, and newspapers as possible sources, and don't overlook the Yellow Pages of your telephone book as a means of locating businesses, special interest organizations, and public service groups that may be useful to your research efforts.

The Value of Writing Down Your Research

You may argue that you have learned all you can or need to know by collecting and sorting through the available information and that once you've found the answers you've been looking for, there's no need to tell yourself in writing what you already know. While such an argument may at first seem to make good sense, it is not necessarily valid. Writing is itself a way of sorting out accumulated information and working through complicated problems. You probably know from your own experience that you learn material more thoroughly and remember it longer if you have to write it down in your own words. Writing gives a concrete form to knowledge that may otherwise remain vague and amorphous. There is some truth to the saying that if you can't explain it in writing, you don't really know it.

The process for writing a research paper itself will probably not differ substantially from the process you've been using for other kinds of writing, but the preliminary work of gathering, evaluating, and organizing material, and the subsequent task of putting it into properly documented form, can present difficulties that you haven't previously encountered. The remaining pages of this chapter are intended to help you develop strategies for doing research in the library and elsewhere and to give you guidelines for shaping your findings into an informative (and perhaps persuasive), readable, and well-documented paper. Mastering those strategies at this early stage of your development as a student and a writer will give you tools that will serve you well not only as you continue your college education, but also later in life, whether you enter a business or professional career, are a member of a community or special interest organization, or simply want to expand your knowledge and satisfy your curiosity as a private individual.

Planning Your Research Paper

Because writing a research paper involves a number of steps and proceeds through several stages, you need to start by working out a master plan that will allow you to see the whole picture and give you a sense of what specific tasks need to be done, in what order, and how long the whole process will probably take. Basically, the process of writing a research paper consists of five major steps (which may overlap and do not necessarily follow one another in an orderly progression):

1. Deciding on a topic
2. Gathering information

3. Planning the paper
4. Writing the paper
5. Documenting your sources

Each of these steps consists of other, smaller steps. For example, deciding on a topic entails making sure you understand all the requirements of the assignment; doing background or exploratory reading, if necessary; narrowing your topic; and posing it in question form. If you divide your task into these smaller steps, the whole process of researching and writing a paper can be much more manageable. It becomes less of an endurance contest and more of the learning exercise your instructor intends it to be.

Clarifying Your Assignment

As in any writing project, you can make your job much easier if you begin by answering these questions fully and precisely before you begin the actual process of conducting research and writing your paper:

1. Why am I writing?
2. Who is going to read it?
3. What specifications must it meet?
4. What is my deadline?

Your purpose may be both informative and persuasive

Purpose Ideally, your research paper reflects your unbiased attempt to discover truthful answers and workable solutions to perplexing questions and problems. As a means of communicating these answers and solutions to interested readers, your research paper will serve a primarily *informative* purpose. But it is very likely that in the course of gathering and examining your information, you will become convinced of the ethical, moral, or factual validity of a particular position. In this event, the paper you write as a result of your research may also be *persuasive* because you wish your readers to adopt the same position and to subscribe to the same truths that you, as an informed researcher, have accepted.

You must be careful, however, not to let persuasion predominate over the primarily informative purpose of research writing. Research papers, in other words, must never become propaganda, seeking to persuade principally by means of emotional or irrational appeals (see Chapter 11). Instead, in writing a research paper or report you must take pains to trace the path of your own reasoning as you examine evidence, weigh testimony, synthesize information from various sources, and finally arrive at an informed conclusion. Persuasion in a research paper results principally from ethical and logical appeals. Your readers must feel confident that you have made an honest attempt to discover the truth and that your research efforts have been sufficient to give you some authority to write on your subject. They must also feel assured that the information you present in the paper is accurate and thorough and that it justifies the conclusions you draw from it.

Audience   When you write a research paper to fulfill a course assignment, your most obvious and immediate audience is your instructor, someone who may know more than you do about your topic. In theory, instructors represent an "audience of colleagues" who share your interests and concerns. But in practice, instructors generally assume the role of superiors, not colleagues. They read their students' research papers not simply for the information they contain, but, perhaps more importantly, in order to evaluate students' performance as research writers.

Your instructor as audience

As a college student, then, you write research papers to demonstrate three important sets of skills to your instructors. First, instructors want you to show that you can proceed on your own to gather information beyond that which textbooks and class lectures and discussions have provided you. In many cases this will require you to use library resources, an activity that entails mastering card catalogue systems, learning how to use indexes and bibliographies effectively, and gaining competence in gleaning pertinent information from the books and articles you consult. Second, instructors generally want to know that you can communicate your findings to other educated people in a clear and organized fashion. And finally, instructors want to know that you have mastered the formal conventions of research writing. These may include fairly trivial matters, such as pagination systems and page format, as well as more substantial concerns, such as organization of content and proper documentation.

Frequently, your instructor's concerns about formal conventions become special criteria that frame your research assignment.

Sometimes, for instance, the first direction instructors give when assigning a research paper concerns length: "Write a ten-page paper on. . . ." You must guard against interpreting this sort of stipulation as an indication that the number of words you write (or the number and kind of sources you cite, or the way you punctuate your footnotes and bibliographic entries) is more important than your ability to conduct a thorough and probing investigation and to present your findings in a clear and readable fashion.

If you're writing on an assigned topic, you may feel that your instructor already knows more than you can hope to learn about the topic and that your most important task is to produce a paper in the proper form, including the proper number and kinds of sources. But this is not necessarily the case. Instructors become bored if the papers they read tell them only what they already know or simply parrot sources to which they already have access. They look forward to learning something from their students' research papers, and if you give yourself time to do a thorough job of research and to think about your topic, you will be in a position to tell your instructor something he or she wants or needs to know.

Specifications   Before you invest a lot of time and effort in research and writing, be sure that you know exactly what your instructor is asking you to do. If you have been assigned a topic, make certain that you understand what it is and that you know how much freedom you have in deciding how to treat it. Find out from your instructor approximately how long your paper should be and translate that into typewritten pages (about 250 words per double-spaced page if you use pica type, 300 if you use elite type). Length may not be important in itself, but it does affect your choice and treatment of topic. You also need to find out what format your instructor wants you to use and what style of documentation he or she favors. Finally, be sure to check little details, such as where your name and other identifying information should go, whether you should make a title sheet and what should be on it, width of margins, and so forth. Some instructors (and later on, perhaps, some employers) find that uniformity in these matters make papers easier to process, and you would be foolish to make a bad impression through carelessness. Your attention to such details reflects your persona, and so affects the ethical appeal of your paper. (See Chapter 4.)

Make sure you understand the research assignment

Deadline Finally, find out precisely when your paper is due and post the date in one or more prominent places, where it will nag you. You might be wise to phrase the deadline in different ways in order to remind yourself that you need to get started. For example:

April 6

five weeks from date assigned

three weeks before end of term

If you know yourself to be a procrastinator, or if you frequently find that you underestimate the amount of time you need to complete a task, try a version of the "setting your watch ahead" strategy. If your paper is due on April 6, plan to finish by April 3, and post your reminders accordingly.

Choosing a Topic

Criteria for a good topic

The way you approach topic selection depends a great deal upon your assignment. In some classes, instructors may simply require that you produce a research paper, leaving the choice of logic entirely up to you. In other instances, you may be given a choice of several general topics to write on, and the decision of approach or focus will be your responsibility. In still other cases, assignments will be much more specific, and you will have very little freedom in determining your topic or your focus. In each of these cases, the decisions you have to make about your topic are different, but in all of them you must be able to formulate your topic as an open-ended question before you are too far into the research process.

The open-ended question format is essential because it gives you a clear idea of what you are looking for when you do your research. Questions, in other words, demand that you *focus* your research efforts and, accordingly, they help you to focus your paper once you begin writing. Material that helps you to answer your question is pertinent to your research and should be retained for your paper; material that, however interesting, does not contribute to your understanding of the question should not find its way into the paper.

Remember, too, that you don't necessarily have to provide a final answer to every question you research. Sometimes it is worthwhile just to *approach* an answer or a solution. In the paper about the quota system mentioned earlier, for example, you would not be able to settle for once and for all the controversy surrounding the issue; nevertheless, you could manage to clarify the issues for your readers and foster clear thinking about an eventual resolution of the conflicting viewpoints. Often it is not possible, nor is it necessary, for you to become the final authority on your subject.

Here are some suggestions to help you formulate research questions in the various assignment situations.

Free Choice of Topic   This can be either the easiest or the most difficult of research paper assignments. On the one hand, you are free to select a subject that is interesting to you and that piques your curiosity. On the other hand, the infinite possibilities opened up by such an assignment may leave you stymied and unable to think of anything at all that you'd care to write about. Here are a few suggestions to get your thoughts going:

Curiosity as a stimulus to writing

1. Let your *curiosity* be your guide. Now is the time to find the answers to questions that have perplexed you or to follow up on subjects that have intrigued you in the past and about which you'd like to know more. For example: How does water witching work? What is the difference between the Republican and Democratic parties? Do animals have emotions? What is deficit spending? Is the quality of American education declining?

Necessity as a stimulus to writing

2. Let *necessity* be your guide. You may be able to exploit circumstances in your own life as a source for your research paper topic. Let's suppose, for instance, that you come from a rural area that has been hard hit by an economic recession. Every week your neighbors, the television, and local newspapers inform you of several more local farmers losing their land. In addition you observe that people who have been long-time employees of farm implement companies and farm service establishments are being laid off. You wonder what is causing this so-called farm crisis and what, if anything, can be done to improve conditions for people like your own family and your neighbors. Here you have a potential research topic drawn from life. Or suppose that the woman you work for is wondering whether she should buy a personal computer for her office and asks you to gather information for her. Since you are also thinking about buying a per-

sonal computer for yourself, you could do some useful research that might help both of you.

3. Let your *other courses* help you with ideas. Sometimes other academic courses you are taking will lead you to topics that arouse your interest but that time does not allow you to study as thoroughly as you'd like to in the class. Often, you can use your research paper assignment as an opportunity to do some follow-up studying on your own. In your human development class, for instance, you learn that the past decade has witnessed a tendency for parents to return to home childbirth assisted by midwives rather than physicians. You wonder why this is the case. Is home childbirth safe and otherwise advisable? If so, why was it "out of fashion" for so many years? Who are midwives and what training do they have? What does the medical community think of this trend? Questions such as these may very well develop into fine research paper topics. And of course it is not only the reading and listening you do for your academic classes that may spark this sort of question. Newspaper articles, television programs, movies, conversations you have with your friends, and reading that you do in your spare time may provide similar possibilities for interesting and satisfying research.

General Assigned Topics   Frequently, instructors will select three or four general topics that have been covered in class lectures and reading assignments and ask you to explore one of them in depth in a research paper. An example might be a sociology course that your instructor has divided into four units, each focusing on a different influence shaping contemporary society: the military-industrial complex, the changing status of women and minorities, the coming of age of computer technology, and the entertainment industry. For your research paper in the course, you are asked to focus on a specific topic from one or a combination of two or more of these categories in order to further explore how these influences affect our present society.

Focusing on an assigned topic

Now let's say that in the unit on the coming of age of computer technology you learned of various ways computers are being used in education. You yourself are taking a self-paced astronomy course in which your tests are administered by a computer, so you have some firsthand experience with computerized instruction. You find this method of learning interesting, enjoyable, and, to the best of your knowledge, successful. But you have heard others complain that computerized instruction is severely limited and should be used with caution if at all. They claim that the human element is vitally important to the educational process and that computers can teach only facts and not the more important understanding of values that is essential to quality education.

Your research on this topic might explore this controversy by pursuing the question, "What are the advantages and disadvantages of computerized instruction?" Or you might wonder whether computerized instruction is really widespread enough to warrant the controversy surrounding it. Your research question, then, might be something like, "When and how is computerized instruction being used in American high schools (or colleges, or businesses)?"

Or let's say that because you are a woman yourself, you were particularly interested in the unit on the changing status of women and minorities. Having learned in your class of the increased participation of women in such spheres as business, politics, medicine, and law, and of the general support for equal rights among politicians as well as the general public, you are curious as to why the ERA was defeated in 1983. Here again you may be able to satisfy your curiosity and the course requirements by doing the appropriate research. In this type of assignment situation you should remember the two main criteria of topic selection: 1) choose an approach with which you are most familiar or have some sort of personal understanding, and 2) choose an approach that is interesting to you and that will help you satisfy your curiosity.

Sometimes doing a little bit of background reading on a general subject will introduce you to some particular aspect of it that sparks your interest and curiosity and raises some questions in your mind you will then want to go on to research more thoroughly. Background reading is a useful strategy for beginning research when you have a general idea about what you want to investigate (or what you are required to investigate) but are undecided as to the particular approach you want to employ.

Start your search for background material in the library by finding out if it has specialized encyclopedias, reference volumes devoted to particular areas of knowledge. Most libraries do have reasonably substantial collections of such volumes. Here are a few with which you might start:

Humanities

Encyclopedia of Religion and Ethics, 12 volumes
Encyclopedia of Philosophy, 8 volumes
Encyclopedia of World History, 15 volumes
Cassell's Encyclopedia of World Literature, 3 volumes
McGraw-Hill Encyclopedia of World Drama, 4 volumes
Oxford Companion to the Theatre
International Encyclopedia of Film
Encyclopedia of World Art, 15 volumes
Praeger Encyclopedia of Art, 15 volumes
Oxford Companion to Music
New Grove Encyclopedia of Music and Musicians, 20 volumes
Encyclopedia of Pop, Rock, and Soul

Social Sciences

International Encyclopedia of Social Sciences, 17 volumes
*International Encyclopedia of Psychiatry, Psychology,
    Psychoanalysis and Neurology,* 12 volumes
Encyclopedia of Bioethics, 4 volumes
Encyclopedia of Social Work, 2 volumes
Encyclopedia of Education
Handbook of Criminology, 2 volumes
Encyclopedia of the Unexplained: Magic, Occultism, and Parapsychology

Science and Technology

McGraw-Hill Encyclopedia of Science and Technology, 15 volumes
Van Nostrand's Scientific Encyclopedia
Cambridge Encyclopedia of Astronomy
Encyclopedia of Biological Sciences
Encyclopedia of Chemistry
Encyclopedia of Ecology
Engineering Encyclopedia

If you can't decide where your chosen topic would fit, ask the librarian. He or she may be able to recommend additional specialized references.

You may also find these general encyclopedias useful, at least for a start.

Collier's Encyclopedia, 24 volumes

Encyclopedia Americana, 30 volumes

Encyclopedia Britannica, 19 volumes

You can update many of these sources by consulting the following yearbooks, usually issued every year to include the most recent material in the field:

Britannica Book of the Year

McGraw-Hill Yearbook of Science and Technology

Yearbook of Science and the Future

Narrowing Your Topic   When you have done enough general reading on your broad topic to give you a good idea of what kind of material is available, you are ready for the crucial step: choosing a limited and specific topic. Remember, the more specific the better. It is almost always a good idea to write more about less, or as one professor has put it, to pick the smallest possible topic out of which you can squeeze the requisite number of words. If you follow that advice, you are more likely to find a topic that will interest both you and your reader because you'll both be learning new information in a specialized area.

Ways to narrow your topic   Some of the limiting strategies you can use to narrow down your topic are these:

time period	specific classification
occupation	individual example
cultural period	gender
religion	specific region or locale
particular economic group	specific nationality or race
specialized discipline	specific age group

Suppose you wanted to narrow the general topic of divorce down to a specific and manageable topic. You might choose to study the causes of divorce among young American (nationality) women (gender) who married in their teens (age group) in the 1970s (time period) and did not finish high school (educational classification). Other topics can be limited in similar ways. You can also get ideas for limiting your topic by considering the questions that follow each of the suggested paper topics at the end of this chapter (pages 440–449), questions that were designed to help you look at a general topic from a specific point of view. And remember that even after you start to do your research and take notes, you may find that you want to narrow or revise your topic again if you make an unexpected discovery.

Specific Assigned Topics   If you happen to be especially interested in a topic you have been assigned for your research paper, so much the better. But even if you believe at the outset that your topic is not particularly intriguing, give it a chance; you may find that as you learn more about it through your research, it becomes more interesting to you. In any case, specific topics, too, must be phrased as questions to help you know just exactly what you are looking for when you begin your research.

Why some topics are not suitable

Topics to Avoid   It has already been mentioned that because research itself is ideally an impartial activity, subjects with which you are emotionally involved or which are matters of faith usually do not make good topics for academic research projects. In addition, you should avoid the temptation to seize upon a topic simply because it looks easy. This usually turns out to be a mistake because you will quickly become bored, and your attitude is bound to show up in the paper you write.

Extremely broad questions, such as "What is socialism?" or "How can the United States and Russia arrive at a disarmament agreement?" or "What is the potential of nuclear energy?" are far too complex to be adequately or authoritatively treated even in a long research paper. Therefore, choose a topic on which you will be able to discover concrete, factual evidence and/or reliable expert opinions and on which you will be able to say something significant in the specified number of pages.

Finally, avoid topics that cannot be adequately researched by using the resources available to you within the specified time constraints. Know the limitations of your college or local libraries and don't underestimate the time it may take to send off for information, to arrange appointments for interviews, or to conduct polls and surveys.

Making a Schedule

Once you have decided upon a question you believe you can research in the time allotted and with the resources that are available to you, you may want to set up a schedule for the various stages of your research so that you can avoid the last-minute panic that is sure to set in if you wait until the final week to do everything. When you draw up a research schedule, begin with the sources you believe will be most fruitful in providing direct and specific information. This way, if you run out of time, you won't have to proceed without having consulted the sources that would have been most valuable to your research.

Gathering Information

Planning your research

Let's assume that you decide to choose the project that would require you to investigate buying a personal computer. First, of course, you must formulate your research question for your paper in such a way that it will have more public appeal than the specific problem you are tackling for yourself and your own small organization. You might, for instance, decide to produce an informative report for owners of small businesses and organizations whose needs and financial considerations are similar to those of your organization, or you might decide to use your organization as a case study to illustrate your more general findings. A schedule for your research, once you have formulated your question, might look something like this:

Week 1

Obtain or produce a clear and detailed set of specifics about your organization's computing needs and financial means. Try to interview some experts on the subject — contact people you know in organizations similar to yours who own or use personal computers. Describe to these people your organization's record-keeping and correspondence needs and ask these users for their recommendations. Use your phone book to help you locate computer dealers who can demonstrate and explain the capacities of a variety of personal computers. Collect from them sales pamphlets and any other available printed information on your subject.

Week 2

Check the *Business Index* in your library for current articles on the selection of personal computers. Also contact someone in the business and computer science departments of your university for information on the selection and use of personal computers. Consult recent issues of *Consumer Reports* for quality ratings on some of the computers that have been recommended by your various sources.

Week 3

Consult the card catalogue to locate books that might inform you about small business finances or personal computers. Check more general indexes, such as *The Readers' Guide to Periodical Literature,* for articles on your subject in popular news magazines such as *Time, Mother Jones,* and *Harper's.* Consult newspaper indexes for recent articles about personal computer sales and recent developments by computer manufacturers. Compare your findings about costs and advantages of possible choices with your organization's needs and financial means.

Weeks 4 and 5

Complete your research. Write a first draft of the paper. Compile the bibliography. Revise the draft. Check the documentation. Write and type the final draft of the paper. Proofread it for typographical mistakes.

Writing out such a schedule will help you realize how much work is involved in producing the final research paper and will remind you to give yourself enough time to complete every step in the process.

Beginning a Focused Search for Information

Your specific research question will determine the types of sources you consult as you conduct your search for information to help you formulate your answers. In the case of the paper about personal computers, for instance, personal computer users are an obvious first choice for experts to be interviewed. In addition, they may be able to direct you to other experts and to helpful printed material, such as users' manuals. It is even possible that the personal computer owners, having done similar research before deciding to invest in a computer, will be able to provide you with users' group newsletters, informational pamphlets and brochures published by companies that manufacture home computers, or literature by consumer information organizations.

In this particular research project, personal computer users and dealerships may be the most direct source for specific and up-to-date information on your topic. The library, too, is a valuable source of information, but your search there is likely to be much more time-consuming, and you may have to dig for pertinent information. To save time and energy in this sorting-out process, begin your library research with facilities that deal as specifically as possible with your subject. In this case, a business or computer science library, if either is accessible, will probably provide you more quickly with the information you need than a general academic or community library.

Most libraries can furnish you with information in three major forms: books, periodicals, and documents. The process of locating information differs slightly for each of these three forms; consequently, the most efficient way for you to search for library materials is to concentrate on one of these categories at a time.

Books   Because the computer industry changes very rapidly, there is probably little up-to-date information about it in full-length books, which, because of the time consumed by the publication process, cannot provide information as current as that which can be found in specialized journals. For this reason, books are more likely to yield general background information that will help you understand, for instance, how personal computers work or how to calculate overhead costs for small organizations such as yours. You have at least two sources for finding books that will help you with your topic: the bibliographies that accompany relevant articles in specialized encyclopedias and the subject section of the library card catalogue.

How to locate information

You may already be familiar with the card catalogue, but if you are not and wonder where to start, consult the two-volume reference book *Library of Congress Subject Headings List;* it will list the subject headings and subheadings in the card catalogue and give you cross-references that can save you a great deal of time. Usually these volumes are kept on a shelf or table very close to the card catalogue. Remember that you may also find useful book titles when you are reading magazine articles on your topic, and in some libraries you can do a computer search for material. More on that later in this chapter.

Your search in the subject catalogue may yield more books than you can use or even skim. You can take steps to avoid this problem by beginning with subject headings that closely describe the information you're looking for. "Personal computers" and "home computers," for instance, will lead you more directly to the information you want than will more general headings, such as "data processing" or "computer science." Once you find cards for books that seem pertinent to your investigation, narrow your search by choosing those titles that sound most directly related to your research question and check publication dates to help you find the most recent books. Make a list of titles, including the date, author's name, and name of the publisher. Try to include at least twice as many books as your instructor has suggested you consult for your paper because inevitably you will find that some of those you want are checked out or lost.

With list in hand, head for the Author/Title section of the card catalogue and start your search. Probably it's most efficient to look for each book by the name of the author. So arrange your list in roughly alphabetical order for a more efficient search and begin looking at the catalogue card for each book. That card will give you specific and useful information that will help you decide if you want to consult it.

```
 ⎧ TX        Lappé, Frances Moore.
 ⎪ 392           Diet for a small planet / Frances
 ⎨ L27        Moore Lappé ; illustrated by Kathleen
 ⎪ 1975       Zimmerman and Ralph Iwamoto. Rev. ed.
 ⎩ UGL        New York : Ballantine Books, 1975.
                411 p. : ill. ; 18 cm.



            ⎰Bibliography: p. 396-397.
            ⎱Includes index.


             1. Vegetarianism.   2. Proteins.
             I. Title
```

If you decide that you want to consult a book, write the *complete* call number beside the title of the book on your list and go on. Later, you can group call numbers together so that if you are working in an open-stack library and are looking for the books yourself, you can do a systematic search.

Two systems of cataloguing

You may have to work in a library that is currently classifying its books in two ways: by the Dewey decimal system and by the Library of Congress system. Many large libraries are now doing this, cataloguing new books that come in by Library of Congress symbols but keeping old books catalogued under Dewey decimal numbers, the kind you may be familiar with from your previous school. The two kinds of symbols look like this:

Dewey decimal
call numbers start with *numbers*

| 813 |
| A75 |

Library of Congress
call numbers start with *letters*

| BD |
| 452 |
| S45 |

Thus, it is particularly important that you write down the full call number before you start looking for books and that you find out where books bearing each kind of symbol are shelved. Books with the Dewey decimal symbols will be shelved in order according to the *number* on the top line of the call number; books with Library of Congress symbols will be shelved alphabetically according to the *letters* on the top line of the call number, then within that category by the number on the second line.

Probably your library will have good directions explaining the system or systems it uses; if it does not, don't hesitate to ask librarians as often as you need to in order to find what you want.

Magazine and Journal Articles   Anyone who does much research soon realizes that one cannot find everything in books. Sometimes the most up-to-date material on a topic can be found only in articles, and often even important older information has appeared only in a periodical. Your library will probably have the most current magazines and journals on the shelves but the older articles may be in bound volumes on the shelves or on microfilm or microfiche. (Don't be intimidated by the latter forms — you can learn how to use them as quickly as you would a simple camera.)

Finding magazine articles requires that you know how to use the periodical indexes — leafing through the tables of contents of even highly specialized magazines consumes too much time.

The same principle of specificity that you used in choosing subject headings in the card catalogue applies to your selection of bibliographies and indexes to consult when looking for journal or newspaper articles. *The Readers' Guide to Periodical Literature* may provide you with some useful citations for articles in general interest magazines, but your subject may require you also to consult more specialized professional periodicals. If, for instance, you were working on the selection of personal computers question, specialized indexes such as *Business Index* would probably enable you to make a more thorough search and help you discover more quickly the information you want. Here are some of the most widely used general and specialized indexes:

General indexes

Magazine Index. 1976 to the present.
Start here for recent articles on topics of general interest in popular magazines. Unlike *Readers' Guide* and the more specialized indexes you will use, all the articles indexed from 1976 to the present are

in one place, rather than year-by-year. Titles are not abbreviated. This index is in a machine format, so follow the instructions for using it that are located on the front of the machine. Although you will be able to use articles found here as a starting point, you will usually need to use a specialized index to find more professional or scholarly articles.

Readers' Guide to Periodical Literature. 1949 to the present.
Use this index for articles on almost any subject. The periodicals covered in this index are general interest magazines. Although you will be able to use articles found here as a starting point, you will usually need to use a specialized index to find more professional or scholarly articles.

Poole's Index to Periodical Literature. 1802–1906.
Use this index to find primary sources for historical studies. This is the nineteenth-century equivalent to the *Readers' Guide*; it contains citations for articles published in general interest periodicals of the previous century.

Specialized indexes

Humanities

Humanities Index. 1974 to the present.
Use this index for information on archaeology, classics, folklore, history, language and literature, performing arts, philosophy, and religion. (Before 1974 this was called *Social Sciences and Humanities Index.*)

Art Index. 1959 to the present.
Articles indexed here cover photography and films, architecture, city planning, fine arts, graphic arts, and design.

Film Literature Index. 1973 to the present.
This index to international publications covers film reviews and articles about specific films, film genres, directors, cinematographers, screenwriters, and other aspects of the film industry. Look under the title of the film to find a review.

Music Index. 1970 to the present.
Look in this index for articles on popular music, dance, jazz, classical music, radio and television, as well as the business aspects of the music industry. A variety of publications is covered, from *Rolling Stone* to *Opera News* and *Journal of Music Theory.*

Social Sciences

Social Sciences Index. 1974 to the present.

This is a good starting place for articles on anthropology, area studies, psychology, public administration, sociology, and related fields. (Before 1974, this was called *Social Sciences and Humanities Index.*)

Public Affairs Information Service Bulletin. (PAIS). 1960 to the present.

This list of articles, pamphlets, and books deals with economic and social conditions, public administration, politics, and international relations. For example, you can use it to find information on the legal aspects of issues like abortion, divorce, child abuse, pollution, and genetic research.

Business Periodicals Index. 1973 to the present.

This index is useful for finding information about business and industries, computer technology, advertising, and business aspects of other subjects.

Current Index to Journals in Education. 1969 to the present.

Over 750 journals containing articles on education and related topics, such as linguistics, sociology, and psychology, are indexed here. The entries include citations and brief summaries of the articles.

Education Index. 1959 to the present.

For material relating to children or to education, this index can be quite helpful. Some examples of subjects covered are busing, child abuse, teen-age pregnancy, adoption, and intelligence.

Business Index. 1979 to the present.

Like *Magazine Index,* this index is in a machine format. It lists articles appearing in business and industry periodicals. Topics covered include market trends, management issues, and international trade. The index cumulates monthly; the most recent articles can be located by using the machine; older entries are stored on microfiche.

Resources in Education. 1966 to the present.

This index contains citations for some of the more obscure and hard-to-locate material on education and related topics. Included are research reports, conference presentations, government reports, and speeches. Entries include citations and abstracts. Arrangement is chronological according to ERIC Document numbers. Instructions for locating entries are given in the front of the index.

Psychological Abstracts. 1975 to the present.

Left-handedness, body language, ESP, and alcoholism are among the many subjects this index covers from a psychological point of view. Most of the articles listed here are scholarly. In addition to the information indexes usually include, *Psychological Abstracts* provides a summary (abstract) of each article, so you can tell if the article will be relevant to your topic. Ask a librarian to explain how to use this index.

Sociological Abstracts. 1975 to the present.

If you are doing research on any aspect of sociology, including studies on poverty, violence, and feminism, try here. Most of the articles summarized here are highly specialized, so you need to have some background knowledge before you will find this a useful source. Ask a librarian to explain how to use it.

Women's Studies Abstracts. 1972 to the present.

If your subject deals with women, you may find this source useful. The books, pamphlets, and periodicals listed here are grouped into broad categories, such as family, employment, and sexuality. However, many topics appear in more than one category, so you must still look for your topic in the index at the back of each issue.

Science

General Science Index. 1978 to the present.

This index covers most of the basic journals in astronomy, biology, chemistry, earth science, environment and conservation, food and nutrition, medicine and health, physics, and psychology. For earlier articles on these topics, select the appropriate index from those listed below.

Applied Science and Technology Index. 1971 to the present.

This publication lists articles on aspects of physics, chemistry, geology, and other industrial and mechanical arts, including the textile industry, computers, the food industry, and energy resources and research.

Biological & Agricultural Index. 1973 to the present.

This indexes scholarly articles in biology, biochemistry, botany, ecology, forestry, nutrition, genetics, zoology, and related sciences. Most of these articles are rather technical and may be found only in specialized libraries.

Engineering Index. 1884 to the present.

This publication indexes a wide range of sources, including international journal articles, proceedings and publications of engineering societies, and reports published by laboratories, universities, and government agencies. Arrangement is according to classified subject, and sources are indexed by author and corporate affiliation.

Index Medicus. 1960 to the present.

This is the major index for medical topics. Sources indexed include journal articles, editorials, and biographies of medical personnel. A wide range of subjects is covered, from heart surgery to veterinary medicine. The index is published in monthly issues. The January issue of every year contains a complete list of the journals listed.

Most indexes follow the same general format. Articles are listed alphabetically by subject. If you don't find your subject listed, try looking under related terms. For instance, if you want articles on Dakota Indians, you might find them listed under "Indians of North America," "Dakota Indians," or "American Indian Movement."

Each entry includes the title of an article, the author's name, title of the periodical, volume, page, and date. For example:

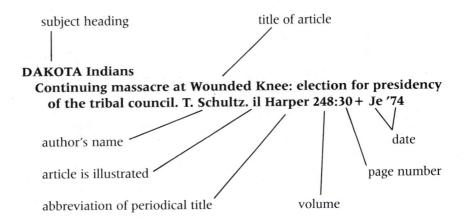

In order to save space, much of the information in the entries is abbreviated. Look in the front of the volume at the "Abbreviations of Periodicals Indexed" to find the full title of the periodical you want. Finding the full title is very important for actually locating the periodical because journals are listed by title in the serials list and in the name/title catalogue. They are also shelved alphabetically by title in your undergraduate library. Other abbreviations used in the entries are also explained at the front of the volume.

Newspapers In addition to journals, newspapers are a good periodical source to consult for information on historical or current topics. Newspapers are especially valuable for their ability to convey public opinion about events and issues when they were current and as indicators of the political climate at any given time. Most sizable libraries house the major newspapers from this country and abroad, and many of these are indexed in special publications. Even if some of these major newspapers are not available in your library, you can use their indexes to discover the dates at which certain events occurred or when certain issues were controversial. You can then consult these same dates in newspapers that are available to you. Here are some of the most widely used newspaper indexes:

New York Times Index. 1851 to the present.
This bimonthly index is a good source to consult for information about topics of national and international importance. It is arranged alphabetically according to subject, and brief summaries are included for many of the articles listed.

Newspaper Index. 1972 to the present.
Four major American newspapers are indexed in this publication: *The Chicago Tribune, The Los Angeles Times, The New Orleans Times-Picayune,* and *The Washington Post.* Because these newspapers are major publications in four different areas of the country, the *Newspaper Index* is a good source of regional as well as national and international news.

London Times Official Index.
This index covers articles from the major English-language European newspaper. It is an interesting source of information about international perspectives on issues and events in the United States as well as about international affairs.

Government Documents Most college libraries of any size have a special section for U.S. Government publications. These publications cover a wide range of subjects, from information on how to construct electric-powered vehicles to the surgeon general's recommendations about prescription drugs to current federal regulations, legislative bills, and congressional hearings. The earliest documents (copies only, of course) available in library collections predate the American Revolution, and the most recent may be less than a week old. Because they are so comprehensive and cover such a lengthy time span, government documents are an especially valuable source of current and official news, statistical data, and historical information.

In most libraries you will find government documents filed according to several systems. Some are listed in the public catalogue and can be located on the shelves according to Dewey decimal or Library of Congress call numbers. Uncatalogued publications are housed separately (usually in a special Government Documents section of the library) and are arranged according to Superintendent of Documents numbers. Finally, some government publications are kept on microform and can be located in collections called microform sets, catalogued by Superintendent of Documents number.

Following are a few of the major indexes you can use to locate government publications. In many libraries a number of other indexes are available as well, and you should ask a librarian to assist you if you have difficulty locating and using them.

Monthly Catalog of United States Government Publications. 1895 to the present.
This index lists all congressional and executive agency reports put out by the Government Printing Office. Entries are indexed by subject, author, and title key word.

The Federal Index. 1976 to present.
This publication indexes the three basic information sources of the federal government: the *Congressional Record, Weekly Compilation of Presidential Documents,* and *U.S. Law Week* (which contains federal court decisions). Additionally, citations are included to the *Federal Register, Code of Federal Regulations, United States Code,* and House and Senate bills. Entries are indexed according to subject and federal agencies.

Index to U.S. Government Periodicals. 1970 to the present.
Citations in this index are to magazines published by the federal government. Subjects covered include economics, political science, sociology, business, education, and public health.

C.I.S.U.S. Serial Set Index.

Here are indexed documents from a collection called the U.S. Serial Set, which contains publications of Congress, some executive agencies, and some civilian organizations. Entries are indexed according to subject and are arranged chronologically by congressional session.

A Descriptive Catalogue of the Government Publications of the United States. September 5, 1774–March 4, 1881.

This is a retrospective index, valuable for historical research. In it are listed selected publications of the executive, judicial, and legislative branches of the government.

Washington Information Directory. 1974 to the present. 2 volumes.

This directory lists executive agencies and private and special interest groups that monitor legislation, government operations, and policy. Entries give the names of organizations, their directors' names, addresses, and phone numbers, and descriptions of the organizations' activities. This is a good source to consult for information about where to write for current information on specialized topics relating to government policy and procedures.

Follow-up on Documented Articles and Books   The footnotes or bibliographies of books or articles that have already proven useful to you can provide leads to other helpful sources of information. This method of locating sources is especially efficient because the book or article in which they have been cited usually gives you a fairly good idea of their content, and you can generally assume that if you have found a particular work to be pertinent to your investigation, the sources that informed that work will also be pertinent.

Computer Searches   An increasing number of libraries have computer facilities for searching for information in periodical articles, and these facilities are often available to students. Many libraries run regular short training sessions that anyone can attend. If your library offers such a service, by all means take advantage of it. It's not difficult to learn the fundamentals, and mastering computer research skills can save you substantial chunks of time, now and later.

Computer searches generally are able to locate articles according to title, author, and subject. Subject searches are often the most helpful, but they are also somewhat more complicated than simple author or title searches and may require the assistance of a trained librarian.

If you decide to run a subject search, it is essential that you have a clear notion of the kind of information you're trying to find. The success of a computerized subject search depends on your ability to describe your topic in terms called *descriptors,* which are similar to subject headings and are included in the indexes searched by the computer. The computer is able to use the descriptors in a cross-referencing system to locate articles that might be pertinent to the user's research. If you were attempting to discover the advantages and the drawbacks of personal computers, for example, you might use descriptors such as "small computers," "microcomputers," "small office equipment," and "word processors."

Cautions about computer searches

While computer-assisted searches can very rapidly produce a large number of sources for you to consult, they do have some limitations that restrict their usefulness to only certain types of research. To begin with, computer searches are usually quite expensive, so you need to find out how much such a service would cost before you decide whether to use it. It might well be that the thoroughness of the search and the amount of time saved would not be worth the expense. Second, computer-assisted searches are not helpful if the library you are using doesn't have most of the sources you turn up. Quite often it is possible to use the services of an interlibrary loan system to obtain materials not available in your own library, but this may be time-consuming and, if a great deal of copying is involved, costly as well.

Last, computer-assisted searches may yield a great many sources you will not find useful, simply because the search relies exclusively upon the descriptor terms that appear in titles and that have been entered for index entries. Obviously, the more precisely you can describe your topic, the fewer irrelevant sources you will be given, but even a very careful selection of descriptors may yield a number of sources that will not help you find the specific information you need.

Serendipity   When you are looking for material, remember *serendipity* (page 50). In research, a person often seems to stumble onto the best leads almost by accident rather than through a methodical step-by-step search. For that reason, stay alert for unexpected findings and follow your hunches. Run your eyes over the books shelved next to the one you are looking for and glance at the table of contents in a magazine that contains the article you want. Pay attention to footnotes; sometimes they will lead you to something more interesting than the text itself. Talk to other people about your research project; they may be able to put you onto some source you hadn't realized existed. In other words, cultivate serendipity by extending your intellectual antennas all around you as you work. Frequently you'll find something you didn't know you were looking for.

Taking Notes

As you begin to accumulate information from the sources you have consulted, you will need to take notes to record what facts and opinions appeared in which sources so that you can document your research when you start to write. In addition, careful note-taking will help you to relocate your sources later on if the need should arise.

Choose a system for notes

Many people find that taking notes on index cards is convenient, and instructors sometimes insist that you use this method. If you are not constrained by such stipulations, you may find that some other method — for instance, keeping all of your notes in a single notebook divided according to individual sources or different categories of information — works better for you. Because the purpose of notes is to help you organize your findings and shape your paper, the form in which you keep them is less important than your ability to use them when you are planning and writing your paper. Regardless of the particular method you choose for keeping track of your notes, the notes themselves should incorporate the following principles:

1. Be selective about the information you decide to retain in your notes. Make a short summary of the main points of the article, book, or interview and record specifically only the information that helps you to develop and explain your research question and answer.
2. Don't rely too heavily on using copying machines and then underlining or highlighting the copied material. This method can save time, especially when you are dealing with articles and books you can't remove from the library or have to share with someone else, but you must avoid the temptation to underline instead of taking notes, for this practice encourages you to lean too much on the original wording once you begin to write your

paper. Also, underlining can prevent you from making the effort really to understand what you read.

3. Master the art of paraphrase — that is, putting the information gathered from other sources into your own words. A good paraphrase involves more than simply changing a few words in the original text; it shows your ability to absorb and comprehend the meaning of the original and to convey that meaning clearly to others. Look carefully at the following paragraph by the child development expert Burton White and the example of a good paraphrase that comes after it. Compare them to the examples given in the section on plagiarism (page 426) to see how true paraphrase differs from mere copying.

Learning how to paraphrase

Original

We have never come across an eight-month-old child who was not incredibly curious. We have never come across an eight-month-old child who needed to be reinforced for exploration of the home once he could crawl. Bear in mind that to have a very strong exploratory drive is vitally important for humans in that unlike most other animals, humans go through a very long developmental period and come equipped with fewer instincts than other animals with which to cope with the world.

Nothing is more fundamental to solid educational development than pure, uncontaminated curiosity.

Paraphrase

Child developmental specialist Burton L. White writes that by the age of eight months, virtually all children are characterized by an insatiable curiosity and an urge to explore their surroundings. This period of curiosity and exploration is vital to the child's learning process, particularly because human infants, unlike the young of other animal species, cannot rely on a complex system of instincts to dictate their responses to their environment.

4. Remember to document your sources, including page numbers, so that you will know where you found the information contained in your notes. Keeping a careful record of your sources from the start will help prevent inadvertent plagiarism and save you from having to return to the library later to check bibliographic information.

5. Use direct quotations sparingly. Quoted material is necessary in the text of your research paper only when the wording of the original itself is important to your argument. This may be the case when the original wording is particularly vivid, colorful, or otherwise effective, or when your argument hinges on some of the terminology used in the original. You can avoid the temptation to overuse direct quotations in your paper by not including them in your notes unless they meet these criteria. When you do decide it is necessary to use direct quotations, be sure that you have an accurate copy in your notes, with wording, spelling, and punctuation *exactly* as they appear in the original. It is also a good idea to include a note about the *context* in which the quotation appeared — that is, where, when, and why the words were spoken or written and, of course, who uttered or wrote the words. This information is important because you will need it to help you introduce the quotation in the text of your own paper.

Definition of plagiarism

Plagiarism   Plagiarism is the use of another person's statements or ideas without acknowledgment. In its most blatant form, plagiarism is an exact duplication of the words and phrases found in the original source, presented without quotation marks to indicate they have been taken from another author and with no reference to the original text, as in this example:

Original

   We have never come across an eight-month-old child who was not incredibly curious. We have never come across an eight-month-old child who needed to be reinforced for exploration of the home once he could crawl. Bear in mind that to have a very strong exploratory drive is vitally important for humans in that unlike most other animals, humans go through a very long developmental period and come equipped with fewer instincts than other animals with which to cope with the world.
   Nothing is more fundamental to solid educational development than pure, uncontaminated curiosity.

Plagiarized Version #1

   There is no such thing as an eight-month-old child who is not incredibly curious. Nor are there any eight-month-old children who need to be reinforced for exploration of the home once they can crawl. To have this strong exploratory drive is vitally important for humans because unlike most other animals, humans undergo an extended developmental stage and are equipped with fewer instincts to deal with their world.

Less-obvious forms of plagiarism

A less obvious but very commonly used form of plagiarism can be seen in the next example. Much of the original wording is changed, but the phrasing, the order in which the information is presented, and the line of argument are so similar to the original that they could not have been written without the original text.

Plagiarized Version #2

All eight-month-old children are extremely inquisitive. Rarely does one encounter children of this age who need to be encouraged to explore their homes once they have mastered the ability to crawl. This strong impulse to explore the environment is especially important for *homo sapiens* who, unlike most animals, have a long infancy and childhood and have fewer instincts to tell them how to deal with their surroundings. Pure, unadulterated curiosity is therefore the most important element in a child's educational development.

Yet another, subtler form of plagiarism is one in which the writer presents someone else's observations, insights, or chain of reasoning without acknowledging the original source. Even though this second version may bear very little resemblance to the words or phrases of the original text, the writer who "borrows" someone else's ideas in this way is still plagiarizing. In this last version of the Burton L. White passage, the content, though not the form, has been plagiarized.

Plagiarized Version #3

Anyone who has watched a young child crawling about and exploring her home cannot deny the importance of a natural curiosity in motivating the child to learn about her environment. No doubt curiosity and the accompanying urge to explore are especially important to young human beings who, unlike other animals, are primarily rational rather than instinctual creatures and must learn through the process of trial and error. The freedom to explore, to act upon this natural curiosity, is therefore crucial to the educational development of any child.

The writer of this version of the passage could avoid the pitfalls of plagiarism by introducing the paraphrase of White's passage with an acknowledgment of the original source and by providing either a footnote or a parenthetical citation to a complete bibliographical entry, as in the following example. Notice that no quotation marks or block indentation is necessary because White's ideas, not his words, are being used.

Version with Acknowledgment

Anyone who has watched a very young child crawling about and exploring her home cannot deny the importance of natural curiosity in motivating the child to learn about her environment. According to child developmental specialist Burton L. White, curiosity and the accompanying urge to explore are especially important to young human beings who, unlike other animals, are primarily rational rather than instinctual creatures and must learn through a process of trial and error. White therefore emphasizes that the freedom to explore, to act upon this natural curiosity, is crucial to the educational development of any child (White 112).

The bibliographic entry for White would appear as follows:

White, Burton L. *The First Three Years of Life*. Englewood Cliffs: Prentice, 1975.

Notice that the page number is given parenthetically in the text, but that no page numbers appear in the bibliography entry. This is always the case except when the source cited is an article within a journal or a section in a collection of essays or an anthology. The page number is necessary in this particular case because a specific part of White's book is being cited, not the whole book.

Planning the Paper

To some extent, planning your paper begins while you are in the process of gathering information. As you accumulate material, you may find that a logical way to organize the paper seems to be emerging in your mind. For instance, in a paper on the causes of teen-age divorce, it would seem logical to divide the causes into economic, social, and emotional and write about them in that order. Or if you are writing a paper on the effects of legalized gambling, you might want to organize it according to different kinds of gambling: state lotteries, off-track betting, and casino gambling. If you were writing a paper on microcomputers, you might want to organize it chronologically, tracing the development of modern small computers from the huge ones of just a few years ago. However, these preliminary ideas about how your paper should be structured may still be vague. This is where writing an outline or plan will help you to solidify and clarify them (see the next section). Most academic research projects are complex enough that you need to have some sort of written plan to help you when you begin writing.

One of the most difficult things about this stage of your project is deciding when it's time to stop looking for information and to begin writing up your findings. Ideally, of course, you would not stop researching until you had thoroughly satisfied your curiosity and found or formulated a definitive answer to your question. Unfortunately, not all questions can be answered definitively, and assigned deadlines often dictate that you stop researching and start writing before you really want to. You should anticipate this problem when you are making your work schedule.

Setting a time to start writing

Set a date to begin writing and stick to it. Don't wait for the library to find the lost book you've been looking for — you may be waiting forever. Instead, be ruthless about adhering to your cutoff date. If you begin writing reasonably in advance of your deadline, you may still have time later on to insert information that you were not able to locate earlier. Or, if you cannot locate a particular source you believe to be important to your study, plan to mention this limitation when you conclude your paper, and let your readers know that further research should take that source — or those sources — into consideration.

One way to begin planning your paper is by reading over your notes and categorizing them into subtopics or individual steps in the logical progression toward your conclusion. If you have taken your notes on cards, you can sort them into subtopic piles, which you can then translate into sections of your written outline. If you've kept your notes in a notebook, you might use some sort of color-coding method to identify different categories of information that will correspond to the sections of your outline and, later on, of your paper. For instance, in reviewing your notes about the reasons for increased crime rates in large urban areas, you might find that the reasons fall into three major categories: economic recession and unemployment, spending cuts for welfare and social services, and the declining quality of education among the urban poor. Each of these would then become a section of your outline.

Outlines

An outline functions as a kind of road map that tells you where you are going as you write your paper. An outline also forces you to arrange in some kind of logical order the divisions you've made in your notes, to verbalize the relationships among these divisions, and to make some decisions about how you will introduce and conclude your paper.

Obviously, an outline is not helpful unless it deals with the specific material that will appear in your paper. For example, the following outline on the causes of teen-age divorce is poor because it does not force you to begin grappling with the arguments you want to present in the final paper:

I. Introduction
II. Causes of teen-age divorce
    A. Emotional factors
    B. Economic factors
    C. Social factors
III. Conclusion

One way to make sure that you begin working with content at this stage is to write a *sentence outline* — one in which every entry is in the form of a complete sentence making a proposition or claim. Such an outline will be very helpful when you begin writing your draft because it forces you to begin thinking about exactly what you want to say. Here is an example of how such an outline might begin:

I. Teen-age divorce is becoming more prevalent in America.
    A. In 1950, 16% of all teen-age marriages ended in divorce (Jenkins 17).
    B. By 1980, that figure had risen to 56% (Jenkins 17).
    C. Today, teen-age marriages are twice as likely to fail as marriages of older couples (Brown 576).

II. Sociologists and religious leaders consider teen-age divorce one of America's most serious social problems.
    A. Young single parents find it extremely difficult, if not impossible, to develop job skills and are therefore destined to lives of poverty and social isolation (Brown 576–80).

....

A sentence outline like this is really a middle step between planning the paper and actually writing it. While it does not require that you have all the transitions, informational details, and references to outside sources that need to be incorporated into the final version, it does start you thinking about the actual wording of your paper and the progression of your argument.

Arrangement of the Text

Purpose of the introduction

Use the question or questions you formulated at the beginning of your research to guide you in arranging the parts of your paper. Your introduction should tell your readers what the question under investigation is and why it needs to be asked and answered. Thus, you might want to emphasize the urgency of a question, perhaps explaining the negative effects that can be expected if the problem goes unsolved or the question continues to be ignored. Or you might want to demonstrate how interesting your question is, arousing your readers' curiosity so that they will want to read on.

Additional information that is appropriate in an introduction includes some discussion of ways in which the problem is commonly misunderstood, previous attempts to solve the problem, progress made to date toward an answer or solution. Finally, you might include some indication of how you will attempt to find an answer or solution. Naturally, you may need more than a single paragraph to accommodate all the information that is necessary to introduce your topic.

The body of your paper is where you relate the findings of your investigation; here you present, interpret, evaluate, and synthesize the material you've gathered from various sources. In organizing this section of your paper, consult your notes and your outline frequently. In addition, it may be helpful to you to reread the section in this book on paragraph development (pages 207–216); the same patterns and principles that create unity in a paragraph can be applied, on a larger scale, to a paper-length discussion.

In the final section of your paper, you should draw a conclusion from the findings you've gathered and presented. It is important to be aware that a conclusion is much more than a simple summary of things you've already said; in essence, it responds to these questions: "So what?" "How does all this information help us answer the question or solve the problem?" "What are the *implications* of this research?" Here again, you will probably require much more than a single paragraph, especially if the material you've presented is complex and the paper itself is long. The important thing to keep in mind as you write your conclusion is that this section of the paper is the final step in completing the question/answer or problem/solution format: first you pose the question (problem), then you search the available sources for information, and finally you distill from that information the answer or solution you were seeking.

Documentation

Reasons for careful documentation
When you write research papers, whether for a class or on the job, you need to document your sources as fully as possible for two reasons. First, you want your readers to know what sources you have investigated, where you found them, and how recent your information is. Second, you want to give your readers enough information so that they can locate and use the material themselves if they wish. After all, people write research reports in order to share information with others, and good documentation makes that easier to do. If you have used the sources listed in the citations or notes of an article or book you have consulted in your own investigation, you already know how helpful clear documentation can be to a fellow researcher. So the question you should keep in mind when you insert reference information into your writing and when you prepare your bibliography or list of works cited is this: "Am I giving my readers the information they need in order to track down the source of this reference?" If you are, then you are doing a good job of documenting your paper.

Keep in mind that when you do research, you gather *ideas* from your sources as well as statistical information and direct quotations, and it is important that your readers be able to tell which contributions are your own, which are reports of someone else's opinions, and which are statements of fact. Making this kind of information clear is not simply a matter of supplying citations for the works you refer to. The text of your paper, too, should tell a reader which material has been gathered from outside sources and which is your own insight and interpretation.

In the case of direct quotations — where you use the exact words of someone else — you supply the information partly by using quotation marks or block indentation. But you also need to provide an introduction to material supplied by outside sources, whether you are paraphrasing that material or quoting it directly. Introductory comments such as the ones in the following example should be used even though the source of the information is given in the list of works cited; they not only make it clear exactly which information is being documented but also help to integrate quoted material smoothly and gracefully into your text:

Original

"Artistic genius is often unsure of itself and yearns for the approval of a respectful public."[1] "Many novelists consider publication of their work as the only reliable proof of its literary worth."[2] Carolyn Kephart, for instance, refused to show the manuscript of *Esme* to anyone before it was finally accepted by a publisher, and even her husband and closest friends had to purchase the novel in a bookstore in order to read it.[3]

Revision

In her book-length study of the creative temperament, psychologist Deborah McRoberts reports that artistic geniuses often need the reassurance of public recognition.[1] Literary scholar Christopher Staples provides evidence that this is frequently true of great novelists. He cites the example of Carolyn Kephart, who needed publication to convince her of the literary value of her work. Although her novel, *Esme,* is now widely acclaimed as a literary masterpiece, Kephart refused to show the unpublished manuscript to anyone, and even her husband and closest friends were forced to purchase the novel in a bookstore in order to read it.[2]

The original version of this paragraph commits the error of using direct quotation when paraphrase would suffice. In addition, a reader cannot tell where the information in the paragraph has come from. The quotation marks indicate that someone other than the writer of the paper is responsible for the first two sentences, but who is that someone? Is he or she a reputable source? Or are there really two different sources? If more than one source is involved, how are these sources related to one another, and why is the writer of the paper using them together in this paragraph? And where does the example of Carolyn Kephart's modesty come from?

The reader might be able to find the answers to these questions by studying the citations, but such an interruption in the reading of a text is awkward, annoying, and unnecessary. The revision eliminates the unnecessary use of direct quotation and incorporates the missing information about the sources smoothly into the text. Citations are still needed, however, because the writer is presenting information that originally appeared in another source and because readers may want to find those sources in order to conduct follow-up research.

Conventions of Documentation

Styles of documentation are likely to vary considerably across academic disciplines, and you need to know which style is preferred in the field for which you are writing. One way to find out this kind of information is to check the form of documentation used in the articles published in scholarly journals in the field you are researching. If you are writing a research paper for a course, check with your instructor to find out what kind of documentation form he or she prefers and which style manual you should consult if you have a question about the correct form for citing your sources.

The format for MLA and APA documentation

Until very recently (1984), the standard guide for writers in English (the *MLA Handbook*) recommended the use of full documentation, the style using superscript numbers in the text of the paper referring readers to the bottom of the page or the end of the paper, where footnotes or endnotes contain complete bibliographic information for the sources cited. With the 1984 edition of the *MLA Handbook for Writers of Research Papers,* however, the MLA (Modern Language Association) adopted an internal documentation style similar to that of the APA (American Psychological Association). Both organizations now recommend that brief citations appear in parentheses in the text immediately after the cited material. Here, for example, is how internal documentation should be styled according to the MLA:

> The intertwining of fact and fiction in the author's craft results in many fictional episodes in Pym's novels which were drawn directly from her own experience. In *No Fond Return of Love,* for example, Dulcie Mainwaring's embarrassing encounter with the woman who had deposited an armload of flowers in the sink at a public restroom (34) repeats a similar incident in Pym's own life (*Autobiography* 121).

Notice that no parenthetical citation is necessary when enough information is given in the text to allow a reader to identify the source in the list of works cited that comes at the end of the book or article. In the example just given, the text identifies *No Fond Return of Love* as one of Pym's novels, so a page number is all the information that is needed parenthetically. Full citations for both *No Fond Return of Love* and Pym's *Autobiography* are included in the list of works cited, of course.

Whenever possible, APA parenthetical citations give the author's name and the date of publication. Sometimes it is necessary to provide page numbers as well.

> Homeopathic medicine has been notoriously critical of the routine administration of the DPT vaccine to infants (Gurrola-Gal 1979; Thigpen 1980; DeVries 1980), advocating instead that more effort be put into helping the body develop its own immune system naturally.

The brief parenthetical citations that both the MLA and the APA recommend must contain enough information to enable the reader to locate the cited sources in the end-of-the-paper list of works cited, where full bibliographic information is given for *all* the sources the writer has consulted in order to produce the paper. This means that footnotes at the bottom of the page or endnotes at the end of the paper need only be used for explanatory material. These *content notes* clarify or justify what has been written in the text. The following example of a content note could appear in a list of endnotes or at the bottom of the page of text to which it refers:

Text

William and Margaret Maxwell's *Denver Chiropractic Notes,* first published in July of 1983, is but one example of a private press publication that has been an influential force in shaping the professional climate of a sizable community.[1]

Note

[1]The name *Denver Chiropractic Notes* was changed to *Backtracking* in September of 1984, at which time the publication was expanded from newsletter to journal format for statewide publication.

The differences that now remain between APA and revised MLA documentation style are principally matters of punctuation, capitalization, and the arrangement of material in bibliographic entries. The following examples show how the same source would be cited in both APA and MLA styles:

MLA Style

Taylor, Dawn, and Jeanne Mahoney. "The Search for Tim Mahoney: Revealing the Masked Man's Identity." *Twentieth Century Folklore* 17(1984):76–92.

APA Style

Taylor, D. & Mahoney, J. (1984) The search for Tim Mahoney: Revealing the masked man's identity. *Twentieth century folklore.* 17, 76–92.

Notice that in both styles, the last name of the first author, when this information is available, is the first item to appear and, therefore, the item that determines the citation's place in an alphabetical listing. In the MLA style, however, the author's full name is used, whereas the APA prefers to use only first initials. Notice too that in APA style the second author's name is entered exactly as the first author's, but in MLA style the second author's name is not inverted because this name is not the one being used for alphabetizing purposes. In both cases a period follows the information about the author or authors, signaling the end of the first unit of bibliographic information.

The second unit of information differs according to the documentation style used. APA places the date of publication in second position, immediately after the author's name, while MLA does not give the date until the end of the entry (followed in some cases by page numbers). The remaining bibliographic information is much the same in both styles except for the way the titles are capitalized. The MLA style follows the conventions that you are probably familiar with: titles of articles or other short works appear in quotation marks, and titles of longer works are italicized (underlined); first, last, and all substantive words in titles of any kind are capitalized. APA style, on the other hand, does not use quotation marks to distinguish the titles of articles and similar short works, nor does it capitalize words in titles except in the following cases: first words, proper nouns and adjectives, and words following a colon.

The sample entries that follow demonstrate the MLA style preferred in most English classes. For a more complete list of sample entries in this style, consult the most recent edition of the *MLA Handbook for Writers of Research Papers,* designed especially for undergraduate students. For a similar listing of APA style entries, consult the *Publication Manual* of the American Psychological Association. Both of these works can be found in the reference section of most libraries, or they can be purchased at the bookstore.

A book by one author:

Koestler, Arthur. *The Act of Creation.* London: Pan, 1975.

A book by two authors:

Singer, Dorothy, and Tracey A. Revenson. *How a Child Thinks.* New York and London: NAL, 1978.

A book compiled by an editor:

Kuhn, Thomas, ed. *The Essential Tension: Selected Studies in Scientific Tradition and Change.* Chicago: U of Chicago P, 1977.

An essay in a book of collected essays:

Judy, Stephen. "On Clock Watching and Composition." Ed. Richard Graves. New Rochelle, NY: Haydn, 1976.

A translation:

Vygotsky, L. S. *Thought and Language.* Trans. Eugenia Hoffman and Gertrude Vakar. Cambridge, MA: MIT P, 1962.

An edition:

Kuhn, Thomas. *The Structure of Scientific Revolutions.* 2nd ed. Chicago: U of Chicago P, 1971.

An introduction to a book:

Geiger, Henry. Introduction. *The Farther Reaches of Human Nature.* By Abraham Maslow. New York: Penguin, 1976.

An article in a reference book:

"Microcomputers." *Encyclopedia Americana.* 1980 ed.

An article in a newspaper:

Palmer, Thomas. "Four Jurors Say They Didn't Intend a Libel Finding in Lakian Verdict." *The Boston Globe* 7 August 1985: 1, 8.

An article in a popular periodical:

Severson, Cindy. "Pack Up Your Troubles." *Texas Monthly* April 1981: 40.

An unsigned article in a magazine or newspaper:

"Working the Rigs." *Texas Monthly* March 1980: 140–46.

An article in a scholarly or professional journal:

Braddock, Richard. "The Frequency and Placement of Topic Sentences in Expository Prose." *Research in the Teaching of English* 8.3 (1974): 28 . (*Notice that for this kind of citation you should give the volume and issue number because the collected journals are bound according to those designations.*)

An unpublished dissertation:

Johnson, Eric. "The Importance of Ethos in the Works of Margaret Gabler." Diss. Temple, 1982.

A government document:

United States. Cong. Joint Committee on the Investigation of Welfare Abuses. *Hearings.* 99th Cong., 2nd sess. 16 vols. Washington: GPO, 1983.

A pamphlet:

Feline Leukemia Virus Infection: Life-saving Information for Cat Owners. Lincoln, NE: Norden Laboratories, 1985.

Material from an information service such as ERIC:

Sandy, Thimothy G., ed. *Survival on the Family Farm: New Possibilities for Multiple Cash Crops.* Cantril: Midwestern Agriculture Conference, 1985. ERIC ED 187 5930.

A specialized encyclopedia:

Hodges, Elizabeth Scott. "Flannery O'Connor and the Quest for Salvation." *Encyclopedia of American Women Authors.* Ed. Erika Obermeier. 3 vols. Pittsburgh: College P, 1983.

A letter to the editor:

Hoffman, Ted. Letter. *Journal of Pharmaceutical Research* 53 (1984):141.

A movie:

Zefferelli, Franco. Dir. *Romeo and Juliet.* BHE Verona Productions, 1968.

A television interview:

Bacall, Lauren. Interview. "Woman of the Year." With Barbara Walters. NBC, New York. 9 June 1981.

A personal interview:

Admiral Bobby Ray Inman. Personal interview. 12 April 1985.

A television program:

"Swimming in a Bad Gene Pool: The Punk Scene in America." Narr. Thomas Roller. Writ. and prod. Susan Shug. CBS Youth in America Series. KBNX, Harrisburg, PA. 3 Feb. 1985.

Preparing the List of Works Cited

The list of works cited comes at the end of your paper. In it you must list all works you have referred to in your paper (that includes interviews, television programs, movies, and so on, as well as articles and books). They should be listed in alphabetical order according to the last name of the author or, in the case of anonymous articles or television programs, by the first word of the title other than *A, An,* or *The.* You may also want to include a list of works consulted, containing works in which you may have done substantial background reading but that you have not actually cited in your paper. You should use the same bibliographical form for that list.

Begin the entry flush with the left margin. If the entry runs more than one line, indent the subsequent lines five spaces. Double-space the entire list, within entries as well as between entries.

Here is the way part of a works cited list might look.

Works Cited

Barzun, Jacques. *Writing, Editing, and Publishing.* Chicago: U of Chicago P, 1971.

Bennett, Patrick. *Talking with Texas Authors.* College Station: Texas A & M P, 1980.

Booth, Wayne. "The Rhetorical Stance." *College Composition and Communication* 1.3 (1965): 221.

Christensen, Francis. *Notes Toward a New Rhetoric.* New York: Harper, 1967.

Flower, Linda. Radio interview by Barbara Fassler. KUT, Austin, TX. 4 June 1983.

Suggested Topics and Model Paper

The final section of this chapter includes a list of fifty topics for research papers, a number of which may interest you or suggest other topics.[1] Following the list is a model research paper.

Suggested Topics for Research Papers

The questions under each topic are intended to serve as probes to help you explore the topic and give you suggestions about various ways in which you might approach your research.

[1]These topics were compiled and annotated by the staff of reference librarians at the Undergraduate Library at the University of Texas at Austin. Copyrighted by the Undergraduate Library, The General Libraries, The University of Texas at Austin, 1980–81.

1. *Gambling*

   Why do people gamble? What are the attitudes toward gambling in our society? Do other societies have similar attitudes toward gambling? Is gambling a legal, a moral, or an economic issue? What are some of the consequences of legalized gambling?

2. *Astrology*

   What is the relationship between astronomy and astrology? Does astrology have a scientific basis? Can belief in astrology cause any harm? How widespread is belief in astrology?

3. *Genetic research*

   What is genetic engineering? What legal, ethical, or safety problems are raised by genetic research? Why is "test-tube birth" controversial? What are the pros and cons of research with recombinant DNA?

4. *Animal communication*

   How do animals communicate with each other? Do certain species have the capacity to talk to humans? What research has been done on teaching language to such animals as apes and dolphins? What are the implications of this research?

5. *Artificial intelligence*

   What is artificial intelligence? Can machines be built that will solve problems, play games, and even demonstrate the ability to learn? What research has been done in this area? What are the dangers of developing artificial intelligence? What is cybernetics? What is the relationship between cybernetics and artificial intelligence?

6. *Equal Rights Amendment*

   When was the Equal Rights Amendment proposed? What progress has been made? What groups are opposed to the Equal Rights Amendment? For what reasons? What impact would the amendment have on women's rights and legal status if it were adopted?

7. *Television*

   How does television violence affect the public? How do TV watchers differ from nonwatchers? What can children learn from television? Who determines what appears on television: advertisers, producers, network officials, the public? How has television programming changed over the years? What impact will cable and satellite dish TV have on television viewers of the future?

8. *Income tax*

   What are some of the criticisms voiced about the federal income tax system? Do the tax laws favor certain groups, such as corporations, the wealthy, or the unmarried individual? If the laws are unfair, why are they so difficult to change? How does our system compare with that of other countries?

9. *Film*

   How have movies been used to influence public attitudes — for example, to encourage patriotism during wartime? Why did certain types of films dominate the screen in certain eras, such as the gangster movies in the thirties? What kinds of social commentary have movies portrayed? What censorship has been imposed?

10. *Population explosion*

    What solutions have been proposed for overpopulation? What are some of the most promising methods of birth control and the problems associated with them? Should sterilization be used as a method of birth control? Are all countries concerned about limiting their populations? How are population trends in other countries going to affect the US?

11. *ESP*

    What is extrasensory perception? What are some of the forms it takes? What kinds of experiments are used to test its validity? Why is there so much skepticism about ESP?

12. *Aging*

    What is it like to be old in the US? How is the age distribution of the population changing? What problems of income, housing, or medical care do old people face? Is mandatory retirement fair? How does the treatment of old people differ in other countries? What factors in our culture contributute to our attitude toward old age? What is "gray power"?

13. *Death and funeral rites*

    What are some of the historical changes in attitudes toward death and the customs associated with it? How are American attitudes toward death changing? What can be done to help terminal patients prepare for death? What are some ways to cope with grief? What functions do funeral rites and ceremonies serve? How do a society's rites reflect its concept of death? What can be learned about life after death and the moment of death from people who survive an apparent death experience?

14. *Cults and religious movements*

    What accounts for the rise in participation in various evangelical religions and cults? How does the increasing interest reflect American society and its values? What is the "human potential" movement? Is it a new religion in America? What is deprogramming? What are the pros and cons of its use on cult members?

15. *Popular music*

    Choose a form of popular music, for example, jazz, country and western, rock, or blues. How did this type of music originate and develop? How has it changed from its original form? What influence has it had on other forms of music? How does it reflect other aspects of contemporary society?

16. *Life on other planets*

    What evidence exists to suggest the possibility of life on other planets? Is the search for extraterrestrial life an important goal in our space program? What methods are used to detect life? What forms is life elsewhere likely to take? Have recent planetary explorations changed our views? What can we learn from contact with other life forms?

17. *Parent and child*

    What role does each parent have in the child's development? How have ideas about raising children changed in the last twenty years? How has our changing society affected the family? Is the family becoming obsolete? What new roles is the father playing in child rearing? Why? What special problems does the single parent face in raising a family?

18. *Utopia*

    What is utopia and how did the term originate? Do ideas of utopia change as society changes? What are some of the famous utopian experiments? Were they successful? Did they have any impact on society? What are some of the famous literary utopias?

19. *Pesticides, herbicides, and industrial poisons*

    What are some of the effects of pesticides on the environment? On people and wildlife? What are some of the chemicals being attacked by environmentalists? How important are pesticides and herbicides in protecting our food supply? What are the limitations or advantages of "natural pesticides"? How have government, industry, or farmers reacted to the controversy? What are the risks or dangers of chemical waste disposal, such as at Love Canal?

20. *Solar energy*

Is solar energy a feasible alternative to fossil fuels? How does it work? What are its limitations? What is the government doing to stimulate research into solar energy? What are the merits of passive design? How has architectural design been affected by solar energy use?

21. *Computers*

How has the computer changed since its invention? What impact has the computer had on business, education, communication, or other aspects of society? What benefits does the computer bring? What problems? How has the invention of the microprocessor revolutionized the computer industry?

22. *Contemporary sexual ethics*

How are sex customs changing in the US? How has sex research contributed to our understanding of human sexuality? What are the pros and cons of sex education in the schools? Are men feeling threatened by changing sex roles?

23. *Wiretapping and the right to privacy*

What legislation has been passed to protect the right to privacy? Is it legal for private citizens to tap, bug, or record private conversations? When did government wiretapping originate? Is it legal? Is it justified?

24. *Endangered species*

What species are endangered? What is being done to save rare animals or plants? What is the history of an animal that is either already extinct or in danger of extinction? Are zoos part of the answer or part of the problem? What is the role of the hunter? Conservationist? Government?

25. *Photography*

Is photography an art or a technology? Trace the development of a style or movement in the history of photography. Who were some of the earliest photographers and how do their methods compare with today's? What is photojournalism? How can it influence the public's perception of current events? How do photographers choose and compose a subject for a photograph? How has photography portrayed various eras in American history, such as the western expansion or the depression?

26. *Vampires*

What is the origin of the vampire legend? Who was the original Count Dracula? What does the vampire represent? How have vampires been portrayed in nineteenth- and twentieth-century literature and in films? Is there any factual data to support the existence of vampires?

27. *Gun control*

What are the arguments for and against gun control? Does the availability of guns lead to their use in crime? How is the phrase "the right to keep and bear arms" interpreted by the National Rifle Association or by gun control advocates? Why is gun control such a controversial issue in the US when it is practiced successfully in many other countries?

28. *The press and politics*

What effect does television and radio coverage have on elections? Have campaign strategies changed as a result? Does television, radio, and newspaper coverage make politicians more open to ridicule and scandal? What effect does television, radio, and newspaper coverage have on political events? Is legislation to control the political use of the press desirable? Can the press "make" or "break" a political figure?

29. *Sports and society*

What are some of the psychological and sociological aspects of being a participant or spectator of sports? How and why have some sports ceased to be "fun" and become big business? Is violence in sports becoming excessive? What are the advantages and disadvantages of amateur versus professional status in various sports? How important are sports and its heroes to the public? Do world political conflicts endanger international sports competitions such as the Olympics and similar events?

30. *Inflation*

What is inflation? What causes it? Is it a recent phenomenon or a historic one? What are its effects? What has the US done to reduce inflation? How do the opinions of particular politicians or economists differ? What effect does the status of the dollar abroad have on the economy here?

31. *Adoption*

Why do people decide to adopt a child? What difficulties are they likely to encounter before and after adopting? What special considerations are involved in the adoption of multiracial, handicapped, or other "special" children? What problems are created for the adopted parents and the birth parents when adopted children search for their "roots"? What obstacles do the children face in their search?

32. *Pyramids and ancient megaliths*

Who built the pyramids of Egypt or Stonehenge in England or the great stone faces on Easter Island? How do these ancient monuments reflect the cultures of their makers? What is one theory of how the pyramids were built? What are some of the legends and curses of the pyramids? Do these structures indicate high levels of civilization? What happened to the builders? What is the relationship between astronomy and these ancient monuments?

33. *Divorce*

How are patterns of marriage and divorce changing in the US? What changes have there been in attitudes toward divorce? What kinds of psychological, legal, financial, or social problems does divorce cause and what help is available to deal with these problems? How does divorce affect children? How should child custody be handled? How can problems in marriage be resolved without divorce?

34. *Origin of the universe*

What are some of the scientific explanations for the origin of the universe? What theory does most of the available evidence seem to support? Is there agreement on the way planets are created? What new evidence has been turned up by the space program?

35. *Consumer protection*

What rights do consumers have? Historically, how has the government regulated such things as food, appliances, alcohol, cars, and cigarettes? What effects has Ralph Nader had on American consumer protection? If a product or service has been unsatisfactory, what can a consumer do about it? Are laws necessary to protect consumers?

36. *Laughter*

What makes people laugh? What are some of the theories of humor? What is the difference between humor and comedy? What role does laughing play in the release of tension? Are some things universally funny? What comparisons can be drawn between contemporary jokes, comedy films, or TV shows and those in the past?

37. *Body language*

What is nonverbal communication? Can you really read a person like a book? How does nonverbal communication differ in other cultures, for example, Latin America? What effect can this have on intercultural communication? Of what practical use is the study of nonverbal communication? What has research on kinetics contributed to understanding the importance of body movement in communication?

38. *Cancer*

What do doctors think causes cancer? Is there likely ever to be a single cure or treatment? What are some of the most promising areas of cancer research? Can cancer be predicted? Can it be prevented?

39. *The airplane and society*

How safe is flying? What are the major causes of aviation accidents? What are some of the safety measures being taken to prevent accidents? What impact has the development of aviation had on business, warfare, or public transportation? What are the pros and cons of deregulation for the airline industry?

40. *Suicide*

Is suicide on the increase? In what groups of people is it most common? Have recent social attitudes toward suicide changed? How do attitudes toward suicide differ among cultures?

41. *Animals that capture the imagination*

Choose an animal and discuss its habitat, behavior, or position in the world today. For example: What is the controversy surrounding whale hunting? Should there be a moratorium on the killing of seals? What has research discovered about the intelligence of dolphins or chimpanzees?

42. *White collar crime*

What is white collar crime? How does it differ from other crime? Do white collar criminals receive special treatment? What are some of the most famous cases of white collar crime? Is white collar crime on the increase in this country? Do computers provide more opportunities for white collar crime?

43. *Child abuse*

How widespread is the problem of child abuse? What are its causes? Is it a moral, legal, or psychological problem? What is being done to prevent child abuse and help the abuser? What are the various forms child abuse can take, such as physical, emotional, or sexual abuse? How does one kind of abuse, such as incest, affect the child in later life?

44. *The twenty-first century*

What are some of the predictions about life at the end of this century and in the twenty-first century? How should we prepare for the future now? Does our future depend on space exploration, increased technology, or new constraints on our use of resources? What nations will be most affected by the future? Who will fare best? Why? What changes will the future bring in terms of social attitudes, such as the changing nature of sex roles or the function of the family?

45. *Smoking*

How serious a health hazard is smoking to smokers and non-smokers? Has smoking always been considered unhealthy? How influential is the tobacco industry? What impact has the surgeon general's report *Smoking and Health* had on smoking habits? What are some of the methods recommended for people trying to give up cigarettes, and how effective are these methods?

46. *Prison reform*

Why do American prisons need reform? What are some specific reforms suggested? What part have the prisoners themselves played in the demand for reform? What are the "liberal" and "conservative" views on this issue? How do penal systems differ in other countries? What progress has been made to improve conditions?

47. *Vitamins*

How do vitamins affect people's health? How accurate is the Minimum Daily Requirement? Does megavitamin therapy work? What are the diseases it is being tried on? What are the arguments against it? How do natural and synthetic vitamins differ?

48. *Art forgeries*

What have been some notorious art fakes and hoaxes? How can forgeries be detected? What are some of the methods used in art forgery? Is there a way to protect valuable art from forgery?

49. *UFOs*

What are some current theories about the existence of UFOs? Do UFO sightings follow a pattern? Is there any evidence of government cover-up of UFO sightings? What serious research has been done on UFOs?

50. *Climatic change and weather modification*
Is modern civilization inadvertently changing the earth's climate? How can pollution, industrialization, or urbanization influence the weather? What do scientists predict the impact of a worldwide climatic change would be? In what cases would weather modification be beneficial? What are the limits of weather modification technologies?

Matt Holicek

E 306 Rhetoric and Comp.

December 6, 1984

TELEVISION VIOLENCE AND AGGRESSIVE CHILDREN

A sixteen-year old boy is arrested for breaking into a house. He says he wore gloves because he saw on television that characters wear gloves so as not to leave finger prints. Another boy age nine gives his teacher a box of poisoned sweets after receiving a bad report card. He claims he saw the technique used on a television show the previous week when a man used it to kill his wife. A seven-year-old child sprinkles ground glass into his family's lamb stew, wondering if it would really work as it did on television (Howe 71).

Television. Ninety-six percent of all the households in the United States have one (Brown 285). It affects all of us in different ways. But the single most affected audience is children. According to FBI figures, between the years of 1952 and 1972, "...the number of juveniles arrested for serious and violent crimes increased 1600%" (Winn 65). That was a time when television became immensely popular and was heavily viewed by children. The programs aired during those times were saturated with crime and destruction. John Heinz, writing in *American Psychologist*, reports, "...children spend more time in this country watching television than they ever spend in school, and, very likely in direct communication with their parents" (816). It is obvious that, given so much time spent in front of the television set, children will be affected by it in some way. As many studies have proved, children who view violent programs on television begin to imitate the violent acts they see, and become significantly more aggressive in their behavior.

The concern about televised violence and its links to childhood aggression has been around for a very long time. In 1952 Senator Estes Kefauver's Subcommittee on Juvenile Delinquency heard psychiatrists who "forcefully expressed their conviction that television violence can lead children into displays of aggression and even to acts of violence of irrationality that directly imitate what they have seen on the screen" (Bogart 493). But their testimony was not enough to warrant further studies on the subject. It was still unclear to the committee exactly how the children were affected and what direct results occurred.

The most popular theory of the television-aggression link centers around the child's early instinct to imitate. Adults are able to understand the difference between the make-believe they see on television and real life situations. Children, unfortunately, are not. To them, seeing is believing (Garry 9). And so, just as they imitate their father and mother in different ways, children begin to imitate what they see on the television screen. Through television, children learn different ways human beings can hurt each other (Singer and Singer 99). If a child is frustrated and finds himself in a situation similar to one he has seen on television, it is likely that he will act out that behavior. An experiment by Albert Bandura tested the possibility that children imitate actions which they see on television. Ninety-six children between the ages of three and five years were separated into three groups (Howe 86). One group watched an adult model hit a weighted inflatable doll with a mallet in the children's play room. A second group watched a *film* with the same adult model hitting the same doll. A third group featured a similar situation, yet with cartoon characters instead of humans. Afterwards, each child was placed into a room with many attractive toys and told to play. Soon after, the experimenter informed the child that he had to play in another room, which had ordinary toys, but also an inflatable doll like the one seen before. This made the children somewhat angry; those who had viewed the film of the real person hitting the doll showed a much higher level of imitation than those who watched the live model or cartoon (Howe 86). The famous Bandura experiment proved that children do imitate some of the violent acts they see on television.

Not only do children imitate the violent acts television portrays; they also learn their attitudes towards violence from television. Randall P. Harrison wrote in *Parents' Magazine,* "The problem is not just that a child may learn how to deliver a karate chop or write a bomb threat; he may learn that the most effective answer to a problem is violence" (60). When children view a show, they are not yet able to realize the motives or consequences of the violent acts they see. For example, if a child sees a television program in which a villain kills a couple of people, robs a bank, and escapes with millions of dollars, it is likely the child will not realize that in the end the criminal will usually die or go to jail. Children just remember the part about the man becoming rich after murdering the people.

Most violent shows have the hero beating up or killing the villain at the end of the movie, causing children to believe that violence is an appropriate way of resolving conflicts. Children become more aggressive in response to violence, even if the intended message is crime does not pay (Bogart 501). One attempt to prove that children believe violence is an appropriate way of solving problems was made through a 1970 survey examining the viewing habits of a sample of about 400 boys ages nine through twelve (Murray 79). They were measured in a number of categories: the amount of violence they watched, their beliefs in the effectiveness of violence as a means of solving conflicts, their willingness to use violence themselves to deal with problems, their approval of violence in others, and their tendency to suggest violent methods of solving problems (Murray 79). It was concluded from the results that "the greater the quantity of television violence to which a boy was exposed, the more likely he was to express a willingness to resort to violence himself, to consider violence to be effective and to suggest violent solutions to problems" (Murray 79). Naturally, the children who watched few or no violent programs generally did not believe violence was an appropriate means of resolving conflicts. In a similar study in 1977 by Greenberg and Atkin, 45 percent of the children between the ages of nine and thirteen who were heavy viewers of television chose responses favoring the idea of aggression as a conflict solver as compared to 21 percent of light violence viewers (Murray 32). Michael Howe, author of *Television and Children,* best summarized those and other studies when he wrote, "If a child comes to believe that acting violently is the normal way of dealing with a range of problems, and at the same time learns *how* to act violently from watching violent situations on television, he will be more likely to acquire violent habits than an individual whose exposure to violence is comparatively limited" (75). Children who view violence on television accept that violence and believe it to be a good way to resolve conflicts.

The previous studies, however, only showed an association between children's *attitudes* to the use of violence and televised violence. Studies were needed to actually prove the link between violence on television and later childhood aggression. It wasn't until 1969 that Senator John Pastore, Chairman of the Senate Subcommittee on Communications, went to the Surgeon General (who had just proved that smoking is dangerous to one's health) to launch a series of studies to prove exactly that link (Palmer and Dorr 115). What followed was a two-year, million-dollar project which produced five volumes of results, plus a summary report of the entire project (Harrison 53). It also created controversy which in turn spawned countless other studies.

In *Television and Youth*, John P. Murray discusses an interesting experiment that tested young people's willingness to hurt one another. Robert M. Leibert and Robert A. Brown showed children either violent segments from *The Untouchables* or segments from a track race (30). After viewing, the children were placed in a room and told to push either a "help" or "hurt" button that would either help or hurt a child in another room's game-playing ability. The results showed that the children who watched *The Untouchables* were more inclined to hurt another child than the children who watched the track race (30). In the following free-play period, the children who viewed *The Untouchables* tended to play with weapons and more aggressive toys. The Leibert and Brown experiment showed that violence on television causes children to act hostilely towards others.

Children who view violent programs on television can become more aggressive in their play. A nine-week study of ninety-seven preschool children by Stein and Friedrich tested children's aggressive behavior following violent viewing. Children were shown either "anti-social" cartoons such as *Batman* and *Superman,* "pro-social" segments from *Mr. Rogers Neighborhood,* or "neutral" travelogue films. The results showed that the children who viewed *Batman* and *Superman* later became more aggressive in play, while those who viewed *Mr. Rogers* were more willing to share toys and cooperate with each other (Murray 35). Viewing action and violence, "tends to lead young children to a state of heightened excitability and to an increase in subsequent displays of aggression" (Bogart 494). Children's aggression in behavior is in part caused by viewing aggressive material (Singer 98).

Most of the studies done only showed a short-term effect of television violence. There were, however, a few studies that tested the long-term effects of television violence on children. In 1972 researchers Eron, Lefkowitz, Huesmann, and Walder were able to go back and study children they had studied ten years earlier (257). The children in the third grade who preferred violent programs were more aggressive in school than children who preferred less violent shows. Ten years later, 427 of the original 875 subjects showed that violence preferred by the male subjects in the third grade was even more strongly related to aggression ten years later (258). There was a causal link between the amount of television violence a child sees at eight or nine and the aggressiveness he shows ten years later.

In 1978 William Belson also showed the long-term effects of television violence and antisocial behavior. A six-year investigation classified 156 teenage boys in London as either heavy or light viewers of television violence. The evidence demonstrated that "long-term exposure to violence increases the degree to which boys engage in violence of a serious kind" (Myson 50). This study related actual antisocial behavior to watching televised violence, whereas earlier studies only showed aggressive behavior as the consequence of viewing violence on television.

The Surgeon General's Committee included many similar studies accounting for some 10,000 children, in all parts of the country, of different ages, and from different socioeconomic backgrounds (Harrison 53). It was demonstrated that even small doses of television violence led to measurable increases in antisocial behavior. These effects were not limited to children who were disturbed or abnormal but were apparently in perfectly normal children as well (Harrison 53). Even the updated version of the studies in 1980 by the National Institute of Mental Health (NIMH) came up with the same conclusion: television violence causes childhood aggression (Rubenstein 820). The NIMH reports stated there was "overwhelming evidence" proving that excessive television violence viewing causes children to act aggressively ("Warning from Washington" 77). However, the best summary of the NIMH reports was stated in Eli A. Rubinstein's article featured in a July 1983 article in *American Psychologist:*

Television can no longer be considered as a casual part of daily life, as an electronic toy. Research findings have long since destroyed the illusion that television is mainly incidental rather than direct and formal. It is a significant part of the total acculturation process. (820)

That conclusion summarizes what almost twenty years of research and more than 3,000 scientific studies have found (820). Experiments have been carried out in large numbers and their findings show with no shadow of a doubt that children's behavior can be influenced by the actions of people they see on television. The violence children witness on the television causes them to behave more violently and aggressively than children who watch little violent programs.

Jesse L. Steinfeld, the Surgeon General, in his memorable testimony before the Senate subcommittee emotionally summed up the entire investigation and also presented his views on the outlook for the future:

> While the committee report is carefully phrased and qualified in language acceptable to social scientists, it is clear to me that the causal relationship between televised violence and antisocial behavior is sufficient to warrant appropriate and immediate remedial action. The data on social phenomena such as television and violence and/or aggressive behavior will never be clear enough for all social scientists to agree on the formation of a succinct statement of causality. But there comes a time when the data are sufficient to justify action. That time has come. (Bogart 521)

Through all of the studies since the early years of television it is now possible to conclude that television violence definitely causes aggression in children. Unfortunately, violence still continues to clutter the television airwaves, and children still continue to watch it. These studies must and will be carried out until enough pressure is finally put on networks to limit violent content and program more quality shows for children. When one considers how long these studies have proved the link between violence and childhood aggression, and the amount of violent content that remains in programs today, it looks as if that day is a long way away.

WORKS CITED

Bogart, Leo. "Warning: The Surgeon General Has Determined That TV Violence is Moderately Dangerous to Your Child's Mental Health." *Public Opinion Quarterly* Winter 1972–1973: 491–521.

Brown, Ray, ed. *Children and Television.* Beverly Hills, CA: Sage, 1976.

Eron, Leonard D. et al. "Does Television Violence Cause Aggression?" *American Psychologist,* April 1972: 253–63.

Garry, Ralph. *Children and T.V.* Association for Childhood Education International 1967.

Harrison, Randall P., Ph.D. "The Violent Shows," *Parents' Magazine* Oct. 1974: 32–33, 52–53, 60.

Heinz, John. "National Leadership for Children's Television," *American Psychologist* July 1983: 817–19.

Howe, Michael J. A. *Television and Children.* London: New University Education, 1977. 71–104.

Morgenstern, Joseph. "The New Violence." *Newsweek* 14 Feb. 1972: 66–69.

Murray, John P. *Television and Youth.* Stanford: The Boys Town Center for the Study of Youth Development, 1980.

Myson, Howard. "Teenage Violence and the Telly." *Psychology Today* March 1978: 50–54.

Palmer, Edward L. and Aimée Dorr. *Children and the Faces of Television.* New York: Academic, 1980.

Rubinstein, Eli A. "Television and Behavior." *American Psychologist* July 1983:

820–25.

Singer, Jerome L. and Dorothy G. Singer. *Television, Imagination and Aggression.* Hillside, NJ: Lawrence Erlbaum 1981.

"Warning from Washington." *Time* 17 May 1982: 77.

Winn, Marie. *The Plug-In Drug.* New York: Viking, 1977. 65–74.

APPENDIX · Tips for Reading Expository Prose

Many of the difficulties that students encounter in college courses are directly connected to reading. They find themselves responsible for understanding, analyzing, and writing about a new kind of material — essays and books that focus on ideas rather than on information. Mastering such material requires more than routine reading; it requires careful, active reading, reading that is purposeful.

The first step is to ask yourself what you expect to get out of your reading. The answer should include at least four points:

1. To discover and be able to state in one or two sentences the author's main idea. What is the thesis or principal point of the book or essay?
2. To understand why the author has taken this position. You should be able to state the chief reasons that the author gives to support the thesis.
3. To decide whether the author's approach is primarily rational, emotional, or some combination of the two. If it is rational, is the reasoning sound? If it is emotional, what specific emotions are appealed to?
4. To evaluate how well the author presents and supports the thesis. Is the writing effective? Why or why not?

Next, before you begin on the text itself, take time to examine whatever nontextual material accompanies the article. You should look for the following information:

1. The name of the author. Is he or she living? If not, what are the dates of birth and death? What is the author's nationality? What qualifications does this person have to write on this particular topic. What else has he or she written? Information of this kind may be in a footnote, in the preface, in a special biographical section of the book, or at the beginning or end of an article.
2. Date and place of publication. You should know this in order to put the work in its historical context.
3. Title. Does it seem to have special significance? Does it give you a clue to the content of the book or essay?
4. Titles of subdivisions, sections, or chapters. Can you tell from this what points the author is going to make?

Begin reading the text with the assumption that you will have to read it at least twice, probably three times if the material is difficult. Although the first reading should be more than just a skimming, you can do it fairly quickly. Read the introduction carefully to get an idea of the author's purpose; then read through the rest of the essay or chapter without stopping to underline or make notes. As you read, note key words that recur frequently because they will give you a clue to the author's chief concern. Pay special attention to italicized words or phrases, noting if possible why they have been stressed. Carefully read the concluding paragraph or section because it is here that the author will probably pull together the main points.

If you find that your mind is wandering as you read and that you are covering large sections without really absorbing the content, make yourself stop and go back to the point where your attention began to wander. Sometimes you may have to take a break, get up and move around for a few minutes, before you go back to refocus on the task at hand. And if on this first reading you encounter words you don't know, stop and look them up. This is particularly important when you are reading expository material, for although you may be able to skip over unfamiliar words in fiction and still grasp the meaning, when you read nonfiction the very word you failed to look up may be essential to understanding the essay.

After reading the whole essay over once, you should have a reasonably good grasp of the author's main idea, but you are probably not prepared either to write on the essay or to discuss it intelligently. In order to do that you need to reread the material slowly and actively with a pencil or highlighter in your hand. I prefer a pencil because I can use it to make notes as I go along: I also use a six-inch plastic ruler as a pacer and an aid to underlining.

Begin your second reading with the conscious intention of stopping at frequent intervals in order to absorb the material and make notes on what you have read. You should time your pauses according to the difficulty of the material. If it is clearly written and deals with relatively simple ideas, you may be able to read several paragraphs or even a whole section at once; if, however, the ideas are complex or totally unfamiliar and the writing rather abstract, you will probably need to stop after each paragraph.

As you are reading, ask yourself these questions: What is the main assertion in this section? What are the key words? Which sentences in the material are primary and which sentences are secondary in the sense that they restate, expand, illustrate, or support the main idea? In all expository writing, much of the material is illustrative or explanatory, and it is essential that you learn to distinguish between the main statements and elaborations on them. Fortunately, authors often give you useful clues that help you to spot important sentences or passages. Watch for signal words and phrases such as *It is essential, An important point, The primary reason, Significantly;* watch for definitions and for words that announce conclusions: *Consequently, Therefore, As a result, Thus,* and *We must conclude;* also look for words signaling order: *first, second,* and *finally.*

When you have finished a unit of the reading, stop and force yourself to summarize what you have just read. If you cannot do it or are confused about the author's meaning, go back and reread; then try again. As tedious as this method may seem, this *immediate recall,* as it is labeled by educators, is probably the most important step in your reading. Experiments have shown that most forgetting takes place immediately after one learns something; thus, in the long run you will save yourself time and retain far more of what you read if you reinforce your learning by stopping to summarize as you go along. Moreover, as writers develop a thesis, they build on and refer back to concepts they have set forth earlier. If you have not grasped those concepts, you will have to go back and reread in order to understand the whole. So make it a rule to understand every paragraph and section as you read.

When you are sure you understand a unit of the material, *and only then,* stop to underline or mark and take notes. If you stop to underline before you have fully grasped the key points in a section, you may find that you have emphasized the wrong things, and the work will have to be done again. Waiting to underline until you are sure you know what is important will insure your marking your book in a way that will be instantly useful to you when you want to review for a paper or exam. Underline thoughtfully but sparingly, marking only crucial passages. If you find that you are underlining half the sentences on a page, you are probably not reading as carefully as you should. Occasionally, of course, an entire paragraph or passage contains essential material. In that case, draw a line down the margin and star the section.

Writing notes and capsule summaries in the margins of your book is another major aid to comprehension and review. Sometimes a note may be just a reminder about the contents of a section: for example, if you are reading an essay on existentialism, you might jot down "despair," "anguish," and "forlornness" in the margins beside the sections dealing with those concepts. Such notes would help you remember the author's main points. More extensive notes that sum up content are an even greater help for both immediate retention and future review. For instance, you might expand your note on existentialism by writing "anguish; uncertainty and distress about decisions and their consequences." Or you might sum up key ideas in an essay by S. I. Hayakawa with notes like these: "hasty judgments block thinking"; "need to be aware of basis of our inferences." *Studying* a book or essay almost necessarily involves making these kinds of marginal notes. Ask your teacher to show you the teaching copy of the text you are using, and you will find a book that is underlined and annotated. From long experience your teacher has learned that the quickest and surest way to comprehend an essay thoroughly is to read it slowly, actively, and with a pencil in hand.

When you have finished this step-by-step reading of an essay, you should then go back and view the material as a whole. Think about what you have read and reflect on it. What have you learned? Was it worth reading? Why do you think so? Do you agree or disagree with the author? Why? Finally, ask yourself the questions that you started out with. By now you should be able to answer them clearly and make a thoughtful, supported criticism of what you have read.

The initial reaction of a student who has never done this kind of reading is nearly always, "But it's so slow! I'll never get through all I have to read if I go at it this way." Well, it is slow; there is no denying that. It is also, however, remarkably efficient. When you have prepared a reading assignment in this way, you have learned it thoroughly. You are ready for class discussion, a quiz, or writing a paper. If you need to review the material for a major examination, you can do so quickly by rereading underlined portions and marginal notes. In the long run the process takes less time and produces far better results than the kind of passive reading and rereading that many students depend on.

Sample Passages of Annotated Reading

1. The object of this essay is to assert one very simple principle, as entitled to govern absolutely the dealings of society with the individual in the way of compulsion and control, whether the means used be physical force in the form of legal penalties, or the moral coercion of public opinion. That principle is, that the sole end for which mankind are warranted, individually or collectively, in interfering with the liberty of action of any of their number, is self-protection. That the only purpose for which power can be rightfully exercised over any member of a civilized community, against his will, is to prevent harm to others. His own good, either physical or moral, is not a sufficient warrant. He cannot rightfully be compelled to do or forbear because it will be better for him to do so, because it will make him happier, because, in the opinions of others, to do so would be wise, or even right. These are good reasons for remonstrating with him, or reasoning with him, or persuading him, or entreat-

Marginal annotations:

purpose: to state rule of way society should deal with individual

* Assertion: only reason soc. can interfere with liberty is self-protection

expansion can't interfere for his own good

ing him, but not compelling him, or visiting him with any evil in case he do otherwise. To justify that, the conduct from which it is desired to deter him, must be calculated to produce evil to some one else. The only part of the conduct of any one, for which he is amenable to society, is that which concerns others. In the part which merely concerns himself, his independence is, of right, absolute. Over himself, over his own body and mind, the individual is sovereign.

only conduct soc. should control is what hurts others

It is, perhaps, hardly necessary to say that this doctrine is meant to apply only to human beings in the maturity of their faculties. We are not speaking of children, or of young persons below the age which the law may fix as that of manhood or womanhood. Those who are still in a state to require being taken care of by others, must be protected against their own actions as well as against external injury. For the same reason, we may leave out of consideration those backward states of society in which the race itself may be considered as in its nonage. The early difficulties in the way of spontaneous progress are so great, that there is seldom any choice of means for overcoming them; and a ruler full of the spirit of improvement is warranted in the use of any expedients that will attain an end, perhaps otherwise unattainable. Despotism is a legitimate mode of government in dealing with barbarians, provided the end be their improvement, and the means justified by actually effecting that end. Liberty, as a principle, has no application to any state of things anterior to the time when mankind have become capable of being improved by free and equal discussion. Until then, there is nothing for them but implicit obedience to an Akbar or a Charlemagne, if they are so fortunate as to find one. But as soon as mankind have attained the capacity of being guided to their own improvement by conviction or persuasion (a period long since reached in all nations with whom we need here concern ourselves), compulsion, either in the direct form or in that of pains and penalties for noncompliance, is no longer admissible as a means to their own good, and justifiable only for the security of others.[1]

rule applies only to mature people, not children

not savages or the uncivilized

despotism OK for barbarians

when people are rational and civilized

compulsion not legit except to protect others

2. The United States was born in the country and has moved to the city. From the beginning its political values and ideas were of necessity shaped by country life. The early American politician, the country editor, who wished to address himself to the common man, had to draw upon a rhetoric that would touch the tillers of the soil; and even the

U.S. political values shaped by country life

[1]John Stuart Mill, *On Liberty* (Indianapolis: Bobbs, 1956) 17–18.

spokesman of city people knew that his audience had been in very large part reared upon the farm. But what the articulate people who talked and wrote about farmers and farming — the preachers, poets, philosophers, writers, and statesmen — liked about American farming was not, in every respect, what the typical working farmer liked. For the articulate people were drawn irresistibly to the noncommercial, nonpecuniary, self-sufficient aspect of American farm life. To them it was an ideal. Writers like Thomas Jefferson and Hector St. Jean de Crèvecoeur admired the yeoman farmer not for his capacity to exploit opportunities and make money but for his honest industry, his independence, his frank spirit of equality, his ability to produce and enjoy a simple abundance. The farmer himself, in most cases, was in fact inspired to make money, and such self-sufficiency as he actually had was usually forced upon him by a lack of transportation or markets, or by the necessity to save cash to expand his operations. For while early American society was an agrarian society, it was fast becoming more commercial, and commercial goals made their way among its agricultural classes almost as rapidly as elsewhere. The more commercial this society became, however, the more reason it found to cling in imagination to the noncommercial agrarian values. The more farming as a self-sufficient way of life was abandoned for farming as a business, the more merit men found in what was being left behind. And the more rapidly the farmers' sons moved into the towns, the more nostalgic the whole culture became about its rural past. The American mind was raised upon a sentimental attachment to rural living and upon a series of notions about rural people and rural life that I have chosen to designate as the agrarian myth. The agrarian myth represents a kind of homage that Americans have paid to the fancied innocence of their origins.

Like any complex of ideas, the agrarian myth cannot be defined in a phrase, but its component themes form a clear pattern. Its hero was the yeoman farmer, its central conception the notion that he is the ideal man and the ideal citizen. Unstinted praise of the special virtues of the farmer and the special values of rural life was coupled with the assertion that agriculture, as a calling uniquely productive and uniquely important to society, had a special right to the concern and protection of government. The yeoman, who owned a small farm and worked it with the aid of his family, was the incarnation of the simple, honest, independent, healthy, happy human being. Because he lived in close communion with beneficent nature, his life was believed to have a wholesomeness and integrity impossible for the depraved populations of cities. His well-being was not merely physical, it was moral; it was not merely personal, it was the central source of civic virtue; it was not merely secular but religious, for God had made the land and called man to cultivate it.

4. yeoman best citizen

agrarian myth came from upper class

strong in U.S. late 18th century

Since the yeoman was believed to be both happy and honest, and since he had a secure propertied stake in society in the form of his own land, he was held to be the best and most reliable sort of citizen. To this conviction Thomas Jefferson appealed when he wrote: "The small land holders are the most precious part of a state."

In origin the agrarian myth was not a popular but a literary idea, a preoccupation of the upper classes, of those who enjoyed a classical education, read pastoral poetry, experimented with breeding stock, and owned plantations or country estates. It was clearly formulated and almost universally accepted in America during the last half of the eighteenth century. As it took shape both in Europe and America, its promulgators drew heavily upon the authority and the rhetoric of classical writers — Hesiod, Xenophon, Cato, Cicero, Virgil, Horace, and others — whose works were the staples of a good education. A learned agricultural gentry, coming into conflict with the industrial classes, welcomed the moral strength that a rich classical ancestry brought to the praise of husbandry. In France the Physiocrats preached that agriculture is the only true source of wealth. In England the rural entrepreneurs, already interested in breeding and agricultural improvements, found the praise of husbandry congenial.[2]

[2]Richard Hofstadter, "The Yeoman and the Myth," *The Age of Reform*, pp. 23–25. Copyright © 1955 by Richard Hofstadter. Reprinted by permission of Alfred A. Knopf, Inc.

APPENDIX · Journals

Many writers, both amateur and professional, find that maintaining a journal helps them to get started writing and keeps them in the habit of writing. Spending twenty or thirty minutes a day writing down impressions or reflections can stimulate a writer's mind and help him or her to discover connections or insights that might very well not surface at all without the act of writing to trigger them. For many professional writers who must write consistently, having a journal seems to help to keep the creative juices flowing.

What do you write in a journal? Anything and everything. It's more than a diary but much less than an essay. Writers use journals to record their impressions of what goes on around them, to respond to new ideas they may read or hear about, to reflect on an experience they have or an unusual occurrence they witness. They use them to capture images or conversations or to philosophize. Many writers use their journals as "commonplace books" in which they record quotations and ideas or jot down random thoughts or analogies that they think may prove useful when they want to write. The journal becomes a storehouse for material they may want to use in their work.

Keeping a journal also has another major bonus for you as a student: it keeps you writing under low-risk conditions. You can develop an idea without worrying about structure or punctuation. Under such circumstances you can enjoy writing for its own sake, be amazed at what you find in your own experiences to write about, and have a good time experimenting with different kinds of writing. Most important, you can practice your writing and play with ideas. A journal provides an opportunity for freewriting or whimsy that may not fit anywhere in the regular structure of a class.

Journals can also serve as an important tool for learning and understanding. If you keep a journal in your history course and write down your impressions of a lecture or of a book you read, you will find that the act of writing helps you to absorb the material. If you keep a journal in a literature course and write down your responses to an author's ideas and to the characters in a novel, or your impressions of an author's style, you will find that you understand the book better and can enjoy it more. You'll also have valuable resource material if you need to write a paper on the book.

Writing teachers use journals in their classes in a variety of ways. They may ask students to respond to quotations or comment on the day's assignments, to reflect on their own writing processes, to comment on an issue of current interest, or to ask questions that they might not want to ask in class. Some instructors ask students to turn in their journals to be read and responded to but not graded. Such an exchange can help students and teachers get to know each other better and discuss topics of particular interest. Sometimes teachers collect journals only occasionally and don't comment on them. Sometimes they consider them students' private records and don't look at them at all, feeling that they have served their purpose by getting students to write for themselves. However they are handled, journals can be a good way to work expressive, unstructured writing into a composition class.

· A Glossary of Usage

accept — except

Accept means "receive" or "agree to."
Except as a preposition means "excluding"; as a verb it means "omit" or "make an exception."

Examples:
They *accept* the conditions of the treaty.
Everyone came *except* John.
The registrar *excepts* handicapped students from the schedule.

access — excess

Access means "admission to" or "approach."
Excess means "too much" or "more than is necessary."

Examples:
He has *access* to the building.
The accident happened on the *access* road.
She smokes to *excess*.
There will be an *excess* profits tax.

affect — effect

Affect is a verb meaning "change" or "influence."
Effect may be a verb meaning "bring about," but in most writing is used as a noun meaning "result."

Examples:
Changes in the weather *affect* his mood.
The black lights produced a startling *effect*.

aggravate

In formal usage *aggravate* means "to make worse" or "intensify." Informally it is used as a synonym for "annoy" or "exasperate."

Formal:
His insolence *aggravated* an already difficult situation.

Informal:
George's habits *aggravate* me.

all right — alright

All right is the preferable spelling for this phrase indicating agreement. Many dictionaries now give alright as acceptable, but your audience might not agree. It is best to remember that *all right* takes the same form as "all wrong."

Example:
Mary is *all right* now.

allusion — illusion

The similarity in sound between these two words sometimes confuses students. *Allusion* means "reference"; *illusion* means "misconception" or "misleading image."

Examples:
The author's *allusion* to Prometheus was confusing.
He is under the *illusion* that she loves him.

a lot — alot

A lot is a colloquialism that is acceptable in informal writing, but it must be written as two words. *Much, many,* or another modifier expressing quantity is preferable in more formal writing.

Formal:
He has *many* friends.

Informal:
She went to *a lot* of trouble to arrange the party.

already — all ready

Already means "prior to a certain time"; *all ready* means "prepared."

Examples:
John was *already* in bed.
The train had *already* left.
The car is *all ready* to go.

among — between

See **between.**

amount — number

Amount generally refers to a bulk quantity or to a mass; *number* refers to several units. *Number* as a subject takes a singular verb.

Examples:
The *number* is rising steadily.
He has a large *number* of friends.
He has a large *amount* of money.

as — like

See **like — as.**

as — that

The use of *as* as a substitute for *that* in introducing a clause is too colloquial for most writing.

Colloquial:
I don't know *as* I will go.

Acceptable:
I don't know *that* I will go.

bad — badly
Bad is an adjective that modifies nouns or acts as a complement to linking verbs. *Badly* is an adverb used to modify verbs or adjectives. People who are trying too hard to speak elegantly frequently make the mistake of completing a linking verb such as *feels* or *looks* with badly.

Correct:
Jim feels *bad* about the accident.
George looks *bad* since his illness.
The team played *badly* tonight.

Incorrect:
Joan looks *badly* without make-up.
I feel *badly* about not going.

between — among

Purists use *between* when referring to two persons or objects, *among* when referring to more than two. The distinction is a comparatively minor one.

Examples:
The quarrel was *between* Joe and me.
The money was distributed *among* the members of the team.

can — may

Traditional grammarians specify that *can* should be used only to indicate capability and *may* to indicate permission. The distinction is rapidly disappearing, and in all but the most formal writing, the terms may be used interchangeably.

Examples:
John *can* lift a 150-pound weight.
You *may* take the book home with you.

center around — center on

Center around is an illogical expression. *Center on* is preferable.

Illogical:
The talk *centered around* the war.

Preferable:
The talk *centered on* the war.

cite — site — sight

Students frequently confuse these three words. *Cite* is a verb meaning "refer to," *site* is a noun meaning "location" or "place," and *sight* as a noun means "view" or "spectacle."

Examples:
He will *cite* two other occasions on which the play had been used.
Fred showed them the *site* of the new building.
The children had never seen such a wonderful *sight*.

collective noun

A collective noun refers to a group of individuals or things considered as a single entity, for example, *team, platoon, congregation, jury.* It may take a singular or plural verb according to the context of the sentence.

Examples:
The *team* is going to win.
The *jury* were divided in their opinion.

complement — compliment

Complement as a verb means "complete" or "fit with"; as a noun it means a "word or phrase that completes."
Compliment as a verb means "speak favorably of"; as a noun it means "favorable remark."

Examples:
That dress *complements* her dark hair.
Linking verbs must be followed by a *complement*.
He *complimented* them on their foresight.
Jack is always ready with a *compliment*.

could of

An incorrect form of *could have.*

Correct:
We *could have* taken the bus.

Incorrect:
We *could of* taken the bus.

data, media, criteria, phenomena

These are plural forms of the singular nouns *datum, medium, criterion,* and *phenomenon* and take plural verb forms. Except in formal usage, however, a singular verb is acceptable with *data.*

Acceptable:
The *data are* inaccurate.
The *data is* reliable.

Correct:
The mass *media are* influential in our culture.
His *criteria are* clearly stated.
These *phenomena indicate* the presence of oxygen.

different from — different than

The preferred usage is "different *from,*" but most dictionaries give either form as acceptable.

double negative

Regardless of its acceptance in other languages, the construction is considered substandard in English. *Hardly* and *scarcely* are negative words and should not be used with other negatives.

Unacceptable:
He *didn't* do *nothing* wrong.
Jane *can't hardly* pass English.

Correct:
He *did nothing* wrong.
Jane *can hardly* pass English.

due to

Although widely used, this phrase is usually avoided by careful writers. *Because of* is preferable.

Acceptable:
Due to icy roads, she could not come.

Preferable:
She was unable to come *because* of icy roads.

effect

See **affect — effect.**

etc.

Etc. is a contraction of the Latin phrase *et cetera,* meaning "and other things." Although it is acceptable in informal speech, too often it is a lazy substitute for writing out a full list. Because many teachers find the expression unacceptable, students would do well to avoid it.

except

See **accept — except.**

fact

Use *fact* only to refer to that which can be tested and verified. *The fact that* is an overworked and often inaccurate phrase that should be avoided whenever possible. When you do use it, be sure that it refers to something that is indisputably true, not a matter of opinion.

Incorrect:
The *fact* that busing to integrate schools is a failure was mentioned again and again.

Acceptable:
The *fact* that Germany was defeated at Stalingrad changed the course of the war.

Preferable:
Germany's defeat at Stalingrad changed the course of the war.

fewer — less

Fewer should be used when one is referring to individual units, *less* when one is referring to a smaller amount of a substance or quality. The distinction is a comparatively minor one.

Examples:
They had *fewer* applicants this year.
He had *less* money than he realized.
A Ford costs *less* than a Buick.

first — firstly; second — secondly

The *-ly* form for numerals is awkward and unnecessary. The straight form is preferable.

Awkward:
Firstly, I should say thank you to my colleagues.

Preferable:
First, I should thank my colleagues.

formally — formerly

Formally means "in a proper manner"; *formerly* means "at a previous time."

Examples:
We have not been *formally* introduced.
He *formerly* played football for Alabama.

infer — imply

Although one major dictionary suggests that these words may be used interchangeably, the practice is not generally accepted. *Infer* means "conclude from the evidence," and *imply* means "suggest" or "hint." In college writing you should observe the distinction.

Examples:
He *inferred* from conversation that Jones was a Democrat.
The article *implied* that the students were responsible.

irregardless

An incorrect form of *regardless*; not acceptable in standard English.

its — it's

Confusion of these two forms causes one of the most common student writing errors. *Its* (in spite of its not having an apostrophe) is a possessive pronoun; *it's* is a contraction of *it is.*

Examples:
The company increased *its* profits.
It's time that something was done.

lay — lie

Lay is a transitive verb that must take an object; it means "place" or "put." Its principal parts are *lay, laid, laid.*
Lie is an intransitive verb that means "recline"; its principal parts are *lie, lay, lain.*

Correct:
The dog *lay* peacefully on the floor.
She *laid* the pattern on the material.

Incorrect:
I *lay* the book on the table yesterday.
He *laid* on the ground for an hour.

like — as

The confusion of these words causes great distress to purists. In formal English *like* should be used only as a preposition, not as a conjunction to introduce a clause. *As, as if,* or *as though* should be used before clauses. The distinction is disappearing, but your teacher may want you to observe it.

Informal:
It looks *like* there will be trouble.

Formal:
It looks *as if* there will be trouble.

Correct:
He looks *like* an athlete.
Mary talks *like* her mother.

loose — lose

Confusion between these terms causes one of students' most common spelling errors. *Loose,* although it can be used as a verb to mean "release" or "make loose," is most often an adjective meaning "unconfined." *Lose* is a verb only.

Examples:
The bindings were too *loose.*
John may *lose* his scholarship.

media

Media is a plural noun and takes a plural verb; see **data.**

myself

Myself should not be used as a substitute for *I* or *me.* Its proper uses are (1) as a reflexive pronoun and (2) as an intensive pronoun.

Correct:
I build it *myself.*
I cut *myself* badly.

Incorrect:
Mary and *myself* are going to do it.
He gave instructions to Jim and *myself.*

one

An impersonal pronoun used more often in formal than informal writing. In strictly formal writing it must be used consistently and not mixed with *his* or *hers.*

Formal:
One has the feeling that *one* is helpless.

Informal:
One has the feeling that *he* is helpless.

only

An adverb or adjective meaning "solely" or "exclusively." It should always come next to the word it modifies.

Correct:
He has *only* two more years of college.
John comes *only* in the mornings.

Incorrect:
He *only* has two more years of college.
John *only* comes in the mornings.

prepositions

There is nothing inherently incorrect about putting a preposition at the end of a sentence if the context seems to call for it. "These were the only figures he had to work *with*" is a perfectly good sentence. So is "There is the man you need to speak *to.*"

principal — principle

These two quite different words are often confused. *Principal* may be a noun or an adjective. As a noun it means "chief administrative officer of a school," "leading character," or "sum of money." As an adjective it means "first" or "main."

Examples:
Jones is the *principal* of the high school.
Fonteyn was the *principal* in Swan Lake.
He invested the *principal.*
Clark is the *principal* suspect in the case.

Principle is a noun only; it means "a rule" or "theory."

Examples:
We must act according to our *principles.*
The *principle* of economy should come first.

reason is because — reason is that

The reason is because is an awkward and redundant construction. *The reason is that* is preferable.

Awkward:
The *reason* John didn't come *was because* his car wouldn't start.

Preferable:
The *reason* John didn't come *was that* his car wouldn't start.

shall — will

Trying to make a distinction between these forms is no longer realistic or useful. They may be used interchangeably in both formal and informal writing.

should of

An incorrect form of *should have*.

Correct:
We *should have* gone yesterday.

Incorrect:
We *should of* gone yesterday.

supposed to — used to

See **used to.**

sure — certainly

Sure should be used to express certainty or assurance.

Example:
I am *sure* that his report is accurate.

Sure should not be used in formal or informal writing to replace *certainly.*

Colloquial:
Alabama *sure* has a great team.

Informal:
Alabama *certainly* has a great team.

their — there — they're

Students sometimes fail to distinguish among these homonyms.
Their is a possessive pronoun.

Tom and Jane will drive *their* own car.

There is a demonstrative pronoun.

There is the woman we saw yesterday.
Tell me when we get *there*.

They're is a contraction of *they are*.

They're scheduled to arrive at noon.

to — too — two

This is another set of homonyms that is often confused.

To is a preposition.

We are going *to* Chicago tomorrow.

Too means "also" or "in addition."

Jane will be there *too*.

Two is a numeral.

There are *two* mistakes on that page.

unique

Unique, like perfect, describes a condition that is absolute. Modifiers should not be used with it.

Correct:
Her problem is *unique*.

Incorrect:
Her problem is *rather unique*.
This dress is *more unique*.

used to — supposed to

Because the final *d* of these verbs disappears when they are pronounced, students sometimes forget to write the complete form.

Correct:
He is *used* to starting on time.
We *used* to get there early.
This is *supposed to* be an open meeting.

Incorrect:
We *use* to get there early.
John is *suppose* to serve as president.

where — that

The colloquial construction *I saw where* or *I read where* should not be used in writing, formal or informal.

Colloquial:
I heard *where* the chairperson died.

Acceptable:
I heard *that* the chairperson died.
I read *that* the building had burned.

who — whom

Who is the nominative pronoun and should be used when the noun it
is replacing would be acting as the subject of a sentence or clause.

Example:
This is the man *who* came with Joe.

Whom is the objective form and should be used when the noun it replaces would be an object.

Example:
There is the man *whom* we saw Friday.

In practice, *who* is generally acceptable in informal writing except when
it occurs directly after a preposition.

Acceptable:
There is the man *who* I need to see.
Jones is the man to *whom* I will write.

will — shall

See **shall — will.**

Avoid attaching *-wise* to a word as a suffix.

Jargon:
Moneywise she is having troubles.
Gradewise Joan is doing well.

Correct:
She is having money troubles.
Joan gets good grades.

would of — would have

Would of is an incorrect form of *would have.*

Correct:
We *would have* come if we had known.

Incorrect:
We *would of* come if we had known.

Would have should not be used to replace *had*.

Correct:
If I *had* known, I would have told you.

Incorrect:
If I *would have* known, I would have told you.

HANDBOOK OF GRAMMAR AND USAGE

SS • Sentence Structure

SS1   Sentence Fragments

> Get rid of fragments in your writing by combining them with other sentences or by revising them into complete sentences.

Sentence fragments — sometimes called broken sentences — are groups of words that do not include enough of the elements of a sentence to express an idea adequately. Readers in business and the professions usually notice sentence fragments and don't approve of them. That's not surprising because fragments can leave the reader in suspense, wondering what is missing; they can frustrate the reader by not giving him or her enough information to grasp the idea; or they can simply irritate a reader because they seem choppy and unfinished. Almost all sentence fragments fall into one of these categories: (1) sentence fragments from verbals, (2) sentence fragments from dependent clauses, and (3) sentence fragments from disconnected phrases and clauses.

Sentence Fragments from Verbals

The three kinds of verbals are

- **Infinitives**   To + the simple verb: *to swim, to drive, to write*
- **Participles**   Modifiers made from verbs: *sailing* ships, *running* horses, *condemned* prisoners, *recognized* experts
- **Gerunds**   Nouns made from verbs: *running* the election, *seeing* people off at the airport, *preparing* a meal

Examples

Sentence fragments from verbals

Faulty   Young people need to be on their own. To show their parents that they can manage. ("To show" is an infinitive and cannot be the verb of the second part.)

Corrected   Young people need to be on their own to show their parents that they can manage.

Faulty   To eliminate corruption in government. That is the claim of almost every political candidate. ("To eliminate corruption in government" is a noun clause that is acting as a subject.)

Corrected   To eliminate corruption in government is the claim of almost every political candidate.

Faulty   They were the most tragic kind of veteran. Prisoners released after the war. ("released after the war" is a phrase that modifies "prisoners," not the predicate of the sentence.)

Corrected   Prisoners released after the war were the most tragic kind of veteran.

Faulty   The governor would not sign the pardon. Considering the man a menace to society. ("Considering the man a menace to society" is a gerund phrase that modifies "governor.")

Corrected   Considering the man a menace to society, the governor would not sign the pardon.

If you remember two rules, you can virtually eliminate verbal sentence fragments from your writing.

- First, *an infinitive can never act as the main verb in a sentence.*
- Second, *an -ing verb form can never act as the verb for a sentence unless it has an auxiliary verb with it.* (For example, "is being," "was running," "were swimming.")

Sentence Fragments from Dependent Clauses

Writers sometimes create sentence fragments from dependent clauses because they don't realize that certain words usually signal dependent, subordinate, or relative clauses. The most common of these words are

- For dependent clauses, *if, although, while, even, when, in spite of,* and *since.*
- For subordinate clauses, *that, thus, therefore, so, as, for,* and sometimes *because.*
- For relative clauses, *who, which, what, where,* and sometimes *that.*

If you have frequent problems with sentence fragments, when you read over your draft watch for these words to see that you haven't begun a fragment with one of them.

Examples

Sentence fragments from dependent clauses

Faulty   Divorce usually upsets children. Although they are more adaptable than their parents sometimes believe. (This is a dependent clause that should be attached to the main part of the sentence.)

Corrected   Although children are more adaptable than parents sometimes believe, divorce usually upsets them.

Faulty   People often assume that rock-and-roll musicians are rich. As they wear such lavish costumes. ("As" signals that even though the fragment has a subject and verb, it depends on another idea for its meaning.)

Corrected   People often assume that as they wear such lavish costumes, rock-and-roll musicians are rich.

Faulty   That scholarship, which would allow me to attend Yale Divinity School, the school of my choice. (Everything that comes after "scholarship" modifies "That scholarship," so the sentence has no verb.

Corrected   That scholarship would allow me to attend Yale Divinity School, the school of my choice.

Examples

Sentence fragments from disconnected phrases

Faulty   God's blessing. That is what leaders who want to make war always claim. ("God's blessing" is simply a noun phrase. It cannot act as a sentence.)

Corrected   Leaders who want to make war always claim they have God's blessing.

Faulty   The contestants did not seem to realize how they looked. Foolish and greedy. ("Foolish and greedy" is a modifying phrase that can't act as a whole sentence.)

Corrected   The contestants did not seem to realize that they looked foolish and greedy.

Faulty   They weren't aware of it at first. The ominous silence, more threatening than any noise. (Since "The ominous silence, more threatening than any noise" isn't attached to anything, the reader at first mistakes it for the beginning of another sentence.)

Corrected   At first, they weren't aware of the ominous silence, more threatening than any noise.

Exercise • **Rewrite the sentences to eliminate sentence fragments.**

Because I had been bored too many times in the past by conversations among parents who seemed to have little else to talk about except their children's latest accomplishments, difficulties, and illnesses. I vowed never to become a parent. Or to become the type of parent who kept quiet about my children and instead conversed

with my colleagues on a loftier plane, about politics, philosophy or literature. That was before I actually became a parent. Now occasionally catching myself in the act of describing in minute detail my daughter's progress in learning to walk or showing pictures of her to relative strangers. At such times I remember how I once despised people who did these sorts of things. The kind of person I myself seem to have become. No longer bored by those child-centered conversations and even occasionally initiating them myself. Or casually speaking to another parent with a baby in the park or shopping center and within minutes finding myself involved in a fascinating conversation about teething remedies and introducing new foods into a baby's diet. Another symptom of my transformation being my changed reading habits. Now often browsing through *Parents* magazine or *American Baby* and quite familiar with Dr. Spock and some of the other well-known child development specialists. Amazing how a baby can change one's life!

SS2   Run-on Sentences

> Correct run-on sentences by dividing them into two separate sentences or by inserting a conjunction or semicolon between the independent clauses.

Run-on sentences (sometimes called "fused sentences") occur when writers fail to use appropriate punctuation or conjunctions to separate two independent clauses, that is, clauses that could act as sentences by themselves.

Examples

Faulty We got to the stadium on time they hadn't even turned the lights on. (Because there is no mark of separation after "time," the reader runs right into the next main idea.)

Corrected We got to the stadium on time, but they hadn't even turned the lights on.

Faulty Women almost never went to medical school fifty years ago if they wanted to cure people they became nurses. (Since the reader finds no mark after "fifty years ago," at first reading she assumes "if they wanted to cure people" goes with the first sentence.)

Corrected Women almost never went to medical school fifty years ago; if they wanted to cure people, they became nurses.

Rewrite these run-on sentences and punctuate them correctly.

1. Ms. Rhoades didn't know what the world was coming to in her day young people had not dressed so tastelessly, nor played their music so loudly, nor spent all their time in video arcades.

2. As a university librarian she found it most distressing to witness the steady erosion of American values among college students every day it was getting more and more difficult to come onto campus and face the Philistine hordes.

3. She found herself increasingly reluctant to entrust books and journals to students of such obviously questionable moral character there really was no telling what they might do to library materials.

4. One day a group of students came into the special collections reading room and asked to see a number of the star charts for an astronomy project they wore studded leather bands on their wrists and had safety pins through their ear lobes one young man had shaved his head and two of the young women had brilliantly colored hair protruding in spiked ridges along their scalps.

5. As they pored over the maps, taking copious notes and conversing among themselves in serious and subdued tones, Ms. Rhoades hovered about them like an agitated vulture finally she could stand it no longer she whisked the pile of maps from the table and through clenched teeth demanded of the students, "Do your parents know how you look?"

SS3 Comma Splices

> Get rid of a comma splice by replacing the comma between two clauses with a coordinating conjunction or a semicolon, by making one of the clauses a dependent clause, or by separating the sentence into two sentences.

A comma splice occurs when a writer joins two independent clauses with a comma, a mark of punctuation that is too weak to show a clear separation between what in effect are two sentences.

Examples

Faulty Laughter has great value in treating illnesses, Norman Cousins gives actual case studies in his book *The Anatomy of an Illness.*

Corrected Laughter has great value in treating illnesses as Norman Cousins shows with actual case studies in his book *The Anatomy of an Illness.*

Faulty The hotel is ugly and old-fashioned, it is the fashionable place to stay.

Corrected The hotel is ugly and old-fashioned, but it is the fashionable place to stay.

Faulty Congress has refused to face up to the problems of the deficit, the members are afraid to vote for higher taxes.

Corrected Because the members are afraid to vote for higher taxes, Congress has refused to face up to the problems of the deficit.

Faulty The author Richard Rodriguez claims his book *Hunger of Memory* is an honest account of his childhood struggle to come to terms with his ambivalence about his heritage, his critics claim the book demeans that heritage.

Corrected The author Richard Rodriguez claims his book *Hunger of Memory* is an honest account of his childhood struggle to come to terms with his ambivalence about his heritage; his critics claim the book demeans that heritage.

Faulty In spite of equal opportunity legislation, women's economic status hasn't changed that much in ten years, in 1985 they were still earning only 60 percent of what men earn for comparable work in nongovernment jobs.

Corrected In spite of equal opportunity legislation, women's economic status hasn't changed that much in ten years. In 1985 they were still earning only 60 percent of what men earn for comparable work in nongovernment jobs.

Exercise • **Rewrite these sentences to eliminate the comma splices.**

1. More than any other people in continental United States, Texans seem to be state-proud, they consider themselves to be Texans first and Americans second.

2. It is not uncommon for Texans to display their state flag in their own front yards, in fact you are probably more likely to see a Texas flag than Old Glory in such a setting.

3. In Texas you are also apt to see many and varied bumper stickers proclaiming the driver's status as a native Texan, some simply display the word "native" against the background of the Texas flag, and others bear more aggressive slogans, such as "If you ain't from Texas, you ain't nothin'."

4. Another way in which Texans express their pride in their state is by using the Texas motif in their home decorating schemes, bathroom sinks and backyard swimming pools, for instance, are sometimes made in the shape of the Lone Star state.

5. And finally, Texans frequently advertise their home state by their

personal attire, such items as Texas-flag jogging shorts, armadillo T-shirts, and Lone Star belt buckles are popular among native Texans.

SS4   Dangling Modifiers

> Get rid of dangling modifiers by checking to see that the word that the modifying phrase is supposed to modify is in the sentence, and that the modifying phrase stands next to it. If it does not, rearrange the sentence.

Dangling modifiers — that is, modifying phrases that are misleading or amusing because they do not modify the correct element in the sentence — occur because English is a word-order language. In English the meaning of a word or phrase is usually determined by its place in the sentence. When the word or phrase is misplaced, or "dangles," its meaning is easily misunderstood.

Examples

Faulty   When leaving high school, ideas about clothes suddenly change. ("When leaving high school" seems to modify "ideas.")
Corrected   When leaving high school, a young person suddenly changes his or her ideas about clothes.

Faulty   Once over the fence, the adventure seemed considerably less attractive. ("Once over the fence" cannot modify "adventure.")
Corrected   Once they were over the fence, the adventure seemed considerably less attractive. (Changing the modifying phrase to a subordinate clause solves the problem.)

Faulty   The job requires a man like Roosevelt McDougal, lucrative and challenging. (The phrase "lucrative and challenging" automatically attaches itself to the words it follows, creating a misunderstanding.)
Corrected   Lucrative and challenging, the job requires a man like Roosevelt McDougal.

Faulty   The proposed tax reforms will bog down in Congress, being opposed by too many special interests. ("Congress" is not what is being "opposed by too many special interests," but the arrangement of the sentence at first gives that impression.)
Corrected   Being opposed by too many special interests, the proposed tax reforms will bog down in Congress.

Faulty   Having argued all morning, a decision was reached by afternoon. ("Having argued all morning" does not refer to "decision.")

Corrected   Having argued all morning, they reached a decision by afternoon.

Most of the time, you can avoid dangling modifiers in your writing by following two suggestions made earlier in the book (Chapter 5) for improving your writing. First, when you can, use people as the subject of your sentences. If you do, you are much less likely to get the modifier in the wrong place. For instance, one student wrote "When hiring waiters and waitresses, their appearance is a major concern." If the student had used "employer" as the subject of the sentence, almost certainly he would have written something like, "When an employer hires waitresses and waiters, their appearance is a major concern."

Second, avoid using passive verbs when you can because they also frequently lead to dangling modifiers. That is what happened in this sentence: "By forcing students to conform to strict rules, creativity is stifled." If the writer had substituted an active verb, the problem could have been solved like this: "Teachers who force students to conform to strict rules stifle creativity."

Exercise   •   Rewrite the following sentences to eliminate dangling modifiers.

1. Crumpling up page after page and tossing them in a pile in the corner of his study, this single short project was taking forever to type.

2. After spending three and a half days in a vain attempt to type a clean copy of a ten-page report, it was clear to Alan that he would have to invest in a word processor.

3. He simply couldn't bring himself to confront his error-ridden text again, frustrated, hungry, and desperate for a good night's sleep.

4. Longing for the comfort of his own bed, yet realizing the necessity of submitting the report early the next morning, his aching fingers pounded on into the morning.

5. In deciding which type of word processing equipment would best meet his needs, Alan's impoverished circumstances loomed as a major obstacle to this solution to his problem.

6. Nonetheless, after considering long-term finances, buying a home computer would obviously be more efficient than hiring a personal secretary.

7. He finally settled on a Japanese-made model with 356K memory and a printer that would allow him to make his own characters after agonizing over the enormous down payment he would have to make.

8. Having saved for years to buy a new used car, his hard-earned money was hard to part with.

9. Considered hopelessly old-fashioned by his colleagues, they were in for a real surprise when they learned that he had entered the computer age.

10. His bank account showed the price one had to pay to keep up in the age of technology now that it had shrunk to a mere husk of its former self.

SS5   Faulty Parallelism

> Make elements of a sentence that are parallel in function also parallel in form.

When you keep the elements of a sentence parallel you help your readers move easily through the sentence because everything in it fits a pattern. When you break the pattern by inserting a word or phrase that doesn't match the others, you disrupt the sentence and distract your readers' attention. You can also confuse them because they may not be immediately able to understand that portion of the sentence that doesn't fit.

Three important kinds of sentence structure that call for parallel form are (1) elements in a series, (2) elements being compared or contrasted through the use of *either/or* or *not only/but also,* and (3) the elements in a balanced sentence. The elements in a list should also have parallel form. Each of these kinds of parallelism is illustrated in the following examples.

Examples

Elements in a series

Faulty   The Changs were noted for their devotion to duty, their strong sense of family, and also had good business intuition.

Corrected   The Changs were noted for their devotion to duty, their strong sense of family, and their good business intuition.

Faulty   When Maria Martinez started college at the age of thirty, she determined to overcome her anxiety, her shyness, and having no confidence.

Corrected   When Maria Martinez started college at the age of thirty, she determined to overcome her anxiety, her shyness, and her lack of confidence.

Faulty   I have chosen to attend a community college because its program is flexible, varied, and fits my schedule.

Corrected   I have chosen to attend a community college because its program is flexible, varied, and suited to my schedule.

Elements being compared or contrasted

Faulty   Hans will either take the exam or be failed in the course.
Corrected   Hans will either take the exam or fail the course.

Faulty   She loved Julio not because he was daring, but his hair was curly.
Corrected   She loved Julio not because he was daring, but because he had curly hair.

Faulty   You will find that Jenny is not only a superb violinist but is also a talented composer.
Corrected   You will find that Jenny is not only a superb violinist but that she is also a talented composer.

Elements in a balanced sentence

Faulty   For them, the issue is power; for us, we want to be recognized.
Corrected   For them, the issue is power; for us, it is recognition.

Faulty   Almost everyone is in favor of increasing government services; most people don't want to pay more taxes.
Corrected   Almost everyone is in favor of increasing government services; almost no one is in favor of increasing taxes.

Faulty   In order to get to the Coliseum, do this:
Take the crosstown bus at 50th Street.
Transfer to the A train at Greely Square.
Get off at 89th Street and turn west.
Arrows will indicate the entrance.
Corrected   In order to get to the Coliseum, do this:
Take the crosstown bus at 50th Street.
Transfer to the A train at Greely Square.
Get off at 89th Street and turn west.
Follow the arrows to the entrance.

Faulty   Experts on stress say that these events head the list of sources of stress:
Death of a spouse or child
Divorce
Loss of a job
Change of residence
When people are bored
Corrected   Experts on stress say that these events head the list of sources of stress:

Death of a spouse or child
Divorce
Loss of a job
Change of residence
Boredom

Exercise • Rewrite these sentences to make the elements parallel.

1. She decided at last to get rid of the dog because it chewed the living room rug, chased the cats, and the mailman was terrified of it.

2. Unfortunately, most career women really have two jobs: their professional work and still do the housework at home, too.

3. When Peter and Melinda learned that Ben and his family were coming for an extended visit, they didn't know whether they should clean out the guest rooms, or should they write and say they would be out of town for the summer?

4. Being a professional athlete is more financially rewarding than a teaching career.

5. Five weeks after the wedding it was beginning to dawn on her that despite his accumulated wealth and his connections to royalty, her new husband was boring, a slob, and not really very good-looking.

6. She yearned for the halcyon days of her youth and to regain the musculature she had then developed as a roller derby queen.

7. They couldn't have planned a better day for an outing, clear, crisp, and enough breeze to keep the bugs away.

8. At the tender age of seventeen Margaret was forced to admit that she was not a genius, then becoming morose and resigning herself to a career in horticulture.

9. The advantages of the temperate climate were offset by the ever-present swarms of mosquitos, and the roaches were so big they could carry you away.

10. Until Bruce saw Sheila Daly play the lead in *The Bovine Madonna,* he had never appreciated opera and believed it was not a suitable form of entertainment for anyone but the highbrows he had grown to despise.

SS6 Faulty Predication

> Correct faulty predication by making the elements that complete the verb in the sentence match logically with the verb.

The relationship between the verb and other elements of the sentence is called *predication*. When a sentence is constructed in such a way that the relationship between the subject and the verb or verb and complement is confusing or illogical, the error is called *faulty predication*. Errors of this kind fall into three classes: (1) faulty subject/verb combinations, (2) faulty verb/object combinations, and (3) faulty linking verb/complement combinations.

Examples

Faulty subject/verb combinations

Faulty Athletic scholarships promote personal achievement and seek out students of high quality. (Notice that "scholarships" cannot "seek" anything.)

Corrected Athletic scholarships promote personal achievement and attract students of high quality.

Faulty The wishes of the voters approved the Articles of the Constitution but then changed their minds. (Notice that "wishes" can't "approve" or "change.")

Corrected The voters approved the Articles of the Constitution but then changed their minds.

Faulty Her desire to be popular fantasizes about being a big TV star. (Notice that a "desire" cannot "fantasize.")

Corrected Her desire to be popular makes her fantasize about being a big TV star.

Faulty verb/object combinations

Faulty The company disconnected people who hadn't paid their bills. (The "company" doesn't "disconnect people"; it disconnects services.)

Corrected The company disconnected the service of people who hadn't paid their bills.

Faulty Such policies intimidate the applications of minority candidates. ("Applications" can't be "intimidated"; only people can.)

Corrected Such policies intimidate minority candidates who might apply.

Faulty Going to Mexico City frustrates the admiration for an exotic city. (One cannot "frustrate admiration.")

Corrected Going to Mexico City will frustrate the person who admires exotic cities.

Faulty linking verb/complement combinations

Notice here that linking verbs set up equations; that is, they signal that the words on each side of the verb match with each other. When they don't, the result is faulty predication.

Faulty   Hate is never acceptable behavior. ("Hate" is an emotion, not a "behavior.")

Corrected   Hate is never an acceptable emotion.

Faulty   Hungry is an incentive to work harder. ("Hungry" is an adjective and cannot be matched with "incentive," a noun.)

Corrected   Being hungry is an incentive to work harder.

Faulty   Plagiarism is when you use someone else's work without giving that person credit. ("when" is an adverb and cannot be matched with "plagiarism," a noun.)

Corrected   Plagiarism is using someone else's work without giving that person credit.

Exercise   •   **Rewrite these sentences to correct faulty predication.**

1. What Mr. Hodges hated most of all was when his wife would wish the cat good morning before she spoke to him.

2. It had happened again this morning when her disregard for him fed Fluffy her breakfast first, apparently without even considering that he might need some sustenance, too.

3. Finally, Mr. Hodges threatened his wife's affection for the worthless animal by saying he was going to take Fluffy to the pound.

4. His threats gave her pause and eventually decided that perhaps she ought to rearrange her priorities.

5. The first step in her campaign to soothe his offended ego was when she served him his tuna in a silver bowl before she gave Fluffy her milk.

6. This tactic offended his wishes to be treated as a human being.

7. Seeing the cat in Mildred's arms every morning felt as though he were an outsider in his own home.

8. He wanted a marriage where no animals came between husband and wife.

9. A true marriage, according to Mr. Hodges, is when you don't have to wipe cat hairs from your face every time you kiss your wife.

10. If Mildred couldn't learn to empathize with his demands, the cat would have to go.

SS7   Subordination

> Show the correct relationship between ideas in a sentence by incorporating the less important ideas into subordinate clauses.

Using subordinate clauses can help you construct a compact sentence that gives the reader a lot of information and organizes it in a way that quickly shows how its ideas are related. Such clauses usually begin with subordinating conjunctions — for example, *although, since, before, when, until, after, because* — or with relative pronouns — for example, *who, that,* and *which.*

Examples

Faulty   The Smithsonian Institution sponsors fine educational tours, and many of its members know nothing about them.

Corrected   Although the Smithsonian Institution sponsors fine educational tours, many of its members know nothing about them.

Faulty   Henry Ford was a man with a strong social conscience. Today the Ford Foundation gives money to improve education in a wide variety of fields.

Corrected   Because Henry Ford was a man with a strong social conscience, today the Ford Foundation gives money to improve education in a wide variety of fields.

Faulty   Beautiful women are not always popular. Sometimes men feel intimidated by them and often they assume women cannot be both beautiful and intelligent. Nancy Baker says this in her book *The Beauty Trap.*

Corrected   As Nancy Baker points out in her book *The Beauty Trap,* beautiful women are not always popular because men may feel intimidated by them or may assume they cannot be both beautiful and intelligent.

Faulty   She had lived in Texas a long time and she knew what the weather was like in July and she advised anyone who wanted to exercise to get up early in the morning.

Corrected   Because she had lived in Texas a long time and knew what the weather was like in July, she advised anyone who wanted to exercise to get up early in the morning.

Faulty   Abdul Fahoud took first place in the departmental poetry contest. He was a poet in his own country and he started to write in English only three years ago.

Corrected   Abdul Fahoud, who was a poet in his own country, took first place in the departmental poetry contest although he started to write in English only three years ago.

Notice that a writer can shift the emphasis in a sentence by rearranging the subordinate clauses. For example, which is the more positive statement in each of these pairs?

A-1   Although all musicians who aspire to be concert artists must practice several hours a day, only a few will ever really succeed.

A-2 Although only a few musicians who aspire to be concert artists will ever really succeed, all of them must practice several hours every day.

B-1 Some hint of corruption has touched almost every bureau head in that state even though the governor herself is above suspicion.

B-2 The governor herself is above suspicion although some hint of corruption has touched almost every bureau head in that state.

C-1 Hayakawa's "ladder of abstraction" illustrates a key concept in linguistics even though it first appeared in his books more than thirty years ago.

C-2 Even though Hayakawa's "ladder of abstraction" illustrates a key concept in linguistics, it has been more than thirty years since it first appeared in his books.

Exercise • Rewrite these sentences to subordinate one or more of the elements in a way that clarifies their relationship.

1. A university education used to be a privilege reserved for young men who were very wealthy, and now university students are likely to be from a wide range of social backgrounds and ethnic groups.

2. English speakers usually find Dutch an easier language to learn than German. English is not a highly inflected language and neither is Dutch.

3. For years, Faustina had admired Dr. Moses from afar. Finally she became personally acquainted with him and he sank rapidly in her esteem.

4. He witnessed the maid's furtive glance at the butler. As a result his mood shifted from lethargy to ire.

5. As a girl she had enjoyed the prospect of a bright future. As the years passed she became disillusioned.

Exercise • Rewrite the following sentences and change the subordination in a way that will change the emphasis.

1. Although the students in Mr. Sibler's class learned very little about geometry, they learned a great deal about life.

2. Even though the damage estimates were not yet complete, Mr. DeVries feared that his involvement in the barroom brawl might spell financial ruin for him.

3. I shall never respect a man who sports a toupee, although I can't help feeling attracted to you.

4. He is usually slow to anger, even though he is now succumbing to a fit of pique.

5. Although Reginald's parents insist that he is not spoiled, he has been petulant and whiny every time I've invited him for tea.

SS8   Comparisons

> 1. Check to see that comparisons in your sentences are unambiguous and logical and that the terms being compared are similar. Use *like* and *as* appropriately in comparisons.

Examples

Ambiguous comparisons

Ambiguous   Carlos likes opera better than Juanita.
Clear   Carlos likes opera better than Juanita does.

Ambiguous   Hepzibah forgot her lines more quickly than her husband.
Clear   Hepzibah forgot her lines more quickly than her husband did.

Illogical comparisons

Illogical   She earned higher commissions than any other man in the company.
Logical   She earned higher commissions than any man in the company.

Illogical   I trust my own sense of direction more than anyone else on the trip.
Logical   I trust my own sense of direction more than that of anyone else on the trip.

Comparison of similar terms

Faulty   Kim Sun-ha found American bicycles more expensive than the British. ("Bicycles" and "the British" are not comparable.)
Corrected   Kim Sun-ha found American bicycles more expensive than British bicycles.

Faulty   I like the rituals of Christmas better than the Fourth of July. ("Rituals" and "the Fourth of July" are not comparable.)
Corrected   I like the rituals of Christmas better than those of the Fourth of July.

Comparisons with *like* and *as*

The guidelines for standard English usage recommend that you use *like* when you are introducing a comparison with a phrase — that is, a group of words that does not have a subject and a verb and could not act as a sentence. Use *as* when you are introducing a comparison with a clause — that is, a group of words that has a subject and a verb and could be a sentence.

Examples

Faulty   Henri acted like he had been there before.
Corrected   Henri acted as if he had been there before.

Faulty   Historians have said that the Mayan kings acted like they were gods.
Corrected   Historians have said that the Mayan kings acted as if they were gods.

Faulty   Johanna always carries herself as a winner.
Corrected   Johanna always carries herself like a winner.

Faulty   Maximillian reacted to other people's success as a bear with a sore head.
Corrected   Maximillian reacted to other people's success like a bear with a sore head.

Exercise   •   **Rewrite the following sentences to make the comparisons appropriate and logical.**

1. "I don't mean to alarm you," she murmured to her host, "but something in this room smells as bilgewater."
2. As he watched the water pouring off the roof of the lean-to, Edgar began to wish that he had dressed like his mother's warning and had worn his raingear.
3. Radiology intrigues me more than any branch of the medical sciences.
4. The promise of an evening given over to reckless abandon and Bohemian excess appealed to Carol more than Steve.
5. A baby's sense of taste is far more acute than adults.
6. Like Manfred said, this pie tastes like it's homemade, but it just isn't the same as mother and her ground cherry pies every fall.
7. I am more interested in the feeding habits of vampires than sharks.
8. Undaunted, the heroic seamstress hemmed like her life depended on the garment's completion, as in fact it did.
9. The cannibals savored the roast pig more than the anthropologists.
10. More than all the presidents of the United States, Abe Lincoln is respected for his honesty.

> 2. When drawing a comparison between two things, use the comparative form of the adjective or adverb, not the superlative form.

When you are making a comparison between only two things (or people), it is not logical to say that one of them is the "best" or the "worst," the "oldest" or the "youngest," the "most interesting" or the "least interesting," and so on. Since you are comparing only two, the correct form of the adjective or adverb is "better," "younger," "more interesting," "less original," and so on.

Examples

Faulty   McEnroe was the best player in that singles match.
Corrected   McEnroe was the better player in that singles match.

Faulty   Juan is the oldest of two sons.
Corrected   Juan is the older of two sons.

Faulty   Kissinger definitely got the best of the other speaker.
Corrected   Kissinger definitely got the better of the other speaker.

Faulty   Chan-li was the most talented one of the twins.
Corrected   Chan-li was the more talented one of the twins.

Exercise • **Rewrite these sentences to make the comparisons logical.**

1. If it comes to a choice between discretion and valor, Eduardo will probably say that discretion is always the best course to follow.
2. I was piqued because she offered the biggest half of the watercress sandwich to Ernest and the smallest half to me.
3. Although I had never witnessed Sir Gawain or Sir Lancelot in action, I was certain that the best man would win when they faced each other in the jousting match.
4. First, my car broke down, then I lost my job, and last but not least, I found out that my bank account was overdrawn; it was the worse week of my entire life.
5. Kari refused to have pictures taken for the book cover until she had obtained the photographer's written guarantee that he would photograph only her best side.

Comparisons Using *unique* and Other Absolute Terms

Some purists about usage hold that certain kinds of modifiers cannot be compared because they express absolute states. The most common of these words are *unique, perfect, empty,* and that favorite, *pregnant.* The reasoning behind this view is that the word *unique* means one of a kind; therefore to say that something is "more unique" is a contradiction. The word *perfect* falls into the same category; it means best. Similarly, a woman is either pregnant or she is not; one cannot logically be a little pregnant.

In everyday speech and writing, of course, educated people do say "That is the most unique design in the competition," or "She is very pregnant." And since the preamble to the U.S. Constitution begins "In order to form a more perfect union," the strictest grammarian is hard put to say that such an expression is wrong. Still, it is useful to remember that, logically, words that express absolute states are not comparable.

Examples

Illogical   She has the most perfect complexion I have ever seen.
Logical   I think she has a perfect complexion.

Illogical   Cantu was deader than a fossil.
Logical   Cantu was as dead as a fossil.

Illogical   Schmidt's design is more unique than mine.
Logical   Schmidt's design is more original than mine.

Exercise   •   **Rewrite these sentences to correct the faulty use of absolute words.**

1. "How Are Things in Guacamole?" is my most favorite parody of a Broadway tune.
2. When Ted awoke and saw sunshine streaming through his tent flap, he knew that the weather would be more ideal for camping than it had been the previous day.
3. On her third and final attempt, Rosalinda performed a swan dive that was less flawless than her first dive.
4. When Carlo saw how his bean rows converged at the far end of the garden, he realized he should have taken precautions to make them more parallel.
5. With grim satisfaction, Miss Bostick acknowledged that the second applicant was even more adequate than the first had been.

SS9   Completeness

1. In sentences that have multiple constructions, be sure that you have not omitted any verb or preposition that is necessary to the meaning of the sentence.

Sometimes the predicate of a sentence may contain two or more idiomatic phrases that call for different prepositions. If so, it is important that you include the correct preposition for each idiom.

Examples

Incomplete   He is both disposed and capable of destroying her illusions.
Complete   He is both inclined toward and capable of destroying her illusions.

Incomplete   I am aware and sympathetic to her problem.
Complete   I am aware of and sympathetic to her problem.

---

2. If you use *so, such,* or *too* in a comparison, be sure that you express the idea completely or change the construction to make it clear what is being compared.

Although in conversation or personal writing we frequently use sentences like "It was *so* hot!" or "Geraldine is *such* a fine pianist," the proper use of those terms, as well as *too,* are modifiers that show comparison. In written English they should not be used as loose intensifiers. To avoid the problem, either rewrite the sentence to get rid of the inappropriate terms or recast the sentence to complete the comparison.

Examples

Incomplete   Jasper is such a fine piano player.
Revised   Jasper is an unusually fine piano player.
Complete   Jasper is such a fine piano player that he could be a professional.

Incomplete   The accident was too devastating.
Revised   The accident was very devastating.
Complete   The accident was too devastating to be forgotten.

Incomplete   The Chinese are so mysterious.
Revised   The Chinese are extremely mysterious.
Complete   The Chinese are so mysterious that they have long puzzled historians.

Completeness

Exercise • Rewrite these sentences to make all elements complete.

1. Both Jessica and Belinda had a propensity and an aversion to affairs of the heart.
2. She was ignorant and oblivious to her suitor, who was entangled in the rose trellis.
3. Money was both the source and solution to his predicament.
4. He was the recipient and shy respondent to her enigmatic smile.
5. His hastily written essay abounds and suffers from the careless mistakes he was warned to avoid.

V • Verbs

V1 ## Verb Forms

All verbs have three principal parts. For example:

Infinitive	Past tense	Past participle
run (to run)	ran	ran
go (to go)	went	gone
kiss (to kiss)	kissed	kissed

Regular and Irregular Verbs

Regular verbs add *-ed* to the infinitive form to make the past and past participles; *irregular verbs* make the past and past participles by changing letters and sometimes whole words (*eat, ate, eaten*).

Tense

The *tense* of verbs refers to the time it expresses.

Present	Past	Future
is	was	will be
give	gave	will give
run	ran	will run

Active and Passive Voice

Verbs have *active voice* when the subject of the verb is acting or being. They have *passive voice* when the subject of the sentence is being acted upon.

Mood

Verbs have three moods. The *indicative mood* expresses a statement or fact. The *imperative mood* expresses a command or directive. The *subjunctive mood* expresses a wish or a condition contrary to fact, for example, "If I were you."

Transitive and Intransitive Verbs

Transitive verbs take objects: Hector *buried* the ox. *Intransitive verbs* do not take objects: She *developed* early.

Auxiliary Verbs

Auxiliary verbs are helping verbs. They are used with other verbs to show tense, voice, and mood: *has* gone, *will* sleep, *are* swimming.

Linking Verbs

Linking verbs are verbs that link or join the subject with a predicate noun or adjective: Harry *is* a woman chaser. The day *seemed* endless. Jackie *looks* tired.

> Check to see that you are using the correct form of all verbs in your sentences.

Regular English verbs have three principal parts: present, past, and past participle. For regular verbs the past tense and the past participle are formed by adding *-ed* to the present form of the verb. For example, *cook, cooked, has cooked; fear, feared, has feared.*

Unfortunately, many of the most common English verbs are irregular; that is, their past tenses and past participles are formed by changing letters within the verb or even by changing the whole word. For example, *go, went, gone; eat, ate, eaten.*

Using an incorrect verb form of a common verb is such a conspicuous error that it provokes a strong negative reaction in readers. For that reason, you need to memorize the principal parts of the most common verbs so well that their use becomes automatic. For the forms of less common irregular verbs, such as *strive, arise,* or *tread,* check the dictionary. If the verb is regular, the dictionary will give only the present form; if it is irregular, you will find all three parts.

Here is a chart of the most common irregular verbs.

Principal Parts of the Common Irregular Verbs

Present	Past	Past participle
awake	awoke, awaked	awoke, awaked
be	was	been
bite	bit	bitten
blow	blew	blown
break	broke	broken
bring	brought	brought
buy	bought	bought
catch	caught	caught
choose	chose	chosen

Present	Past	Past participle
come	came	come
cost	cost	cost
cut	cut	cut
do	did	done
dive	dove, dived	dived
drag	dragged	dragged
drink	drank	drunk
drive	drove	driven
eat	ate	eaten
fall	fell	fallen
freeze	froze	frozen
give	gave	given
grind	ground	ground
grow	grew	grown
hang (execute)	hanged	hanged
hang (suspend)	hung	hung
hurt	hurt	hurt
keep	kept	kept
know	knew	known
lay	laid	laid
lead	led	led
leave	left	left
let	let	let
lie	lay	lain
lose	lost	lost
ride	rode	ridden
ring	rang	rung
rise	rose	risen
see	saw	seen
shake	shook	shaken
shrink	shrank	shrunk
sing	sang	sung
speak	spoke	spoken
steal	stole	stolen

Present	Past	Past participle
swear	swore	sworn
swim	swam	swum
swing	swung	swung
take	took	taken
write	wrote	written

Exercise • Revise the underlined verbs in these sentences to make their form correct.

1. The minister <u>awaked</u> with a start, remembering only snatches of the dream he had <u>dreamed</u> as he <u>lied</u> with his head upon the half-<u>wrote</u> sermon on his desk.

2. He had <u>dreamed</u> that he had <u>hanged</u> his cassock in its usual place and had <u>lain</u> his hymnal on the stand beside his desk.

3. Suddenly, the hymnal, as if it had a life of its own, <u>leap</u> from the stand and <u>smited</u> him on the head.

4. As he <u>set</u> on the floor where he had been <u>casted</u>, the hymnal <u>fleed</u> from the office and <u>disappear</u> into the dark corridor that <u>lead</u> to the sanctuary.

5. Dazed, the minister <u>heave</u> himself to his feet and <u>sweared</u> a mighty oath, uttering words that didn't <u>became</u> a man of his office.

6. He gingerly <u>feeled</u> his forehead and realized that a lump had <u>arose</u> where the hymnal had <u>smote</u> him.

7. Glancing at himself in the mirror, he <u>weeped</u> to see how his forehead had <u>swelled.</u>

8. Vowing revenge, he <u>tread</u> cautiously down the dark, damp corridor and was dismayed to discover that someone had <u>strew</u> the hall with pieces of broken furniture.

9. There was a musty odor in the corridor, too, and he was <u>remind</u> of the root cellar in the house where he had <u>dwellen</u> as a boy, a place that always <u>stinked</u> of the mildew and fungus that <u>thriven</u> there.

10. It was at this point that the minister had <u>awoke</u>, relieved that he had only been dreaming and wondering if perhaps he had <u>drank</u> a little too much of the sacramental wine.

A Pair of Troublesome Verbs: *lie* and *lay*

Lie is an intransitive verb that means to lie down or recline. It cannot take an object. The principal parts of *lie* are *lie, lay, lain;* the present participle is *lying*.

Examples

She *lies* there helplessly.

She *lay* there yesterday.

She *is lying* there still.

She *has lain* there before.

The book *lies* on the table.

Charles *is lying* on the ground.

We *lay* on the deck.

The dogs *have lain* there all night.

When you use *lie* you should think of a person or thing lying on something, even if the "on" is not stated.

Lay is a transitive verb that means to place something on a surface. It must take an object. The principal parts are *lay, laid,* and *laid;* the present participle is *laying.*

Examples

Joe can *lay* the box on the floor.

Joe *laid* the box on the floor.

Joe *had laid* it there two days ago.

Joe *is laying* the box down.

I will *lay* my coat here.

The brothers *have laid* their cards on the table.

Montgomery *laid* his plans carefully.

Chauncey *is laying* carpet in their bedroom.

When you use *lay* you should think of someone actually handling an object and putting it down, although the word can also have a less literal sense — that is, people *lay* plans, they *lay* down rules, and so on.

Exercise • **Use the correct forms of *lie* and *lay* in these sentences.**

1. He <u>lay</u> his cards on the table before she could ask what <u>laid</u> at stake.
2. He <u>lie</u> writhing on the rug which someone had been kind enough to <u>lie</u> there for him.
3. He <u>lay</u> himself down on the banks of red roses.
4. How many times have I myself <u>lay</u> where she was now allowing her gerbils to <u>lay</u>?
5. I hope that we can finally <u>lie</u> this ugly incident to rest.

Tense Shifting

Make verb tenses consistent in your sentences.

The tense of a verb indicates the time when an action takes place, and in most cases if you have more than one verb in a sentence, they should be in the same tense. You should shift tenses only when the logic of the sentence requires it.

Examples

Inconsistent   After they heard the main speaker, they are ready to leave.
Consistent   After they heard the main speaker, they were ready to leave.

Inconsistent   As the crowd gathers, Jim became more and more excited.
Consistent   As the crowd gathered, Jim became more and more excited.

Inconsistent   Jennifer always expects to be the victim, and of course she was.
Consistent   Jennifer always expects to be the victim, and of course she is.

You should also make tenses consistent from one sentence to the next within a paragraph so that readers don't feel they are jumping back and forth in time.

Examples

Inconsistent   The author's examples are not randomly chosen. He told of conversations and interviews, but he does not mention conversations with enlisted men. He says his sample is adequate, but this kind of bias invalidated his reasoning.
Consistent   The author's examples are not randomly chosen. He tells of conversations and interviews, but he does not mention conversations with enlisted men. He claims his sample is adequate, but this kind of bias invalidates his reasoning.

Inconsistent   When the country faced a huge budget deficit in 1985, the president is determined to lower taxes. His proposals were popular with many people, but it is the Congress who refuses to go along. They claim that the time had come to impose a national excise tax.
Consistent   When the country faced a huge budget deficit in 1985, the president was determined to lower taxes. His proposals were popular with many

people, but the Congress refused to go along. They claimed that the time had come to impose a national excise tax.

If, however, the logic of your writing demands that you speak of certain events in the past, you *may* mix your tenses.

Example

We now know that Hitler was more than a dictator; he was also a master psychologist.

Historical Present Tense

It is customary to use the present tense throughout a paper or essay when writing about a literary work or historical document.

Examples

In the *Republic* Plato asserts that poetry is an inferior art because it is, by definition, an imitation of real life.

The Constitution is written to restrict the power of the individual states.

Exercise • Mark verbs in this paragraph that are in an inappropriate tense and substitute appropriate verbs.

> Havelock wrote that before the Greeks invented the alphabet, the human brain was used as an internal record of much that is now preserved externally in written form. Poetry, for instance, had been produced orally by bards such as Homer. These bards use their memories as a record of their culture's history and values. Sometimes bards had to retain in their memories thousands of lines of poetry, a feat that modern man would have found virtually impossible today. Havelock went on to explain that the *Phaedrus* reveals Plato's mistrust of the relatively new technology of alphabetic writing. According to Havelock, Plato fears that with the advent of writing, people would rely on this new technology and would no longer exercise their memories. Plato's position, it seemed, was similar to that of parents who fear the technology of television because they are afraid it will discourage their children from engaging in the mental exercise required by reading.

V3   Voice

> Use the active voice (that is, the verb form showing that the subject is acting) when you want to emphasize the person or thing acting; use the passive voice (the verb form showing that the subject is being acted upon) when you want to emphasize the action rather than the agent who is acting.

In general, use active verbs in your writing. Try to avoid overusing the passive voice because not only can it make writing seem bland and lifeless but too often it conceals the identity of the person acting. It is appropriate when describing a *mechanism or action* in which the agent acting is not known or not relevant.

Examples

Ineffective passive voice   The congregation *was told* by the minister to picket the book store.
Effective active voice   The minister *told* the congregation to picket the book store.

Ineffective passive voice   Historically, artists have been subsidized and controlled by the church and the nobility.
Effective active voice   Historically, the church and the nobility subsidized and controlled artists.

Effective passive voice   When they arrive on campus, students are given a voucher to buy their computers. (Who gives the voucher isn't important here.)

Effective passive voice   The motors are inspected and stamped at the end of the process. (Who does the inspecting and stamping is not important.)

Exercise • **Revise these sentences to eliminate the inappropriate passive voice.**

1. An attack of insomnia was experienced by me last night.
2. During my period of sleeplessness, several troublesome issues were mulled over and many unsolved problems were analyzed in agonizing detail.
3. Even small annoyances and minor concerns were made by my fatigued mind to seem overwhelming.

4. In the wee hours of the morning it was felt by me that my unfinished projects would never be completed.

5. The annoying background to these troublesome thoughts was furnished by a continuing recurrence of jingles from television commercials — the very ones that were most loathed by me.

V4   The Subjunctive Mood

> Use the subjunctive mood of verbs when expressing wishes, conditional states, or ideas that are contrary to fact.

In contemporary writing and speaking, people use the subjunctive mood of verbs much less than they did in the past; nevertheless, knowing how to use the subjunctive correctly is convenient when you are writing for a well-educated audience and when you want to express nuances or to moderate the tone of your writing. The subjunctive mood is expressed by the verb forms *were, would, could, might, may,* and sometimes *should,* and, in certain constructions after the word *that,* by the present form of the verb: for example, *be, come,* or *deal.*

Examples

Expressing wishes

Colloquial   I wish I was that lucky.
Preferable   I wish I were that lucky.

Colloquial   Every player on the team wished that he was going.
Preferable   Every player on the team wished that he were going.

Examples

Expressing conditional statements

If I were you, I would consider changing my plans.

Should that happen, General Foods will be in trouble.

In the best of all possible worlds, things like that couldn't happen.

Were it possible for them to come, they would.

It might be that we can eliminate that hazard at very little cost.

May I ask you to consider that there may be another side to the issue?

Were it my responsibility, I would act differently.

Could it be that the inventory was wrong?

Might we reconsider that proposal another time?

It may be that we should try another approach.

Notice that using the subjunctive mood in sentences like these softens and moderates the writer's tone so that he or she does not seem dictatorial or overbearing. When you want your writing to have a gracious and conciliatory tone, it's good to use subjunctives.

Examples

Indicating a condition that is contrary to fact

Colloquial   He wishes that he was a better runner.
Preferable   He wishes that he were a better runner.

Colloquial   It would be nice if Jules was as honest as he is handsome.
Preferable   It would be nice if Jules were as honest as he is handsome.

Certain Constructions After *that*

In formal writing, certain *that* clauses that demand, request, recommend, or express necessity call for the subjunctive in the form of the infinitive of the verb.

Examples

It is important that they be informed of the change.

We recommend that everyone in the neighborhood be given adequate information on the chemical spill.

If this be treason, make the most of it.

The emperor asks that everyone be required to come see his new clothes.

Jaime implored that Juanita give him her answer.

Exercise •   Replace the underlined verbs in these sentences with the appropriate subjunctive form.

1. André wished he <u>was</u> better with words, as he struggled to compose his letter to Charlotte's father.

2. It was essential that Mr. Aubach's suspicions of his intentions <u>were</u> laid to rest.

3. If this letter <u>wasn't</u> successful, he <u>can</u> forget about the future he had planned for himself as the husband of the beautiful and wealthy Charlotte Aubach.

4. If she <u>was</u> to become his bride, he <u>didn't</u> need to worry any longer about his creditors' ugly threats.

5. He had to convince Mr. Aubach that it was Charlotte herself that he loved; after all, he mused, he still <u>wanted</u> to marry her even if she <u>wasn't</u> beautiful.

Exercise • Replace the underlined verbs in these sentences with subjunctive forms that will change the tone of the sentences.

1. "Dear Mr. Aubach," he wrote, "<u>Can</u> you spare a few moments from your busy schedule to learn of my esteem for your daughter?"

2. "I assure you my intentions <u>can't</u> be more honorable."

3. "If I <u>can</u> only have your daughter's hand in marriage, I <u>will be</u> the happiest man on earth."

4. "I humbly beg that you <u>are</u> patient with me while I attempt to convince you of the depth of my affection for your daughter."

5. "If I <u>was</u> you, I <u>was</u> honored to have an upstanding young man like myself as a son-in-law."

V5   Subject/Verb Agreement

Check your sentences to see that single subjects are matched with single verbs and plural subjects are matched with plural verbs.

Examples

Single subject/single verb

George believes in voodoo.

Catastrophe usually strikes unexpectedly.

The best organized book exhibit is that one.

Plural subject/plural verb

Four nights in the emergency room require great stamina.

Millions of refugees wander through the world today.

Husbands of this decade are different from their fathers.

Compound Subjects

When two or more subjects are joined by *and,* the subject is compound and takes a plural verb.

Examples

Incorrect   Building a savings account and lowering one's tax bracket is the advantages of the tax-sheltered annuity.
Correct   Building a savings account and lowering one's tax bracket are the advantages of a tax-sheltered annuity.

Incorrect   She and Margery goes to the opera frequently.
Correct   She and Margery go to the opera frequently.

Incorrect   The price of his clothes and the size of his house shouts of money.
Correct   The price of his clothes and the size of his house shout of money.

Exception: Some compound phrases are used so often that they act as a single term — for instance, "law and order," "scotch and soda," "cheese and crackers." When such phrases act as the subject of a sentence, they should be regarded as a single term.

Examples

"Law and order" is the judge's campaign slogan.

Scotch and soda is Gerald's favorite drink.

When two or more subjects are joined by *or,* they are considered separate and take a single verb.

Examples

Incorrect   Dr. Janice Woods or Professor Marybeth Green are going to be our next president.
Correct   Dr. Janice Woods or Professor Marybeth Green is going to be our next president.

Incorrect   Aerobic jazz or body toning are good for the circulation.
Correct   Aerobic jazz or body toning is good for the circulation.

When a compound subject is joined with *either . . . or, neither . . . nor,* or *not . . . but,* the verb agrees with the part of the subject that is nearest to it.

Examples

Incorrect   Either his cows or his bull are sterile.
Correct   Either his cows or his bull is sterile.

Incorrect   Neither the man close to him nor the one standing in the door are members.
Correct   Neither the man close to him nor the one standing in the door is a member.

Intervening Modifiers

Any modifier that comes between the subject and verb of a sentence does not affect the subject/verb agreement.

Examples

Incorrect   Skiing or backpacking, two of the area's most popular sports, are sure to be included in the trip.
Correct   Skiing or backpacking, two of the area's most popular sports, is sure to be included in the trip.

Incorrect   The student, along with friends who had joined him from all around the country, were surprised to be arrested.
Correct   The student, along with friends who had joined him from all around the country, was surprised to be arrested.

Exercise   •   Rewrite these sentences to make subjects and verbs agree.

1. A party made up of several convicted felons and one or two otherwise unsavory characters are having an audience with the queen.
2. The host, as well as his guests, are hoping that the plumbing holds out for the rest of the evening.
3. Every inflection and innuendo were noted by the nervous linguist.
4. Neither his mustache nor his eyebrows was the same color as his beard.
5. The world's largest collection of grammar and usage exercises are preserved in that time capsule.

6. I don't care what your horoscope says, I still think four hundred guests is a few too many.

7. Economics are the cause of many a business major's decision to leave school.

8. His was one of those tentative proposals that never seems to merit any attention.

9. "Lethargy and Squalor" were chosen as the unlikely theme of the prom.

10. Rickets are the one disease he has not yet contracted.

Guidelines for Determining Correct Agreement

In sentences that begin with *there* or *here* followed by a linking verb, the verb should agree with the subject that follows it.

Examples

Incorrect   There is numerous objections to his plan.
Correct   There are numerous objections to his plan.

Incorrect   Here is the guidelines we are being asked to follow.
Correct   Here are the guidelines we are being asked to follow.

In sentences that follow a subject/verb/complement pattern, the main verb should agree with the subject of the sentence.

Examples

Incorrect   Literary agents is a necessary evil.
Correct   Literary agents are a necessary evil.

Incorrect   The chief drawback of going to visit Tokyo are the high prices.
Correct   The chief drawback of going to visit Tokyo is the high prices.

Group nouns — team, legislature, class, brigade, and so on — can take either singular or plural verbs, depending on the context in which they are used.

If you are using the group noun to refer to the members of the group acting as individuals, use a plural verb.

Examples

The class are discussing their papers in small group conferences.

The executive committee were divided on their recommendations.

If you are using the group noun to refer to the components of the group acting together as a unit, use a singular verb.

Examples

The team competes in the regional playoffs almost every year.

The New York audience is conditioned to expect several curtain calls from an artist.

Sometimes the choice between a singular or plural verb to go with a group noun seems arbitrary; in that case, you can choose the kind of verb that seems more logical to you, or you can rewrite the sentence to get around the problem. For example, in the sentences above, you could write "the members of the team" or "those in the audience" and use a plural verb.

Words that are plural in form but singular in meaning take single verbs.

Examples

The evening news is often distressing.

Politics is the art of the possible.

Athletics is overemphasized at many schools.

Reminder: Remember that *data, media, phenomena, memoranda,* and so on are plural nouns and should take plural subjects, at least in formal usage.

Examples

The data are unreliable.

The media generally follow the polls.

When the subject is an indefinite pronoun, it usually takes a singular verb. The most common indefinite pronouns are

each	either
one	anyone
everyone	someone
anybody	nobody
everybody	somebody
no one	neither

Even though some of these terms — for instance, *everyone* and *everybody* — refer to groups of people, in formal English such a term requires a singular verb. Problems with this kind of construction usually occur when the subject pronoun is followed by a phrase that has a plural noun in it; often it is necessary to check carefully to identify the subject in sentences with this kind of structure.

Examples

Incorrect   Everyone in the room were stunned.
Correct   Everyone in the room was stunned.

Incorrect   Neither of them are suitable for the job.
Correct   Neither of them is suitable for the job.

Incorrect   Each of the participants were at the stadium early.
Correct   Each of the participants was at the stadium early.

Incorrect   Any one of the candidates are a good choice.
Correct   Any one of the candidates is a good choice.

A few indefinite words may take a singular or a plural verb, depending on their context in the sentence. Those words are *none, all, part, some,* and *half.*

Examples

Some of my anger comes from frustration. ("Some" refers to a specific portion so it takes a singular verb.)

Some of the players believe the referee was unfair. ("Some" refers to more than one player so it takes a plural verb.)

Half of what you earn is mine. ("Half" is a specific amount so it takes a singular verb.)

Half of the sales force win prizes every year. ("Half" refers to more than one person so it takes a plural verb.)

The pronouns *any* and *none* can refer to either one or several items and thus may take either singular or plural verbs.

When a relative pronoun follows the subject of a sentence, the verb agrees with the antecedent of the pronoun. The relative pronouns are *who, which,* and *that.*

Examples

Incorrect   She is one of the girls who plays on the soccer team. (The "who" refers to "girls" so the verb should be plural.)
Correct   She is one of the girls who play on the soccer team.

Incorrect   The promises that was made at that meeting were never kept. (The first "that" refers to "promises" so the verb should be plural.)

Correct   The promises that were made at that meeting were never kept.

A verb agrees with its subject, not with its complement or with its object.

Examples

Incorrect   Fitzgerald's focus in the story are the illusions of naive lovers.
Correct   Fitzgerald's focus in the story is the illusions of naive lovers.

Incorrect   Lucchese were honored by many awards.
Correct   Lucchese was honored by many awards.

When writing a sentence with inverted word order, make sure that you identify the subject and that the verb agrees with it.

Examples

Incorrect   Is there any paintings here done by famous artists?
Correct   Are there any paintings here done by famous artists?

Incorrect   Sitting on the other side of the room was all the hopeful relatives.
Correct   Sitting on the other side of the room were all the hopeful relatives.

Exercise • **Rewrite these sentences for correct agreement.**

1. **There is sometimes too many items on the agenda.**
2. **The band was putting away their instruments when the fire alarm sounded.**
3. **Everyone in the audience were astonished by the speaker's lack of sensitivity.**
4. **Gary is one of those persons who thinks winning is everything.**
5. **Remembering his slights in the past, none of my relatives plan to attend the funeral of John McGinty.**
6. **Street musicians is a common sight on the streets of Boston.**
7. **Each of us believe that Mary has the right to return to school.**
8. **I cannot believe his statement that higher fees is the reason he transferred from Wabash to Purdue.**
9. **Standing at the rear of the platform was all the winners of previous pageants.**
10. **Some of the cast was in favor of having an opening-night party.**

N • Nouns

Terminology and Functions of Nouns

The classes of nouns are

- **Proper nouns**   Names of specific people, places, or things are always capitalized. For example, *Sarah, Mr. Williams, Paris, June, Tuesday, Constitution.*
- **Common nouns**   All other nouns that do not name specific things or individuals are written with lower-case letters. For example, *mud, cat, tomatoes, road, happiness.*
- **Goncrete nouns**   These are names of things that can be perceived with the senses — tasted, seen, felt, heard, smelled. For example, *stairway, automobile, water, lion, cup.*
- **Abstract nouns**   These are names of concepts, ideas, traits, and qualities that can be conceived by the mind. For example, *loyalty, misery, principle, intelligence, belief.*
- **Collective nouns**   These are names of collections of things or individuals. For example, *team, congregation, navy, committee, class.*
- **Compound nouns**   These are combinations of words. For example, *commander-in-chief, sister-in-law, member-at-large, theater-in-the-round.*

Nouns are *plural* or *singular,* and they have *possessive* forms. Nouns in English do not have gender as they do in other languages, except in a few obvious cases: *sister, mother, daughter,* or *actress, waitress,* for example.
   The functions of nouns are

Subject of a sentence or clause: *Vanessa* bought it.

Object of a verb: Sheila broke the *glass.*

Indirect object of a verb: The company gave the award to an *accountant.*

Complement: Elaine is the *vice-president.*

Object of a preposition: Chaos came after the *revolution.*

Object of a verbal: She tried to find *comfort.*

Appositive: Ringling Brothers, the world's most famous *circus,* comes next week.

Modifier of another noun: A *submarine* detector; a *classroom* teacher; a *garden* tractor.

N2   Plurals of Nouns

> Use the correct plural noun form.

Most nouns have regular plural forms that are made by adding -s to the singular form: *books, records, shoes, dogs.* For words that require an extra syllable for pronunciation, -es is added: *glasses, beaches, masses, circuses, Jameses.*

A few English nouns have irregular plurals: *men, children, women, mice,* for example. Others form their plurals according to the rules for Latin: *datum, data; medium, media; alumnus, alumni; fungus, fungi.*

Some nouns ending in -f form their plurals by changing the -f to -v and adding -es: *wolves, scarves, wharves, leaves.*

Many nouns ending in -y or -ey form their plurals by changing the -y or -ey to -i and adding -es: *stories, monies, industries, factories, families.*

Some nouns are the same in both singular and plural forms:

Words that end in -ics: *athletics, politics, economics, gymnastics.*

Names of certain animals: *deer, fish, sheep.*

Certain words that seem to be plurals, but in fact are never used in the singular and always take plural verbs: *trousers, scissors, manners.*

Since there are no consistent or easily remembered rules for forming the plural of nouns, check the dictionary if you have any doubt about the correct form. If the plural is made by adding -s or -es, no plural form will be given; if the plural takes any other form, it will be given.

N3   Possessive Forms of Nouns

> 1. Use the correct possessive form with nouns.

The possessive form for nouns can be expressed in two ways: (1) by adding an apostrophe with an -s or (2) by inserting an *of* before the noun.

The dog's collar, the star's bouquet, the head of a man, the sleeve of the coat

This seems simple enough, but difficulties can arise when one tries to choose the proper place to put the apostrophe or to decide when to use an apostrophe and when to insert *of.* Here are some guidelines.

The position of the apostrophe in the possessive form signals whether the noun is singular or plural. In most cases, the apostrophe comes *before* the -*s* for a singular noun and *after* the -*s* for a plural noun. (Exceptions for irregular noun forms are given below.)

Examples

The mother's warning (warning of one mother)

The boat's mooring (the mooring of one boat)

A student's grades (the grades of one student)

But note that the possessive for a few plural nouns is also made this way:

The men's concerns (the concerns of several men)

The children's cries (the cries of several children)

The possessive form for regular plural nouns ending in -*s* looks like this:

The cooks' implements (the implements of several cooks)

The engineers' reports (the reports of more than one engineer)

Our parents' wishes (the wishes of both parents)

The possessive form for singular nouns ending in -*s* may be formed by adding an apostrophe after the final -*s* or by adding another -*s* and inserting an apostrophe before it.

Examples

James' father, or James's father

Hans' business, or Hans's business

The stewardess' uniform, or the stewardess's uniform

The possessive of compound nouns is formed by adding an apostrophe plus -*s* to the last word in the construction.

His brother-in-law's firm.

The sergeant-at-arms' position

Our chief justice's office

If two nouns joined by *and* or *nor* form the subject, the possessive is formed by adding an apostrophe and -*s* to the second noun if both subjects are possessors. For example:

Jerry and Jean's apartment was robbed.

The captain and lieutenant's office.

But, if the two nouns are each possessors of something, an apostrophe plus -s should follow each noun. For example:

We recognized Patricia's and Margaret's motorcycles.

Viola's and Kenneth's houses are up for sale.

Do not use an apostrophe after the plural noun in expressions in which the noun acts as a noun modifier rather than as a possessive. For example:

mechanics lien

farmers market

teachers union

United States passport

criminal courts building

Choosing Between the Apostrophe + s Form and the *of* + Form

2. In general, use the apostrophe + s form of the possessive with the names of people or countries and for animate creatures, people, or animals. Use the *of* + form with concepts or inanimate objects.

Examples

Tom's job fascinates him.

The whale's breathing apparatus is remarkable.

Yugoslavia's economy has improved.

He gave Tim the synopsis of the story.

The background of the violence has just come out.

The critics of the play wrote scathing comments.

This rule is flexible, however, and you may ignore it if one construction or the other sounds more natural to you in certain instances, particularly in idiomatic expressions, such as "the sins of the fathers," "a month's salary," or "the bearing of a queen."

When using the titles of books, plays, movies, magazines, or newspapers in a possessive construction, use the *of* construction.

Examples

Clumsy   *Amadeus*'s popularity has been phenomenal.
Preferable   The popularity of *Amadeus* has been phenomenal.

Clumsy   The *Iliad*'s story is the basis for Adams' novel *Blind Man's Bluff.*
Preferable   The story of the *Iliad* is the basis for Adams' novel *Blind Man's Bluff.*

In a few instances both the *of* + possessive construction and the apostrophe + *s* construction are used. Although the construction can scarcely be called logical, some possessive idioms call for both indicators.

Examples

Those tears of Veronica's

Some classmates of my mother's

Color photographs of Mary's (notice here that the extra apostrophe + *s* is needed to distinguish the phrase from "photographs of Mary")

Many friends of my husband's

Common Problems with Noun Possessives

Do not add *-s* + apostrophe to irregular noun plurals to show possession.

Examples

Incorrect   The childrens' books were lost. (The form "children" is already plural and does not need another *-s* added to show possession.)
Correct   The children's books were lost.

Incorrect   The gentlemens' agreement had fallen apart.
Correct   The gentlemen's agreement had fallen apart.

Do not confuse possessive forms with apostrophes with straight plural forms. The latter never require an apostrophe.

Examples

Incorrect   The Harrises' are at home. ("Harrises" is not a possessive here.)
Correct   The Harrises are at home.

Incorrect   You will find him at the drycleaners'. ("Drycleaners" is not a possessive here.)
Correct   You will find him at the drycleaners.

Exercise • Substitute the correct possessive form for each of the underlined terms.

1. The suspense was trying the <u>ladies-in-waiting</u> patience and destroying all four <u>maid-of-honor</u> sense of humor.
2. At his <u>cronies</u> urging, Horace agreed to describe his <u>day off</u> goings-on.
3. Jealousy destroyed <u>Desdemona and Othello</u> honor.
4. Sloth is <u>one of my brother</u> best attribute.
5. The <u>day in the park</u> relaxing effects proved to be the <u>captain of the guard</u> downfall.
6. I hope you will never have to suffer the stings of <u>several Portuguese man-of-war</u> at once.
7. *The Women's Room* conclusion enraged me more than any other <u>novel</u> ending that I have read.
8. Do you remember what happens in *Romeo and Juliet* final scene?
9. The <u>botanists</u> tea group holds its meetings in one of <u>Mr. Valdes mother</u> greenhouses.
10. <u>The man who would be king</u> reputation was on the line.

N4   Using *a* and *an* Before Nouns

> Make your choice about using *a* or *an* as the article before a noun on the basis of the *sound* of the first letter, not on the basis of the letter itself.

Use *a* before words beginning with a consonant sound. These include the initial sounds in words like *union* or *united*.

Examples

a perfect day	a useful tool
a national scandal	a euphoric mood
a C in the course	a U-joint
a winter's dream	a young man
a handsome woman	a high price

Use *an* before words beginning with a vowel sound. These include the initial sounds in words like *hour* and *honor*.

Examples

an astronaut	an interesting idea
an honest account	an F in the course
an omen	an aura of mystery
an unparalleled success	an escrow account
an essential element	an ACT score

Exercise • **Choose either *a* or *an* as the appropriate article before each underlined word or phrase.**

1. Merry has ————— <u>unique</u> opportunity to excel in the race.
2. She will be able to race around ————— <u>empty</u> barrel.
3. Then she can swoop down to the ground in ————— <u>unprecedented</u> maneuver.
4. Then she can gallop back down the stadium and make ————— <u>U-turn</u> and screech to a halt.
5. The display should bring her at least ————— <u>honorable</u> mention.

PN • Pronouns

The Terminology of Pronouns

Agreement   A pronoun must agree (that is, correspond) in number, gender, and person (first, second, or third person) with the noun that it replaces in a sentence.

Reference   A pronoun must refer to a specific and identifiable word, phrase, or clause in the same sentence or in a previous sentence.

Case   There are three pronoun cases: subjective, objective, and possessive.

- Subjective pronouns act as subjects and complements in sentences: They are

I	we
you	you
she, he	they
it	who

- Objective pronouns act as objects in sentences. They are

me	us
you	you
her, him	them
whom	

- Possessive pronouns show possession. They are

my, mine	our, ours
your, yours	your, yours
her, hers	their, theirs
his	whose
its	

Kinds of Pronouns

Demonstrative Pronouns

this	that
these	those

Indefinite Pronouns

all	either	nobody	someone
another	everybody	none	something
any	everyone	no one	such
anyone	everything	nothing	
anybody	few	one	
anything	many	other	
both	most	several	
each	much	some	
each one	neither	somebody	

Interrogative Pronouns

who	which
what	whom
whose	

Personal Pronouns

I, me, my, mine	he, him, his
we, us, our, ours	it, its
you, yours	they, them, their, theirs
she, her, hers	

Reflexive and Intensive Pronouns

myself	ourselves
yourself	yourselves
herself, himself	themselves
itself	
oneself	

Relative Pronouns

that	whom
who	whose
which	

Reciprocal Pronouns

each other	one another

PN2   Pronoun Agreement

> A pronoun must agree in number, gender, and case with the noun to which it refers.

Number and Gender

Use a singular pronoun when the antecedent is single; use a plural pronoun when the antecedent is plural. If the pronoun and its antecedent are separated by several words or groups of words, it is particularly important to check on agreement.

Examples

Incorrect   The Parisian, who has always been noted for culture and sophistication, love their opera and ballet.

Correct   The Parisian, who has always been noted for culture and sophistication, loves her opera and ballet.

Note: You can avoid the problem of specifying a pronoun of one gender or the other by writing the sentence differently.

Examples

Correct   The Parisian, who has always been noted for culture and sophistication, loves opera and ballet.

Correct   Parisians, who have always been noted for culture and sophistication, love their opera and ballet.

Incorrect   After driving five hundred miles to see the Grand Tetons, the Tanaguchis did not find it very impressive.

Correct   After driving five hundred miles to see the Grand Tetons, the Tanaguchis did not find them very impressive.

Incorrect   The average student at this university takes their studies quite seriously.

Correct   The average student at this university takes his or her studies very seriously.

Use a plural pronoun to refer to two antecedents that are joined with *and*.

Examples

Incorrect   Students should attend the college or university that best meets his needs.

Correct   Students should attend the college or university that best meets their needs.

Incorrect   That book shows how women are conditioned to put everyone else's needs above hers.

Correct   That book shows how women are conditioned to put everyone else's needs above theirs.

Use a singular pronoun when two subjects of a sentence are connected by *or.*

Examples

Incorrect   If Mario or Julio meets the train, give them the directions I have written out.

Correct   If Mario or Julio meets the train, give him the directions I have written out.

Incorrect   Diana Ross or Tina Turner always put their best into a performance.

Correct   Diana Ross or Tina Turner always puts her best into a performance.

Use a singular pronoun to refer to a group noun when the context indicates that the members of the group are functioning as a unit. Use a plural pronoun when the context indicates they are functioning individually.

Examples

Incorrect   The team advanced their position in the tournament.
Correct   The team advanced its position in the tournament.

Incorrect   The family was disappointed at its shares of the inheritance.
Correct   The family was disappointed at their shares of the inheritance.

Use a singular pronoun when the antecedent is one of these indefinite pronouns: *another, any, anybody, anything, each, either, everybody, everyone, everything, nobody, neither, no one, nothing, one, other, somebody, someone, something,* or *such.* Use a plural pronoun when the antecedent is one of these indefinite pronouns: *all, both, few, many, most, several,* or *some.*

Examples

Incorrect   Everybody who was invited had to show their invitation.
Correct   Everybody who was invited had to show his or her invitation.

Incorrect   Somebody in the sorority had obviously violated their pledge of secrecy.
Correct   Somebody in the sorority had obviously violated her pledge of secrecy.

Incorrect   Neither of the contestants wanted to release their scores.
Correct   Neither of the contestants wanted to release his scores.

Exercise • **Make the underlined pronouns agree with their antecedents in number.**

1. Each person in the choir was charged for cleaning their robe.
2. When Mary or Phyllis wanted theirs cleaned, however, they took them home and washed them.
3. That practice so upset the choir director that he issued orders and said everyone must follow it.
4. He took to inspecting everyone's robe as they came to choir practice.
5. The upshot of the whole dispute was that every one of the girls in the choir refused to wear our robes for the Christmas cantata, and the town was scandalized.

Use the relative pronoun *who* when the antecedent is a person; use the relative pronouns *which* or *that* if the antecedent is an animal or thing. In informal usage, *that* is occasionally used to refer to a person, but *who* is preferable.

Examples

Incorrect   Santini is the man which led the raid.
Acceptable   Santini is the man that led the raid.
Preferable   Santini is the man who led the raid.

Incorrect   The corporate officers which traveled frequently collected many bonus plane trips.
Correct   The corporate officers who traveled frequently collected many bonus plane trips.

Incorrect   Arabian horses who win international shows become extremely valuable.
Correct   Arabian horses that win international shows become extremely valuable.

Exception: Because *which* has no possessive form, *whose* can be substituted when you need a possessive form in a sentence about animals or things.

Examples

Those are the planes *whose* engines have caused so much trouble.

Chimpanzees are the animals *whose* habits and feelings most resemble those of humans.

Exercise • **Choose the appropriate pronoun from those in parentheses.**

1. The sales people (which/who) are most respected are those (that/who) don't sleep during sales presentations.
2. My friend (which/who/that) maintains a live-and-let-live stance is nonetheless alternately terrified and enraged by mice (who/which/that) leap out of her kitchen trash can.
3. Kilroy is the parrot (who/that) screamed raucously throughout Laetitia's entire recitation of *The Prophet* by Kahlil Gibran, a poet (that/which/who) excelled in expressing sentimentality.
4. People (who/that) live in glass houses need all the protection they can get.
5. Lady Bracknell in *The Importance of Being Earnest* is the character (that/which/who) is most nearly my ideal.

Case

Use the subjective case for a pronoun when it serves as the subject of a sentence or as a subjective complement.

Examples

Incorrect Jim and me were the first ones on the scene.
Correct Jim and I were the first ones on the scene.

Incorrect Her and I thought the movie was superb.
Correct She and I thought the movie was superb.

Incorrect That's him over there.
Correct That's he over there.

Incorrect The qualified applicants are Hawkins and me.
Correct The qualified applicants are Hawkins and I.

Incorrect This is her speaking.

Correct   This is she speaking.

If a pronoun acts as the subject of a clause in a sentence, it should be in the subjective case.

Examples

Johnson claims that *he* will be the new chairman.

We will have to change our plans if *he* is not accepted.

If you use a pronoun in an appositive phrase, it should be in the same case as its antecedent.

Examples

Incorrect   The chief opponents in this battle, Carlos and me, are not willing to compromise.
Correct   The chief opponents in this battle, Carlos and I, are not willing to compromise.

Incorrect   McShepherd caught the culprits, Jena and she, in a hair-raising chase on the highway.
Correct   McShepherd caught the culprits, Jena and her, in a hair-raising chase on the highway.

If you use a pronoun after *like* or *as* in a clause in which a comparison is implied, its case should be the same as it would be if the clause were completely expressed.

Examples

Incorrect   The latest arrivals in camp suffered as much as them.
Correct   The latest arrivals in camp suffered as much as they. (As "they had suffered" is implied.)

Incorrect   Contessa de Miguel complimented no other child as much as she.
Correct   Contessa de Miguel complimented no other child as much as her. ("as she complimented" is implied.)

Use the objective case for a pronoun that serves as the object of a preposition.

Examples

Incorrect   Plenty of opportunities were offered to Linda and I.
Correct   Plenty of opportunities were offered to Linda and me.

Incorrect The choice will be between Mohammed Ali and he.
Correct The choice will be between Mohammed Ali and him.

Note: Writers usually choose the wrong pronoun only if there is more than one person in the object; for instance, "my daughter and I" or "Ralph and she." You can check by asking yourself, "Would I say "She invited I?" and using the pronoun that would be correct if it were the object by itself.

Be particularly careful when a modified word or phrase follows the pronoun after the preposition.

Example

Incorrect The majority of we travelers had never been to Italy before.
Correct The majority of us travelers had never been to Italy before.

Exercise • **Choose the appropriate pronoun from those in parentheses.**

1. The one who most closely resembles the description of the witness is (he/him).
2. Those who suffered the most from her ingratitude, Olga and (I/me), still bore her no ill will.
3. Between you and (I, me), I think his taste in ties is atrocious.
4. Many of (we, us) jurors had never been in a courtroom before.
5. Dominick admired no one else as much as (she, her).

PN3   *Who* and *Whom*

Even among educated people, the strict distinction between *who* and *whom* is gradually disappearing from English, particularly the spoken language, and in another decade or so, it may also largely disappear from written language. Already a well-known English professor repeats the question "Who's kicking who?" throughout a popular text.* Nevertheless, it's still useful to know the distinction between the two forms and to observe it in most kinds of formal writing, particularly when you are addressing an academic audience.

> 1. Use *who* or *whoever* when the pronoun is the subject in a sentence or clause, even though the subordinate clause in which it appears is itself an object.

*Richard Lanham, *Revising Prose* (New York: Scribners, 1979).

Examples

Correct   Who steals my purse steals trash.

Incorrect   I will prosecute whomever steals my purse.
Correct   I will prosecute whoever steals my purse.

Incorrect   He asked whom was available.
Correct   He asked who was available.

> 2. Use *whom* or *whomever* when the pronoun replaces a word or phrase that is acting as an object in the sentence, especially if the pronoun is the object of a preposition and comes directly after it.

Examples

Incorrect   Who we appoint to that position is a matter of indifference to me.
Correct   Whom we appoint to that position is a matter of indifference to me.

Incorrect   Who did the President choose as ambassador?
Correct   Whom did the President choose as ambassador?

Incorrect   Cox is the man to who we owe all this.
Correct   Cox is the man to whom we owe all this.

Incorrect   In the nineteenth century, an actress was inevitably a woman about who everyone gossiped.
Correct   In the nineteenth century, an actress was inevitably a woman about whom everyone gossiped.

The best way to determine whether you should use *who* or *whom* is to recast the sentence or question using another relative pronoun. For example, "There is the man (who, whom) I met yesterday." Ask yourself, "Would I say, 'I met he'?" Since the answer is that you would say "I met him," you should use the objective *whom.* Or perhaps you want to say, "This is the man (who, whom) will run for president." Ask yourself if you would say, "he will run for president," or "him will run for president." Since you would say "he," you choose the subjective *who.*

Exercise   •   Insert *who, whom, which,* or *that* in the blank spaces in each of these sentences.

1. Beauregard was the very model of a southern gentleman ———— always called his elders "Sir" and rose when ladies came into the room.

---

2. He always wore a large-brimmed white hat, a hat ————— could be recognized from one hundred feet away.

3. He took pride in raising his hat whenever he saw a lady ————— he knew.

4. And of course he always removed his hat indoors — any southern gentleman ————— was properly brought up would do so.

5. Imagine his shock, then, when he went to a dance at the Broken Spoke to see dozens of men ————— kept their hats on.

6. Not only that, they were wearing large black hats, any of ————— would make his hat look small.

7. It was a new experience for him to see men ————— not only kept their hats on indoors but even wore them while they were dancing.

8. As a southern gentleman, Beauregard felt anyone ————— would wear his hat while dancing was insulting the gentler sex.

9. To protest the barbaric practice he tapped one black-hatted dancer on the back and said, "I am a man ————— will not tolerate this insult to southern womanhood."

10. When Beauregard regained consciousness, he found himself on the ground outside the Broken Spoke looking up at a saddled and tethered horse ————— was wearing a large-brimmed white hat ————— looked familiar.

Exercise • Change the underlined words to the appropriate form of *who* or *whom* when necessary.

1. A hero is not a person to <u>who</u> things happen, but rather one <u>whom</u>, as I understand it, makes things happen.

2. Heroic deeds may be accomplished by <u>whomever</u> has the initiative and the desire to rise above the rest of humanity.

3. The crowd grew restless as it awaited <u>whoever</u> was going to lead the way to the fire exit.

4. You don't give away a good dog like Yellow to <u>whoever</u> comes along and volunteers to feed him.

5. <u>Whom</u> was she trying to impress by calling herself K. Blythe?

6. He stood on the street corner, casting aspersions at <u>whomever</u> passed within earshot.

7. The woman to <u>whom</u> he was married was not the one <u>who</u> he thought he had wed.

8. <u>Who</u> can you turn to if not your rich uncle Harry?

9. At <u>whom</u> was the menacing stare directed?

10. <u>Who</u> will I have to put up with this time?

PN4 ## Possessive Pronouns

> Do *not* use an apostrophe with the possessive forms of personal pronouns.

Personal pronouns have two forms for the possessive. One form is used when the pronoun acts as a modifier before the noun: *my* hat, *his* graduation, *their* problems, *her* success. The other form is used when the pronoun comes after the noun: that hat is *mine*, the mistake was *hers*, the responsibility is *theirs*.

Many writers have a special problem distinguishing between *its*, the possessive form of *it*, and *it's*, the contraction of *it is*. Be particularly careful to check that construction.

Examples

Incorrect   Bicycling had it's origin in England.
Correct   Bicycling had its origin in England.

Incorrect   Its always a good idea to confirm your flight ahead of time.
Correct   It's always a good idea to confirm your flight ahead of time.

Incorrect   The scientific method has it's own built-in validation.
Correct   The scientific method has its own built-in validation.

Use *whose* as the possessive form for *who*.

Examples

Incorrect   Georgia O'Keeffe is the woman painter who's work I admire most.
Correct   Georgia O'Keeffe is the woman painter whose work I admire most.

Incorrect   Brian was always the person who's car we used.
Correct   Brian was always the person whose car we used.

(See p. 536 for additional information about *whose*.)
In most cases, use the possessive case for a pronoun that precedes a gerund. A gerund is an *-ing* verbal acting as a noun.

Examples

Incorrect   Me winning the contest surprised everyone.
Correct   My winning the contest surprised everyone.

Incorrect   Them staying so long almost ruined the friendship.
Correct   Their staying so long almost ruined the friendship.

PN5   Reflexive and Intensive Pronouns

> 1. Use the reflexive form of pronouns when you are referring to the subject in a sentence and want to show that the subject and person being acted on are the same.

Examples

Incorrect   The Inmans accompanied my husband and myself to the concert.
Correct   The Inmans accompanied my husband and me to the concert.

Incorrect   When I was an adolescent, I criticized me constantly.
Correct   When I was an adolescent, I criticized myself constantly.

Incorrect   My brother and myself were fortunate enough to be there.
Correct   My brother and I were fortunate enough to be there.

> 2. Use a reflexive pronoun form as an intensifier when you want to stress a personal noun or pronoun in the sentence.

Examples

The president of the university taught the class himself.

Einstein himself was not a good mathematician.

She herself was not implicated in the scandal.

Exercise • **Rewrite these sentences to use the correct forms of reflexive and intensive pronouns.**

1. No one but Shahid knows about Shahid's midnight trysts. (Make it intensive.)
2. And now if you'll excuse me, I'm going to peel me some grapes.
3. I didn't think he was the kind of person who would discredit his self in public like that.

4. The ones in charge of this experiment are Igor and myself.

5. How can they deny the charges of gluttony when they theirselves have admitted to consuming more than half of last night's smorgasbord?

PN6   ## Pronoun Reference

A reader should never have to guess at the antecedent for a pronoun. The antecedent should be clearly stated in the same sentence or the sentence before it.

---

1. When using *this, that, it,* or *which,* be sure it refers to a noun, noun phrase, or noun clause. If necessary, change the pronoun to a noun or rewrite the sentence to make the reference clear.

Examples

Unclear   Didion is a moralistic writer, which is the basic theme of her books.
Clear   Morality is the basic theme of Didion's books.

Unclear   The accounts of teenage drug addiction are certainly plausible because this happens every day.
Clear   The accounts of teenage drug addiction are certainly plausible because one hears of similar cases every day.

Unclear   Coles was a fine horse trainer, but he couldn't explain it to others.
Clear   Coles was fine at training horses, but he couldn't explain it to others. ("Training horses" is now the antecedent for "it.")

Exercise •   **Rewrite these sentences to eliminate ambiguous pronoun references.**

1. My aunt Pauline's letters usually told of wardrobe selections, luncheon menus, and news recently printed in the obituary column of the local paper, which we found increasingly annoying to read.

2. Aunt Pauline used to keep large sums of money and important legal documents in her icebox, and she stored her vegetables under her four-poster bed. This earned her a reputation as a local eccentric.

3. Her home was crowded with valuable but fragile antique furniture and breakable knickknacks, which always made my mother nervous when she took us kids to visit Aunt Pauline.

4. One time my brothers and I went with my parents to visit Aunt Pauline in her home in Paris, Missouri, which was customary in the summertime.

5. Although we could very easily have caused a great deal of damage to her home, Aunt Pauline didn't worry about the way we climbed on the rickety furniture or played tag and hide-and-seek in the house. It made visits to her house especially exciting for us.

6. Her house offered a selection of daybeds, fainting couches, trundle beds, and chaise lounges for children to sleep in. That was always one of the most exciting parts of our visits.

7. The guest bedroom where the vegetables were stored was a hard place in which to maneuver because it was crowded with especially beautiful but uncomfortable old furniture, which was really quite inconvenient for my parents, who usually slept there when we visited.

8. One might we were awakened by a loud crash that originated from the room where my parents were sleeping. It was especially memorable to us kids, for whom "things that went bump in the night" were a constant concern.

9. Apparently the four-poster bed had collapsed during the night, leaving my parents sprawled on the floor in a pile of tangled bedsheets and scattered turnips, squash, and potatoes, which was to be expected, considering the age and condition of the bed.

10. The mattress had been suspended by a web of ropes laced back and forth from wooden pegs protruding from the sides of the bedframe. This used to irritate my father because he was always hitting his shins on them when he got into bed.

---

2. Make sure that the pronoun in a sentence can refer to only one antecedent. If necessary, revise the sentence to make the antecedent specific.

Examples

Unclear The doctor told Jacques that he was a lucky man.
Clear The doctor told Jacques to consider himself a lucky man.

Unclear Freud first met Jung when he was a young man.
Clear Freud first met Jung when the latter was a young man.

Unclear   When Vincent couldn't please his father, he thought he was a failure.

Clear   When Vincent couldn't please his father, he thought himself a failure.

> 3. Streamline and tighten your writing by cutting out superfluous *who*'s, *which*'s, and *that*'s when you can.

Often a writer can get rid of a *which, who,* or *that* without altering the meaning of the sentence and actually improve his or her writing by making it more concise and more pleasant to read. For that reason it is a good idea to get in the habit of checking to see if you can cut those pronouns when you are reading a draft. If you can, you may also eliminate the problems of deciding whether to use *who* or *whom* or *which* or *that.*

Examples

Wordy   The program which he wanted to see was canceled.
Improved   The program he wanted to see was canceled.

Wordy   When he found the person whom he was looking for, she turned out to be a former classmate.
Improved   When he found the person he was looking for, she turned out to be a former classmate.

Wordy   Kincaid thought that education was the cure to every problem.
Improved   Kincaid thought education was the cure to every problem. (Notice the revision also prevents the reader potentially mistaking "that" for a demonstrative pronoun modifying "education.")

Wordy   Anyone whom they choose will indeed be fortunate.
Improved   Anyone they choose will indeed be fortunate.

Wordy   The judges thought that he should have chosen a more difficult piece for the recital.
Improved   The judges thought he should have chosen a more difficult piece for the recital.

Wordy   The achievement of which he is most proud is making his marriage work.
Improved   The achievement he is most proud of is making his marriage work.

Exercise • Rewrite the following sentences to eliminate unnecessary relative pronouns.

1. Jasper is someone whom I hope never to see again.
2. The things that he did while he was here were unbelievably bizarre.
3. For one thing, he compulsively washed everything that he touched or any food that he put into his mouth.
4. He also told everyone whom he met that he was a follower of the Aztec religion and believed in animal sacrifice.
5. I knew the time had come for him to leave when he began to build an altar in the backyard and look hungrily at a dog that he had found in the park.

ADJ/ADV • Adjectives and Adverbs

ADJ/ADV 1   Definitions of Adjectives and Adverbs

Adjectives are modifiers that give information about nouns and pronouns.

Jim likes his coffee *warm*.

The *glorious* Fourth of July is my *favorite* holiday.

Healthy children are a joy.

Adverbs are modifiers that give information about verbs, adjectives, other adverbs, or, sometimes, an entire sentence.

Kevin spoke *evasively*.

Fortunately, such events are rare. (Modifies the whole sentence)

The conversation started rather *awkwardly*.

The upper-class English are *exquisitely* courteous.

It is important that writers distinguish between adjectives and adverbs and choose the appropriate word as a modifier.

ADJ/ADV 2   Adjectives

Position of Adjectives

> 1. Check the position of the adjective to see that it modifies the correct word.

Since English is a word-order language in which the position of a word strongly affects its meaning in a sentence, writers must be careful to place adjectives next to the words they modify.

Examples

Confusing   The dark girl's room was frightening. (Does "dark" refer to "girl" or to "room"?)

Clear   The girl's dark room was frightening.

An ancient Scotsman's sword hung on the wall. (Does "ancient" refer to "Scotsman" or "sword"?)

A Scotsman's ancient sword hung on the wall.

Usually an adjective comes before the word it modifies, but other positions are possible and sometimes desirable if one wants to draw attention to a noun or pronoun.

Examples

Conventional   The hearty and blonde Helga exemplifies the typical Scandinavian woman.

Variation   Helga, who is hearty and blonde, exemplifies the typical Scandinavian woman.

Conventional   The cupboards were overflowing with colorful and sparkling preserved jellies.

Variation   The cupboards were overflowing with preserved jellies, colorful and sparkling.

Conventional   The legislative halls reverberated to the sound of impassioned but ill-considered speeches.

Variation   The legislative halls reverberated to the sound of speeches, impassioned but ill-considered.

Predicate Adjectives

Predicate adjectives are adjectives that complete the linking verbs (various forms of *to be, has, have been, seem, appear, become, grow, prove*) and verbs like *feel, taste, smell,* and *look* which describe sensations. They modify nouns.

> 2. Use a predicate adjective, not an adverb, to complete linking verbs or verbs that describe sensations.

Examples

Incorrect   The corners must be swept *cleanly.*

Correct   The corners must be swept *clean.* ("Clean" modifies "corners," not "swept.")

Incorrect   Jana felt *badly* about the mistake.

Correct Jana felt *bad* about the mistake. ("Bad" modifies "Jana," not the act of feeling.)

Incorrect The natives have felt *insecurely.*
Correct The natives have felt *insecure.* ("Insecure" modifies "natives," not "felt.")

Understandably, writers can sometimes become confused about choosing the correct words to complete a linking verb because linking verbs can also be completed by an adverb that modifies the action in the sentence rather than an adjective that modifies the subject. For example, in the following pairs, both constructions are correct:

The animals grew *rapidly.*

The animals grew *restless.*

Ted looked *enviously.*

Ted looked *envious.*

To determine whether you should use a predicate adjective or an adverb to complete a verb, check to see if the word you are going to use modifies the subject or the verb of the sentence. If it modifies the subject, use an adjective; if it modifies the verb, use an adverb.

Examples

The prisoners looked *miserable.* (A predicate adjective describing the prisoners)

The prisoners looked *miserably* through the bars. (An adverb describing the way in which the prisoners looked)

The weather feels *warm* today. (A predicate adjective modifying the weather)

He feels *warmly* toward his fellow runners. (An adverb modifying the way in which the subject feels)

Use of *good* and *well*

Writers sometimes have difficulty choosing between *good* and *well.*

3. *Good* is an adjective and should be used only to modify nouns directly or as a predicate adjective completing a linking verb or verb of sensation.

Examples

Jason looks good.

That's a good movie.

He earns a good salary.

But it is incorrect to write

That job pays good. (As an adjective "good" should not modify "pays.")

The car runs good. (As an adjective "good" should not modify "runs.")

The sentences should be completed with *well*, which is an adverb.

That job pays well.

The car runs well.

One can, however, use the adverb *well* to refer to the way a person feels when the reference is to the person's health.

Examples

Harvey is feeling well again.

Margery is now a well woman.

Exercise • **Choose the correct word in each set in these sentences.**

1. He waxed (poetic, poetically) when he described the charming domestic scene: his wife on her hands and knees, (poetic, poetically) waxing the kitchen floor.

2. If he had looked (close, closely), however, he would have seen that she looked (close, closely) to tears.

3. Although a victim of olfactory hallucinations, Hamlet smelled (good, well) enough to know that something did not smell (good, well) in the state of Denmark.

4. In the dark he felt (clumsy, clumsily) for his cane; although he didn't really need it, he felt (clumsy, clumsily) without it.

5. When Charlie applied for the job at the vineyard, he was given several tests to determine if he could taste (good, well). "Here," said the vintner, handing him a glass. "Does this taste (good, well) to you?"

6. He proved (satisfactory, satisfactorily) to the jury that the maid had proven (satisfactory, satisfactorily) in her position.

7. "I'm sorry you're not feeling (good, well)," said the witch, giving Hansel's arm an investigative squeeze. "Because you feel (good, well) enough to eat."

8. You have to learn to act (professional, professionally) during an in-

terview if you ever expect to get a job acting (professional, profession-ally) with a reputable company.

9. "Don't play (coy, coyly) with me," he said, as his fingers played (coy, coyly) with her ear lobe.

10. He grew (quiet, quietly) when she revealed the rose bushes growing (quiet, quietly) in the secluded courtyard in the middle of the noisy and bustling city.

Use of *this* and *that*

4. Use the demonstrative adjectives *this* or *these* to refer to things, ideas, or persons that are close or of immediate interest. Use the demonstrative adjectives *that* and *those* to refer to things, ideas, or persons that are relatively distant or of secondary interest.

Examples

This woman is my mother.

That woman is the dean of students.

These concepts are important to his theory.

Those concepts were disproved years ago.

5. When using *this* or *that* as a modifier for the terms *kind* or *sort,* remember that they must agree in number with those terms, not with the object of the preposition *of.*

Examples

Incorrect   I am infuriated by these kind of pranks.
Correct   I am infuriated by this kind of pranks.

Incorrect   It takes time to get used to those sort of exams.
Correct   It takes time to get used to that sort of exams.

Incorrect   Whenever you find these kind of flowers, you will find hum-
    mingbirds nearby.
Correct   Whenever you find this kind of flowers, you will find humming-
    birds nearby.

Correct   Whenever you find these kinds of flowers, you will find humming-birds nearby.

ADJ/ADV 3   Adverbs

Forms of Adverbs

Most adverbs are formed by adding *-ly* to an adjective: *consciously, viciously, absent-mindedly,* and so on. There are a few, however, that have two forms — one with an *-ly* and one without.

Examples

slow, slowly	deep, deeply
tight, tightly	fair, fairly
quick, quickly	rough, roughly
even, evenly	soft, softly

The first form of each of these pairs could be used as either an adjective or an adverb. For example:

She talks rough.

That is rough talk.

It was tied tight.

She walked a tight rope.

He probed deep.

They used a deep probe.

These adverbs are unusual, however, and in most cases it is necessary to add *-ly* to an adjective to form the appropriate adverb.

---

1. In most cases, be sure that you use the *-ly* form of a modifying word when you are using that word to modify a verb.

Some of the adjectives most commonly misused as adverbs are *real, considerable, different, sure,* and *serious.*

Examples

Incorrect   The Trojans worked real hard on that horse.
Correct   The Trojans worked really hard on that horse.

Incorrect   Capital and labor think different.
Correct   Capital and labor think differently.

Incorrect   Marvin takes himself too serious.
Correct   Marvin takes himself too seriously.

Incorrect   The congregation has thought about it considerable.
Correct   The congregation has thought about it considerably.

Incorrect   That stallion is sure a fine horse.
Correct   That stallion is surely a fine horse.

Exercise   •   **Rewrite these sentences using the correct adverb forms.**

1. They were exceeding pleased to have found the real, bubbling Fountain of Youth.
2. Gregory's chant echoed lonely in the monastery's stone corridor.
3. Had I known that you could liberate the silver so easy, I wouldn't have tried to do it so sneaky myself.
4. I hope you won't hold it against Karlina that she eats so messy.
5. If you treat me nice, I'll let you down easy.
6. For an octogenarian he moves pretty spritely.
7. Elvis implored her to love him tender and true.
8. Although he had just returned triumphant from battle, I despised him nevertheless when I heard him talking mean to his hounds.
9. Tonight the children are nestled snug in their beds; last night they were nestled cozy on their ottomans.
10. He was sure proud of his polyester leisure suit, which he had ordered special from the Sears, Roebuck catalog.

Position of Adverbs

Adverbs are more flexible than adjectives and can often move around freely in a sentence, allowing writers to change emphasis or vary their style.

Examples

James spoke excitedly of his experiences.

James spoke of his experiences excitedly.

Excitedly, James spoke of his experiences.

Sometimes, however, changing the position of an adverb confuses or distorts its meaning.

> 2. Be careful to place adverbs so that their meaning cannot be misinterpreted.

Examples

Ambiguous   Killing a deer cruelly exploits animals. ("Cruelly" could modify either "killing the deer" or "exploits.")
Clear   Killing a deer exploits animals cruelly.

Ambiguous   Coming on the ruins unexpectedly cost us a great deal of money. ("Unexpectedly" could modify either "coming on the ruins" or "cost.")
Clear   Unexpectedly coming on the ruins cost us a great deal of money.

In careful written English, the adverb *only* should be placed directly before the word it modifies.

Examples

Incorrect   James only wants to go if he has enough money. ("Only" does not modify "wants.")
Correct   James wants to go only if he has enough money.

Incorrect   Swann only thinks of his own pleasure. ("Only" does not modify "thinks.")
Correct   Swann thinks only of his own pleasure.

Exercise •   **Rearrange the adverbs in these sentences to clarify the meaning.**

1. He believed finally man could fly.
2. The man who wrote poetry at home surreptitiously in his spare time did needlework.
3. The woman scratching her head vigorously picked up her pen and began doodling.
4. Your apologizing sincerely touched her.
5. It was a good idea to move furniture only onto the sun porch for the children.

ADJ/ADV 4   Comparison of Adjectives and Adverbs

Adjectives and adverbs have three degrees of comparison: positive, comparative, and superlative. The comparative form is usually made by adding *-er* to the positive form or using the words *more* or *less* before the form. The superlative is made by adding *-est* or using the words *most* or *least* before it.

Forms of Common Adjectives

Positive	Comparative	Superlative
white	white	whitest
slow	slower	slowest
agile	more agile	most agile
clean	cleaner	cleanest
active	less active	least active
friendly	friendlier	friendliest

As a rule of thumb, add *-er* or *-ier* to adjectives and adverbs of one syllable and use *more* and *most* with longer words. Often, however, you just have to trust your ear. If it sounds awkward to add *-er* to a word, use *more* or *most*.

> Use the comparative form of the adverb or adjective when comparing two things. Use the superlative form when comparing more than two things.

Examples

Incorrect   His brother is smart, but James is smartest.
Correct   His brother is smart, but James is smarter.

Incorrect   Of the two mountain peaks, Everest is highest.
Correct   Of the two mountain peaks, Everest is higher.

Incorrect   If you are choosing between a philosophy course and an astronomy course, choose the one that is the most stimulating.
Correct   If you are choosing between a philosophy course and an astronomy course, choose the more stimulating.

Incorrect   Every horse in the race was fast, but the black one was more fast.
Correct   Every horse in the race was fast, but the black one was fastest.

Exercise • Write the correct form of the adjectives in parentheses in these sentences.

1. Your pen may be (mighty) than my sword, but his truncheon is the (mighty) weapon of all.
2. I care little for your supplications and even (little) for your demands.
3. The (thankless) task of all was plucking lint from his lapels.
4. His hangers-on were actually (fun) to dance with than he.
5. A canine that is (timorous) than most is a terrier (scared) than the rest.
6. He couldn't imagine a (benign) demeanor than the extortionist's.
7. The (wicked) ruler in history led a (chaste) life than they.
8. He had (few) students in his class this year than in previous years, probably because there is (little) demand now than before for classics scholars.
9. I didn't think anyone could tell (awful) jokes than Brian, but your shaggy-dog story is the (awful) I've heard.
10. Although her hem is (even) than yours, your skirt is generally (well-made) than hers.

PUNC • Punctuation

The purpose of punctuation is to mark writing in a way that will help the reader understand the divisions within the writing; that is, figure out which groups of words belong together and how some groups relate to others. Thus punctuation is a set of signals for the reader; it takes the place of the pauses, inflections, gestures, and intonation that help us understand spoken language. A piece of writing with no punctuation would be a nightmare for a reader. It might be an even worse nightmare if writers didn't agree on a set of signals for all writing but instead punctuated their writing in any way they pleased. For that reason, scholars and editors have, over a period of time, compiled a system of punctuation that serves as a set of signals we can all rely on to mean the same thing. This section of the handbook describes that system.

PUNC 1   End Punctuation

Three kinds of punctuation marks signal the end of a sentence: periods, question marks, and exclamation points. Every complete sentence must terminate with one of these marks. (The period also serves other functions that will be discussed later.)

Periods

---

1. Use a period at the end of a declaratory statement or a command.

Examples

Calhoun hopes to take a new job this year.

Go get your raincoat.

God helps those who help themselves.

Since a period is a mark of terminal punctuation, it should never appear within a sentence unless it is marking an abbreviation — for example, *Mrs.*, *Dr.*, *M.A.* — or serving as a decimal point in a figure — *2.5* yards, *98.6* temperature.

> 2. Use a period after abbreviations.

Periods are used after letters in an abbreviation to indicate that a title, month, state, or name of an organization has been abbreviated.

Examples

Ph.D., M.D., LL.D. (doctor of laws), Ms., Mr.

Feb., Jan., Dec.

F.B.I., I.R.S., P.L.O. (Palestine Liberation Organization)

If the abbreviation is the last term in the sentence, the period that marks the last letter can also be used as the end punctuation for the sentence.

Gustave has always wanted to work for the I.R.S.

Question Marks

> 3. Use a question mark to indicate the end of a sentence that is a direct question.

Are you prepared for the trip?

When can the French expect new elections?

A question mark can also be used within a sentence under some circumstances, notably when it marks off a direct quotation inside a sentence.

"Isn't that what you expected?" she asked.

"Are oil prices ever going to stabilize?" Carl asked.

The only other case in which you would be likely to need a question mark within a sentence would be for indicating a date about which there is dispute. For instance:

The duchess lived from 1610 to 1689(?).

> 4. Do not use a question mark to indicate the end of a question that is stated in a sentence indirectly.

Examples

A question was raised about what would happen if the plan failed.

Keith asked if the issue can ever be settled.

Exclamation Points

> 5. Use an exclamation point to indicate strong emphasis at the end of a sentence or after an interjection within a sentence.

Use exclamation marks sparingly throughout your writing because they will lose their force if the reader encounters too many of them.

Good heavens! How can the team overcome such a handicap?

What a wonderful conference that was!

Exercise • **Insert the appropriate end punctuation for these sentences.**

1. Did you know that every year thousands of domestic animals are euthanized under the auspices of the S.P.C.A.

2. It breaks my heart to think of all those homeless cats and dogs

3. In our city, the executive board of the Humane Society is headed by Dr. Christine Baumann, D.V.M.

4. At one of the recent meetings she introduced a panel presentation on the theme, "Why don't more pet owners neuter their animals"

5. She and other board members wanted to find out what they could do to make pet owners take responsibility for curbing the growing number of homeless animals

6. They knew that enlisting the aid of veterinarians was an effective first step toward solving the problem, but what else could they do

7. In addition to sponsoring educational programs and providing shelter for stray animals, doesn't the S.P.C.A. publish a list of films that have not met acceptable standards for humane treatment of animals during filming

8. And how about that new pet-therapy program they are planning to start

9. It's such a wonderful idea to bring cats and dogs to rest homes and retirement centers so the residents can enjoy the company of animals

10. How interesting it is to discover that animal companionship can actually reduce stress and prolong human lives

PUNC 2   Commas

Aside from the question mark and exclamation point, writers use four marks of punctuation whose principal functions are to mark divisions in a piece of writing and keep words from bumping into each other.* They are the comma, the semicolon, the colon, and the period. The comma is the weakest of these marks and thus the one that indicates the slightest pause or least interruption in the flow of the sentence. For that reason, it is used entirely *within* sentences and independent clauses to clarify meaning and to separate elements in a sentence that need to be set off for accurate meaning.

Commas are tricky, and learning to use them appropriately is rather complicated. They're important, though, and in the long run writers need to master their uses. And it is important to learn when *not* to use commas if you want to avoid confusing your reader.

> 1. Use commas to separate independent clauses that are joined by a coordinating conjunction.

Although a separating comma is not always needed between independent clauses to clarify meaning, it is just as well to establish the good habit of inserting one in order to avoid any confusion. The comma comes *before* the joining conjunction.

Examples

He is an ambitious man, but he is not a scrupulous one.

I hope she is in class early, for her report is one that interests me. (Notice that if the comma is omitted, "early" joins with "for her report" and the reader is temporarily confused.)

The lawyer withdrew the objections, but they had already had their impact on the jury.

Exception: If both independent clauses are short and their relationship is clear, you may omit the comma without causing problems.

Examples

We had won but victory was bitter.

They followed instructions and they got lost.

*Dashes, parentheses, and brackets also are used to mark off units of writing; their functions will be discussed later.

> 2. Use a comma after a conjunctive adverb (*however, nevertheless, therefore, consequently,* and similar words) when that adverb comes after a semicolon that joins two independent clauses.

Examples

The Russians have never ratified that treaty; nevertheless, they insist that others honor it.

Jorge's reaction is understandable under the circumstances; however, he still needs to apologize.

When she took French many years ago, most colleges did not use language labs; consequently, although she reads French well, she speaks it poorly.

> 3. Use a comma to separate a subordinate clause at the beginning of a sentence.

If the pipeline is not repaired, the city will soon run out of fuel.

Until we have settled that issue, there can be no peace.

As we drove toward the river, we saw that it was flooded.

If the subordinate clause comes *after* the main clause, a comma is not necessary because the writer does not need to stress the separation so strongly.

We will get to the convention if the plane arrives on time.

The investigators cannot publish a definitive report until they have finished their research.

> 4. Use a comma to set off long modifying phrases at the beginning of a sentence.

Even if the sentence doesn't need an interrupting comma for clarity, the rhythm of such sentences demands one.

Examples

Given the circumstances under which Kim Li-Sung had lived, she adapted to prosperity remarkably well.

If you want to train horses well, it is almost necessary to serve an apprenticeship with a master trainer.

Exercise • **Insert commas where they are needed in these sentences.**

1. Oddly enough many otherwise well-informed people don't seem to know very much about the state of Iowa nor do they seem eager to remedy their ignorance.

2. In fact it seems that Iowa is mainly recognized only for its obscurity.

3. The title of the novel, *But Will They Get It in Des Moines?,* **and the popular phrase about the "little old lady from Dubuque" are references to the popular belief that Iowa is a remote outpost and its people are all somewhat provincial and old-fashioned.**

4. As I learned from a British travel guidebook to the United States Iowa also has the reputation abroad of being a fairly nondescript if not a downright boring state.

5. When I looked to see what sites and events the British were being directed to in Iowa I found only the following terse comment.

6. "If you find yourself in Des Moines you may be on your way north or south or you may be headed east or west; in either case keep going."

7. It's true Iowa has never been a trend setter and you will hear of few fashions or fads that originate there; in fact there is some truth to the rumor that hula-hoops are still the best-selling recreational device in Iowa.

8. When the *Des Moines Register* **recently held a contest to solicit a new motto to put on Iowa license plates one of the most popular suggestions was "Iowa: Gateway to Nebraska."**

9. If you ask non-Iowans what they know about Iowa they are likely to tell you about relatives in Toledo or they will smile and say, "Potatoes, right?"

10. These types of responses are so common that the campus shops in Iowa City sell T-shirts that bear the words, "University of Iowa, Idaho City, Ohio" but many out-of-state students at the university don't get the joke.

> 5. Use a comma to indicate a separation in a sentence that might be misinterpreted if that comma were missing.

When you read your draft, be alert for places where words run together and the meaning becomes confused.

Examples

John stood by the door where Joe had come in, and waited. (If the comma is omitted, the reader gets the impression that it was Joe who waited.)

If grumpy, Henry forgets his manners. (If the comma is omitted, the sentence may be read as an introductory clause.)

To the insecure, female education poses a great threat. (Without the comma, the opening phrase might be read as "To the insecure female.")

---

6. Use a comma to set off interrupting, nonrestrictive phrases or clauses in a sentence.

A *nonrestrictive* or nonessential phrase or clause is one that gives information that is supplementary, rather than essential, to the main idea of the sentence. The sentence would make sense even if the restrictive phrase or clause were omitted.

A *restrictive* or essential phrase or clause is one that gives essential information in the sentence. The meaning of the sentence would be seriously altered if it were omitted. The distinction between nonrestrictive and restrictive is not always easy to make, but the following examples should help clarify it.

Examples

Nonrestrictive A convicted felon, no matter how good his record, may not serve on a jury.

Restrictive Anyone who has been convicted of a felony may not serve on a jury.

Nonrestrictive Students, who compose one-third of registered voters in this precinct, will not be allowed to vote in this election.

Restrictive Students who have not registered in this precinct will not be allowed to vote in this election.

Nonrestrictive Hundreds of thousands of Southeast Asians, many of them once-respected professionals in their native countries, are now having to rebuild their lives in the United States.

Restrictive Hundreds of thousands of Southeast Asians who were professional people in their own countries are now having to rebuild their lives in the United States.

Sometimes you can distinguish between a restrictive and nonrestrictive phrase or clause only when you review the context in which it is used. Then

---

you have to make a judgment call according to the meaning you want to convey.

Example

Restrictive   The soldiers who couldn't read were not allowed to operate the machinery.

Nonrestrictive   The soldiers, who couldn't read, were not allowed to operate the machinery.

Here you have to decide whether your meaning is that soldiers had not been allowed to operate the machinery unless they could read. If it is, you want the restrictive clause without commas.

Restrictive   A medallion blessed by the old priest was reputed to have magical powers.

Nonrestrictive   A medallion, blessed by the old priest, was reputed to have magical powers.

Here you have to decide whether you mean that the medallion was supposed to have magical powers because it had been blessed. If you do, you want the restrictive clause.

Exercise •   **Insert commas in these sentences where they are needed to prevent misinterpretation.**

1. When Lucia married her father knew that she was not going to have an easy life.
2. As far as he could tell Alvin was a no-account who had never held down a job for more than six months at a stretch.
3. His good points, on the other hand, were well hidden and seldom revealed themselves to Lucia's father.
4. Although Lucia's father wanted to protest her marriage to Alvin was made official on the scheduled day.
5. Although Alvin didn't seem concerned about two hundred dollars was all that stood between him and abject poverty.
6. While he sat and smoked Lucia's father learned of the method by which Alvin proposed to become a millionaire without working.
7. The plan was confusing his son-in-law told him only because it was not the sort of scheme a conventional businessman would think of.
8. Thus far the lucrative potential of chain letters had not been exploited on a large scale by anyone but Alvin intended to change all that.

9. As he spent his time writing complaints from his father-in-law fell on deaf ears.

10. The pressures of arranging to buy postage stamps for Alvin and her father's determination to have her marriage annulled were beginning to take their toll on Lucia's health and appearance.

---

7. Use commas to set off appositives in a sentence.

An appositive is a explanatory phrase inserted after a noun to give additional information about it. It is usually nonrestrictive and thus is set off by commas.

Examples

Her uncle, the chairman of the board, gave her that information.

Blackwell, an ex-policeman, is their security guard.

Tokyo, the world's largest city, has crushing traffic problems.

---

8. Use commas to set off various kinds of minor interrupters such as qualifying phrases, introductory sentence adverbs (see p. 554), and words or expressions that compare and contrast.

Qualifying Phrases

Examples

You must get people believing, even in small ways, that they are winners.

Maigret, despite the myths, never did have a secret method for solving crimes.

It is customary, however, to pay for extra service.

Introductory Sentence Adverbs

Examples

Happily, she was still able to join the group.

Not surprisingly, the chairman was furious at her colleagues.

Understandably, Brian didn't want to go back there.

Expressions that Compare and Contrast

Examples

Microcomputers, on the other hand, fit conveniently on an office desk.

In the same way, Central Loan and Savings has taken over the outstanding loans of private banks.

Janice's second reaction, however, was anger.

Marketing stocks requires knowledge, not charm.

Exercise • Insert commas in these sentences where needed to mark off appositives.

1. My psychologist told me that I needed assertiveness training the way Attila the Hun needed the atom bomb.
2. Bob Dylan wailer of songs and ballads proved that you don't have to be able to carry a tune to become a famous singer.
3. There are some nasty rumors all of them untrue circulating about the Archangel Gabriel.
4. Melvin the Magnificent the man of my dreams has left me in the lurch a spot I never expected to occupy.
5. Clarence Witherspoon professor of classics threatened to leave academia and offer his talents to industry if the board rejected his demands for a raise.

---

9. Use commas to separate words, phrases, or clauses in a series.

Most editors prefer that writers insert a comma after every element in a series except the last; however, omitting the commas after the word that comes before the connecting term is permissible.

Examples

Traditional   The early explorers were searching for gold, spices, and precious stones.

Permissible   The early explorers were searching for gold, spices and precious stones.

Other examples of traditional punctuation:

The recipe called for cream, cheese, onions, and marjoram.

The volunteers took down the decorations, swept the floor, and replaced all the chairs.

The semester has been exhausting, frustrating, and generally difficult.

> 10. Use commas to separate adjectives in a series when they modify the same noun.

Adjectives that modify the same noun are called *coordinate adjectives;* that is, they are serving the same kind of function. To test whether the adjectives you are using are coordinate, ask yourself if they could be joined by *and* or if their positions could be changed without altering the sense of the sentence. For example, in this sentence the adjectives could be moved about: "It had been a long, dreamy, romantic summer." Thus they are coordinate.

In this one, however, the adjectives could not be moved or linked by *and:* "Melissa appeared in a shockingly tight dinner dress." Thus they are not coordinate.

Examples

The cruise liner was a sumptuous, elegant, clean ship.

Norman Cousins writes of crippling, mind-numbing panic experienced by heart attack victims.

Cassandra was fated to be a misunderstood, mistrusted woman.

Exercise • **Insert commas where needed to mark off items in a series.**

1. She jilted the lawyer spurned the judge disappointed the IBM executive and finally accepted the proposal of the refrigerator repairman.

2. Her unlikely suitor was younger shorter and less intelligent than she.

3. We didn't know if her decision to marry him should be taken as a cruel joke an indication of madness or a pointed social comment.

4. Despite our grave misgivings we wished them health happiness and a long life together.

5. The newlyweds gulped their cake swilled their champagne and bolted from the reception hall to the waiting van.

> 11. Use commas in the conventional ways to mark off units in numbers, addresses, titles, dates, and salutations, and within sentences to introduce quotations and separate terms of direct address.

In writing numbers, commas are used to mark off units of three digits:

5,689   2,100,000   48,500

Commas are not used to separate digits in serial numbers or street addresses:

S5728933   5001 North Lamar   Apt. 2026

In addresses:

Carstairs House, Culloden, Scotland
12 Hampingdon Mews, London SW 3, England
Route 1, Box 70, Taylor, Texas

In titles:

Tabitha Hunter, M.D., F.A.C.S.
Admiral Ralph Cousins, U.S.N., ret.
Lucy Hairston, M.D., Ph.D.

In dates:

January 6, 1987
May 5, 402 B.C.

In salutations and closings of letters:

Dear Ms. Cutright,
Dear General Hood,
Cordially,
Sincerely yours,

In introducing or attributing quotations:

Nora said, "Won't that testimony be challenged?"
"Never get in the way of progress," Clark wrote.
"Given the circumstances," said Lee, "we have no choice."

Exception: Commas are not necessary if a short phrase is being quoted as part of a sentence.

The revolution proved to be "a sordid boon."
In England the expression for a fatal accident is "He bought the farm."

---

12. Use commas to set off terms of direct address in a sentence.

Given your qualifications, Nancy, you should get the job.

Colleagues, we have serious deliberations before us.

Fellow workers, you have nothing to lose but your chains.

Exercise • **Insert commas in these sentences where required by conventional usage.**

1. On May 20 1953 she was borne, kicking and screaming, to an early grave.

2. I knew from the aggressive slant of her handwriting that Caverna Dunn Ph.D. was not the woman for the job.

3. Before opening the envelope, I tried to think whom I knew at 100 Main Street Normal Illinois 42500.

4. She had read almost 4000 pages of the 8974388-page manuscript before she finally heaved it aside in disgust and began to compose a rejection letter to its author.

5. Whom are you trying to intimidate by calling yourself Julian T. Potterspell III Ph.D. D.D.S.?

Misuse of Commas

Since a comma is a interrupting mark and always indicates a slight pause, writers have to be careful where they insert them. They should not be used when they will interrupt the flow of thought or signal an unwanted stop between two elements that go together: between subject and verb, subject and complement, verb and object, or preposition and object.

---

13. Do not insert a comma between main sentence elements in a way that interrupts the flow of the idea.

Examples

Incorrect   One mark of an educated person is, an appreciation of the classics. (The comma signals a pause between a verb, "is," and its complement, "appreciation," two words that must not be divided here.)

Correct   One mark of an educated person is an appreciation of the classics.

Incorrect   Today most women who have careers, also want to have families. (The comma interrupts the direct connection between the subject "women" and the verb "want.")

Correct   Today most women who have careers also want to have families.

Incorrect   Drake's soldiers defeated, the Spanish Armada. (The comma makes the reader stop between the verb "defeated" and its immediate object, "armada.")

Correct   Drake's soldiers defeated the Spanish Armada.

Incorrect   Steve has every good quality one could want except, a sense of responsibility. ("A sense of responsibility" is the object of the preposition "except" and should not be separated from it by a comma.)

Correct   Steve has every good quality one could want except a sense of responsibility.

---

14. Do not insert a comma between two words or phrases joined by *and*.

Examples

Incorrect   The office is divided into avid smokers, and militant nonsmokers.

Correct   The office is divided into avid smokers and militant nonsmokers.

Incorrect   The trappings of success, and the status that went with them were dear to Jeffrey.

         The trappings of success and the status that went with them were dear to Jeffrey.

Exercise • **Remove commas from these sentences where they interfere with the flow of the meaning.**

1. Living on a dairy farm, we always had enough milk, to support a huge, herd of cats.
2. Cats are, usually, able to figure out how they can live a comfortable life, without having to pay for it.
3. Cats, that live on a dairy farm, quickly figure out where their food is coming from, and, rapidly, form a close attachment, to the cows.
4. Our cats learned to gather around the cows, at milking time, sometimes even, lining up beside the empty buckets, to meet my father, when he came to the barn, to do the morning chores.
5. From time to time, my father, would break the rhythm of his milking,

to shoot a stream of milk sideways, into the open mouth, of a hungry cat, hovering, politely, nearby.

A Final Caution About Commas

In the editorial offices of most magazines, newspapers, and publishing houses today, the tendency is to use fewer commas than are called for by strict rules of usage. The reasoning is that an excessive number of commas can make writing choppy and difficult to read. Thus, if editors believe that a sentence doesn't need a comma to clarify meaning, they are inclined to omit it. And since editors in these places are the people who gradually change the rules of usage, their lead is worth following.

If you have a tendency to put in commas everywhere you think they may be needed just to be on the safe side, you may be overpunctuating your sentences and making them more difficult to read than they need to be. So when you are editing your last draft, consider whether you could improve your writing by eliminating some commas where they seem to be clogging up your writing.

Examples

Overpunctuated Last night, when the meeting was over, Randall, tired and, therefore, irritable, made a serious, though not fatal, error. (That's hard to read!)

Improved Last night when the meeting was over, Randall, tired and therefore irritable, made a serious though not fatal error.

Overpunctuated Of course, given what we know now, we realize that Francisco made his debut too early, but, in light of the circumstances, we will have to do the best we can.

Improved Of course given what we know now, we realize that Francisco made his debut too early, but in light of the circumstances, we will have to do the best we can.

Exercise • **Remove excess commas from these sentences to avoid overpunctuation.**

1. When Elizabeth, late, and, therefore, flustered, tried to sneak behind stage of the large, dark, concert hall, she caught her heel and, to her chagrin, stumbled into the orchestra pit.

2. Franz, the orchestra leader, looking splendid but, for a number of reasons, flustered himself, looked up, and, trying to stay calm, went on conducting the William Tell Overture.

3. But, as the violins played the melody, and the French horns took up the subtheme, he saw Elizabeth, struggling with all her strength, trying to extricate herself from the clutches of a folding chair.

4. The chair, a wooden relic of earlier days and, consequently, rickety and rattly, began to splinter and disintegrate as Elizabeth flailed about.

5. And, as the overture thundered to a climax, Elizabeth and the chair collapsed on the floor, but, as she proudly pointed out later, she and the cymbals struck at the same time.

PUNC 3   Semicolons and Colons

Semicolons

A semicolon is a more forceful mark of punctuation than a comma, signaling a more significant pause and a stronger interruption. Because it should be used only between coordinate sentence elements, it has many fewer uses than a comma. Those uses are important, however, and worth mastering since writers who know how to use semicolons can solve many of their punctuation and transition problems. Some of the nineteenth-century writers like John Stuart Mill were masterful wielders of the semicolon, and as a result, their prose was tightly unified and gracefully balanced.

Example

> As it is useful that while mankind are imperfect there should be different opinions, so it is that there should be different experiments of living; that free scope should be given to varieties of character, short of injury to others; and that the worth of different modes of living be proved practically, when anyone thinks fit to try them. (John Stuart Mill, *On Liberty*)

> 1. Use a semicolon to connect coordinate clauses that are independent but very closely related.

Examples

Incorrect Johnson is not at her best when she lectures, she communicates best in small seminars. (comma splice)

Correct, but choppy Johnson is not at her best when she lectures. She communicates best in small seminars.

Correct and smooth Johnson is not at her best when she lectures; she communicates best in small seminars.

Other correct examples:

Yesterday we were confronted with the waste of our natural resources; today we are confronted with pollution as well.

The issue is not who is right and wrong; it is who can make their views prevail.

A painter with taste will trust his eye to tell him what needs to be on his canvas and what doesn't; the one without taste will give us a landscape that's too pretty, or too cluttered, or too gaudy in its colors — anyway, too something. (William Zinsser, *On Writing Well*)

The independent clauses in any of these sentences could be separated and marked as sentences (and that should be one of your tests for this kind of construction), but the ideas being expressed in each case are so closely related that joining them with a semicolon makes more unified writing.

---

2. Use a semicolon to precede a transition word that connects independent clauses.

Examples

Incorrect Hawkins will make a good district attorney, moreover, she will make an effective candidate. (comma splice)

Correct Hawkins will make a good district attorney; moreover, she will make an effective candidate.

Other correct examples:

The statute of limitations on that crime expired over a year ago; as a result, Morenci cannot be tried.

Johann has no interest in taking over the Taj Mahal; nevertheless, he will participate in negotiations.

Joan was wearing a splendid new jogging suit; however, she collapsed after the second mile.

> 3. Use semicolons as separation marks when you want to connect several clauses or phrases that have internal punctuation.

If you use commas to mark off elements in a series that already have commas in them, the result will be total chaos; if you use semicolons, however, the feat can be managed easily.

Examples

Chaotic   The people who gathered at the swimming pool were Grant Rock, a former Harley-Davidson racer, Mondy Koontz, who was a disc jockey at L.A. in the seventies, Sam Santos, who did great imitations of Woody Allen, and Lily Lopiano, the rodeo sweetheart from Laramie.

Controlled   The people who gathered at the swimming pool were Grant Rock, a former Harley-Davidson racer; Mondy Koontz, who was a disc jockey in L.A. in the seventies; Sam Santos, who did great imitations of Woody Allen; and Lily Lopiano, the rodeo sweetheart from Laramie.

Other correct examples:

Those who participated in the meeting were Gerald Young, president of the company; Moralia Young, principal stockholder; Robert Mills, the inventor of the new device; and Mrs. Herbert Cohn, the widow of the former chairman of the board.

Robinson told of the experiments with monkeys, who responded unusually well; with rats, who didn't respond at all; and with pigs, who refused to cooperate.

> 4. Use semicolons to connect a series of closely related parallel clauses into one tight sentence.

Examples

Correct   There are several advantages to the plan: if we lose our director, we can easily find another one; if one of the participants drops out, we will still have enough people to work with; if we should fail, we have not invested a great deal of money.

Correct   Professional basketball fans are the most loyal of all; they show up for every home game, even when the team is losing; they charter planes for out-of-town games so their team will always have rooters; they reserve their season tickets years ahead; they never bet against their own teams; and they donate funds when recruitment time comes around.

> 5. Do not use a semicolon between clauses or sentence elements that are not coordinate.

Examples

Incorrect   Although the house had been heavily promoted and on the market for six months; they refused to lower the asking price.

Incorrect   Murphy never understood that he had lost the respect of all of his coworkers; because of his failure to take responsibility.

Exercise •   Insert semicolons at the appropriate places in these sentences.

1. Christoph wasn't crazy about the idea of hitchhiking across a strange country however there seemed no other alternative.
2. The ancient and dilapidated pick-up groaned to a halt at the side of the highway it was his first ride however uncomfortable it might prove to be.
3. The cab of the pick-up was already filled to capacity it seemed, with a large radio wedged between the driver and her companion, two lively kittens scampering from one lap to the other, and a litter box on the floor in front of the passenger seat, but the two women, smiling and nodding and hastily trying to make their belongings more compact, assured Christoph that there was plenty of room for him.
4. He would have to put his bag in the back however, and this made Christoph somewhat nervous his passport and all his money were in that bag.
5. He surrendered his bag to the crowded depths of the pick-up, fearing the worst, nevertheless it came as a shock to him when, several hours later, the driver pulled her vehicle to a halt and informed him, "Your luggage seems to have fallen onto the interstate."

Colons

The colon is a strong mark of punctuation that says, in effect, "Stop and pay attention. Something is going to follow." What follows may be an entire piece of writing, such as a letter, a list, an explanation or expansion, an illustration, a quotation, or a summary. Be careful, then, to use the colon only when you want to draw the reader's attention to what is coming.

> 6. Use a colon to separate an introductory element and signal that something else is coming.

Examples

Salutations for a business letter

Gentlemen:

Dear Customer:

Heading for a memorandum

To: All personnel in Unit 4

From: Commanding Officer Inkster

Subject: Recent changes in leave policy

Introduction of a list or series of items

These cities participated in the training program: Chicago, Dallas, New Orleans, Minneapolis, and Seattle.

The company will insist on these conditions: abundant water, reasonably priced housing, low taxes, and a supply of skilled labor.

To make gazpacho, throw the following ingredients in your food processor: ripe tomatoes, green peppers, garlic, cucumbers, a small onion, and tomato juice.

An explanation or expansion

New Yorkers are mad for Texas chic: they love cowboy boots, chili parlors, Lone Star beer, and Texas performers like Willie Nelson and Jerry Jeff Walker.

Some psychologists say that today's young men are the postponing generation: they fear commitments, they postpone marriage while waiting for the perfect woman, and they are reluctant to commit themselves to one career.

In titles to indicate expansion in a subtitle

The Serial: A Year in the Life of Marin County

Creative Separation: The Dividends of Splitting

"The Winds of Change: Thomas Kuhn and the Revolution in the Teaching of Writing"

At the end of a sentence to introduce an illustration

One attribute is necessary for living in Mexico: patience.

Our throw-away culture makes a mockery of two old-fashioned virtues: thrift and self-restraint.

At the end of a sentence to summarize content

All these developments can be summarized in one word: disaster.

The account of folly in the book *The March of Folly* can be summed up simply: governments are extraordinarily stupid.

To introduce a quotation

One of Galbraith's comments illustrates my point: "Faced with the choice of spending time on the unpublished scholarship of a graduate student and the unpublished work of Galbraith, I have seldom hesitated."

Kennedy's inaugural address concluded with this statement: "With a good conscience our only sure reward, with history the final judge of our deeds, let us go forth to lead the land we love, asking His blessing and His help, but knowing that here on earth God's work must truly be our own."

---

7. Do not use a colon as a mark of anticipation after a grammatically incomplete expression, especially after a preposition or a linking verb.

Examples

Incorrect   The requirements for the job are: union membership, five years' experience, and a high school diploma. ("The requirements are . . ." is not a grammatically complete expression and thus should not have a colon as a mark of anticipation.)

Incorrect   The movie is about: organized crime, drug smuggling, and graft. ("The movie is about . . . is an unfinished sentence element and should not have a colon at the end of it.)

Exercise   Substitute colons for other marks of punctuation at appropriate places in these sentences.

1. The following businesses have opened up in the new Superhealth Shopping Center, Weight for Me, Fit or Fat, Nautilus Forever, and The Magnificent Metabolism.
2. All of these establishments have one motto — Live Forever!
3. The proprietor of one shop put it this way, "We haven't ratified getting old."

---

4. A banner over the entrance of another proclaims; "If It Sags, We Can Fix It."

5. Ultimately, this is their philosophy, there's money in youth.

PUNC 4   Dashes, Parentheses, and Brackets

Dashes

Dashes are convenient marks of punctuation when you want to signal a kind of temporary detour in your writing. They should be used sparingly, however, because they are rather imprecise marks of punctuation, and the guidelines about using them are hazy.

> 1. Use dashes to set off parenthetical material when you want to emphasize the contrast between that material and the rest of the sentence.

Examples

To lose one's temper because of a slighting remark — and certainly there are times when it is difficult not to do so — is a self-defeating indulgence.

In spite of the delays and interruptions — and God knows there were plenty of them — we managed to finish the project on time.

> 2. Use a dash to indicate any sudden change in the structure or the direction of a sentence.

Examples

As a stern Calvinist, Jordan believed in predestination, original sin, the election of saints — and his own infallibility.

Michael had everything Jane admired in a man: humor, ability, elegant manners, rugged good looks — and a great deal of money.

If one looks at the issue from the communists' point of view — but of course we are not capable of doing that.

> 3. Use a dash to indicate that what follows is a summary of the previous material in the sentence.

Examples

Too much rain, insects, an early frost — all contributed to the crop failure that year.

Good grades, high test scores, strong recommendations — the person who hopes to get into graduate school must have all of these.

Notice in these examples that a colon would not have been appropriate because the part of the sentence before the dash is not a complete sentence element.

> 4. Use dashes to mark off a phrase that has been inserted to add an extra element of emphasis to a sentence.

Examples

Whatever one's stand on the issue — and one must take a stand — the problems will not be resolved soon.

Given their tendency to procrastinate — a tendency that seems to be getting worse — we can hardly expect a decision this week.

Note: In typing or using a word processor, indicate a dash by two hyphens on the typewriter or screen; there should be no space between the dash and the words next to it.

Parentheses

> 5. Use parentheses to enclose explanatory remarks or digressive remarks in a sentence.

Remember that you must always use two parentheses because they represent signs that signal enclosure; to use only one would be like using one book end to hold up a group of books. Often parentheses serve almost the same function as a set of dashes; they enclose explanatory remarks.

Examples

Lately when I go to London (and I have been there just recently), I have been disappointed at the caliber of the plays in the West End.

Robison never thought that he would want to return to the house on Euston Avenue (long since converted into a funeral home), but he found himself drawn toward it as soon as he arrived in the city.

This year I have learned French by listening (cassette tapes, records, and French movies), by reading (novels and a biweekly newspaper), and by studying (a workbook and grammar text).

Notice that in these sentences the commas come *after* the completed parentheses. Punctuation should come after the parentheses and be placed outside.

Brackets

The functions of brackets are different from those of parentheses, and the two kinds of marks should not be used interchangeably. Brackets indicate that whatever is enclosed in them does not actually belong in the text but has been put in to provide necessary explanation or editorial comment.

---

6. Use brackets to set off explanations by an editor or author.

Examples

Brooks said, "I think that she [Emily Dickinson] was the finest poet of her time." (The author has inserted the words in brackets to give the readers information they need but do not get from the quotation.)

The report focused on the material that he had published the year before [a biography of Thomas More] under another name. (The author is giving the reader important information that the straight sentence does not provide.)

Anthony West's new book focuses on the difficult relationship between his father [the famous H. G. Wells] and his mother, Rebecca West.

---

7. Use brackets to enclose material that you are providing to give the reader a context for a statement or to fill in material that is missing from a quotation.

Examples

When Jefferson referred to his "splendid misery" [his term for the presidency], one never knew if he was being ironic.

Cousins has been both honored and scorned for his aggressive challenge to the medical establishment [his claim that laughter is a legitimate treatment].

Viola suggests, "Read those flyers [from the life insurance companies] if you want a blatant example of misleading statistics."

---

8. Use brackets around the word *sic* to indicate that you are reproducing an exact quotation, and that the mistake or lapse in the quotation is in the original document.

Examples

The document on display at the archives says, "This manuscript is attributed to Shakespeer [*sic*]."

In his speech to promote more funds for teaching English, the senator distributed a brochure that claimed "The starting celery [*sic*] of teachers in this state is a scandal."

Exercise • Insert dashes, parentheses, or brackets where appropriate in these sentences.

1. Have you ever wondered probably not who writes the grammar and punctuation exercises for handbooks like this one?

2. One of the most famous writers of exercises if there can be any fame in such a profession was Hiram Rothschild 1867–1926.

3. We cannot underestimate the value of his contributions to the profession the creation of several heuristics for inventing grammatical infelicities, the unionization of professional exercise writers and the organization of the first National Conference for Grammarians and Usage Experts NCGUE.

4. It was Rothschild whose life story was the inspiration for the best-selling novel soon to be released as a major motion picture *The Exercist* this is the term preferred over "exercise writer" by members of the profession.

5. Yet another esteemed past member was Winston Churchill whose classic exception to the rule about prepositions occupying the final

position in sentences is an inspiration to us all: "That is an impertinence up with which I will not put" or was it Mark Twain who said that?

6. One of the more eccentric exercists of this country devoted more than fifteen years of her life to the task of embedding her autobiography in the grammar exercises of three major handbooks an accomplishment that to my knowledge has never been duplicated by any other exercist.

7. Other professional writers tend to discount the abilities of exercists that is especially true of novelists and journalists claiming that it takes no great talent to product grammatical errors.

8. A little known fact, however, is that many exercists, Karen Elizabeth Gordon, for example, are also novelists themselves.

9. Although even the most ignorant and unschooled can produce usage violations and punctuational atrocities with no trouble whatsoever, making mistakes deliberately is more difficult far more difficult than you might imagine.

10. As Rothschild himself once observed, "Its *sic* like having to be funny on command."

PUNC 5   Quotation Marks and Ellipsis Marks

These two types of punctuation are signals that give a reader useful information about the writing that he or she is reading. They can tell the reader whether that writing represents the author's own words or those of someone else and whether anything has been omitted from a passage that is being quoted. Quotation marks are also used to indicate the title of an article or a chapter in a book. (See the section on italics for conventions concerning titles of books and magazines.) Without these signals, readers would often be confused about who wrote what and to what item a specific group of words is referring.

Knowing the conventions for these marks is especially important when you are writing a research paper and must indicate clearly when you are quoting and when you have omitted something.

Quotation Marks

The conventions of quotation marks sometimes seem mysterious and arbitrary, and indeed sometimes they are. Anyone would be hard pressed to explain why one must always put commas and periods inside quotation marks but semicolons outside, or why a quotation mark at the end of a sentence should not come before the period. But those are the conventions, and it is useful to memorize most of them so you don't have to look them up constantly.

> 1. Use quotation marks to indicate spoken passages when you are writing dialogue.

Examples

"Clean hit," George said. "Not an inch off mark." He pulled the arrow out of the target and walked back to the toe line, a little smug.

"My turn to shoot. I'm going to match your shot."

"Sweep, sweep, sweep!" Melanie cried at me as we headed toward the rapids with the rock looming directly before us. "Get over! We've got to eddy out."

"I can't! I'm not strong enough — we're going over," I hollered back at her. And in ten seconds we did, into the fast, cold waters of the Chatooga.

Writing dialogue requires that the author pay close attention to the fine points of using quotation marks. If you are writing stories and need to use dialogue frequently, you would do well to study the patterns in a novel or short story or consult a manual about writing fiction.

> 2. Use quotation marks to set off spoken passages when you are directly quoting what someone else has written or said.

Examples

What he saw there I saw now. It appeared to me to be a hill of fur. "Big boar grizzly," Fedeler said in a near whisper. (John McPhee, *Coming into the Country*)

The other man was not, after all, much different from her husband. They both gave orders: she followed. "If you tell your family, I'll beat you. I'll kill you. Be here again next week." (Maxine Hong Kingston, *The Woman Warrior*)

Eldridge Cleaver says, "There is in James Baldwin's work the most grueling, agonizing, total hatred of blacks . . . that one can find in the writings of any black American writer of note in our time."

If you quote a long passage from a work, one that would run to more than three lines in your paper, you should omit the quotation marks and signal that you're quoting by indenting the whole passage. (You will notice that pattern many times in the main part of this book.) For instance:

> There is practically no exchange of words among riveters. Not only are they averse to conversation, which would be reasonable enough in view of the effect they have on the conversation of others, but they are averse to speech in any form. The catcher faces the heater. He holds up his tin can. The heater swings his tongs, releasing one handle. The red iron arcs through the air in one of those parabolas so much admired by the stenographers in the neighboring windows. And the tin can clanks. (*Fortune Magazine*, "Riveters")

---

3. Use single quotation marks to mark off a quotation within another quotation.

Examples

James remarked, "My father's favorite quotation is 'There's a sucker born every minute.'"

"I will always remember that counselor's advice: 'Take what you want and pay for it,'" said Hannah.

---

4. Use quotation marks around the titles of short works such as poems, short stories, magazine or newspaper articles, essays, and chapters in books.

Examples

Her favorite poem is Robert Frost's "Home Burial."

Dickson referred to the chapter in McGill's book titled "Why Men Fear Intimacy." (Notice that the quotation marks around the title signal that it refers to the chapter, not the book.)

Fitzgerald's story "Winter Dreams" prefigures the famous *The Great Gatsby*.

The classic statement about Doublespeak is Orwell's essay "Politics and the English Language."

The *Newsweek* article "And Man Created the Chip" is a kind of primer of microcomputers.

Two cautions:

- Do not put quotation marks around the title of your own papers.
- In a sentence do not put a comma before a title marked off by quotation marks.

> 5. In certain instances, use quotation marks to set off special words within a sentence: for example, words used ironically or words that need to be identified as a term of some kind.

Examples

Words used ironically

Their "benefactors" fled with the last of their savings.

The language of the petition was, you might say, "down to earth."

You should use this device sparingly; otherwise you will seem to be apologizing for your word choice. And you should not use quotation marks around slang words. As Strunk and White say in an elegant little guide for writers, *The Elements of Style:*

> If you use a colloquialism or a slang word or phrase, simply use it; do not draw attention to it by enclosing it in quotation marks. To do so is to put on airs, as though you were inviting the reader to join you in a select society of those who know better.

Examples

Words identified as terms

"Hopefully" is a word often used incorrectly.

The spelling checkers that come with word processing programs will not tell you when you write "allusion" for "illusion" or "except" for "accept."

In this context the word "discipline" refers to a special field of study.

> 6. Put quotation marks *outside* of periods and commas; put quotation marks *inside* semicolons and colons. Check the context to see where to put them with question marks, exclamation points, and dashes.

Probably no one claims the system is logical, and at times even people who should be last-word experts disagree on where to put quotation marks. So don't try to decipher the system rationally — just learn the rules, especially the one prescribing that commas and periods always go *inside* the quotation marks.

Examples

Commas and periods

He made frequent use of the terms "wired," "space cadet," and "in the fast lane."

"If I can come," he said, "it will be on Tuesday."

Hawkins claims in his book, "The childish side of the American character surfaced during the postwar period," but he does not go on to support this claim with evidence.

To everyone's great surprise, Sam concluded his speech by saying, "Hurray for the C.I.A."

Fontaine made this criticism: "I believe it is a romantic oversimplification to say, as Wordsworth does, that poetry is 'emotion recollected in tranquillity.'"

The last story that Jack had read was Faulkner's "Barn Burning."

Examples

Semicolons and colons

Marx had always thought of himself as a "man of reason"; nevertheless, Marxists often appeal mainly to the passions.

The terms Selzer favors are "invasive procedures" and "treatment of choice"; the terms his critics use are "cutting" and "radiation."

A resident in internal medicine assists at many "Code Blues": the medical term for a cardiac arrest emergency.

Question marks, exclamation points, and dashes can be placed inside *or* outside of the quotation marks, depending on the situation. They come *inside* when they apply to the quotation only. They come *outside* the final quotation mark when they apply to the whole statement.

Examples

Is this an instance of "checks and balances"?

She said, "He is absolutely insane!"

Harold broke in to protest, "But I never ——" but got nowhere.

Don't they always end up saying, "But that's the bottom line"? (Question mark applies to the whole statement.)

It's an outright scandal that half the teachers didn't get the so-called "merit raises"! (Exclamation point applies to the whole sentence.)

A final caution about the ins and outs of quotation marks: you can never have *two* end punctuation marks. So, for example, if you end your sentence with a question mark inside quotations, you shouldn't add a period. The examples below are correctly punctuated.

The last thing that his counselor said as he left was "Do you think you can handle the guilt?"

In the end, the crucial question that a business person has to ask about any proposed new product is "Will it sell?"

Exercise • Insert quotation marks where needed in these sentences, and insert punctuation marks where needed in sentences in which quotation marks are used.

1. "What would you get" he queried idly "if you crossed Lassie with a cantaloupe"
2. "A melancholy baby" she guessed.
3. He felt a momentary contempt for the weatherman as he looked out his bedroom window at four inches of partly cloudy rushing down his driveway.
4. Have you ever heard him sing Where Have All the Flowers Gone?
5. Lascivious was the word that best described his advances.
6. Watch out he screamed, just in time to prevent her from straying absentmindedly into the path of an oncoming bread truck.
7. She consistently typed resulted as resluted.
8. Keith's lifestyle had always been what my mother would call intemperate; he denied himself nothing and indulged himself in easy vices.
9. Alas she mourned the scoundrel has absconded with my camshaft.
10. The phrase I remember from Saki's short story, The Open Window, is Birdie, why do you bound?

Ellipsis Marks

An ellipsis mark is a series of three dots used to indicate that something has been omitted from a quotation. The responsible writer uses it scrupulously every time he or she leaves out anything from quoted material; otherwise that writer is vulnerable to the charge of distorting or misrepresenting someone else's words. An ellipsis gives the reader a signal that what he or she is reading has been edited and is not the complete original text.

> 7. Use three separated dots (. . .) to indicate that something has been omitted from a sentence being quoted.

Examples

An edited quotation from John Stuart Mill

Unless anyone who approves of punishment for the promulgation of opinions flatters himself that he is a better man than Marcus Aurelius . . . let him abstain from that joint assumption of infallibility of himself and the multitude, which the great Antoninus made with so unfortunate a result. (*On Liberty*)

An edited quotation from Berton Roueche

The belief that alcoholism stems directly from some personality derangement is the oldest of the explanatory theories still in scientific vogue. . . . Among those on active duty in alcohol research, its vogue, however, has waned. That is not to say they reject it. They merely regard it as incomplete. Alcoholism, in their opinion, is far too dark and prickly to be accounted for so simply. (*The Neutral Spirit*)

The second example uses four dots in the ellipsis to show that an entire sentence has been left out.

> 8. Use a full line of ellipsis dots to indicate that an entire paragraph or more, or an entire line or more of poetry, has been left out.

Example

An edited quotation from Carol Gilligan

While women thus try to change the rules in order to preserve relationships, men, in abiding by these rules, depict relationships as easily replaced. Projecting violence . . . they write stories about infidelity and betrayal that end with the male acrobat dropping the woman, presumably replacing the relationship and going on with the act.

. . . .

The prevalence of violence in male fantasy, like the exploitive imagery in the moral judgment of the eleven-year-old boy and the representation of theft as the way to resolve a dispute, is consonant with the view of aggression as endemic in human relationships. (*In a Different Voice*)

PUNC 6   Hyphens

Except for the convention that a hyphen is used to divide a word at the end of a line, there are few absolute rules for hyphens. There are, however, some useful guidelines.

> 1. Use a hyphen to divide a word that must be broken because it comes at the end of a line.

Although hyphens are used in this way less in these days of word processors that justify lines, it is still useful to hyphenate words occasionally. There are correct and incorrect ways to divide words; when in doubt, consult a dictionary for the proper form.

> 2. Use a hyphen between words to form common compound nouns.

Examples

mother-in-law

ten-year-old

sergeant-at-arms

representative-at-large

There are few rules for making this kind of compound nouns and even editors cannot always agree on which word groups should be hyphenated and which should not. As a rule of thumb, hyphenate those in which the words seem to you to be most closely connected, like *secretary-treasurer* and *father-in-law*. For others, use your own judgment.

> 3. Use hyphens to connect the words in compound adjectives.

Examples

a hang-dog look

a go-to-hell attitude

a run-of-the-mill movie

a ten-year-old boy

a play-by-play description

self-styled liberal

self-contained package

a once-in-a-lifetime chance

> 4. Use a hyphen between the prefix *ex-* and a noun; use a hyphen with any prefix that comes before a proper noun.

Examples

ex-football player

ex-wife

ex-governor

pro-American sentiments

anti-European feeling

super-Texan

anti-Semitic

pre-World War I styles

> 5. Use a hyphen to connect the two words of many compound modifiers.

Examples

a twentieth-century painter

a dyed-in-the-wool conservative

a card-carrying liberal

In general, in the editing departments of newspapers, magazines, and publishing firms, the tendency is toward fewer hyphens and toward joining more compound words. If you are not sure whether to hyphenate and the term seems clear without hyphenation, either leave it alone or try joining the two words. If you're really in doubt, check the dictionary. And if you haven't time to do that, gamble on what looks right to you.

Exercise • **Insert hyphens where needed in these sentences.**

1. Seeing Stagger Lee in concert was a once in a lifetime experience.
2. Ever since I first learned to like rock and roll, I've wanted to hear this top notch band.
3. In particular, I dreamed of meeting their curly haired drummer at some after the concert party.
4. A notorious man about town and coauthor of many heartstring twanging lyrics, he was my all time favorite musician.
5. Of course it was not so much his celebrity status that attracted me or even his he man physique, but rather his reportedly above average intelligence.

PUNC 7   Apostrophes

Rules for using apostrophes are few and fairly straightforward, even though there seems to be a good deal of confusion on the issue.

---

1. Use an apostrophe in contractions to indicate that something has been omitted.

Example

Karen can't go.

That dog won't hunt.

He'll never make it.

That's where you're wrong.

I'm hoping we can't get there.

It's going to be a long, cold winter.

An apostrophe is also used to signal omissions in expressions like these:

ten o'clock (originally "of the clock")

the summer of '59

Examples

Singular

the cat's pajamas

a bride's book

our doctor's husband

that child's toy

Plural

the boys' meeting

those students' books

the women's movement

these mothers' concerns

(Review section on possessives, p. 526 for more on these forms.)

Remember that personal pronouns have their own possessive forms: *mine, your/yours, her/hers, his, its, our/ours, their/theirs.* They do not use an apostrophe + *s* to form the possessive.

Examples

Maria has trouble with *s*'s.

The early 1700's was an era of great discovery in science.

Joseph is a scholar who dots all his *i*'s and crosses all his *t*'s.

In the era of the '30's, jazz was reinvigorated.

Exercise   **Insert apostrophes in these sentences where needed to indicate omissions, possessives, or plurals.**

1. Poetry of the 1800s frequently used abbreviated words in order to preserve a strict meter.

2. An example of this phenomenon is found in these lines from Henry Pontets ballad, "Saved by a Child":

> And the child, in faltring accents told
> To the Heavns his touching plea;
> And a wave of comfort oer me rolld,
> Like the tide of some deep sea!

3. The students were nonplussed when they saw that there were no As and very few B + s on Mrs. Kepharts grade sheet.

4. If shes not back by four o clock, were going to St. Johns Woods without her.

5. She was a relic from the 60s with her Beatles albums, her granny glasses, and her peace symbols.

6. "Thats right sportin of you," he acknowledged, "but I still aint changin my mind."

7. With our old car its always something; either its spark plugs are bad or its tires are flat or the starter doesnt work.

8. The Granthams were the first ones to tell me about St. Elmos fire.

9. The flower that youve always known as "Avon" is what we call "grandfathers whiskers," and what you call "bleeding-heart" is "Dutchmans britches" to us.

10. Im tempted to find a place in this handbook for a sentence that has ten "hads" in a row.

MECH • Mechanics

MECH 1 Italics

Italic is a typeface used to draw special attention to particular words, phrases, or groups of words. In handwritten or typed material, italics are indicated by underlining; in printed material they are indicated by a special slanted typeface like this: *italics*. There are fairly well-established conventions about what kinds of terms should be italicized; a list and some examples appear below.

Use italics to emphasize appropriate terms and phrases.

Examples

For titles of books, magazines, newspapers, movies, long poems, and musical compositions

Camus' *The Stranger*

Williams' *The Glass Menagerie*

Milton's *Paradise Lost*

New York Times

Rossini's *The Barber of Seville*

Prizzi's Honor (the movie)

Gourmet (magazine)

For names of ships, aircraft, trains, spacecraft, theaters, and television programs

The Flying Cloud

Airforce I

Orient Express

Challenger IV

Rialto, Strand

Dynasty

For foreign words and phrases

¡Qué barbaridad!

idée reçue

Sanguinaria canadensis

au courant

Many foreign words have been incorporated into the English language and do not require italics in print (for example, simpatico, bête noire, hubris). If you are in doubt, consult a dictionary. Foreign words are usually given a label (*French, Spanish,* etc.), which means they should be italicized.

For emphasizing special words, terms, or statements

Justice, not legality, is the issue here.

The concept of *due process* is of particular significance here.

Perleman talks about a quality of writing that he labels *presence.*

Right side up; Do not use hooks

Note that throughout this handbook principles of usage and punctuation are italicized for emphasis. Other terms that might be italicized are those that the writer wants to single out for attention or those that illustrate a point.

Exercise • **Underline words that should be italicized in these sentences.**

1. Dismayed, he watched his companion's joie de vivre turn to Weltschmerz.
2. Star Trek has made the starship Enterprise familiar to thousands of viewers.
3. This Splendid Stupor seemed a risky title for her novel, but she used it anyway, recalling how her earlier work, Narcolepsy and Other Delights, had been a best-seller for months.
4. Unwilling to reveal to the readers of the National Inquirer the sordid nature of her dispute with Amin, she referred to his offending remark vaguely, as a casus belli.
5. Unable to come up with a more inspired appellation, he called the last movement of his Concerto for Kazoo and Triangle allegro ma non tropo.
6. Mrs. Knight was unsettled when her husband, Harold, broke into a chorus of Four-and-Twenty Virgins during the closing scene of The Guest Who Wouldn't Leave.
7. Like Gaul, my paper will be divided into tres partes.

8. Before our cat Pancho came on the scene, our house was overrun with mus musculi.

9. He reclined listlessly upon the causeuse, a victim of amoebic dysentery and Angst.

10. Owing to a bizarre and unavoidable set of circumstances, A Moribund Affair will not be shown tonight.

MECH 2   Capitalization

> Capitalize appropriate words and phrases; make lower case all appropriate words and phrases.

The conventions for capitalizing words and phrases are well standardized in English. This section gives the chief instances in which one should use capitals.

Examples

For proper nouns and the words derived from them

George is a native of Chicago.

France is a member of the United Nations.

The Mississippi flows into the Gulf of Mexico at New Orleans.

His command of English is poor.

Alaska and Hawaii were the last states to join the Union.

The United States entered World War II in 1941.

My German class is fascinating.

For words referring to God, other sacred deities, and major religions; the titles of major sacred texts and political documents

the Koran, the Bible

Buddhism, Mohammedism

Christ and His disciples

the Virgin Mary

the Magna Carta

the Constitution

the Articles of Confederation

the Methodist Church

For proper names, days of the week, months, and holidays

Mary Cousins, Jane Henderson, John Walter

Tuesday, Friday, Sunday

January, March

the Fourth of July, Christmas, Thanksgiving

For titles used with a name and degrees after a name

Admiral Inman, President Lincoln, Dr. Watkins

Steven Clark, M.D., Janet Fox, LL.D., Margery Sharp, Ph.D.

For the names of organizations (but not a common noun that designates a kind of organization)

Name of organization   American Red Cross, Sierra Club, Department of Public Safety, University of Iowa, Better Business Bureau, Tenneco, Inc., Federal Bureau of Mines

Kind of organization   a university, a corporation, a fraternity, the state hospital

For titles of works

The Return of the Native

Death in the Afternoon

All's Well That Ends Well

The Jewel in the Crown

"On Natural Death"

"Red-Headed Stranger"

"To His Coy Mistress"

Note that only the first word and the most important words in the titles of books, articles, essays, song titles, short stories, plays, and so on are capitalized. Usually that means all words except prepositions and articles.

For major historical periods, events, and philosophies

the American Revolution

the Industrial Revolution

Social Darwinism

Existentialism

Marxism

the Enlightenment

Platonism

For abbreviations of organizations, bureaus, and associations

I.R.S.

U.S.A.

T.V.A.

MADD (Mothers Against Drunk Driving)

F.I.P.S.E. (Fund for the Improvement of Post Secondary Education)

N.E.H. (National Endowment for the Humanities)

Sometimes the first letters in an abbreviation are run together without periods to create an *acronym,* or a term made up from the first letters of several words (as MADD, above). When you use either an abbreviation or an acronym in a piece of writing, you should spell out the words at first use, unless the abbreviation is so familiar that everyone will recognize it immediately.

For the first word of every sentence and every line of poetry

Exercise • **Capitalize words in these sentences as needed.**

1. The most interesting topic our professor, dr. marini, introduced us to in our american history class was the victorian "cult of sentimentality."

2. One of the literary genres that the followers of this cult made popular was "empty cradle" poetry, which commonly appeared in newspaper obituary columns.

3. Typically written by and for women and clergymen, "empty cradle" poetry was a highly sentimentalized attempt to address the domestic crisis of bereavement.

4. Like harriet krenshaw's "o the sweet smiles we shall nevermore see" or dr. george root's "the vacant chair," most "empty cradle" poems focused on articles of clothing, favorite possessions, or other mementos the departed loved one had left behind.

5. Children were especially prominent figures in the poetry and songs of sentimentalists, often serving as mouthpieces for the moral admonitions of the christian church and leaders of the temperance movement.

6. Sometimes the children of these works reawakened a sense of christian hope and goodness in the heart of a disillusioned adult, as in piccolomini's "saved by a child."

7. In other cases, tales of a child's bereft state were intended to stimulate the spread of charitable works, as in "won't you buy my pretty flowers?" — a song whose heroine is directly descended from charles dickens' little nell.

8. "Come home, father" and "father's a drunkard and mother is dead"

are examples of songs in which the persona of a child contributes pathos to the temperance message.

9. As might be expected, mothers, too, are highly revered in sentimental songs and poems of the nineteenth century, as is evident in songs such as "just before the battle, mother," "a boy's best friend is his mother," and "my mother was a lady."

10. The unstinting sentimentality of this victorian genre is aptly illustrated by the following lines which conclude dr. george root's "the vacant chair":

> sleep today, o early fallen!
>   in thy green and narrow bed,
> dirges from the pine and cypress,
>   mingle with the tears we shed.

Houston, Sam (student paper), 110
Hyphens (handbook), 589–590

Illumination, 20
Incubation periods, 19–20
Indefinite pronouns (handbook), 532
Indexes
  newspaper, 420
  periodical, 415–420
  specialized, 416–419
Induction, 322–332
  criteria for, 326–331
Inductive arguments, 322–333
  constructing, 331–332
  how to judge, 331
Inductive leap, 332
Infer-imply, 478
Informal logic, 333–345
  claims in, 333
  in college papers, 342–345
  elements of, 333
  kinds of support, 340–341
  strength of, 341–342
  terminology for, 333
Informal outlines, 53–54
Informal tone, 276
Information, revising to add, 125
In Search of Excellence (Peters and Waterman), 341
Inspiration, myth about, 16
Institute for Propaganda Analysis, 384
Intensive pronouns (handbook), 532, 542
Interrogative pronouns (handbook), 532
Intransitive verbs, definition of (handbook), 507
Irregardless, 478
Irregular verbs, principal parts of (handbook), 508–510
Italics (handbook), 594–595
Its-it's, 478

Jargon, 246–251
  coping with in reading, 251
  definitions of, 246
  guidelines for avoiding, 250–251
  reasons for, 248–250
Johnson, Lyndon B., 269–270
Johnson, Rita, 207a

Journal articles, using in research, 415–420
Journalists' questions, as a strategy for discovery, 48–49
Journals, student, 470–471

Kahn, Russel, 208n
Kearns, Doris, 270
Kenner, Hugh, 374
Killian, Michael, 310n
King, Larry, 202n
King, Martin Luther, Jr., p. 63, 296, 301
Kingston, Maxine Hong, 213n

Lacy, Dan, 211n
Ladder of abstraction, 240
Language in Thought and Action (Hayakawa), 240
Lax, Eric, 220n
Lay-lie, 478, (handbook), 510–511
Leggett, John, 294n
"Legholds and Limbs" (student paper), 110–113
Leighton, Alexander, 218n
Length, paragraph, 216–220
  deciding about, 217–220
"Letter from Birmingham Jail," 296–301
Levels of generality, 204–206
Library of Congress Subject Headings List, 413
Library of Congress system, 414–415
Like-as, 479
Like/as, comparisons with (handbook), 501
Linking verbs, definition of (handbook), 508
Links in writing, *see* Transitions
Lists, as an aid to organization, 57–58
Local revising, 125–133
  to change words and phrases, 127–128
  to improve transitions, 129–130
  to make language more concrete, 126
  meaning of, 119
  of opening and closing paragraphs, 131–132

to rearrange sentences, 130–131
to reduce wordiness, 128–129
steps for, 126
Logic, informal, 333–345
Logical definition, 290–291
Loose-lose, 479

Magazine articles, using in research, 415–420
McCullough, David, 339
McGinniss, Joe, 385–387
McMurtry, Larry, 66–67
Mechanics in writing, 10–13, (handbook), 594–599
  reasons for their importance, 10–13
  spelling, 12–13
Media as a plural noun, 476
Mein Kampf (Hitler), 379
Message writing, 22–25
Metaphor, 268–273
  effects of, 273
  extended, 269–270
  how it works, 268
  purposes of, 271
  rhetorical purposes of, 271–273
  submerged, 268–269
  and unifying writing, 63
Mill, John Stuart (*On Liberty*), 466–467
MLA Handbook for Writers of Research Papers, 434, 437
Models for writing, 13–16
  finding good ones, 14–16
  misconceptions about, 13–14
  problem of, 13–15
Modes of argument, 288–315
  ways of using, 288–289
Mood, in verbs (handbook), 507
Myself, 479
Myth(s)
  about inspiration, 16–17
  about rules, 17
  about writing, 16–17

Narration, in paragraphs, 212–213
Narratives, as a strategy for discovery, 49
Natanson, George, 222n
Newspaper indexes, 420
Newsweek magazine, 209n, 212n
Nixon, Richard, 386–387